American Violence

A Documentary History

American Violence

A Documentary History

edited by

Richard Hofstadter

and

Michael Wallace

Vintage Books
A Division of Random House/New York

Acknowledgment is gratefully extended to the following for permission to
reprint from their works:

Arno Press, Inc.: From Revolt Among the Sharecroppers, by Howard Kester,
and The Great Steel Strike and Its Lessons, by William Z. Foster, 1969, Arno
Press Editions.

Colonial Society of Massachusetts publication: From "Tar and Feathers, The
Adventures of Captain John Malcolm," XXXIV, April 1941 by Frank Hersey.

Augustus M. Kelley, Publishers: From Seventy Years of Life and Labor, by
Samuel Gompers. Published in 1925 by E. P. Dutton & Co., Inc., and reprinted in 1967 by Augustus M. Kelley, Publishers.

Doubleday & Company, Inc.: From For Us. The Living, by Mrs. Medgar
Evers with William Peters. Copyright © 1967 by Myrlie B. Evers and
William Peters.

Henry E. Huntington Library and Art Gallery, San Marino, California: From
Peter Oliver's Origin & Progress of the American Rebellion: A Tory View,
edited by Douglas Adair and John Schutz.

Look Magazine: From "How a Secret Deal Prevented a Massacre at Ole
Miss," by George B. Leonard, T. George Harris, and Christopher S. Wren,
December 31, 1962. Copyright © 1962 by Cowles Communications, Inc.

An excerpt from North From Mexico by Carey McWilliams (1949) is reprinted by permission of the author.

At a time of unprecedented concern over American violence the value of a documentary reader on the history of our domestic violence needs little explanation. No doubt it will be most useful if the least extravagant claims are made for it, and if its role as a sampler and an introduction to a complex major problem is made entirely clear. Some explanation is needed of the principles governing the selection of material. Our subject is *domestic* violence. The editors have not forgotten that war is by far the most destructive of all the forms of violence; but we have not tried here to represent the history of our wars, which, unlike the history of our domestic violence, is quite familiar to educated readers and is represented in many documentary collections. However, in the belief that they shed some light on our national ways of behavior, a few episodes of gratuitous brutality in warfare with Indians and Filipino insurrectionaries have been included in Part III under the general heading of racial violence. They are rather arbitrarily classified here only because we believe that racial antagonism had much to do with them. This should not be taken to suggest that we consider such episodes to be fully explained by their racial aspect. As with warfare, we have not tried to deal with violent individual crimes but only with collective acts of violence or with individual acts, such as assassination, that have an obvious public importance. The exclusion of violent crime, once again, is an act of convenience and does not represent any conviction about its irrelevance, since the pattern of crime and the use of violence both by criminals and the police plainly shed a good deal of light upon the temper of a civilization.

Usually an episode qualifies for inclusion here because of a considerable toll in lives or extensive property destruction, or both. However, a few episodes of very limited violence, among them the Whiskey Rebellion, have been included simply because of their historical importance. At times in our history major violence has taken place with an ostensible or easily traced effect upon the course of political events;

and yet there are other instances in which minor violence has had major historical consequences. We have tried to make our selections representative, without being entirely sure how, in the present state of historical inquiry, representativeness itself could be precisely determined. The many unresolved questions in the historical study of violence were a constant reminder of the tentativeness of our undertaking. A few omissions pehaps require a word of explanation: the assassination of John F. Kennedy has been left out because it has been so exhaustively reported and written about, that of Martin Luther King, Jr., because there is no eyewitness account of the act of assassination itself.

Readers are urged not to take too literally our efforts at classification, for which we claim no more than convenience and partial validity. We have been aware from the first that what we choose to call political violence often has ethnic, religious, or social overtones, that economic violence has frequently been complicated by racial or ethnic differences, and that racial violence has been inspired at times by economic rivalries. Over the whole history of American violence, indeed, the fact of racial and ethnic hatreds hovers as an ominous presence.

All those who have had occasion in any capacity to evaluate the testimony of eyewitnesses know of their fallibility; and fallibility is often magnified when especially intense emotions are involved and where horrifying experiences are endured. We do not present these documents, then, as definitive or balanced accounts. What we have looked for is material of distinctly reportorial character and value, rather than editorialized. These documents, however limited, are the kinds of materials that historians have to work with when they sift evidence. In a few instances there are factual discrepancies between our explanatory headnotes and the documentary narratives. These occur where we believe we have found in other sources sufficient reasons to depart from the document. Seventeenth- and eighteenth-century documents have been partially modernized as to capitalization and punctuation.

This book was planned jointly by the editors. A calendar of almost 2,000 violent episodes was compiled by Michael Wallace, who then searched out and assembled the documents from among many possibilities. He also did the research for the headnotes. His first drafts of headnotes were then redrafted by both editors. To their great benefit the headnotes and documents were also searchingly scrutinized and edited by Beatrice K. Hofstadter. The general introduction was written by Richard Hofstadter, who alone must be considered responsible for it. For indispensable and enthusiastic help in research the editors thank

Paul Berman, David Osher, and Dennis Van Essendelft. We also acknowledge the cordial interest and cooperation of Ashbel Green and Jane Slater.

January 1, 1970   R.H.
                                                            M.W.

CONTENTS

Part I

Political Violence

Part II

Economic Violence

Part III

Racial Violence

Slave Revolts and Their Suppression

Race Riots

Ghetto Riots

Some Casualties of Conquest

Part IV

Religious and Ethnic Violence

Part V

Anti-Radical and Police Violence

Part VI

Personal Violence

Part VII

Assassinations, Terrorism, Political Murders

Part VIII

Violence in the Name of Law, Order, and Morality

American Violence

A Documentary History

Reflections on Violence
in the United States

The United States, it has been said, has a history but not a tradition of domestic violence. A history, because violence has been frequent, voluminous, almost commonplace in our past. But not precisely a tradition, for two reasons: First, our violence lacks both an ideological and a geographical center; it lacks cohesion; it has been too various, diffuse, and spontaneous to be forged into a single, sustained, inveterate hatred shared by entire social classes. Second, we have a remarkable lack of memory where violence is concerned and have left most of our excesses a part of our buried history. In our time, with riots and arson a summertime commonplace, with the whole course of our public life changed by three strategic and terrible assassinations, with political murder a disturbingly frequent practice in the Southern states, and with campuses rent by force and violence and invaded by guns, firebombs, and police, we have wakened to curiosity as well as anxiety about our own violent ways. The rediscovery of our violence will undoubtedly be one of the important intellectual legacies of the 1960's.

Yet there is nothing new in our violence, only in our sudden awareness of it. The 1960's marked only another peak moment in a long and crowded history. Educated Americans, always fully aware of their country's foreign wars and familiar with the history of its Civil War, have hardly a hint of its striking legacy of domestic turbulence. Shirked by our historians, the subject has been repressed in the national consciousness. We have been victims of what members of the National Commission on the Causes and Prevention of Violence have called a "historical amnesia." Yet it is not simply that historians have found a way of shrugging off the unhappy memories of our past; our amnesia is also a response to the experience of a whole generation. For the long span from about 1938 to the mid-1960's, despite the external violence of World War II and the Korean War, the internal life of the country was unusually free of violent episodes. Industrial violence and lynching had almost disappeared. Rioting in the cities—despite the Harlem riot of 1935, the Detroit riot of 1943, and the Los Angeles zoot-suit riot of the same year—occurred less often than in many past periods. Americans who came of age during and after the 1930's found it easy to forget how violent a people their forebears had been.

Historians have done little to remind them. For historians violence is a difficult subject, diffuse and hard to cope with. It is committed by isolated individuals, by small groups, and by large mobs; it is directed against individuals and crowds alike; it is undertaken for a variety of purposes (and at times for no discernible rational purpose at all), and in a variety of ways ranging from assassinations and murders to lynchings, duels, brawls, feuds and riots; it stems from criminal intent and from political idealism, from antagonisms that are entirely personal and from antagonisms of large social consequence. Hence it has been hard to conceive of violence as a subject at all. The first collective multi-volume social history of the United States, the *History of American Life Series*, edited by Arthur M. Schlesinger and Dixon Ryan Fox and appearing mainly in the 1920's and 1930's, gave only the most casual attention to violent episodes. The old *Encyclopedia of the Social Sciences* did not have an entry under "Violence" and neither does the recent *International Encyclopedia of Social Science*.

For this reason, a documentary anthology of episodes in the history of American violence is pertinent now, not least as a stimulant to inquiry. However, a general view of the subject must still be purely prefatory, since most of the studies upon which it might rest more securely are yet to be written. We do not yet know much about the patterns of American violence, and even our awareness of its past frequency is almost certain to be expanded as new areas of historical inquiry are opened. There are, for example, descriptive and statistical books on lynching, as well as works of moral protest; but there is no great history of the subject that assesses its place in the political culture of the South. Many riots have been described by historians, but there is no general work that compares or analyzes them; nor is there such a work tracing the development of police systems or the history of the National Guard. There are many special studies that contribute to our understanding of the history of vigilantism, but as yet no work that puts this institution in its place among the questionable American practices. There are a few sources of insight into the militancy and violence of the South,[1] but there are no histories of regional 'violence to illuminate the peculiar patterns of the South and the West. There is no full historical explanation of the peculiar stubbornness with which Americans have clung to their feeble and outmoded gun control laws. There are books on episodes or periods of violence in the history of labor, but there is no master work that explains the particular patterns of American industrial violence or sets it into comparative perspective with the labor movements of other countries. There is no sociological work that informs us very fully about the place of violence in the assimilation cycles of ethnic groups in America.[2] There is no general study, to my knowledge, of verbal and ideological violence, from which we might begin to differentiate between rhetoric that acts as a benign substitute for extreme action and rhetoric that is only a prelude to such action.[3]

In the future, no doubt, much of this inattention will be remedied. Today we are not only aware of our own violence; we are frightened by it. We are now quite ready to see that there is far more violence in our national heritage than our proud, sometimes smug, national self-image admits of. Our violence frightens us, as it frightens others, because in our singular position uncontrolled domestic violence coincides with unparalleled national power, and thus takes on a special significance for the world. It is not only shocking but dangerous for a primary world power to lose three of its most important and valuable public leaders within a few years, and with them to lose an immeasurable part of its political poise. Violence in Colombia or Guatemala is of life-or-death concern to Colombians and Guatemalans. Violence in the United States has become of life-or-death concern to everyone. It is, again, disturbing to many Americans that the recent outbreaks coincided with the most sustained economic boom we have ever had. Although the American creed has been built upon the efficacy of riches, it has now become alarmingly clear that some of our social discontents, instead of being relieved by prosperity, are exacerbated by it. Although Americans are

---

[1] See John Hope Franklin: *The Militant South* (1956); and the essay by Sheldon Hackney: "Southern Violence," *Violence in America: Historical and Comparative Perspectives* (1969), A Report to the National Commission on the Causes and Prevention of Violence, ed. Hugh D. Graham and Ted R. Gurr (hereafter cited as *Violence*), 479–500.

[2] Daniel Bell: "Crime as an American Way of Life," in *The End of Ideology* (1960), is immensely suggestive as to the possibilities here.

[3] But see the illuminating essay by John R. Howe: "Republican Thought and the Political Violence of the 1790's," *American Quarterly*, XIX (Summer 1967), 147–65.

richer than ever, they have not found a way to buy themselves out of trouble.

Americans certainly have reason to inquire whether, when compared with other advanced industrial nations, they are not a people of exceptional violence. Any American who has lived for a time in England, for example, can hardly fail to notice there a gentleness and a repugnance to violence that underlines our own contrasting qualities. Americans, however they may deplore and fear violence, are not so deeply *shocked* by it as the English are. Our entertainment and our serious writing are suffused with violence to a notorious degree; it is endemic in our history. Americans, apparently taking it as a part of the stream of life's events, do not as a rule very promptly rise up in large numbers and in lawful ways to protest, oppose, or control it. They are legendary for their refusal to accept the reality of death, but violence they endure as part of the nature of things, and as one of those evils to be expected from life.

How does the United States really stand today among the nations of the world in the level of its domestic violence? Here it is important not to succumb to the conventional and maudlin anti-Americanism of our era, and not to be parochial even in self-denigration. For good or ill, violence has been a common agent of historical change almost everywhere; it occurs at decisive moments even in the history of those nations that have otherwise enjoyed long periods of gradual and relatively peaceful change. While we may find violence undesirable, we can hardly find it unnatural. The United States, even with its considerable record of violence, appears not as some mutant monster among the peoples of the world but rather as a full-fledged and somewhat boisterous member of the fellowship of human frailty. What is most exceptional about the Americans is not the voluminous record of their violence, but their extraordinary ability, in the face of that record, to persuade themselves that they are among the best-behaved and best-regulated of peoples.

They are neither among the best nor among the worst. There are far worse things than the spontaneous mob violence of which we have had so much. After all, the greatest and most calculating of killers is the national state, and this is true not only in international wars, but in domestic conflicts. Nothing in the experience of the United States or any other democratic state can compare with the wholesale violence wreaked by the totalitarian powers upon their people. All the violence of all kinds committed on American soil from the first settlements to the most recent clash between demonstrators and police could be tucked away in a small corner among the casualties of Stalin's terror, which are estimated at about twenty million, or among the six million or more Jewish victims of the Nazis' genocidal mania. Even the civil violence of recent years, which is surely one of our most tumultuous periods, pales before the contemporary experience of Algeria, Nigeria, Indonesia, or Venezuela.

Few of us will be so parochial in our anti-Americanism as to fail to see that large-scale violence is so commonplace in the histories of societies that the American record, when put in a world-historical perspective, is not so remarkable as it first seems. What is impressive to one who begins to learn about American violence is its extraordinary frequency, its sheer commonplaceness in our history, its persistence into very recent and contemporary times, and its rather abrupt contrast with our pretensions to singular national virtue. What must also be observed about it, however, is the circumscribed character and the small scale of the typical violent incident. America has experienced one major internal war on an exceptionally costly scale. But its riots and massacres and other spontaneous outbursts of savagery do not otherwise loom inordinately large when projected against the long backdrop of history. It is horrifying to read of the heads of 16 slaves exposed on poles at intervals up the Mississippi River as a warning to blacks after the slave insurrection of 1811. It is still more horrifying to think of the aftermath of the Spartacus uprising, when, after inflicting well over 30,000 battle casualties on the slaves, the Romans crucified about 6,000 of them along the road from Capua to Rome. It is, again, depressing to read of the repeated mobbings of Irish Catholics in nineteenth-century American cities, but it may not be wholly irrelevant to recall that in the massacres of Huguenots attending and following St. Bartholomew's Night of 1572 in France, the uncounted and uncountable murders are believed by some modern scholars to have reached about 8,000 or 10,000 or that in the massacres of English and Scotch settlers in the Irish uprising of October 1641, some 12,000 to 15,000 were murdered or died of subsequent ill treatment. The deaths in the Indonesian massacre of Communists and their sympathizers in 1965-6 may well have exceeded 150,000. If the quantitative dimension of such human tragedies is to concern us, as I think it must, America's episodic violence does not rank notably large.

Still, our civil violence is quite out of keeping with our image of ourselves as one of the world's most advanced political cultures. Our new sense of this disparity finds support in the attempts of the experts of the National Commission on the Causes and Prevention of Violence to measure the nations of the world against each other.[4] In some ways their comparisons are crudely mechanical. The "measurement" of civil strife by the numbers of participants, the duration of incidents, or the casualties per 100,000 of population has no way of taking account of the decisive *qualitative* aspects of violence. The political importance of an act of violence need not be at all proportionate to its cost in casualties—witness the Boston Tea Party, in which not a soul was hurt. Like so many other positivistic inquiries in social science, such "measurement" jars our sense of proportion by setting down with mathematical exactitude data that have in actuality little of the precision apparently conveyed by the figures in which they are reported. It is a bit hard to understand what we are being told when we learn that the "magnitude of civil strife" in Venezuela for the troubled five-year period 1961-5 was 20.3 while that of France was 12.1, and that of the United States for the five years 1963-8 was 13.8. The fact that the estimated casualties for the United States per 100,000 were five, whereas those for France were four may not tell us quite what we want to know about the comparative importance of violence in the polities of the two countries. There were more casualties in the local encounter over the "People's Park" in Berkeley in May 1969 than in the convulsive upheaval throughout France a year earlier.

Nonetheless, the figures compiled by the National Commission's experts constitute the only check we have thus far against arbitrary impressions, and they confirm our sense that the United States is far from being the most peaceful among the Western or other industrial nations with which comparison seems most appropriate.[5] These experts find in the United States of recent years a magnitude of civil strife that compares very unfavorably with most other nations of a high level of economic development, and somewhat unfavorably even with some nations of a medium level of economic development. This country has been, for example, less strife-ridden than Indonesia, Algeria, Rhodesia or Venezuela, about as strife-ridden as France, India, and Ecuador, and far more so than the United Kingdom, West Germany, the U.S.S.R., Puerto Rico, Taiwan, and the Scandinavian countries, to choose more or less at random from a large number of countries with less domestic violence than our own.

[4] See Ted R. Gurr: "A Comparative Study of Civil Strife"; and Ivo K. Feierabend, Rosalind L. Feierabend, and Betty A. Nesvold: "Social Change and Political Violence: Cross-National Patterns," *Violence*, 541–668.
[5] See, for example, the tables compiled by Gurr in *Violence*, 550, 600–2. On Gurr's scale of 114 nations, the United States ranked 41st for its magnitude of civil strife in 1961–5, but 24th for the years 1963–9.

There is another respect in which such data should be looked at carefully: the level of civil strife has no consistent relation to political freedom. The United States in the 1960's showed a relatively high level of freedom and permissiveness in its policies toward domestic protest at a time when it had profoundly divisive domestic problems and a simultaneous unsuccessful and unpopular foreign war. This reads like a prescription for violent disturbances. By contrast, nations governed by dictators or firmly installed authoritarian systems—Portugal and Spain, the U.S.S.R., Poland, Yugoslavia, and Rumania, as well as Saudi Arabia and the United Arab Republic—all stand well below the United States in the dimensions of their civil strife. Yet the internal peace enjoyed by some polities rather resembles that of the graveyard, and here invidious comparisons with American violence would have little meaning. One might well prefer to endure occasional and limited violence if the only alternative is a state of almost unlimited repression.

II

Before looking at the historical forms of American violence, it is important to offer a definition and to establish one distinction. Acts of *violence*, as I use the term here, are those which kill or injure persons or do significant damage to property. Acts of *force* are those which prevent the normal free action or movement of other persons, or which inhibit them through the threat of violence. The two are often confused, and certainly the relation between them is often intimate, but the distinction is necessary not only for our own clarity but because it has come to have such tactical and moral importance to authorities and dissidents alike. A line of policemen arrayed against, say, demonstrators or strikers, represents force. Violence begins when they use their weapons. Similarly, when strikers sit down in a factory, or when a group of students seizes a university building, or when pacifists throw themselves on the ground before a convoy of army trucks, they have, however non-violently, used force. In a democratic state, it is vital that the informal legitimation of authority be wide and deep enough so that its power is not too often challenged, and that when it is challenged it can be asserted successfully merely by a show of force without repeated and excessive episodes of violence. Often force used by dissenters touches off violence, and the competition for legitimacy then proceeds as each side tries to throw the public onus for unacceptable violence upon the other. This game, though perhaps not altogether new, is being played today with an unprecedented recklessness.

An arresting fact about American violence, and one of the keys to understanding of its history, is that very little of it has been insurrectionary. Most of our violence has taken the form of action by one group of citizens against another group, rather than by citizens against the state. The sheer size of the country, the mixed ethnic, religious, and racial composition of the people, and the diffuseness of power under our federal system have all tended to blunt or minimize citizen-versus-state conflicts and to throw citizen-versus-citizen conflicts into high relief. And this is one of the reasons why so much of our violence has been buried away in our historical memory: for historians, conflicts between groups of citizens, no matter how murderous and destructive, have been forgettable; attacks upon state power, no matter how transient and ineffective, win historical attention. Hence such low-key and almost charmingly benign episodes as the Boston Tea Party, Shays' Rebellion, and the Whiskey Rebellion find a place, as indeed they should, in our history books. But other episodes, often of startling savagery and destructive effect, like the suppression of the slave rebellion in New York in 1712, are readily forgotten.

Again, our federal structure has deflected violence from the symbols of *national* power. Although much of our violence has been carried out by, or launched in response to, local police or military power, very little has been directed against the power of the several states, and practically none against the power of the national government. On occasions, it is true, state legislatures have been threatened or even seized, though usually by groups with objectives too limited in scope to be called "revolutionary." But the most common form of American violence, bringing citizen into conflict with citizen, has usually brought the power of authority into play as a third party (though by no means as a "neutral" one) to protect property or end crowd violence; and there have been countless occasions when the truly costly violence, in human terms, has occurred only when the police act. But the important point here—important in part because we may now be witnessing a change in the pattern—is that crowd actions have hardly ever been coupled with a flat challenge to the legitimacy of the whole American system. Since our violence did not typically begin with anyone's desire to subvert the state, it did not typically end by undermining the legitimacy of authority.

The United States has thus been able to endure an extraordinary volume of violence without developing a revolutionary tradition, and indeed while maintaining a long record of basic political stability. With the striking—and admittedly very important—exception of the Civil

War, our political development has taken place for over 175 years under relatively free conditions, with a stable Constitution, free (if not always quiet or uncorrupted) elections, orderly and effective political parties, and working parliamentary institutions. We have brought a vast continental area together under a free government and combined in one polity people from several parts of the world. The coexistence of stability and violence poses a paradox: most of the countries we regard as acutely violent we also regard as suffering from chronic upheaval and political incapacity. But not the United States, which has long shown a political stability that compares favorably with, say, that of England or the bland polities of Scandinavia, and yet has a level of civil violence that rather resembles some Latin American republics or the volatile new states of Asia and Africa.

Finally, one is impressed that most American violence—and this also illuminates its relationship to state power—has been initiated with a "conservative" bias. It has been unleashed against abolitionists, Catholics, radicals, workers and labor organizers, Negroes, Orientals, and other ethnic or racial or ideological minorities, and has been used ostensibly to protect the American, the Southern, the white Protestant, or simply the established middle-class way of life and morals. A high proportion of our violent actions has thus come from the top dogs or the middle dogs. Such has been the character of most mob and vigilante movements. This may help to explain why so little of it has been used against state authority, and why in turn it has been so easily and indulgently forgotten. Our new concern about violence today is, among other things, a response to a sharp increase in its volume, but it is also a response to its shifting *role*. Violence has now become, to a degree unprecedented in the United States, the outgrowth of forcible acts by dissidents and radicals who are expressing hostility to middle-class ways and to established power. Many people see it as newly dangerous because it is politically more purposive than in the past, more intimately related to basic social issues, and because it touches the vulnerable sensibilities of the comfortable middle class.

III

It inevitably will be asked why advanced industrial America has so violent a history, but this is not, I think, either as difficult or as interesting as another question: How could America have combined such a substantial degree of popular domestic violence with such a high degree of political stability? The conventional attribution of American violence to our long frontier history should not be given too much credence. It is true, of course, that frontier conditions somewhat enhanced the American disposition to violence, as they did, for example, in the history of Indian warfare and the attitudes it engendered. And before the era of the gangster hero, it was the frontier that gave this country one of its central images of justified violence and some of its archetypal heroes of violence. Yet it is worth emphasizing that over the whole course of our history only a small portion of the total American population—and always a decreasing portion—has ever seen or been on a frontier. Again, all frontiers do not automatically produce similar patterns of violence, as a comparison of American with Canadian and Australian behavior would show. The prominence of violence in the South, far behind the advancing frontier, should inspire further skepticism on this count. But also, as it happens, most American domestic violence has been urban. If we are to understand it, then, we must turn away from the preoccupation with the frontier and from explanations based on the natural environment to look at the conditions of American urban life. And when these are examined, one is quickly driven to the conclusion that ethnic, religious, and racial mixture—above all the last of these—are the fundamental determinants of American violence. And they have been exacerbated by other national circumstances: weak government, localism, and the diffusion of authority and power; extraordinarily rapid urban growth, large-scale migrations, and rapid social change; the inability or unwillingness of urban Americans to relinquish their gun culture; and finally, the development in the nineteenth century of a type of socially unchecked industrial baron, often an absentee, lording it over a distant and heterogeneous "alien" working force with which he felt no ethnic, institutional, social, or religious ties.

I do not hope, for reasons which I trust I have made clear, to say anything in a brief historical review of the specific forms of American violence that will survive the intensive inquiries into the subject that are now almost certain to be made by historians and others. Yet to give some body to our sense of the subject, I propose to review briefly a few major chronic forms of group violence. I omit criminal violence, frontier brawling, gangster shoot-outs, feuds, and assassinations (though the latter have had important effects). I also omit our Indian wars, on the ground that they have been wars rather than a part of our domestic violence, though in the main they had the character of guerilla warfare punctuated by massacres and counter-massacres. All these forms of violence deserve attention, but for the sake of brevity I confine myself here to some of the most costly and symptomatic varieties: riots of several kinds, industrial violence, lynching, vigilantism, and slave revolts and their suppression. These categories will serve at least to illustrate some of the problems inherent in the subject.

Riots, I suppose, have been the most important single form of domestic violence in American history, certainly when measured by their historic duration, and probably when measured by the cost in casualties. But rioting in itself is not a single category that will yield us very much understanding: rather it is a broad rubric that covers a wide variety of types of social conflict. Rioting has taken place chiefly in the cities, but in earlier days it was not unknown in the countryside. We have had political riots (particularly important in the Revolutionary period and in the heated moments of the Federal era), election riots, food riots, anti-abolitionist and other anti-radical riots. We have had riots arising out of industrial disputes—which I will discuss in connection with industrial violence. But by far the greatest number of riots have arisen out of ethnic-religious or racial antagonisms; and even many of the riots that seem to stem from other issues, when examined more closely, turn out to be shaped by such antagonisms. What may be called election riots, for example, often prove to be the result of an effort to keep some minority group from voting. What seem to be riots arising from labor disputes may turn out to have a strong racial coloration, when one finds white workers attacking black scabs or imported Chinese laborers. An examination of violent episodes impresses one with the delusive and superficial character of the "melting-pot" image as it has been so often applied to our history. The truth is that all too often, especially under urban conditions, the contents of the melting-pot did not melt; or when they did, it was only under fire. And so far as the blacks are concerned, the melting never took place: the preponderance of our crowd violence has been a case of whites against blacks.

To an extraordinary degree class conflict in American history has been overshadowed by ethnic-religious and racial conflict. Intermittent group warfare has been our substitute for, or alternative to, class war, and class war itself, when it has flared up, has seldom taken place in a clear atmosphere, unclouded by our racial-ethnic antagonisms and by our complex hierarchy of status based upon religious-ethnic-racial qualities.

When riots began to reflect ethnic mixture, they took on an especially lethal quality. Americans, it is true, had a considerable heritage of violent action in the colonial period. In the seventeenth and early eighteenth centuries, the English were a rough lot, and most Americans were transplanted Englishmen. Violence, and the threat of violence, marked at their peak by New York and New Jersey tenant riots and Bacon's Rebellion in Virginia, were significant in colonial life, and when Americans entered the Revolutionary era, they had a well-established habit of moving into forcible action. But their ways had also somewhat softened, and the violence that prevailed in the late eighteenth century and the first decades of the nineteenth was limited in its destructive consequences, even though often of decisive political importance. The town or country demonstration was a common thing, and in the resistance to taxes or mortgages, in the protests against the Stamp Act and the excises, it rose often enough to the level of violence. But as Howard Mumford Jones has remarked of mobs in the pre-Revolutionary era: "American mobs were curiously lacking in furious, deep-seated, and bloodthirsty resentment. No royal governor was hanged or shot by a drumhead courtmartial. No stamp collector or customs official was summarily executed, though some of them suffered physical injury. No 'tyrant' was decapitated as the unfortunate Governor of the Bastille was decapitated, and nobody's head was borne about the streets of Philadelphia or Boston on a pole. There was no American parallel to the Jacqueries, the Noyades, the September Massacres, or the Reign of Terror."[6] Nothing in American experience in the eighteenth century approached the Gordon riot of 1780 in London, in the course of which 285 rioters were killed and enormous physical damage was done.

What Jones observes about the crowd actions of the pre-Revolutionary period seems largely true of such action as took place during the domestic political conflicts of the 1780's and the 1790's. But after 1830, with increasing ethnic mixture in the Northern cities and the quick suppression of slave restiveness—or of attacks upon slavery—the tempo and destructiveness of violence increased. The next major period of riots, rising with the growth of cities and the development of large slum areas, Irish immigration, and the abolitionist movement, came in the 1830's, 1840's, and 1850's, which Richard Maxwell Brown has described as "a period of sustained urban rioting particularly in the great cities of the Northeast." This, he suggests, "may have been the era of the greatest urban violence that America has ever experienced."[7] Brown has counted in the four cities of Baltimore, Philadelphia, New York,

---

[6] Howard Mumford Jones: *O Strange New World* (1964), 290.

[7] "Historical Patterns of Violence in America," *Violence*, 50. Here he may be in error, since urban violence during Reconstruction must be weighed against that of this earlier period.

and Boston at least 35 "major riots," and there were other riots in the cities of the Midwest and the lower Mississippi Valley, like Cincinnati. But if we had more complete histories of smaller communities, the number of identifiable riots would probably grow considerably.

The fiercest riots arose out of religious-ethnic and racial conflict, but a few important ones were waged against abolitionists. The great abolitionist orator Wendell Phillips was converted to abolitionism in 1835 by seeing a mob drag William Lloyd Garrison down Court Street in Boston with a rope around his neck. In 1837 a mob in Alton, Illinois, attacked the office of Elijah P. Lovejoy, and after a brief battle killed the anti-slavery editor. It was partly in response to this episode that Abraham Lincoln issued his famous warning of 1838 against American lawlessness to the young men of Springfield. Lincoln was aware not only of the anti-abolitionist riots but also of nativist riots directed mainly against the Irish. Touched off by the burning of the Ursuline Convent at Charlestown, Massachusetts, in 1834, they continued well into the 1850's. The Anti-Catholic Know-Nothing Party encouraged the use of violence, not least in attempting to keep foreign-born voters from the polls. Clashes between Know-Nothing Clubs and Democratic organizations over the voting rights of immigrants were frequent in the 1850's. One fracas in Baltimore, in which organized platoons were set against each other, cost the lives of eight and a toll of fifty wounded. As Ray Allen Billington has written: "In every American city the story was the same. In New Orleans four men were killed when native and foreign factions clashed. In Lawrence, Massachusetts, 1500 Americans stormed the Irish section and destroyed homes and churches. In St. Louis the 1854 elections led to a riot in which ten men were killed and several wounded. More serious was a battle which developed in Louisville on August 5th, 1855. There the native factions had been aroused by a no-popery campaign being carried out by the Louisville *Journal*. When a group of them marched through the German sector, fighting began which only ended after more than twenty men had been killed and several hundred wounded."[8]

Nativist riots were followed by riots between the Irish and the Negroes. In the New York City draft riots, which raged for five days in mid-July 1863, and which owed more to inter-racial tensions than to anti-war feeling, there was wholesale murder and lynching of blacks. Estimates of those killed, which vary widely because of the clandestine burial of victims, range up to 1200.

[8] Billington: *The Protestant Crusade* (1938), 421.

Reconstruction in the South was marked by frequent episodic violence on both a large and small scale. As Otis Singletary has remarked, any definitive history of Reconstruction will "contain deep and depressing undertones of violence."[9] Radical Reconstruction leaders in several Southern states organized Negro militias (actually often racially mixed) both to defend the interests of the freedmen and to patrol and control elections. Southern whites reacted to this challenge to their supremacy by forming, under various names, White Leagues, politico-military organizations which, unlike the Ku Klux Klan, operated quite openly, conducting military drills and laying public plans for resistance. The White Leagues were, in effect, the armed wing of the Democratic Party. Their members seem to have welcomed, and on some occasions probably planned, riots as occasions upon which they could strike back against the Negro militias. In some areas violence became commonplace. An investigation by the Texas legislature showed that between the close of the war in 1865 to June 1868, 509 whites and 486 freedmen had been killed. Most of the deaths had been inflicted by whites, and only a tiny fraction of the white deaths resulted from attacks by freedmen.[1] Between 1868 and 1876, lethal riots of considerable consequence took place in Opelousas, Louisiana, Laurens, South Carolina, Pine Bluff, Arkansas, Clinton, Vicksburg, Yazoo City, Mississippi, and Hamburg, South Carolina, and there were many lesser disturbances. The most extraordinary encounter took place in New Orleans on September 14, 1874. In this affair, which rose above the level of a riot or shoot-out to that of a pitched military battle in the streets of the city, two factions were battling for control of the state. In this encounter a Gatling gun and some regular artillery were deployed, and the clash of the two armed groups left over 20 dead and over 100 wounded. By 1877, with the defeat of radical reconstruction, the last of the Negro militias was dissolved.

Although there was never any long hiatus in rioting, the next major episode after the 1870's occurred during the violent period of 1915 to 1919, when there were twenty-two major inter-racial disturbances, many of them arising out of Northern wartime migration of Southern Negroes. These were, in the main, large-scale inter-racial conflicts in which the initiative was taken by whites. In most instances, Negroes fought back. The worst of the post-war riots took place in Chicago.

[9] Otis A. Singletary: *Negro Militia in Reconstruction* (1957), 3; this book is one of the most illuminating studies of Reconstruction violence.
[1] *Ibid.*, 18.

It began late in July 1919, when a young Negro "encroached" upon a swimming area the whites had (without legal authority) marked off for themselves, and was stoned until he drowned. By the time the riot was over, a week later, thousands of both races had been involved in a series of frays, fifteen whites and twenty-three Negroes had been killed, and hundreds injured. The riots of the 1919 period established a certain pattern: whites were resisting the rapid growth of Northern Negro communities; on occasion they seemed to welcome an incident that would give vent to their feelings; Negroes, it was made clear (though there were earlier precedents for this), would fight back; and the police exacerbated the situation by their obvious unneutrality.[2]

The riots of that era were fully inter-racial, with the blacks mainly on the defensive. In this respect, the riots of the 1960's have thus far established a new pattern. Today the initiative comes from within the Negro community, and the action is not precisely inter-racial in the old pattern (though it does strike at white representatives of authority and occasionally singles out whites) but is directed more at property (particularly white property) than persons, and is largely confined within the ghettos. The earlier inter-racial riots were touched off to a large degree by white resentment of an increasing black presence. The ghetto riots, though they seem too spontaneous to be *planned* for this or any end, serve the purpose of expressing social protest. In this respect they appear to have been successful: it is rioting on a large scale that has, more than anything else, alerted national and community leaders to the seriousness of Negro grievances and the hardships of life in the black slums. There is, of course, a cost and a danger in the riot as a vehicle of protest: riots inflict their primary casualties and property losses on those who live in the ghetto; they also tread a dangerous line in that they risk setting in motion a popular backlash that might undo the gains that come from forcing white elites to become aware of black grievances. Negro leaders, including many militants, are distressed at the racial self-image that emerges from the riots. For the moment, preponderant black sentiment suggests that riots may have spent themselves. A national poll of Negroes taken in the spring of 1969 showed (omitting those who answered uncertainly) that while a very substantial majority predicted further riots (64% as against 9%), a minority (31% as against 48%) thought riots justified, and only a small minority (11% as against 68%) thought they would take part in one.[3]

---

[2] See Arthur I. Waskow: *From Race Riot to Sit-in, 1919 and the 1960's* (1966).
[3] *Newsweek*, June 30, 1969.

IV

In respect to its social consequences, if not actual casualties, industrial violence appears to rival rioting—though there are times, as in the great railway strike of 1877, when the two merge. Although there had been violence arising out of capital-labor disputes long before, the major phase of our industrial violence opened with the activities of the Molly McGuires in the anthracite coal towns[4] and with the strikes of 1877, and continued to the time of World War I. The great railroad strike of 1877 led to riots and violent encounters in more than a dozen cities; it resulted in at least 90 deaths and in injuries it would be futile to try to count, as well as in extensive property damage.[5] The ranks of strikers and sympathizers, swelled characteristically by adolescents and erupting in several cities in rapid succession, were almost more than the limited police and military forces of the country could contain.[6] For the first time, the event raised the spectre of an unmanageable national insurrectionary power (though nothing of the kind seems to have been in the minds of the strikers), and led to the very considerable strengthening of the National Guard and the establishment of a chain of armories in key cities.

There was to be no comparable threat again (though the railroad strike of 1886 was also violent), but the industrial history of the country was punctuated by fiercely fought strikes, like those at Pullman and Homestead. The beginning of the twentieth century brought many more episodes of violence, especially where the Western Federation of Miners and the I. W. W. were influential. Bouck White remarked in 1911 that the "vital and arresting point" in the case of the Los Angeles *Times* bombing by the McNamara brothers was "its disclosure of a state of internecine war in our civilization." The long struggle in the Colorado coalfields in 1913-14 was climaxed by an atrocious attack by militiamen upon a tent encampment of workers at Ludlow in which, besides the several victims of rifle fire on both sides, eleven children and two women of the colony were burned to death when

---

[4] In the case of the Molly McGuires the coal towns had a kind of Irish labor Mafia, which provided a good deal of murder and melodrama but did nothing to improve the condition of the miners. The best study is Wayne G. Broehl: *The Molly McGuires* (1964).

[5] I have tallied the deaths from Robert V. Bruce's fascinating account: *1877: Year of Violence* (1959), but it is clear from his report that the tables of mortality did not record all those who were killed.

[6] On the response to this event, see Gerald Grob: "The Railroad Strikes of 1877," *Midwest Journal*, VI (1954-5), 16-34.

militiamen poured coal oil on the tents and put them to the torch. When the Industrial Relations Commission met in 1914 to study the fierce industrial violence of the Progressive era Walter Lippmann remarked, in words which today sound strikingly contemporary, that its members "have before them the task of explaining why America, supposed to become the land of promise, has become the land of disappointment and deep-seated discontent."[7]

The most recent phase in industrial violence came with the organizing campaigns of the 1930's. The national cotton textile strikes of 1934 resulted in probably as many as 13 deaths and required the deployment of 10,000 troops. The Little Steel Strike of 1937 cost the lives of 15 strikers and seriously injured over 100. The last memorable episode of violence in labor history was the Memorial Day Massacre in the Republic Steel Strike during 1937 when police charged a crowd of demonstrating strikers, killing 10 men and injuring many others. No one has ever attempted to take a full toll of the casualties arising out of industrial violence, nor has anyone made a close comparative study of violence in American labor disputes and that in other industrial countries. However, I believe no student of labor history is likely to quarrel with the judgment of Philip Taft and Philip Ross: "The United States has had the bloodiest and most violent labor history of any industrial nation in the world."[8] Taft and Ross have identified over 160 instances in which state and federal troops have intervened in labor disputes, and have recorded over 700 deaths and several thousands of serious injuries in labor disputes, but one can only underline their warning that this incomplete tally "grossly understates the casualties."[9] The rate of industrial violence in America is striking in light of the fact that no major American labor organization has ever advocated violence as a policy, that extremely militant class-conflict philosophies have not prevailed here, and that the percentage of the American labor force organized in unions has always been (and is even now) lower than in most advanced industrial countries. With a minimum of ideologically motivated class conflict, the United States has somehow had a maximum of industrial violence. And no doubt the answer to this

[7] Bouck White and Lippmann quoted by Graham Adams, Jr.: *Age of Industrial Violence, 1910–15* (1966), 27, 50. On Ludlow and other violence, see Samuel Yellen: *American Labor Struggles* (1936); and Louis Adamic: *Dynamite: The Story of Class Violence in America* (rev. edn., 1934).
[8] "American Labor Violence: Its Causes, Character, and Outcome," *Violence*, 270; *cf.* 360. See also Taft's essay: "Violence in American Labor Disputes," *Annals* of the American Academy of Political and Social Science (March 1966), 128.
[9] *Violence*, 360.

must be sought more in the ethos of American capitalists than in that of the workers.

v

Lynching and vigilantism have so few parallels or equivalents elsewhere that they can be regarded as distinctively American institutions. Lynchings—open public murders conceived and carried out more or less spontaneously by a mob—seem to have been invented here. In the first scholarly study of the practice, written in 1903, James E. Cutler remarked that "lynching is a criminal practice which is peculiar to the United States." The nearest approach he could find to it—its similarity is slight—was in the rural districts of Russia where peasants sometimes took it upon themselves to execute accused horse thieves.[1] However, the Eastern European pogrom may in fact be more comparable. While lynchings began in this country with early nineteenth-century vigilantism and again took place on a considerable scale in the South during Reconstruction, it was not until 1882 that the Chicago *Tribune* first began to take systematic account of them, and in later years the record was continued by the N.A.A.C.P. Of necessity the figures cannot be complete, but there is reason to think that they were nearly so, and from 1882 to 1927 they show 4,950 recorded lynchings. Many hundreds more were attempted and were stopped by authorities—over 700 just between 1914 and 1932. During the nineteenth century a significant minority of lynching victims were white; but after the turn of the century they were almost all blacks. Victims were not always men: there are reports of the lynchings of at least 92 women, 76 black, 16 white. Nor was lynching confined to the South: there are only four states—Massachusetts, Rhode Island, New Hampshire, and Vermont—that have been free of it.[2]

The extraordinary lawlessness prevalent in the South, the Southwest, and some parts of the West is reflected in the relation between lynchings and legal executions. In all but a few years from 1882 to 1903, the number of lynchings exceeded, usually to some considerable degree, the number of lawful executions for capital crimes. From 1882 to the end of the nineteenth century there were rarely fewer than 135 lynchings annually, and in the worst year, 1892, there were 235. Lynchings declined quite steadily from that year to about 1905, when

[1] James E. Cutler: *Lynch-Law* (1905), 1, 3.
[2] On the history of lynching statistics, see Cutler: *Lynch-Law;* and Walter White: *Rope and Faggot* (1929).

there were 65. No material change occurred for nearly twenty years (there was an average of 62 lynchings for the years 1910-19), but beginning with 1923 lynchings again began to grow markedly fewer, and in the late 1930's and 1940's trailed off and became rarer. No one has yet written a full account of lynching which explains the rhythm of its occurrence or the reasons for its final decline.

The lynching of blacks, although apparently spontaneous, seemed also to manifest a desire to establish beyond any doubt the point that the caste system of the South could not be challenged. In this respect there is a suggestive psychological similarity, even if no easily established historical affiliation, between the psychology of lynchings and the pattern of suppression of slave revolts. The extraordinary harshness with which slave revolts, or suspected or alleged conspiracies to revolt, were suppressed, supplies a suggestive analogue to lynching, and on a few occasions to vigilantism as well. By and large, slaves under the American slave system were deemed entitled to a trial, but where rebellions, real or imagined, were concerned, the law was swift, and the punishment was often harsh or even barbarous. From the beginning whites seemed to be determined, through the brutality of reprisals, to impress upon slaves the futility and the extraordinary danger of rebellion or otherwise resisting slavery. Such occasional tactics as pulling runaways out of jail and lynching them, burying a slave alive for the murder of his master, tortures to get confessions of slave revolt plots, and whipping to near the point of death bespeak a certain purposive brutality. As early as 1712 when slaves rose up in New York City and killed several whites, reprisals were unrestrained: rebels were burnt, hanged, and hung alive in chains as a public example of the fate of slave rebels. In 1741 a rumor, probably false, that slaves were planning to poison the city water supply was followed by the burning alive of thirteen slaves and the hanging of eighteen others. In one New Orleans revolt of 1811 the heads of sixteen captured rebels were posted on poles as a warning to others. The abortive Gabriel plot in Virginia in 1800 was suppressed with the hanging of as many as thirty-five blacks, and a like number were hanged in Charleston, South Carolina, after the disclosure of the abortive Denmark Vesey plot of 1822. The well-remembered Nat Turner insurrection in Virginia in 1831, which resulted in the deaths of at least fifty-seven whites, ended with a massacre of reprisal whose victims ran well over a hundred and included scores of innocent blacks.

Vigilante groups may be defined as organizations formed to create and enforce laws of their own making in the supposed absence of adequate law enforcement. Penalties inflicted by vigilantes were at times devised to fit the alleged crimes, and they often followed an informal trial; but a peremptory lynching was more likely to be the result of a vigilante arrest. In the main vigilantism was a frontier phenomenon, although it could appear in urban areas that had been affected by frontier traditions. In fact the largest of all such organizations was the San Francisco Vigilance Committee of 1856, which may have had from 6,000 to 8,000 members. Richard Maxwell Brown, in his informative study of the subject, considers the South Carolina Regulators, a frontier movement organized to put down a backcountry crime wave in the 1760's, as the first precedent for vigilantism. But this movement, which largely succeeded in its purposes and disbanded in 1769, seems hardly to have started a tradition, since the next notable vigilante organizations, which appeared in Illinois and Indiana, did not emerge until the period 1816-30. In the main, vigilantism, which moved westward with the frontier, was a mid-nineteenth-century phenomenon. The 236 movements Brown has recorded killed at least 729 persons. Almost half of these killings took place in Texas, California, and Montana, and all but a small fraction of them were committed in the half century between 1840 and 1890.[3]

Vigilante groups were rarely led by rowdies or thugs. Indeed it is testimony to the extent to which informal and violent substitutes for law were accepted in many parts of the country that such organizations often drew their leaders from the top levels of local society, sometimes from prominent merchants and able young men on the make, and that their following came largely from the solid middle class. They were organized, after all, to defend property, as they saw it, and to maintain order. To justify themselves they invoked self-preservation, popular sovereignty, the need for efficient and inexpensive justice, and even at times the sacred right of revolution. Very commonly they salved their consciences by holding informal trials, and sometimes the larger movements were quite formally organized and governed. Most vigilante organizations seem to have accelerated in violence, moving rather rapidly from whipping and expulsion to hanging. On occasions too their organizations led to near anarchy, when a vigilante movement would be met by an anti-vigilante coalition, and two rival groups would settle into a feud not altogether unlike the gangster feuds of the twentieth

3 Brown's essay: "The American Vigilante Tradition," *Violence*, 144–218, is the source of my information; for early vigilantism, Cutler: *Lynch-Law*, chapters II-IV, is also informative.

century, but sometimes intermingled with local partisan politics. Yet the larger vigilante movements won a surprising acceptance in the respectable world. Pointing out that at one moment (in 1890) four ex-vigilantes were serving in the Senate, Brown enumerates among prominent men who were ex-vigilantes, or who at some time strongly approved of vigilantism, two Presidents (Jackson and Theodore Roosevelt), five Senators, eight Governors, and a considerable number of writers.[4]

No doubt defenders of vigilantism like Theodore Roosevelt, Ray Stannard Baker, and H. H. Bancroft thought of vigilantism as an expression of a kind of old-fashioned popular American hardihood, and as an informal, basically well-intentioned, sometimes necessary and benign extension of the law. We may wonder what they would have thought of the vigilantism of the modern Ku Klux Klan, whose members in the main also thought themselves to be acting in the name of patriotism, law and order, and moral decency. Appealing to Americans devoted to these old-fashioned virtues, as well as to the domination of the old-fashioned white, Anglo-Saxon, Protestant type, the Ku Klux Klan probably had over two million members pass through its ranks between 1915 and 1944, over four fifths of them in the South, Southwest and in the older North Central states of Indiana, Ohio, and Illinois. The Klan was strong in cities and in small towns, particularly in areas of rapid growth and social dislocation. In order to intimidate Negroes, Catholics, Jews, labor leaders, "loose women," and in some cases to enforce Prohibition as well as its own notions of religion, morals, and racial and ethnic purity, the Klan resorted to some techniques, like lobbying, that are quite legitimate in the American canon, but also to extensive violence in the vigilante tradition. As early as 1921, before the Klan had reached its peak membership, the New York *World* listed 152 outrages it believed had been committed by the Klan, including 27 tar-and-feather parties, 41 floggings, and 4 murders.[5] In addition, the Klan on occasion resorted to kidnapping, house-burning, simple assault, branding, and mutilation. The intimidating force of its

[4] *Violence*, 178–83.
[5] For estimates of the Klan membership and other facts, I have relied on *The Ku Klux Klan in the City, 1915–1930* by Kenneth T. Jackson (1967), which also has an excellent critical bibliography of writings on the Klan. Jackson gives ample attention to Klan violence, as does David M. Chalmers: *Hooded Americanism: The First Century of the Ku Klux Klan* (1965) and Charles C. Alexander: *The Ku Klux Klan in the Southwest* (1965).

activities in those parts of the country where it was strong can hardly be overemphasized.

Starting with the 1960's a new type of urban vigilantism has appeared in a few American cities. Chiefly with the purpose of opposing organized crime, and out of a sense of dissatisfaction with existing police protection, various groups, some black and some white, have begun to organize to patrol the streets. Unlike earlier vigilante organizations the urban vigilantes organized in the 1960's have tended to cooperate with the police and the authorities, and thus far have shown little disposition to resort to violence. They have shown, however, some tendency to direct their attention toward race relations, and there is always a certain dangerous potential in the existence of groups of armed civilians, however well-intentioned.[6]

VI

In reading of the crowd actions of the nineteenth century, one notices how readily large portions of urban crowds became armed with guns. Every aspect of violence in our history, from riots to presidential assassinations, has been exacerbated by the fact that ours is a gun culture—a thing without parallel among the industrial nations of the world. In some measure our gun culture owes its origins to the needs of an agrarian society and to the dangers and terrors of the frontier, but for us the central question must be why it has survived into an age in which only about 5% of the population makes its living from farming and from which the frontier has long since gone. Why did the United States, alone among modern industrial societies, cling to the idea that the widespread substantially *unregulated* availability of guns among its city population is an acceptable and a safe thing?

Much of it has to do with an ideology widely shared since colonial times and seemingly confirmed by the supposed success of the militiamen in the Revolution and the War of 1812 (their dismal failures were swept under the rug): the classic radical Whig conviction that a standing army, along with the potential Caesars and Cromwells who command it, is one of the greatest dangers to free government, while an armed populace is one of freedom's primary safeguards. It is this political doctrine that was embodied in the Second Amendment, with its injunction that "the right of the people to keep and bear arms not be infringed"—though the Second Amendment also made it clear that this

---

[6] See the summary of these groups by Richard Maxwell Brown in *Violence*, 187–93.

right was not a categorical prerogative of the *individual* but was linked
to the *civic* need for "a well regulated militia."[7]

At any rate, as the United States became more and more industrial
and urban, its people, even in the towns, still continued to exercise,
and indeed grow emotional, about their "right" to go armed, and it
is a safe guess that there have been very few peacetime periods in our
nineteenth-century history during which guns in the hands of civilians
did not outnumber those in the hands of soldiers and policemen. The
Founding Fathers were in dead earnest in their fear of a standing army.
In the mid-1780's, after they had just won their independence by the
force of arms, Secretary of War Henry Knox found himself managing
an army of about 700 men under the Articles of Confederation, and a
few years later, when the Washington administration under the new
Constitution proposed to add only 512 more, the Pennsylvania democrat, Senator William Maclay, grew nervous at the thought that the
government might be "laying the foundation of a standing army."
Even in 1811, when the country was clearly headed toward war with
England, the army numbered only 5,600 officers and men.

Historically, therefore, the United States long exhibited the interesting spectacle of an armed population juxtaposed to feeble police
and military establishments, a remarkable testimony to public confidence in the loyalty of the citizens and in their disposition, if they were
to use their arms at all, to use them only against each other and not
against civil authority. But the notion that the citizen needs a gun to
protect himself, a notion now nourished by a gun lobby which is as
powerful as it is indifferent to the public safety, is still very widely
and intensely felt in the United States. Today, despite the anguished
memory of recent assassinations and the expressed interest of a great
majority of the public in stronger gun laws, despite the appearance of
armed rioters and mounting complaints about criminal and political
violence, the nation still lives under the chaotic governance of 20,000
permissive and porous federal, state, and local laws regulating guns;
and the state of the laws still abets assassins, maniacs, impulsive murderers, and potential political terrorists at the expense of the general
population and the civic order.

[7] Despite the assertion of gun lobbyists, the clear intent of the framers of the Second
Amendment was to make an organized *militia*, and not an armed populace, possible.
That this amendment does not bar gun controls has been repeatedly adjudicated by
the Supreme Court. The leading case now is *U.S.* v. *Miller*, 307 U.S. 174 (1939), in
which the Court upheld the principle of prohibitions by Congress on arms which have
no relation to the organized militia of the states.

Comparative figures show that the United States, wedded to its gun culture, shows a higher homicide rate, and in particular a higher gun-homicide rate, than any advanced nation we would care to be compared with. Some measure of the unnecessary cost may be arrived at by setting our total civil casualties against our comparative rate of gun fatalities. An incomplete tally of firearm fatalities shows that we have suffered in the twentieth century over 750,000 deaths, embracing over 265,000 homicides, over 330,000 suicides, and over 139,000 accidents.[8] The grand total of 750,000 is considerably more than all the battle fatalities (i.e., armed service losses excluding deaths from disease) suffered by American forces in all our wars combined.

Other industrial nations have very stringent laws governing the possession of guns by private citizens, a fact which has much to do with our unenviable leadership in gun fatalities. The gun-homicide rate of the United States, for example, is forty times as much as the rates of Scotland, England and Wales, Japan, and the Netherlands. In 1963, when the United States had 5,126 gun murders, England and Wales had 24, and there are several American cities which annually have more gun homicides than all of England, Scotland, and Wales put together.

In the nineteenth century presumably fewer Americans in the cities could afford guns than today, but even then armed crowds usually had more lethal weaponry at their disposal than bats and rocks (they often looted gun stores), and most of the deaths in the railroad strike riots of 1877 were inflicted by gunfire. Today the supplies for an armed crowd are more accessible than ever. Because it is the only great nation that will permit their import and sale, the United States provides the only large and rich market for militarily obsolescent but still usable weapons. World War II surplus guns and N.A.T.O. discards have flooded into the country for many years, many of them selling for $15 or less (the one that killed President Kennedy was sold for $12.78). It is estimated that from 1959 to 1963, between five and seven million foreign weapons were imported, and the *urban* population of the country is probably more heavily armed than at any time in our history. A few years ago a Gallup poll showed that about half of the nation's households had guns, though a more recent national poll by Opinion Research (September, 1968), taken after the national revulsion caused by the Martin Luther King and Robert Kennedy assassinations and the passage of a few tighter local gun ordinances, found that among whites

[8] These figures are explained by Carl Bakal: *The Right to Bear Arms* (1966), 354–5.

34% and among blacks 24% reported owning guns. The most stringent federal law (1968) still goes no further than to prohibit the mail-order sale of guns and ammunition, and the strongest state laws tend to bar only the carrying of *concealed* weapons.[9]

The history of America's gun culture—the casualness with which we extend country and frontier ways to the urban milieu, the stunning aplomb with which for so long we lived with an armed populace and negligible official forces—is at once a symptom of political negligence and yet a token of deep political self-confidence. American authorities discovered only in the frequent riots of the 1830's how lightly policed their cities were; it was not until the sudden apparition of anarchy in 1877 that they concluded that a substantial National Guard was necessary. Americans seem always to have been quite sure that, whatever might happen up the alleys where the modern equivalents of the James and Dalton brothers meet each other and draw, nobody will do anything to challenge the power of government or subvert the American way of life. It is unfortunate if the citizens insist on attacking each other from time to time with lethal weapons, but past experience shows that such disorders will not shake the government. Blood-letting is republican high spirits in action. The tree of liberty has to be watered by the blood of tyrants and martyrs. And it is true that for most Americans so much of the worst violence has taken place so far from home—so many of the violent labor struggles, for example, in out-of-the-way places like Cripple Creek, Centralia, Ludlow, Coeur d'Alene, Everett, Gastonia, McComb—that one hardly believes it will affect the population centers of the nation. From the beginning there was a benign and wise disposition to let bygones be bygones, where uprisings, even those with insurrectionary overtones, were involved: there were easy pardons and no official vindictiveness after the Shays' Rebellion, the Whiskey Rebellion, the Fries Rebellion. The old American tolerance for the violent act may have been founded on some secret sympathy for it—D. H. Lawrence believed that "the essential American soul is hard, isolate, stoic, and a killer"—but it was also and more certainly based upon an uncommon confidence in the stability and security of the country, the confidence that almost any kind of mess could be brought under control quickly enough if one suddenly had to ex-

[9] There is valuable information on the current state of the gun culture in *Time*, June 21, 1968, and *Newsweek*, June 24, 1968, as well as Bakal: op. cit., and Thayer's book on arms merchants. In the spring of 1969, 25% of Negroes questioned on the matter thought that they should arm themselves, 59% that they should not, and the remainder were uncertain. *Newsweek*, June 30, 1969.

tend oneself, and that if a few people died in the meantime, that was just the way of the world.

And then, after the terrible decades of violence from the late 1870's to about 1914, some forms of violent action had reassuringly tended, despite some fluctuations, to go sharply downward until almost yesterday. Lethal vigilantism (despite a few murders by the Klan in the 1920's) went out with the last century; lynching, long in slow decline, decreased sharply in the 1920's and all but disappeared by the end of the 1930's; violence in labor disputes flared up in a last ugly climax in the 1930's and then abruptly died away. Perhaps we came to take it for granted that, as all things are supposed to get better, violence would take care of itself too. No historian or sociologist has yet tried to find an answer to the question: how is a particular form of violence, once firmly rooted in the ways of society, done away with? If we were to examine vigilantism, lynching, and industrial violence with this question in mind, I am not at all sure what form our answers would take, but it seems reasonably clear that they would be upsetting to one of the most modish ideas of our era, the idea that our basic social problems will best be solved if they are turned back to management by local communities where "participatory democracy" can come into action. Whatever may happen in the future, in *our* past, at any rate, local control and the action of the people in the streets has had gory consequences time after time. The story of our diminished violence, in those areas of our life where it has in fact largely been brought under control, has been in good part the story of the submergence and defeat of arbitrary, bigoted, self-satisfied local forces by the advancing cosmopolitan sentiment of a larger, somewhat more neutrally minded state, or, better, national public. It has been marked by the replacement of small-town vigilantes by state authorities or national troops; the subordination of local sheriffs harboring secret or even open mob sympathies to the external forces of relatively neutral law, by the supremacy of national laws and standards over state and municipal laws and practices; the replacement of hometown sentiment by metropolitan ways of criminal justice; the subjection of local abuses to the spotlight of national, and even world, opinion; the concentration of nationwide attention on employers and police officers who had counted on being able to terrorize miners, textile hands, or lumberworkers in remote towns on the assumption that nobody would be looking; the establishment of national legal authority over a system of recognized collective bargaining. This is a country in which the whole is likely to be better than the sum of its parts.

VII

On the cover of the June 30, 1969, issue of *New Left Notes,* the organ of the Progressive Labor faction of Students for a Democratic Society,[1] there is a large woodcut illustration which must surely be one of the minor signs of the times. Two young men, one white, one black, are seen crouching on a roof-top above a city in flames. Both are armed with automatic rifles, and both wear, Mexican-fashion, the crisscrossed bandoleers of the rural insurrectionary or bandito. They are revolutionaries, urban guerillas. Alongside them is the legend: "We are advocates of the abolition of war, we do not want war; but war can only be abolished through war, and in order to get rid of the gun it is necessary to take up the gun." One must, I think, pass by the resemblance of this promise of a war-to-end-war to other such promises in the past; one must pass by also its hauntingly perverse echo of the words of the American officer in Vietnam that "In order to liberate the village we had to destroy it," to consider its larger meaning for American political culture.

There is in America today[2] a rising mystique of violence on the left. Those who lived through the rise of European fascism, or who have watched the development of right-wing groups in this country over the last generation, or have fully recognized the amount of violence leveled at civil rights workers in the South, are never surprised at violence cults on the right. They still see them in action in such crank groups as the Minutemen and hear their accents in some of the uninhibited passages in George Wallace's speeches. What has been more arresting is the decline of the commitment to non-violence on the left, and the growth of a disposition to indulge or to exalt acts of force or violence. What was once the Student Non-Violent Coordinating Committee has taken the "Non-Violent" out of its title. Frantz Fanon's full-throated defense of the therapeutic and liberating effects of violence has been one of the most widely read books of our time. During a summer of frequent rioting, *The New York Review of Books,* one of the most influential and fashionable periodicals on the

[1] Not to be confused with the organ of an opposing faction, the Revolutionary Youth Movement, which is also entitled *New Left Notes.*
[2] This Introduction was completed in the opening weeks of 1970, and I have not tried to update it, even though the Cambodian invasion and other events of the spring might easily require modification of some of my speculative remarks. These events, however, do not in my mind affect the main burden of the following pages, which is to make a largely prudential argument against the use of violence by dissenters.

American campus today, elected to feature on its cover a fully instructive diagram for making a Molotov cocktail. In its columns a widely-read left-wing journalist, Andrew Kopkind, has told us that morality comes out of the muzzle of a gun. The Weatherman faction of SDS has made a primary tactic of violent encounters with the police. A young leader of the Black Panthers rose at the 1969 summer convention of the SDS to taunt the white delegates with the boast that the Panthers had "shed more blood than anyone" and that white leftists have not even shot rubber bands. Dotson Rader, a young veteran of Columbia's wars, informed the readers of *The New York Times* in its correspondence columns that the justice the New Left seeks will be won by "fighting in the streets."[3] Some, no doubt, are reminded of the Paris Commune. Others will be reminded of the promises of Mussolini.

Certain ironies in the new cult of violence are inescapable. The sidewalk Sorels who preach violence know very little about it, and sometimes prove pitifully ineffectual in trying to use it. Those who practice it with the greatest effect—the police and the military—find preaching superfluous. The new prophets of violence are almost certain to become its chief victims if it becomes general and uncontrolled, especially when their own romanticism carries them from the word to the deed. Historically, violence has not been an effective weapon of the left, except in that rarest of rare circumstances, the truly revolutionary situation. Under normal circumstances, violence has more characteristically served domineering capitalists or trigger-happy police, peremptory sergeants or fascist hoodlums. And even in our day, I think it should be emphasized, the growing acceptance of violence has been unwittingly fostered from the top of society. The model for violence, which has rapidly eroded the effectiveness of appeals to nonviolent procedures, has been the hideous and gratuitous official violence in Vietnam. And after having created and made heroes of such a special tactical force as the Green Berets, we should not be altogether surprised to find the Black Panthers wearing *their* berets and practicing close-order drill. It may be childishly irrelevant to cite the example of Vietnam as an answer to every reproach for domestic acts of force or violence, but there is in that answer a point of psychological importance that we should not overlook: now, as always, the primary precedent and the primary rationale for violence comes from the established order itself. Violence is, so to speak, an official reality. No

[3] For the Panthers, see *National Guardian*, June 28, 1969; Rader in *The New York Times*, July 6, 1969.

society exists without using force or violence and without devising sanctions for violence which are used to uphold just wars and necessary police actions. But the frequency and the manner in which official violence is used is of signal importance to the legitimation of the civic order. Any liberal democratic state is in danger of wearing away its legitimacy if it repeatedly uses violence at home or abroad when the necessity of that violence is wholly unpersuasive to a substantial number of its people.

Neither establishments nor revolutionary movements can do without sanctions for violence. What any man sees as a just war or a necessary police action will, of course, depend upon his situation and his politics; but only a few pacifists quarrel with the idea that just wars are conceivable, and only a few utopian anarchists are likely to deny that under some circumstances authorities have to use force or violence to keep order. The right of revolution is itself an established and sanctified rationale for violence. It can hardly be banished from the established sanctions in a country like America that was born in a revolution. One of our most sacred texts lays down the circumstances under which revolutionary resistance becomes legitimate. "Prudence," it also remarks (there *were* revolutionaries for whom prudence was a consideration), "will dictate that Governments long established should not be changed for light and transient causes; . . . But when a long train of abuses and usurpations, pursuing invariably the same Object evinces a design to reduce them under absolute Despotism, it is their right, it is their duty, to throw off such a Government, and to provide new Guards for their future security."

In our own time we have no difficulty in thinking of some tyrants against whom the right of revolution was or could have been justifiably invoked, and responsibly so when the circumstances warranted hope of success. Unfortunately, in this age of verbal overkill, the epithet of tyranny can be hurled at any regime that is intensely disliked by a morally self-confident minority, and the prospects of revolutionary success may seem astonishingly good to those who gull themselves with their own miscalculations and fantasies. The classic rationale for revolution is now widely used to sanction piecemeal violence against democratic regimes in which no shadow of a revolutionary situation exists. The word "revolution" has been distended to apply to any situation in which there is rapid change or widespread discontent. Hence acts of forcible or violent adventurism can be given a superficial legitimacy by defining any situation one pleases as a "revolutionary situation." One radical thinker, Barrington Moore, Jr., who cannot be accused of lack of concern for the oppressed or of hostility to revolutions, has deplored the current disposition "to cast some vague universal cloak of legitimacy upon violence—even upon violent resistance to oppression," and has warned against occasions when "revolutionary rhetoric outruns the real possibilities inherent in a given historical situation." Today, in America, he asserts, "talk about revolution is . . . pure talk with potentially dangerous and tragic consequences."[4]

One of the essential difficulties in justifying violence is that its success is an ingredient in its justification, and such success is usually a matter of chance. There *are* some blunders that are worse than crimes, and among these are the blunders of those who, even in a good cause, precipitate violence without reasonable grounds for believing that violence will serve its purpose or that it can be contained within bounds that will be proportionate to the ends in view. No doubt it is tempting to think of putting a final end to some grave and massive social evil by a quick, surgical, limited act of violence. But the difficulty lies in being reasonably sure, before the event, that the evil will indeed be ended and not exacerbated or succeeded by some equal or greater evil; that the violence can really be limited both in time and in the casualties it inflicts, and that the reaction will not be more harmful than the surgery. For this reason all politicians, revolutionary no less than establishment politicians, must work with a terrible calculus in human misfortune.

In order to justify the use of violence as a means toward the accomplishment of some humane and "progressive" end, one must first believe that he knows, roughly at least, two things: first, that so-and-so much violence is in fact necessary to achieve the end; and second, what the countervailing human cost of the violence will be—that is, where its repercussions will stop. There are, of course, many people who imagine that they have this kind of command of the future; but some of us are not so sure, since we are not even sure that we can judge the necessity or usefulness of *past* violence in many cases where all the returns seem to be in hand.

But let us not deceive ourselves. Current credulity about the benefits of violence is rarely based upon a careful concern about when and how violence can be justified, or upon sober estimates of its past role or its prospects of future success. We are not living in a period of moral casuistry or measured calculation but in one of robust political

[4] Barrington Moore, Jr.: "Thoughts on Violence and Democracy," *Proceedings* of the Academy of Political Science, XXIX (1968), 6–7.

romanticism.[5] The protest politics of the 1960's threatened at times to break with the historic politics of liberal American reformers, who aimed to persuade a wide public, had scruples about methods, were willing to compromise, to move patiently from one limited end to another. For a decisive but now perhaps waning segment of the far left, politics has become all too much a matter of self-expression and of style, and such efforts as its more extreme exponents make at calculation and casuistry seem feeble as compared with the full-blown bravado of their actionist creed. There are moments when the aim of the political act seems to have become little more than the venting of a sense of outrage, and there have been activists more concerned with their freedom to carry the Vietcong flag in a peace parade or to use four-letter words than with their ability to persuade. There is less hope that any particular foray will yield visible results or affect public policy, more desire to get a sense of emotional satisfaction out of a mass happening. The demand for programmatic achievement has become less fixed, that of self-assertion central. The distinction between politics and theatre has been deliberately blurred by activists in politics and activists in the theatre.

In the new politics, force or violence has a new place: for some it is satisfying merely to use it, but others have devised strategies to provoke counter-violence to show up the establishment, as they put it, for what it is. In any case, violence has come to bear the promise of redemption. "Violence alone," writes Frantz Fanon in one of the canonical works of the new politics, "violence committed by the people, violence organized and educated by its leaders, makes it possible for the masses to understand social truths and gives the key to them." Fanon, writes Sartre in presenting him, "shows clearly that this irrepressible violence is neither sound and fury, nor the resurrection of savage instincts, nor even the effect of resentment: it is man recreating himself. . . . No gentleness can efface the marks of violence, only violence itself can destroy them."[6]

Violence, then, is not only useful but therapeutic, which is to say indispensable. It seems natural enough for those who have been victims of a great deal of violence, or simply of the constant threat of over-

[5] For a remarkable essay on the changing style of social analysis that has come with the new cult of violence in the international left, see Richard Lowenthal: "Unreason and Revolution," *Encounter*, XXIII (November 1969), 22–34.
[6] Fanon: *The Wretched of the Earth* (1961 ; Evergreen edn., 1968), 148; see Sartre's Preface, 21. One can see here how the Gandhian conception of non-violence as being the therapeutic and healing agent is on the wane. The ability to use or risk violence is now the mark of moral superiority.

whelming force, to conclude that they can restore their dignity only when they use violence themselves. But the restorative power of violence, if indeed violence can have such a power, must surely depend upon its being used successfully. The unsuccessful use of violence, ending in defeat and fresh humiliations, may in fact intensify the original malaise. It is hard, for example, to imagine that the survivors of the grim massacre of the Indonesian Communist party in 1965–66 would have the same enthusiasm for the restorative power of violence as the victorious Algerian rebels. And this is why the existential mystique of violence, which tries to circumvent the rational calculus of tactical probabilities, will not do: its claims for therapy or sanctification through violence rest upon an arbitrary assumption of success. There is no satisfactory refuge from political calculation in psychology or metaphysics.

But of course there *are* examples of success in our time—examples set by Mao, Castro, the Algerian rebels, Ho Chi Minh and the Vietcong. The circumstances in all these cases have a special quality: the successes have been among "backward" peoples with a firm territorial base and a history of colonial exploitation. It is now suggested that violence can be equally successful in modern industrial countries, that guerilla action suitable to the Sierra Maestre or the terror and sabotage that won in Algiers can be adapted to New York, Chicago, Oakland, or even, it appears, Scarsdale. A good deal of tactical ingenuity has in fact been stimulated, but the chief intellectual consequences have been pathetic: many young blacks have begun to think of themselves as being a colonial people, and of their problems of liberation as having exactly the same characteristics.[7] The psychological similarities are, of course, there—and a book like Fanon's *The Wretched of the Earth*, the work of a psychiatrist, argues its case largely in psychological rather than in social structural terms. American blacks may have the psyches of other victims of colonialism but they lack all the essential features of the true colonial situation: a terrain suitable to guerilla action, the prospects of becoming a majority, territoriality, and the promise of integral control of the economy after the colonial power has been expelled. Except for these indispensable elements, the com-

[7] Since so much has been accomplished by strategic minorities, it may not matter for the future of violence in America that the black militants have not yet converted a majority of Negroes. In *Newsweek*'s 1969 poll, 63% (as against 21%) thought that Negroes could win their rights without violence. Overwhelming majorities also repudiated separatism in response to questions about integrated schools and integrated neighborhoods. *Newsweek*, June 30, 1969. The appeal of militant ideas, however, is much higher among the young.

parison is excellent, and therefore we may indulge ourselves in the fantasy that Watts is just like Algiers.[8]

But in the end one must give the prophets of violence their due: violence *is* pervasive in human experience and has been pervasive in American history, and however it repels us, we must see it as an instrument of common use. The creed its proponents put before us is simple but forceful: Violence has been all but universal in the past. Violence changes things and nothing else does. Violence is therefore necessary. "Violence," said Rap Brown in what must surely remain one of the memorable utterances of our time, "is necessary and it's as American as cherry pie." Presumably he did not expect his listeners to be so uncritically patriotic as to think that violence must be good because Americans have so often used it. No doubt his hope was that if a decent respect for the normality and inevitability of violence could be instilled in the minds of his contemporaries, they would be less censorious about the violence supposedly necessary to black liberation. And one should grant all that is sound here: certainly violence that would in fact lead to a full realization of the rights of blacks would have a great deal to be said for it, and would stand in quite a different moral position from the violence, say, that many lynchers used for their own entertainment and for the edification of their children. Here, as always, however, one encounters the latent, the unexamined assumption: violence *will* deliver that which is expected of it. It is an assumption shared more and more among the very young,[9] black or white: Justice will be won by "fighting in the streets." Fighting in the streets as a revolutionary technique—it is one of the few old-fashioned ideas still alive.

Certainly world history yields plenty of cases in which some historical log-jam seems to have been broken up by an eruption of violence, which is then followed by a period of peaceful, gradualist

[8] For a shrewd analysis of the implications of this kind of thinking see Christopher Lasch's essay "Black Power: Cultural Nationalism as Politics," in *The Agony of the American Left* (1969). For a bleak estimate, based on historical experience, of the prospects of transferring guerilla warfare to cities, see Martin Oppenheimer: "Para-Military Activities in Urban Areas," in L. H. Masotti and D. R. Bowen, eds.: *Riots and Rebellion* (1968), 429–38.

[9] The very young: to some considerable degree the current American problem of violence is a demographic problem. Violent solutions—either in politics or crime—appeal mainly to those under 25. Today almost one-half the American population is under 25 and an extraordinary proportion is in the age group 14 to 25, which produces or stimulates most violence. Those politicians who think they can lightly promise a successful campaign against criminal violence have not consulted the demographic returns. For a sober estimate of the prospects here, see Fred P. Graham: "A Contemporary History of American Crime," *Violence*, 460–78.

improvement. It is always possible in such cases to argue (though difficult to prove) that the violence was a necessary precondition of the peaceful change that followed. The trouble is that there are so many other cases in which violence has decided issues in ways we are less likely to applaud. American experience with the large-scale violent resolution of fundamental crises is mixed. The Revolution and the Civil War pose an interesting antithesis. The question of American independence was settled by violence, and, as historical issues go, settled with considerable success. But one of the keys to that success may be found in the minimum of gratuitous violence with which the Revolution was carried out. There could be no regicide and there was no terror. There were frequent incidents, but there was no wholesale mobbing of dissidents. Few Loyalists outside the ranks of the British army were killed, though many were terrorized, many went into exile, and many lost large properties. Even the military action did not characteristically go beyond what we would call guerilla warfare. Most important, the revolutionaries did not turn upon each other with violence or terror. The Thermidor, if the adoption of the Constitution can be correctly called that, was equally mild, and in part simply nationalized and embodied in institutional form some of the principles set forth in the Revolution itself. Not only was independence secured and the political life of the American states markedly democratized but many social reforms were given a strong impetus. In spite of the difficult questions of national organization that were not settled, and in spite of the tumultuous passions raised by the political issues of the Federal era, the episodes of domestic violence that followed the Revolution—and there were quite a number of them—were in a relatively low key and proved eminently controllable. The early rebellions mounted by Daniel Shays, the Whiskey rebels, and Jacob Fries, though of much political consequence, were, as episodes of violence, kept at the level of skirmishes, and their leaders were afterwards treated with judicious consideration. The Revolution was followed by relative social peace: on the whole, the era from 1790 to 1830, though far from violence-free, was one of the least violent periods in our domestic history.

The Civil War stands in marked contrast. Again, it did settle historical issues, the issues of union and of the legal status of slavery. But it was preceded by a decade of searing civic violence and climaxed by a war that cost 600,000 lives, and it left an extraordinary inheritance of bitterness and lethal passion that has not yet ended. The legal liberation of the slave was not followed by the actual liberation of the black man. The defeated states became less rather than more democratic.

The violence of the war was followed by the resounding and horrifying episodic violence of Reconstruction, and the Thermidor in the South went on for a full generation after the guns were stilled. The war seems in retrospect to have been an intensely cruel and wasteful way of settling—if that is the right word—the issues that gave rise to it. I do not agree with the categorical form or exaggerated rhetoric of Barrington Moore's pessimistic world-historical estimate that "violence has settled all historical issues so far, and most of them in the wrong way,"[1] but in the considerable list of historical cases that could be drawn up to support his judgment, the Civil War would surely rank high.

If we look at the use of violence in social situations of less profound consequence than those which led to the Revolution and the Civil War, we can find instances when violence in the United States appears to have served its purpose. And it has been, on the whole, the violence of those who already had position and power. Many vigilante movements, for example, achieved their limited goal of suppressing outlaws. Lynching clearly added a note of terroristic enforcement to the South's caste system. For years employers used violence and the threat of violence against labor with success: in the main, the outstandingly violent episodes in industrial conflict were tragic defeats for labor, although there were occasions when violence initiated on behalf of employers became too blatant for public acceptance and boomeranged. Labor has used violence less often than employers and with only rare success. There was, to be sure, one very effective series of extra-legal actions by labor—the sit-downs of the 1930's. However, in these instances the workers, though using illegal *force*, were using a tactical device that tended to avert rather than precipitate acts of outright violence. This may explain why they won considerable sympathy from the public, which was at the same time becoming acutely aware of the violence, intimidation, and espionage used by employers in many industries. In any case, the sit-downs were a transient tactic which labor leaders abandoned as soon as collective bargaining was achieved, and it is difficult to imagine the sit-downs repeatedly successful as a standard device.[2]

In sum, violence can succeed in a political environment like that

[1] "Thoughts on Violence and Democracy," 11. What he means by the wrong way is made clear: "The violence of the oppressor has generally been far more effective than the violence of the weak and oppressed."
[2] For a penetrating estimation of the sit-downs, which stresses their basic spirit of civility, see Michael Walzer: "Corporate Authority and Civil Disobedience," *Dissent*, XVI (September-October 1969), 395–406.

of the United States under certain conditions. Those who use it must be able to localize it and limit its duration. They must use it under circumstances in which the public is either indifferent or uninformed, or in which the accessible and relevant public opinion (as in the case of vigilantes and, usually, of employers in the nineteenth century) is heavily biased in their favor. If violence is accompanied by exceptional brutality (lynching, employer actions like that at Ludlow), it must be kept a local matter, and the perpetrators must hope that it can somehow be screened from the attention of the larger polity. The conditions for its success, in this respect, seem to have become more problematic in the age of mass communications, where the most vital tactical problem is to set the stage so that the onus for violent action can be made to seem to rest entirely upon one's adversaries.

If violence sometimes works, it does not follow that nothing but violence works. Most of the social reforms in American history have been brought about without violence, or with only a marginal and inessential use of it, by reformers who were prepared to carry on a long-term campaign of education and propaganda. The entire apparatus of the welfare state, from child labor laws, wage-hour regulation, industrial safety laws, and workmen's compensation to legally regulated collective bargaining, social security, and medical care for the aged is the achievement of active minorities which, while sometimes militant and always persistent, were also patient and non-violent. Ours, however, is an age that cannot wait, and it is doubtful that young militants, black or white, are taking much comfort from the example of such predecessors in the tradition of American reform. The activists, according to their temperaments, will argue either that earlier reforms, being props to the establishment, were of little or no value, or that they were all a generation overdue when they came. The first response is simply inhumane, but the second has much truth in it: such reforms were indeed long overdue. However, it does not follow that the use of violence would have hastened their coming. Under some conditions the fear or threat of violence may hasten social reforms, yet if actual outbreaks of violence were the primary force in bringing reform, one might have expected social welfare laws to come in the United States before they came to such countries as Great Britain and Germany where there was considerably less industrial violence. The important element seems to have been not the resort to violence but the presence of powerful labor movements with a socialist commitment and the threat of sustained action through normal political channels.

But the confrontationist politicians of our time have hit upon an approach to violence that surmounts one of the signal disadvantages under which social dissidents have labored in the past: they have learned the value not of committing violence but of *provoking* it. It remains true today, as it has always been, that most political violence is committed by the agents of authority. In the past, for example, labor often got the blame for violent outbursts that were primarily the work of police or other agents of employers. Hence one speaks of "labor violence" but not of "capital violence." Today, however, a technique has been found to put official violence to work in the apparent interests of dissent. A small cadre of determined activists, enveloped in a large crowd of demonstrators, can radicalize a substantial segment of public opinion by provoking the police into violent excesses—if necessary by hurling objects, but better still by hurling nothing more than verbal abuse. The activists have correctly gauged the temper of the police, who are often quite ready to oblige by lashing out indiscriminately against both those who have offended them and those who have not —orderly demonstrators, innocent bystanders, reporters, cameramen. Young radicals have thus found a way to put the police and the mass media to work for them, as the public sees a hideous spectacle of beating, kicking, and clubbing by officers of the law against unarmed demonstrators and witnesses. Outrage becomes the more blatant to those who are aware of and attracted by the milky innocence of the majority of young demonstrators.

Whether the larger public effect of such confrontations will actually work to the ultimate advantage of the activists is problematical. What they can see with their own eyes at the moment of conflict is that many persons, hitherto vaguely sympathetic, become, at least for a time, energized and activated out of indignation. What they choose to ignore is the other, less visible but usually larger public, which puts the full blame on demonstrators and backs the police and the authorities. (The behavior of the Chicago police during the Democratic Convention of 1968, one of the most flagrant police actions of this era, was approved by a substantial majority of the public.) Still, activist leaders are aware of *their* converts, and converts there usually are. Why not rejoice in the converts and dismiss the backlash? Hence the ubiquitous New Left agitator Tom Hayden has called for "two, three, many Chicagos," and the young activists interviewed by Jerome Skolnick's researchers for the National Commission on the Causes and Prevention of Violence show a shrewd if limited understanding of the implications of such tactics. The purpose of confrontations, they argue with striking candor, is to educate the public by staging spectacles of repression.

"Direct action is not intended to win particular reforms or to influence decision-makers, but rather to bring out a repressive response from authorities—a response rarely seen by most white Americans. When confrontation brings violent official response, uncommitted elements of the public can see for themselves the true nature of the 'system.' " The activists also believe that such experience lowers the "cultural fear of violence" natural among young middle-class radicals—a fear that is "psychologically damaging and may be politically inhibiting," and thus prepares them for a serious commitment to revolution.[3] To some degree they have already been proved right: the "damaging" inhibitions against the use of guns, bombs, and arson have begun to break down.

VIII

Can this breakdown be extrapolated into an indefinite future? No doubt most Americans are more curious about where our penchant for violence is taking us than they are about a more precise explanation of its pattern in the past. But here prognosis is as hazardous as anywhere. In the past our violence has always been cyclical, and it is possible to believe that the 1960's will some day appear on the charts of the sociologists as another peak period, rather more pronounced than many, which is followed by relative calm. As the young never tire of reminding us, we live in a situation that is new and in some decisive respects unprecedented. (I sometimes think that *all* American experience is a series of disjunctive situations whose chief connecting link is that each generation repeats the belief of its predecessor that there is nothing to be learned from the past.) In any case, our social violence is not a self-contained universe that holds within itself all the conditions of its future development. In fact almost everything depends upon external forces which no one dares to predict: the tempo at which we disengage from Vietnam, the national and international response to our undisguisable failure there, and our ability to avoid another such costly venture.

Who can really believe that he knows what to expect of the future of American violence? It is easy to draw up two plausible scenarios for the future, one apocalyptic, the other relatively benign though

[3] Jerome H. Skolnick: *The Politics of Protest* (1969), 107–8; for Hayden, see 31. On the ultimate dangers of polarization from the new politics, see Irving Howe: "The New 'Confrontation Politics' Is a Dangerous Game," *New York Times Magazine*, October 20, 1968.

hardly exhilarating. Apocalyptic predictions are conventionally in order—indeed they have become so conventional that they constitute a kind of imperative intellectual fashion. But in them there is more of omniscience than of science, and their function seems more psychological than pragmatic. In a magical gesture one predicts evil in order to ward it off. Or worse, in moments of terrible frustration one threatens one's audience with some ultimate catastrophe by way of saying: This is what you will all get for not having followed the social policies I have prescribed for you. However, over the past generation the visions of the future that have prevailed among the most modishly apocalyptic intellectual circles in this country have been so largely wrong that they could almost be used like odd-lot buying in the stock market as a negative indicator of future realities. Perhaps the most cogent reason (aside from the perverse element of self-indulgence inherent in it) for not yielding too easily to the apocalyptic frame of mind is a pragmatic one: apocalyptic predictions, repeated too often and believed too automatically, could at best reduce men of good will to a useless passivity and at worst turn into self-fulfilling prophecies. Pragmatic wisdom argues for assuming that our difficulties are manageable, so that we may put our minds to thinking about how in fact they can be managed.

Still, it requires no remarkable ingenuity to see how some of the recent trends in American society, continued and magnified, could bring about the eclipse of liberal democratic politics. The danger is not that the alienated young and the militant blacks will wage a successful revolution. The United States is basically a conservative country, and its working class is one of the anchors of its conservatism. Its overwhelming majority is not poor, not black, and not in college. College activists, themselves only a fraction of the college population, command so much attention from the mass media that the actual state of mind of the American young has been obscured. Almost three-fourths of those in the 17-23 age bracket do not go to college, and their political direction is quite different from that of the college activists. Their responsiveness even to the cruder forms of backlash sentiment may be measured by their votes in the 1968 election, in which George Wallace had proportionately somewhat *more* support among white voters in the age groups 29 and under than in the age groups 30 and over.[4]

[4] An American Institute for Public Opinion national sample showed that Wallace had the following support in four age brackets: 21-5, 13%; 26-9, 18%; 30-49, 13%; 50 and over, 11%.

In a nation so constituted, the most serious danger comes not from the activities of young militants, black or white, but from the strength of the backlash that may arise out of an increasing polarization of the society. The apocalyptic scenario spells itself out rather easily: an indefinite prolongation of the war in Vietnam, or a re-escalation, or the launching of yet another such provocative and disastrous foreign undertaking; a continued unwillingness or inability to make adequate progress in accommodating the demand for racial justice; an intensification of confrontation politics in the colleges and on the streets; a heightened alienation of the intelligent young; violent scenes, vividly reported on TV, of provocative conduct by demonstrators and brutal responses by police; a continuing polarization of the political public into right and left which shuts off just such political and social efforts as might relieve the crisis; the formation of numerous armed groups of black and white citizens, highlighted perhaps by a few mass gunfights in the big cities; the breakdown of one or both of the major parties; the capture of the presidency and Congress by a nationwide movement dedicated to political repression at home and a hard line in foreign policy.

Not altogether impossible, one must say, though to me it somehow fails to carry conviction. The particular forms of violence that flourished in the 1960's seem now to be on the decline: ghetto riots have been tapering off, and the crest of violence touched off by campus protest may have been reached in the years 1967–70. Black militancy is certain to be with us for an indefinite future, and it is a sobering thought that the one major breakdown of the American political system came in association with an unresolved problem of race; but black agitation tends to grow more selective about methods and goals, and it is by no means clear that it must involve large-scale violence or mass casualties. Student activism too seems likely to outlast an American withdrawal from Vietnam, since it rests on a profound cultural malaise that goes beyond any political issue, but it may work at a lower level of emotional intensity. An end to the war would bring about a political and economic climate in which the effort to relieve urban blight and poverty and to come to terms with the demand for racial justice can be resumed under far more favorable conditions than those of the past five or six years. It is a rare thing in our experience to be centrally preoccupied with the same problem for two successive decades, and it is quite conceivable that even a persisting and relatively high level of violence in the 1970's will come to be regarded as a marginal rather than a central problem. At some time in the near future the destruction of the environment, and the problems attendant upon pollution and overpopulation, are likely to take the center of the historical stage and to have such a commanding urgency that all other issues will be dwarfed. The styles of thought, the political mood that will be created by such problems, as well as the political alignments they will bring about, may be so startlingly different from those of the 1960's, that the mentality of the 1960's will seem even more strange by 1980 than the mentality of the 1950's has appeared during the past few years.

When one considers American history as a whole, it is hard to think of any very long period in which it could be said that the country has been consistently well governed. And yet its political system is, on the whole, a resilient and well-seasoned one, and on the strength of its history one must assume that it can summon enough talent and good will to cope with its afflictions. To cope with them—but not, I think, to master them in any thoroughly decisive or admirable fashion. The nation seems to slouch onward into its uncertain future like some huge inarticulate beast, too much attainted by wounds and ailments to be robust, but too strong and resourceful to succumb.

RICHARD HOFSTADTER

PART I

Political Violence

Pilgrims versus Puritans

1634

Relations between the Pilgrims of Plymouth and the Puritans of the Massachusetts Bay Colony were sometimes less than cordial. They disagreed about theology, they disputed over land, and they competed for the Indian fur trade. It was the rivalry for furs that led to what was perhaps the first American inter-colonial crisis. John Hocking, of Piscataqua (later Portsmouth, New Hampshire) attempted to intercept the Pilgrims' beaver trade on the Kennebec River by trading upstream from their posts. After he ignored their reproaches, a party set out to cut the moorings of his trading ship. He drew a gun to stop them, killed one man, and was then killed by the attacking Pilgrims. When shortly thereafter John Alden sailed into Boston harbor on a trading mission he was arrested. Hoping to avoid further trouble, the Pilgrims sent Miles Standish to explain why Hocking had been attacked and to establish that an infringement of Plymouth territory had clearly taken place. The dispute was later settled peaceably at a conclave of magistrates and ministers, who, in William Bradford's words, "embraced with love and thankfulness . . . their love and concord renewed." The following account is taken from James Kendall Hosmer, ed.: "Winthrop's Journal," in *Original Narratives of Early American History*, VII (1908); see also William Bradford: *Of Plymouth Plantation*, ed. Samuel Eliot Morison (1967).

May 3. News came of the death of Hockin and the Plymouth man at Kenebeck (and of the arrival of the ship at Pemaquid, which brought thirty passengers for this place).

The occasion of the death of those men at Kenebeck was this: The Plymouth men had a grant, from the grand patentees of New England, of Kenebeck, with liberty of sole trade, etc.

The said Hockin came in a pinnace, belonging to the Lord Say and Lord Brook at Pascataquack, to trade at Kenebeck. Two of the magistrates of Plymouth, being there, forbad him; yet he went up the river; and, because he would not come down again, they sent three men in a canoe to cut his cables. Having cut one, Hockin presented a piece, and sware he would kill him that went to cut the other. They bad him to do if he drust, and went on to cut it. Thereupon he killed one of them, and instantly one in the Plymouth pinnace (which rode by them, and wherein five or six men stood with their pieces ready charged) shot and killed Hockin.

15. At the general court at Boston, upon the complaint of a kinsman of the said Hockin, John Alden, one of the said magistrates of Plymouth, who was present when Hockin was slain, being then at Boston, was called and bound with sureties not to depart out of our jurisdiction without leave had; and withal we wrote to Plymouth to certify them what we had done, and to know whether they would do justice in the cause, (as belonging to their jurisdiction,) and to have a speedy answer, etc. This we did, that notice might be taken, that we did disavow the said action, which was much condemned of all men, and which was feared would give occasion to the king to send a general governor over; and besides had brought us all and the gospel under a common reproach of cutting one another's throats for beaver.

Battle of the Severn
1655

The Battle of the Severn was one episode in the long struggle between Protestants and Catholics for control of the Province of Maryland. The Long Parliament had sent commissioners to bring Maryland under obedience to them, displacing the Maryland proprietor, Lord Baltimore. In July, 1654, the commissioners called a Protestant Assembly, making the Puritan minority, which had long chafed under Catholic control, masters of Maryland.

By January 1655, however, Cromwell was attempting to mend his political fences, and so sent an order forbidding his commissioners to use force against the Catholics. At the same time, Lord Baltimore ordered his agent, Governor Stone, to reassert proprietary authority. Cromwell's order made the commissioners neutral, so the only obstacle to the proprietor was Providence, (later Annapolis) the Puritan settlement on the Severn. Stone gathered a force of 130 men, captured some ammunition, and marched against the town. Captain William Fuller, commander of the Puritan forces, aided by a merchant ship in the harbor, prepared to defend it. In the battle the Proprietary forces were completely routed. Three Puritans were killed and three mortally wounded, but the Catholics lost about 50 killed and wounded, and all their leaders, including Stone, were captured. Ten leaders were condemned to death, of whom four were actually executed.

The Puritan victory was later overturned by the Committee of Trade in England. By 1658 Baltimore had regained full control of the province on condition that there be no reprisals or discrimination.

The following account of the battle was written by Leonard Strong, one of Captain Fuller's Counsel at Providence, in *Babylon's Fall in Maryland . . .* (1655), printed in C. C. Hall, ed.: *Narratives of Early Maryland, 1633-84* (1910). See J. Thomas Scharf: *History of Maryland*, I (1879); John Leeds Bosman: *The History of Maryland from its First Settlement*, II (1837). On early Maryland see also John Barth's novel: *The Sot-Weed Factor* (rev. edn., 1967).

The Province was quiet, and so continued until the later end of January; about which time the ship *Golden Fortune*, whereof Captain Tilman was Commander, arrived in Maryland.

Then the Lord Baltamore's officers, and the Popish party began to divulge abroad, and boast much of power which came in that ship from his Highness the Lord Protector to confirm the Lord Baltamore's patent to him, and to re-establish his officers in their former places under him: which pretended power they assumed to themselves; Captain Stone and the rest giving out threatening speeches, That now the rebels at Putuxent and Severne, should know that he was Governour again;

. . . And further, the said Captain Stone gave several Commissions to the Papists and other desperate and bloody fellows, to muster and raise men in arms . . . presently they mustered in arms two hundred or two hundred and fifty men . . .

. . . They bent all their forces towards Providence, the chief place of the residence of most of the Commissioners, and people that were forced out of Virginia by Sir William Barkely for conscience sake, some of the said company marching by land, others by water; they that marched by land, did much spoil and robbery in all the houses and plantations where they came, breaking open doors, trunks and chests. In this barbarous manner . . . Capt. Stone and his company still drew neerer to Providence. . . .

. . . Now the people at Providence perceiving such a tempest ready to fall upon them, and all messages rejected, prepared for their coming, looking up and crying to the Lord of Hosts and King of Sion, for counsel, strength and courage, being resolved in the strength of God to stand on their guard, and demand an account of these proceedings; seeing no other remedy, for so great a mischief, could be found. . . .

Capt. Fuller and the Council of War appointed at Providence Mr. Wil. Durand, Secretary, to go aboard the *Golden Lion*, which then lay at anchor in the river, and to fix a proclamation in the main mast, directed to Captain Heamans, Commander of the said ship, wherein he was required in the name of the Lord Protector, and Commonwealth, of England, and for the maintenance of the just liberties, lives and estates of the free subjects thereof against an unjust power to be aiding and assisting in this service. . . .

The said Captain Heamans at first was unwilling; but afterwards seeing the equity of the cause, and the groundless proceedings of the enemy, he offered himself, ship, and men for that service, to be directed by the said William Durand . . .

. . . The first day of the week . . . the enemy appeared in a body upon a narrow neck of the land, near their vessels, and with drums and shoutings said, *Come ye Rogues, come ye Rogues, Roundheaded Dogs;* which caused the Captain of the Ship to give fire at them, and forced them to march further off, into the neck of land.

In the meantime Capt. Will. Fuller with his company came up the river with shoutings and courageous rejoycings, and landed with a hundred and twenty men, six mile distant from the enemy: and immediately sent away all their sloops and boats, committing themselves into the hand of God: he marched directly where the enemy lay waiting for him. The enemies sentry shot; immediately they appeared in order. Captain Fuller still expecting that then at last possibly they might give a reason of their coming, commanded his men upon pain of death not to shoot a gun, or give the first onset; setting up the standard of the Commonwealth of England: against which the enemy shot five or six guns, and killed one man in the front before a shot was made by the other. Then the word was given *In the name of God fall on; God is our Strength,* that was the word for Providence; the Marylanders word was *Hey for Saint Maries.* The charge was fierce and sharp for the time; but through the glorious presence of the Lord of Hosts manifested in and towards his poor oppressed people, the enemy could not endure, but gave back; and were so effectually charged home, that they were all routed, turned their backs, threw down their arms, and begged mercy. After the first volley of shot, a small company of the enemy, from behinde a great tree fallen, galled us, and wounded divers of our men, but were soon beaten off. Of the whole company of the Marylanders there escaped onely four or five, who run away out of the army to carry news to their confederates. Captain Stone, Colonel Price, Captain Gerrard, Captain Lewis, Captain Hendall, Captain Guither, Major Chandler, and all the rest of the councellors, officers and souldiers of the Lord Baltamore among whom, both commanders and souldiers, a great number being Papists, were taken, and so were all their vessels, arms, ammunition, provisions; about fifty men slain and wounded. We lost onely two in the field; but two died since of their wounds. God did appear wonderful in the field, and in the hearts of the people; all confessing him to be the onely worker of this victory and deliverance.

Bacon's Rebellion
1676

Bacon's Rebellion was set off by contention between Indians and frontiersmen. In 1676 the Susquehannocks, peaceful Indians driven out of Maryland but mistaken by Virginians for another hostile tribe, were attacked by the settlers. In return, the Indians killed thirty-six settlers in Virginia's western plantations. Governor William Berkeley ordered an expedition to suppress them, but when the Indians offered to make peace he called back his forces. Berkeley then attempted to stabilize the border by barring whites from Indian territory without government approval and constructing a series of forts to enforce his prohibition. While Berkeley seems to have done this because he felt that the grievances of the Indians were just, he also wanted to restrict the profits of the lucrative Indian trade to some of his friends. Furthermore, he and his friends had sizable holdings in unoccupied land, and he saw no necessity for pushing farther into Indian territory. But a sizable number of angry, frightened, and acquisitive frontiersmen joined with a few newly arrived English gentlemen who had not yet acquired estates to oppose Berkeley's policy. The foremost gentleman, Nathaniel Bacon, demanded a commission to lead an expedition of frontiersmen against the Indians. Berkeley refused. After several attempts to get Berkeley to change his mind, Bacon's followers threatened that if Bacon was not given a commission they would pull down Jamestown, the capital of the colony. Bacon led his followers to Jamestown, forced the Governor to commission him, and marched off to fight the Indians. But when some Virginians, irritated by Bacon's levies on their horses and arms, queried Berkeley about the validity of Bacon's commission, Berkeley announced that it had been secured under duress and that Bacon was a rebel. Bacon then turned back and marched against the Governor. Unable to rally support, Berkeley fled to the eastern shore of Virginia and Bacon found himself master of the province. He once more set out against the Indians, but while he was gone Berkeley with a newly recruited army retook Jamestown. For the second time Bacon marched against the capital; the battle which was fought is described below. Although Berkeley lost the battle, Bacon died of dysentery and a plague of lice on October 26th and his movement collapsed. Berkeley had executed fourteen persons under martial law during the rebellion; and after the arrival of new commissioners from London, nine more were hanged, despite a royal pardon which might have been construed to apply to them.

The following account is from *A True Narrative of the Rise, Progresse, and Cessation of the Late Rebellion in Virginia, Most Humbly and Impartially Reported by His Majestyes Commissioners Appointed to Enquire into the Affaires of the Said Colony*, printed in Charles M. Andrews, ed.: *Narratives of the Insurrections, 1675-90* (1915). On the Rebellion, see Bernard Bailyn: "Politics and Social Structure in Virginia," in James Morton Smith, ed.: *Seventeenth Century America: Essays in Colonial History* (1959); Wesley Frank Craven: *The Southern Colonies in the Seventeenth Century, 1607-1689* (1949); Thomas J. Wertenbaker: *Torchbearer of the Revolution: The Story of Bacon's Rebellion and its Leader* (1940); Wilcomb E. Washburn: *The Governor and the Rebel: A History of Bacon's Rebellion in Virginia* (1957).

The Governor . . again proclames Bacon and his party rebells and traytors, threatening them with the utmost severityes of law.

Upon this Bacon calls his few men together which upon a muster made a little after the last skirmish with the Indians . . . were but 136 tyr'd men, and told them how the Governor intended to proceed against him and them.

But this rather animated and provoked new courage in them than any wise daunted them, soe that among other cheerfull expressions they cry'd out they would stand by him their Generall to the last. . . .

Bacon in most incens'd manner threatens to be revenged on the Governor and his party, swearing his soldiers to give no quarter and professing to scorne to take any themselves, and so in great fury marches on towards James Towne, onely halting a while about New Kent to gain some fresh forces, and sending to the upper parts of James River for what they could assist him with.

Having increased his number to about 300 in all, he proceeds directly to towne, as he marcheth the people on the high wayes coming forth praying for his happiness and railing ag't the Governour and his party, and seeing the Indian captives which they led along as in a shew of tryumph, gave him many thankes for his care and endeavours for their preservation, bringing him forth fruits and victualls for his soldiers, the women telling him if he wanted assistance they would come themselves after him.

Intelligence coming to Bacon that the Governour had good in towne a 1000 men well arm'd and resolute, "I shall see that," saith he, "for I am now going to try them."

. . . In the evening Bacon with his small tyr'd body of men comes into Paspahayes old Fields and advancing on horseback himselfe on the Sandy Beech before the towne commands the trumpet to sound, fires his carbyne, dismounts, surveys the ground and orders a French worke to be cast up.

All this night is spent in falling of trees, cutting of bushes and throwing up earth, that by the help of the moone light they had made their French worke before day, although they had but two axes and 2 spades in all to performe this work with.

About day-break next morning six of Bacons soldiers ran up to the pallasadees of the Towne and fired briskly upon the guard, retreating safely without any damage at first (as is reported) the Governor gave comand that not a gun should be fir'd ag't Bacon or his party upon paine of death, pretending to be loath to spill bloode and much more to be beginner of it, supposing the rebells would hardly be so audacious as to fire a gun against him, But that Bacon would rather have sent to him and sought his reconciliation so that some way or other might have bin found out for the preventing of a warr, to which the Governour is said to have shewne some inclination upon the account of the service Bacon had performed (as he heard) against the Indian enemy, and that he had brought severall Indian prisoners along with him, and especially for that there were severall ignorant people which were deluded and drawne into Bacon's party and thought of no other designe than the Indian warr onely, and so knew not what they did.

But Bacon (pretending distrust of the Governor) was so farr from all thought of a Treaty that he animates his men against it, telling them that he knew that party to be as perfidious as cowardly, . . . The better to observe their motion [Bacon] ordered a constant sentinel in the daytime on top of a brick chimney (hard by) to discover from thence how the men in Towne mounted and dismounted, posted and reposted, drew on and off, what number they were, and how they moved. Hitherto their happen'd no other action then onely firing great and small shott at distances.

But by their movings and drawings up about towne, Bacon understood they intended a sally and accordingly prepares to receive them, drew up his men to the most advantageous places he could, and now expected them (but they observ'd to draw off againe for some tyme) and was resolved to enter the towne with them, as they retreated, as Bacon expected and foretold they would do. In this posture of expectation Bacon's forces continued for a hour till the watchman gave notice that they were drawne off againe in towne, so upon this Bacon's forces did so too. No sooner were they all on the rebells side gone off and squandered but all on a sudden a sally is made by the Governor's party, . . . But we cannot give a better account, nor yet a truer (so far as we are informed) of this action than what this Letter of Bacon's relates: . . .

". . . . Yesterday they made a sally with horse and foote in the Van; they came up with a narrow Front, and pressing very close upon one anothers shoulders that the forlorne might be their shelter; our men received them so warmly that they retired in great disorder, throwing downe theire armes, left upon the Bay, as also their drum and dead men, two of which our men brought into our trenches and buried with severall of their armes . . . They shew themselves such pitifull cowards, contemptable as you would admire them. It is said that Hubert Farrell is shot in the belly, Hartwell in the legg, Smith in the head, Mathewes with others, yet as yet we have no certaine account . . ."

After this successless sally the courages and numbers of the Governor's party abated much, and Bacon's men thereby became more bold and daring in so much that Bacon could scarce keepe them from immediately falling to storme and enter the towne; but he (being as wary as they rash) perswaded them from the attempt, bidding them keepe their courages untill such tyme as he found occasion and opportunity to make use of them, telling them that he doubted not to take the towne without losse of a man, and that one of their lives was of more value to him than the whole world.

Having planted his great guns, he takes the wives and female relations of such gentlemen as were in the Governor's service against him (whom he had caused to be brought to the workes) and places them in the face of his enemy, as bulworkes for their battery, by which policy he promised himself (and doubtless had) a goode advantage, yet had the Governor's party by much the odds in number besides the advantage of tyme and place.

But so great was the cowardize and baseness of the generality of Sir William Berkeley's party (being most of them men intent onely upon plunder or compell'd and hired into his service) that of all, at last there were onely some 20 gentlemen willing to stand by him, the rest (whom the hopes or promise of plunder brought thither) being now all in haste to be gone to secure what they had gott; so that Sir Wm. Berkeley himselfe who undoubtedly would rather have dyed on the place than thus deserted it, what with importunate and resistless solicitations of all, was at last over persuaded, now hurryed away against his owne will to Accomack and forced to leave the towne to the mercy of the enemy.

Bacon haveing early intelligence of the Governor and his party's quitting the towne the night before, enters it without any opposition, and soldier like considering of what importance a place of that refuge was, and might againe be to the Governor and his party, instantly resolves to lay it level with the ground, and the same night he became poses'd of it, sett fire to towne, church and state house (wherein were the country's records which Drummond had privately convey'd thense and preserved from burning). The towne consisted of 12 new brick houses besides a considerable number of frame houses with brick chimneys, all which will not be rebuilt (as is computed) for fifteen hundred pounds of tobacco.

Now those who had so lately deserted it, as they rid a little below in the river in the shipps and sloop (to their shame and regret) beheld by night the flames of the towne, which they so basely forsaking, had made a sacrifice to ruine.

Bloody Election in Philadelphia

1742

In eighteenth- and nineteenth-century American elections, one faction often tried violently to prevent another from voting. One eighteenth-century broadside advised: "As soon as your ticket is agreed on, let it be spread through the Country that all your party intend to come well armed to the election." One of the earliest election riots, as distinct from the drunken brawls which were also common on election days, occurred in Philadelphia in 1742.

Two prominent political factions, the Quaker and Proprietary parties, were divided over one notable issue—the reluctance of the Quakers, centered in the East, to authorize the use of force against the Indians in the West. This issue was complicated by an ethnic division; the frontiersmen were mostly Scotch-Irish, and the Quaker party counted many Germans among its allies. Every year, these antagonisms came into focus on election day. The polls in Philadelphia were located on the balcony of the Court House. Voters would ascend a staircase from the street, deposit their tickets, then descend by the opposite staircase. Whoever controlled the stairs could intimidate or reject opponents. For years, the Quakers controlled the stairs, but in 1742 the Proprietary Party hired burly sailors and ships' carpenters to remove them. The sailors were at first successful, but the Germans rallied and drove them off, and the Quaker faction triumphed once again. The following account is from the *Minutes of the Provincial Council of Pennsylvania*, IV (1951), 620-2. See Sister Joan Leonard: "Elections in Colonial Pennsylvania," *William and Mary Quarterly*, XI (1954), 385-401; and William T. Parsons: "The Bloody Election of 1742," *Pennsylvania History*, XXXVI (July 1969), 290-306.

"By a petition lately presented to us from a great number of the freemen of the city and county of Philadelphia, they complain of a very extraordinary riot committed within the said city at the last election. As it is an affair which justly alarmed the inhabitants of this province, and was attended with very uncommon circumstances, it engaged our inquiry and stay much longer than is usual at this season of the year. The discoveries we have been able to make in the course of this inquiry, we apprehend it to be our duty to lay before the Governor as they appear to us from the examinations taken, which are to the effect following:

"Early in the morning of the first of October past, being the day appointed by our charter and the laws of the province for the choice of representatives to serve in Assembly, a number of sailors, consisting of thirty or upwards, mostly strangers lately arrived at the Port of Philadelphia, prepared themselves with large clubbs or truncheons, and armed with them went about through divers parts of the city in a riotous and tumultuous manner, and particularly before the Mayor's door and in his sight, with-

out his taking the care he ought to have done to disperse them. Divers
freemen, inhabitants of the city, observing this, and fearing some outrage
was intended at the election, and judging it unlawful for these men to go
about in the manner before described to the terror of the King's good
subjects, addressed themselves to the Mayor and Recorder the same morning, desiring them to take proper measures for preserving the publick
peace, but did not receive such an answer as might justly have been expected
from gentlemen in their stations. Applications were likewise made to others
of the city magistrates, who promised to attend and use their endeavours to
prevent any disorders which might happen. About the tenth hour in the
forenoon of that day, the freemen and inhabitants of the county being met,
and the Sheriff attending, proceeded in a peaceable manner to choose
inspectors, during which time the sailors before mentioned having joined
themselves with others, also strangers, making in all about seventy, armed
with clubbs and other weapons, which they flourished over their heads with
loud huzzas, and in a furious and tumultuous manner approached the place
of election. Divers of the magistrates present observing this, attended by
some few of the electors, went towards them and let them know they had
no right to appear in that riotous manner, endeavouring to perswade them
to desist going further or giving any disturbance at the election, in which
they, being strangers and not inhabitants, could have no pretence of right,
and desired them to retreat peaceably. This the sailors not only refused,
but struck at the magistrates and others with great violence. The constables
interposing with their staves for some time kept off the rioters, but their
attack was so furious as to break the constables' staves, who were then
obliged to give ground. In this interval, divers of the inhabitants were
knocked down and greviously wounded, and amongst them one of the
aldermen of the city, who in all likelihood would have been barbarously
murthered had it not been prevented. The sailors at length marched away
in the same riotous manner they came, and the inhabitants being unwilling
to be disappointed in their election, and not expecting further abuse,
proceeded in the choice of their inspectors, which was performed in a
very peaceable manner. And soon after the ballot for the choice of representatives was begun, when on a sudden the same sailors, in like furious
and tumultuous manner as aforesaid, made a second and unexpected attack
upon the freemen of the province, throwing stones at them and knocking
down all they were able, without regard to age or station. Many of the
inhabitants having before dispersed themselves to several parts of the city,
and those who remained being unarmed and having nothing to defend
themselves withal, were in the surprize driven away by the sailors some
distance from the place of election, but at length recovering themselves

and provoked by the repeated abuses they had received, turned on their assailants, who seeing this soon fled before them, and being pursued by directions from some of the magistrates, upwards of fifty of them were in a little time apprehended and carried to prison, and the freemen proceeded to finish the election of their representatives, which was done in a very peaceable manner. . . .

"In the course of our examinations it further appears that the recorder and divers other magistrates were present and saw these outrages committed, and were at the time repeatedly requested to exert themselves in suppressing the rioters, and told that numbers of the electors were ready and willing to assist to that end if the magistrates thought fit, but all applications proved wholly inefectual; they refused the least interposition of their authority, and remained unactive spectators of the abuses committed, some of them behaving rather like men that approved of the conduct of the rioters than otherwise. This, however, was not the case of all the magistrates; some there were who exerted themselves laudably, and merit the thanks of all well wishers to the province for the services done their King and country on that day."

Knowles Riot in Boston

1747

To supply the men needed for the Navy, the British Government regularly practiced impressment at home and in the colonies. Navy "press gangs" seized merchant seamen, both on board American vessels and in the streets of American towns; sailors resisted when they could, most successfully when sympathetic townspeople joined them. In the 1740's Boston was plagued by press gangs, and many seamen left the port. This hurt Boston's trade, and the town meeting protested strongly against impressment. On November 16, 1747, several hundred sailors, laborers, and Negroes tried to halt one impressment under Commodore Charles Knowles by seizing a Navy lieutenant. They then assaulted the sheriff who came to rescue the lieutenant, put a deputy in the stocks, stormed the town house where the General Court sat, and demanded the seizure of impressment officers. Governor William Shirley fled to Castle William when the militia failed to respond to orders to put down the rioters. The riot brought a temporary halt to impressment, but in the 1760's there were more impressments and more riots—in New York in 1764, Newport in 1765, Casco Bay, Maine, in 1764, and Norfolk in 1767. Rioting continued until 1775, and impressment continued to be an issue until after the War of 1812.

The following account is taken from a letter written by Governor Shirley to the Lords of Trade, December 1, 1747, reprinted in Charles Henry Lincoln, ed.: *Correspondence of William Shirley* (1912), 412-15. See Jesse Lemisch: "Jack Tar in the Streets: Merchant Seamen in the Politics of Revolutionary America," *William and Mary Quarterly*, XXV (July 1968), 371-407. See also John A. Schutz: *William Shirley* (1961).

A riot, and insult upon the King's government lately happen'd here of so extraordinary a nature, that I think it my duty to give your Lordships an account of it.

It was occasion'd by an impress made on the sixteenth of November at night out of all the vessels in this harbour, by order of Commodore Knowles, then on board the Canterbury, for manning his Squadron . . .

The first notice, I had of the mob, was given me between nine and ten o'clock in the forenoon by the Speaker of the House of Representatives, who had pick'd up in the streets Captain Derby of his Majesty's Ship Alborough, and the Purser of the Canterbury, and brought 'em under his Protection to me for shelter in my house acquainting me at the same time, that the mob consisted of about three hundred seamen, all strangers, (the greatest part Scotch) with cutlasses and clubs, and that they had seiz'd and detain'd in their custody a Lieutenant of the Lark, whom they met with at his lodgins on shoar; The next notice I had was about half an hour after by the Sheriff of the County, who with some of his officers had been in pursuit of the mob in order to recover the Man of War's Lieutenant, and to endeavour to disperse 'em; and who coming up with four of 'em separated from the others, had wrested a cutlass from one and seiz'd two of 'em; but being overtaken by the whole mob, (who were appriz'd of this), as he was carrying those two to goal, was assaulted, and grievously wounded by 'em, and forc'd to deliver up his two prisoners, and leave one of his deputies in their hands, for whose life he assur'd me he was in fear.

Thereupon I immediately sent orders to the Colonel of the Regiment to raise the militia of the town and suppress the mob by force, and, if need was, to fire upon 'em with ball; which were scarcely deliver'd to him, when they appear'd before my gates, and part of 'em advanc'd directly through my court yard up to my door with the Lieutenant, two other sea officers, that part of the mob which stay'd at the outward gate crying out to the party at my door not to give up any of their prisoners to me. Upon this I immediately went out to 'em and demanded the cause of the tumult, to which one of 'em arm'd with a cutlass answer'd me in an insolent manner it was caus'd by my unjustifiable impress warrant; whereupon I told 'em that the impress was not made by my warrant, nor with my knowledge; but that he was a very impudent rascal for his behaviour; and upon his still growing more insolent, my son in law who happen'd to follow me out, struck his hat off his head, asking him if he knew, who he was talking to; this immediately silenced their clamour, when I demanded of 'em, where the King's Officers were, that they had seiz'd; and they being shewn to me, I went up to the Lieutenant and bid him go into my house, and upon his telling me the mob would not suffer him, I took him from among 'em, and putting him before me caus'd him to go in, as I did likewise the other three and follow'd 'em without exchanging more words with the mob, that I might avoid making any promises or terms with 'em; But my son in law, with the Speaker of the Assembly, the Colonel of the Regiment, and Captain of the Massachusetts frigate, who were now come into the house, stood some time at the door parlying and endeavouring to pacify 'em 'till upon the tumult's increasing, and their threatning to recover the sea officers by force, if I did not deliver 'em up again, or the Lieutenant did not come out to 'em and swear that he was not concern'd in the impress, I sent an Under Sheriff, then lately come into my house, to desire the gentlemen to let 'em know that I should consent to neither; and to retire into the house; and arm'd the offiers, who were now seven or eight in number, to stand upon their defence, in case the mob should be so outrageous as to attempt to break into the house, and had the door shut against 'em; upon which the mob beset the house round, made some feint appearances of attempting to force the door open, abus'd the under-sheriff in my court yard (whom they beat and at last put in the publick stocks) and after behaving in a tumultuous manner before the House about half an hour, left it. . . .

. . . the mob now increas'd and join'd by some inhabitants came to the Town House (just after candle light) arm'd as in the morning, assaulted the Council Chamber (myself and the Council being then sitting there and the House of Representatives a minute or two before by accident adjourn'd) by throwing stones and brickbatts in at the windows, and having broke all the windows of the lower floor, where a few of the Militia Officers were assembled, forcibly enter'd into it, and oblig'd most of the officers to retire up into the Council Chamber; where the mob was expected soon to follow 'em up; but prevented by some few of the officers below, who behav'd better.

In this confusion two popular members of the Council endeavoured, but in vain, to appease the mob by speaking to 'em from the balcony of the Council Chamber; after which the Speaker of the House and others of the Assembly press'd me much to speak two or three words to 'em, only promising to use my endeavours with Mr. Knowles to get the impress'd inhabitants and some of the outward bound seamen discharg'd; which, against my inclinations, and to prevent their charging any bad Consequences, which might happen from this tumult upon my refusal, I yielded to; and in this parley one of the mob, an inhabitant of the town call'd upon me to deliver up the Lieutenant of the Lark, which I refus'd to do; after which among other things he demanded of me, why a boy, one Warren now under sentence of death in goal for being concern'd in a press gang, which kill'd two sailors in this town in the act of impressing, was not executed; and I acquaint'd 'em his execution was suspended by his Majesty's order 'till his pleasure shall be known upon it; whereupon the same person, who was the mob's spokesman ask'd me "if I did not remember Porteous's case who was hang'd upon a sign post in Edinburg." I told 'em very well, and that I hop'd they remember'd what the consequence of that proceeding was to the inhabitants of the city; after which I thought it high time to make an end of parleying with the mob, and retir'd into the Council Chamber: The issue of this was that the mob said they would call again at the Council Chamber the next day to know whether the impressed men were discharg'd; and went off to a dock yard upon proposal made among 'em to burn a twenty gun ship now building there for his Majesty; whereupon I went to my own house accompanied with a party of Officers, Sir William Pepperrell, and the gentlemen of the Council; within a quarter of an Hour after which the mob, who had been diverted from their purpose against the King's ship by the sudden coming to shoar of a barge, which they took to belong to one of Mr. Knowles's squadron, seiz'd and carry'd it in procession through the town with an intention to burn it in my court yard; upon which I order'd a party of officers to go out and oppose their entrance at my outward gate, which about ten of 'em immediately did, and upon the appearance of the mob's preparing to force that gate open, cock'd and presented their musketts at 'em through an open palisade fence, and fir'd upon 'em, if Sir William Pepperrell had not instantly call'd out to the Officers to hold, 'till such, who might only be spectators could be warn'd to separate from among the mob; which they perceiving, and that the windows of the house were likewise lin'd with arm'd officers, desisted and immediately alter'd their scheme to that of burning the barge in an out part of the Common, not discovering, 'till after it was burnt, that it really belong'd to a Master of a Scotch vessell, one of their ringleaders.

. . . The day following Mr. Knowles upon hearing of these outrages wrote me word, that he purpos'd to bring his whole squadron before the town the next morning, but I dissuaded him from it, by an immediate answer to his letter: In the evening the mob forcibly search'd the Navy Hospital upon the Town Common in order to let out what seamen they could find there belonging to the King's ships; and seven or eight private houses for officers, and took four or five petty officers; but soon releas'd 'em without any ill usage, as they did the same day Captain Erskine, whom they had suffer'd to remain in a gentleman's house upon his parole, their chief intent appearing to be, from the beginning, not to use the officers well any otherwise than by detaining 'em, in hopes of obliging Mr. Knowles to give up the impress'd men.

Stamp Act Riots
1765

In March 1765, Parliament, in search of revenue to meet the costs of war and empire, passed a Stamp Act to take effect in November of the same year, which required that formally written or printed matter such as deeds, bills, diplomas, and news-papers carry a stamp to indicate that the designated taxes had been paid. The Act raised new questions about the limits and legitimacy of imperial rule; and for the first time the colonies united in a common effort—the Stamp Act Congress—to effect the repeal of the tax.

In Boston the leaders of popular resistance to the Stamp Act were artisans and shopkeepers known as the Loyal Nine, and later as the Sons of Liberty. They persuaded the town gangs who had previously mobbed one another on Guy Fawkes Days to turn their energy against a common enemy, the British. Led with discriminating purposefulness by a shoemaker, Ebenezer MacIntosh, the Bostonians attacked the individuals who were to put the new tax into effect. On August 14, a mob attacked the house of Andrew Oliver, the Stamp Collector-designate. On the 26th they damaged the houses of a judge of the Admiralty Court, the Comptroller of Customs, and completely destroyed the house of Lieutenant Governor Hutchinson.

Boston set the example for the other colonial ports. In Newport a crowd broke up the houses of the designated stamp collector, two men who had written pamphlets advocating sub-mission to Parliament, and the Customs Collector. Elsewhere a show of force was enough to compel resignations, and when the November deadline arrived not a single colony had an official who would distribute the stamps.

The violence was minimal; no one was killed. This is the more remarkable when compared to European riots in these years, and probably can be accounted for by the absence or ineffectiveness of governmental authority. Having insufficient force to suppress rioters, officials capitulated to their demands.

The following account of the destruction of Andrew Oli-ver's property was reported in the Boston *Gazette*, August 19, 1765. On the riots, see Gordon Wood: "A Note on Mobs in the American Revolution," *William and Mary Quarterly*, XXIII (October 1966), 635-42; Edmund S. and Helen M. Morgan: *The Stamp Act Crisis: Prologue to Revolution* (1963); William Ander Smith, "Anglo-Colonial Society and the Mob: 1740-1775," unpublished doctoral dissertation, The Claremont Colleges, 1965.

Early on Wednesday morning last, the effigy of a gentleman sustaining a very unpopular office, viz, that of St—p Master, was found hanging on a tree in the most public part of the town, together with a boot, wherein was concealed a young imp of the Devil represented as peeping out of the top. On the breast of the effigy was a label, In Praise of Liberty, and announcing vengeance on the subvertors of it. And underneath was [sic] the following words. HE THAT TAKES THIS DOWN IS AN ENEMY TO HIS COUNTRY. The owner of the tree finding a crowd of people to assemble, though at five o'clock in the morning, endeavored to take it down; but being advised to the contrary by the populace, lest it should occasion the demolition of his windows, if not worse, desisted from the attempt. the diversion it occasioned among a multitude of spectators who continually assembled the whole day, is surprising; not a peasant was suffered to pass down to the market, let him have what he would for sale, till he had stopped and got his articles stamped by the effigy. Towards dark some thousands repaired to the said place of rendezvous, and having taken down the pageantry, they proceeded with it along the main street to the town house, thru which they carried it, and continued their route thru Tilby Street to Oliver's dock, where there was a new brick building just finished; and they imagining it to be designed for a Stamp Office, instantly set about demolishing of it, which they thoroughly effected in about half an hour. In the meantime the high sheriff etc., etc., being apprehensive that the person of the then Stamp Master and his family, might be in danger from the tumult, went and advised them to evacuate the house; which they had scarcely done, making their retreat across the gardens, etc., before the multitude approached Fort Hill, contiguous thereto, in order to burn the effigy, together with the timber and other woodwork of the house they had demolished. After setting fire to the combustibles, they proceeded to break open the stables, coachhouses etc., and were actually increasing the bonfire with a coach, Booby-Hutch, Chaise, etc. but were dissuaded going so far by a number of spectators present, tho they burnt the coach doors, cushions, etc. But it seems not having completed their purpose, they set about pulling down a range of fences upwards of fifteen feet high, which enclosed the bottom of the garden, into which having entered, they stripped the trees of the fruit, despoilt some of them by breaking off the limbs, demolished the summer house, broke the windows in the rear part of the house, entered the same, went down the cellars, and helped themselves to the liquor which they found there in the silver plate that the house afforded, none of which however was missing the next day, altho scattered over various parts of the house. They then destroyed part of the furniture, among which was a looking glass said to be the largest in North America, with two others, etc.

The next day the transactions of the preceeding night was of course the general topic of conversation; when the Stamp Master, in order to appease the sensations which seemed to possess the breasts of everyone, at the prospect of a future stamp duty, sent a card to several gentlemen, acquainting them that he had absolutely declined having any concern in that office, which being publicly read upon change, it was thought all uneasiness would subside; but the evening following they again assembled, erected a number of stages with tar barrels, etc. in the form of a pyramid, in the center of which was a flag staff, and a Union flag hoisted; whereupon 'tis said, the Stamp Master sent them a letter with the aforementioned resolution of non acceptance, and assurance of endeavors to serve the province, etc. Upon which they thought proper to demolish the bonfire and retire, but did not disperse till they went down to his H–r the L—t G—r's, with whom they said they wanted to have a talk; but not finding him at home, they concluded the business of the night by loud acclamations in every quarter of the town, on account of the resignation of the Stamp Master; which they were assured was forwarded by express to New York to go in the packet from thence.

Boston Massacre
1770

The tensions produced by the Stamp Act relaxed when Parliament repealed the tax, but they were soon rearoused by the Townshend Acts. These laws placed import duties on several previously untaxed items, established a local customs board to collect the duties, and instituted additional vice-admiralty courts to enforce them. Once again, as in the Stamp Act crisis, Americans questioned not only the taxes themselves but the legitimacy of Parliament's power to tax the colonies, and launched a non-importation boycott of British goods. On February 11th, 1768, the Massachusetts House of Representatives approved a Circular Letter denouncing the Townshend Acts and calling for united colonial resistance. Rioting broke out anew; in the *Liberty* Riot of June 10, 1768, for example, customs officials were forced to flee Boston. Realizing that their authority would have to be backed with force, the customs commissioners pleaded with the British government to send troops. By October of 1768, five British regiments had arrived in Boston.

Throughout the following year there were a number of clashes between citizens and soldiers, many of them occasioned by the British Army's practice of allowing its soldiers, who were paid very little, to take extra jobs in their off-duty hours. But times were hard and jobs scarce, so friction with Boston laborers was almost inevitable. In October 1769, what might have been a serious clash was avoided when troops fired a volley into the air. On the evening of March 5, 1770, a crowd of working men whom John Adams later described as "a motley rabble of saucy boys, negroes and mulattoes, Irish teagues and outlandish Jack tars," attacked some British sentries. Although the testimony is contradictory, it appears that the crowd was hurling snowballs at the soldiers when someone, either the leader of the troops, Captain Thomas Preston, or a member of the crowd, yelled "Fire." The soldiers shot into the crowd. Three men were killed at once, and eight were wounded, two mortally. Preston and six of his men were arrested and tried for murder. Defended by John Adams and Josiah Quincy, Preston and four of the soldiers were acquitted, and the other two were found guilty of man-slaughter and punished by branding their thumbs. The incident provided the patriots with a major focus of propaganda: annual commemoration ceremonies led by men like John Hancock, Joseph Warren, and Sam Adams kept public indignation alive.

The first of the following accounts is that of a colonial, Richard Palmes: *A Short Narrative of the Horrid Massacre in Boston* (1770; reprinted 1849), 70-1; The second is that of Captain Preston: *Publications* of the Colonial Society of Massachusetts, VII (April 1900), 6-10. See also Frederick Kidder, comp.: *History of the Boston Massacre, March 5, 1770* (1870); Richard B. Morris: *Government and Labor in Early America*

(1946); and John Shy: *Toward Lexington: The Role of the British Army in the Coming of the American Revolution* (1965).

I

I, Richard Palmes, of Boston, of lawful age, testify and say, that between the hours of nine and ten o'clock of the fifth instant, I heard one of the bells ring, which I supposed was occasioned by fire, and enquiring where the fire was, was answered that the soldiers were abusing the inhabitants; I asked where, was first answered at Murray's barracks. I went there and spoke to some officers that were standing at the door, I told them I was surprised they suffered the soldiers to go out of the barracks after eight o'clock; I was answered by one of the officers, pray do you mean to teach us our duty; I answered I did not, only to remind them of it. One of them then said, you see that the soldiers are all in their barracks, and why do you not go to your homes. Mr. James Lamb and I said, Gentlemen, let us go home, and were answered by some, home, home. Accordingly I asked Mr. William Hickling if he was going home, he said he was; I walked with him as far as the post-office, upon my stopping to talk with two or three people, Mr. Hickling left me; I then saw Mr. Pool Spear going towards the town-house, he asked me if I was going home, I told him I was; I asked him where he was going that way, he said he was going to his brother David's. But when I got to the town-pump, we were told there was a rumpus at the Custom-house door; Mr. Spear said to me you had better not go, I told him I would go and try to make peace. I immediately went there and saw Capt. Preston at the head of six or eight soldiers in a circular form, with guns breast high and bayonets fixed; the said Captain stood almost to the end of their guns. I went immediately to Capt. Preston (as soon as Mr. Bliss had left him), and asked him if their guns were loaded, his answer was they are loaded with powder and ball; I then said to him, I hope you do not intend they shall fire upon the inhabitants, his reply was, by no means. When I was asking him these questions, my left hand was on his right shoulder; Mr. John Hickling had that instant taken his hand off my shoulder, and stepped to my left, then instantly I saw a piece of snow or ice fall among the soldiers on which the soldier at the officer's right hand stepped back and discharged his gun at the space of some seconds the soldier at his left fired next, and the others one after the other. After the first gun was fired, I heard the word "fire," but who said it I know not. After the first gun was fired, the said officer had full time to forbid the other soldiers not to fire, but I did not hear him speak to them at all; then turning myself to the left I saw one man dead, distant about six feet; I having a stick in my hand made a stroke at the soldier who fired, and struck the gun out of his hand. I then made a stroke at the officer, my right foot slipped, that brought me on my knee, the blow falling short; he says I hit his arm; when I was recovering myself from the fall, I saw the soldier that fired the first gun endeavoring to push me through with his bayonet, on which I threw my stick at his head, the soldier starting back, gave me an opportunity to jump from him into Exchange lane, or I must been inevitably run through my body. I looked back and saw three persons laying on the ground, and perceiving a soldier stepping round the corner as I thought to shoot me, I ran down Exchange lane, and so up the next into King Street, and followed Mr. Gridley with several other persons with the body of Capt. Morton's apprentice, up to the prison house, and saw he had a ball shot through his breast; at my return I found that the officers and soldiers were gone to the main guard. To my best observation there were not seventy people in King street at the time of their firing, and them very scattering; but in a few minutes after the firing there were upwards of a thousand. Finding the soldiers were gone I went up to the main-guard, and saw there the soldiers were formed into three divisions, the front division in the posture of platoon firing, and I expected they would fire. Hearing that his Honor the Lieutenant-Governor was going to the Council-chamber, I went there; his Honor looking out of the door desired the people to hear him speak, he desired them to go home and he would enquire into the affair in the morning, and that the law should take its course, and said, I will live and die by the law. A gentleman desired his Honor to order the soldiers to their barracks, he answered it was not in his power, and that he had no command over the troops, and that it lay with Col. Dalrymple and not with him, but that he would send for him, which after some time he did; upon that a gentleman desired his Honor to look out of the window facing the main-guard, to see the position the soldiers were in, ready to fire on the inhabitants, which he did after a good deal of persuasion, and called for Col. Carr and desired him to order the troops to their barracks in the same order they were in; accordingly they were ordered to shoulder their guns, and were marched off by some officers. And further saith not.

RICH. PALMES

11

It is matter of too great notoriety to need any proofs, that the arrival of his Majesty's troops in Boston was extremely obnoxious to its inhabitants. They have ever used all means in their power to weaken the regiments, and to bring them into contempt, by promoting and aiding desertions, and with impunity, even where there has been the clearest evidence of the fact, and by grossly and falsly propagating untruth concerning them. . . . several disputes have happened between the towns-people and soldiers of both regiments, the former being encouraged thereto by the countenance of even some of the magistrates, and by the protection of all the party against government. In general such disputes have been kept too secret from the officers. On the 2d instant, two of the 29th going through one Gray's Rope-Walk, the rope-makers insultingly asked them if they would empty a vault [privy]. This unfortunately had the desired effect by provoking the soldiers, and from words they went to blows. Both parties suffered in this affray, and finally, the soldiers retired to their quarters. The officers, on the first knowledge of this transaction, took every precaution in their power to prevent any ill consequences. Notwithstanding which, single quarrels could not be prevented; the inhabitants constantly provoking and abusing the soldiery. The insolence, as well as utter hatred of the inhabitants to the troops, increased daily . . .

On Monday night about eight o'clock two soldiers were attacked and beat. But the party of the towns-people, in order to carry matters to the utmost length, broke into two meeting-houses, and rang the alarm bells, which I supposed was for fire as usual, but was soon undeceived. About nine some of the guard came to and informed me, the town-inhabitants were assembling to attack the troops, and that the bells were ringing as the signal for that purpose, and not for fire, and the beacon intended to be fired to bring in the distant people of the country. This, as I was Captain of the day, occasioned my repairing immediately to the main-guard. In my way there I saw the people in great commotion, and heard them use the most cruel and horrid threats against the troops. In a few minutes after I reached the guard, about an hundred people passed it, and went towards the Custom-House, where the King's money is lodged. They immediately surrounded the sentinel posted there, and with clubs and other weapons threatened to execute their vengeance on him. I was soon informed by a townsman, their intention was to carry off the soldier from his post, and probably murder him. On which I desired him to return for further intelligence; and he soon came back and assured me he heard the mob declare they would murder him. This I feared might be a prelude to their plundering the King's chest. I immediately sent a non-commissioned officer and twelve men to protect both the sentinel and the King's-money, and very soon followed myself, to prevent (if possible) all disorder; fearing lest the officer and soldiery by the insults and provocations of the rioters, should be thrown off their guard and commit some rash act. They soon rushed through the people, and, by charging their bayonets in half circle, kept them at a little distance. Nay, so far was I from intending the death of any person, that I suffered the troops to go to the spot where the unhappy affair took place, without any loading in their pieces, nor did I ever give orders for loading them. This remiss conduct in me perhaps merits censure yet it is evidence, resulting from the nature of things, which is the best and surest that can be offered, that my intention was not to act offensively, but the contrary part, and that not wthout compulson. The mob still increased, and were more outragious, striking their clubs on bludgeons one against another, and calling out, "Come on, you rascals, you bloody backs, you lobster scoundrels; fire if you dare, G—d damn you, fire and be damn'd; we know you dare not;" and much more such language was used. At this time I was between the soldiers and the mob, parleying with and endeavouring all in my power to persuade them to retire peaceably; but to no purpose. They advanced to the points of the bayonets, struck some of them, and even the muzzles of the pieces, and seemed to be endeavoring to close with the soldiers. On which some wellbehaved persons asked me if the guns were charged: I replied, yes. They then asked me if I intended to order the men to fire; I answered no, by no means; observing to them, that I was advanced before the muzzles of the men's pieces, and must fall a sacrifice if they fired; that the soldiers were upon the half cock and charged bayonets, and my giving the word fire, under those circumstances, would prove me no officer. While I was thus speaking, one of the soldiers, having received a severe blow with a stick, stept a little on one side, and instantly fired, on which turning to and asking him why he fired without orders, I was struck with a club on my arm, which for sometime deprived me of the use of it; which blow, had it been placed on my head, most probably would have destroyed me. On this a general attack was made on the men by a great number of heavy clubs, and snow-balls being thrown at them, by which all our lives were in imminent danger; some persons at the same time from behind calling out, "Damn your bloods, why don't you fire?" Instantly three or four of the soldiers fired, one after another, and directly after three more in the same confusion and hurry.

The mob then ran away, except three unhappy men who instantly expired, in which number was Mr. Gray, at whose Rope-Walk the prior quarrel took place; one more is since dead, three others are dangerously, and four slightly wounded. The whole of this melancholy affair was transacted in almost 20 minutes. . . .

On the people's assembling again to take away the dead bodies, the soldiers, supposing them coming to attack them, were making ready to fire again, which I prevented by striking up their firelocks with my hand. Immediately after a townsman came and told me, that 4 or 5000 people were assembled in the next street, and had sworn to take my life with every man's with me; on which I judged it unsafe to remain there any longer, and therefore sent the party and sentry to the main-guard, where the street is narrow and short, there telling them off into street firings, divided and planted them at each end of the street to secure their rear, momently expecting an attack, as there was a constant cry of the inhabitants, "To arms, to arms,—turn out with your guns," and the town drums beating to arms. I ordered my drum to beat to arms, and being soon after joined by the different companies of the 29th Regiment, I formed them as the guard into street firings. . . . Several officers going to join their regiment were knocked down by the mob, one very much wounded, and his sword taken from him. The Lieutenant-Governor and Col. Carr soon after met at the Head of the 29th Regiment, and agreed that the Regiment should retire to their barracks, and the people to their houses but I kept the piquet to strengthen the guard. It was with great difficulty that the Lieutenant-Governor prevailed on the people to be quiet and retire: At last they all went off excepting about an hundred.

A council was immediately called, on the breaking up of which three justices met, and issued a warrant to apprehend me and eight soldiers. On hearing of this procedure, I instantly went to the sheriff and surrendered myself, though for the space of four hours I had it in my power to have made my escape, which I most undoubtedly should have attempted, and could have easily executed, had I been the least conscious of any guilt.

Battle of Alamance
1771

Colonial government in North Carolina was controlled by the landed gentry of the eastern seaboard. Local officials, particularly on the frontier, were thoroughly corrupt; sheriffs embezzled about half the annual tax revenue of the colony; other local magnates charged exorbitant fees for legal services. Throughout the 1760's the frontiersmen appealed to the government for redress and reform; some took vigilante action against the officials who were defrauding them. In 1768, the sheriffs announced that they would no longer go to the farms to collect taxes; instead, farmers would have to travel the long distances to the sheriffs' offices, or face stiff fines payable to the sheriffs. Now the farmers organized into the formal associations which came to be known as the "Regulators." Their request for a meeting with officials was refused. The fact that the farmers had organized in opposition to the government made their actions indistinguishable, in official eyes, from sedition; Governor William Tryon ordered them to disband. Two of the leaders were arrested and the militia dispersed the organizations. In 1769 more petitions were sent to the assembly, this time asking for ballot voting, taxation in proportion to wealth, collection of taxes in commodities, the registering of votes in the Assembly journals, and the regular publication of laws. Regulators won some elections that year, and were able to enact some corrective legislation, but it proved unenforceable. Finally, in September 1770, the Regulators marched to the county seat of Hillsborough, shut down the court, and demolished the house of one of the obnoxious officials. The Colonial Assembly responded with a law which made the failure of a crowd of ten or more to disperse when so ordered punishable by death. Governor Tryon then moved to crush the uprising by force. He recruited an army of 917 men (paying them bounties since many of the regular militia refused to serve) and 151 officers, among whom were members of most of the leading families of the colony. On May 16, 1771, Tryon's forces engaged an unorganized, poorly armed body of 2,000 Regulators at Alamance, and, making effective use of artillery, routed them. One leader of the insurgents was executed on the battlefield the next day, 6 others were executed for treason later. Thousands of Piedmont settlers were required to take an oath of allegiance to the government, though many moved further west rather than do so. The antagonism of frontiersmen against Easterners led many backwoodsmen to fight on the Loyalist side in the Revolution.

The following account of the battle is taken from Francois-Xavier Martin: *The History of North Carolina from the Earli-*

est Period (1829), II, 28-81. See Elisha Douglass: *Rebels and Democrats* (1955); and John Spencer Bassett: "Regulators in North Carolina," American Historical Association, *Annual Report*, 1894.

On the 15th, a messenger from the regulators brought a petition to the governor; the object of it was to desire, that he would redress the grievances of the people, as the only means of preventing that bloodshed, which, from the ardour of the leaders and of the troops on both sides, must otherwise ensue; his answer was desired within four hours; the governor sent the messenger back, with a promise that an answer would be returned on the following day, by noon. John Ashe and John Walker, who were sent out of camp on duty, were, in the evening, seized by the regulators, tugged up to trees, severely whipped and made prisoners. . . .

The army moved the next morning, at break of day, without beat of drum, leaving their tents standing, and their baggage and waggons in the camp; one company, from the detachment of Johnston county, with such men as were not able to march briskly, remained behind, as a guard to the camp, under the orders of Colonel Bryan; the waggon horses were kept in their geers, and the whole army was drawn into a hollow square.

At a distance of five miles from the camp, the armies being within half a mile from each other, three guns were fired, as a signal to form the line of battle, which was immediately done. . . .

The regulators were encamped at some distance; their number exceeded, in a small degree, those of the governor; they were headed by Hermon Husband, James Hunter and William Butler; they answered the governor's guns by three huzzas and beating to arms. A message was then sent them, in reply to their petition; the purport of it was, that the governor had, in every circumstance, both in his particular and legislative capacity, pursued every measure that was in his power, to quiet them, but without effect; he had now nothing to offer them, but was bound to require of them an immediate submission to government, a promise of paying their taxes, so long withheld from the public, an immediate return to their respective places of residence, and a solemn assurance, that they would no longer protect the individuals who were indicted, from a fair trial for their offences; he concluded, by allowing them one hour to consider, and if they did not then yield and accept so fair a proposal, the circumstances that would follow would be imputed to them alone.

On the arrival of the messenger at the camp of the regulators, they impatiently heard the reading of the governor's answer to their petition, and bid him return to Billy Tryon, and say they defied him, and battle was all they wanted; some of their leaders, however, prevailed on them to listen to a second reading of the paper; but they again expressed their impatience to come to an engagement, with the most violent imprecations. On return of the messenger, the army marched to within three hundred yards of the regulators' camp, and there halted. The regulators advanced also, in order of battle, to a short reach of the road, where they halted likewise, waving their hats as a challenge, to dare their opponents to advance.

Governor Tryon now sent a magistrate and an officer, with a proclamation, commanding the insurgents to disperse within one hour: the magistrate read it aloud, in front of the lines; but they disdained listening to him, crying out battle! battle!! . . . The enemy being tardy in their compliance, and the army complaining of the extreme heat of the sun, and manifesting great impatience to advance, it was thought advisable to lead them on. They marched in profound silence, till the lines of both parties met, almost breast to breast. The governor forbade his men to fire until he ordered them. The first rank were almost mixed with those of the enemy, who were stationed a little before the main body, and who now began to retreat slowly, to join their army, bellowing defiance and daring their opponents to advance. The army kept on till within twenty-five yards of them and then halted. The regulators continued to call on the governor to order his men to fire: several of them advancing towards the artillery opening their breasts and defying them to begin. . . .

An adjutant was now sent, to the enemy's camp, to receive John Ashe and John Walker, who brought for an answer, that they would be surrendered with half an hour. He was sent back to inform the regulators, that the governor would wait no longer, and that, if they did not directly lay down their arms, they should be fired on. Fire and be d—d, was the answer. The governor, ordering his men to fire, was not immediately obeyed; on which, rising on his stirrups and turning to his men, he called out "Fire! fire on them or on me." The action now began, and, almost instantly, became general.

The insurgents, pursuing the Indian mode of fighting, did considerable injury to the king's troops; but, owing to the artillery, and firmness of the latter, were, after a conflict of one hour, struck with a panic and fled, leaving upwards of twenty dead, and a number of wounded. The fugitives were pursued, and several prisoners were made. The loss of the governor was only nine killed, and sixty-one wounded. The laurels which he gained on this day, were sullied by a vindictive and intemperate behaviour. Towards the evening, when every thing was quiet, and the regulators defeated and dispersed, Captain Few, one of the prisoners made in the pursuit, was, by his orders, without a trial, hung on a tree.

Terrorism Against Loyalists
1774-1775

In their efforts to prevent the Loyalists from effectively aiding the British, the American revolutionaries often used violence. There was no American Revolutionary Terror, but there was considerable terrorism. Loyalists were tarred and feathered, ridden on rails (a more painful experience than the phrase itself suggests), branded, imprisoned, and forced into exile, and occasionally shot or hanged.

The following four instances of terrorism against Loyalists are taken from: Douglas Adair and John A. Schutz, eds.: *Peter Oliver's Origin and Progress of the American Rebellion: A Tory View* (1963), 155-7; Lorenzo Sabine: *Biographical Sketches of Loyalists of the American Revolution* (1864), I, 597; Frank W. C. Hersey: "Tar and Feathers, The Adventures of Captain John Malcolm," *Publications of the Colonial Society of Massachusetts*, XXXIV (April 1941), 450-1; Edward A. Jones: *Loyalists of Massachusetts* (1930), 243. See also Wallace Brown: *The Good Americans: The Loyalists in the American Revolution* (1969).

I

The Attorney General, *Mr. Sewall*, living at *Cambridge*, was obliged to repair to *Boston* under the protection of the King's troops. His house at

Cambridge was attacked by a mob, his windows broke, & other damage done; but by the intrepidity of some young gentlemen of the family, the mob were dispersed.

In November 1774, *David Dunbar* of *Hallifax* aforesaid, being an Ensign in the Militia, a mob headed by some of the Select Men of the Town, demand[ed] his colours of him. He refused, saying, that if his commanding officer demanded them he should obey, otherwise he would not part with them:—upon which they broke into his house by force & dragged him out. They had prepared a sharp rail to set him upon; & in resisting them they seized him (by his private parts) & fixed him upon the rail, & was held on it by his legs & arms, & tossed up with violence & greatly bruised so that he did not recover for some time. They beat him, & after abusing him about two hours he was obliged, in order to save his life, to give up his colours.

A parish clerk of an Episcopal Church at *East Haddum* in *Connecticut*, a man of 70 years of age, was taken out of his bed in a cold night, & beat against his hearth by men who held him by his arms & legs. He was then laid across his horse, without his cloaths, & drove to a considerable distance in that naked condition. His nephew Dr. *Abner Beebe*, a physician, complained of the bad usage of his uncle, & spoke very freely in favor of government; for which he was assaulted by a mob, stripped naked, & hot pitch was poured upon him, which blistered his skin. He was then carried to an hog sty & rubbed over with hog's dung. They threw the hog's dung in his face, & rammed some of it down his throat; & in that condition exposed to a company of women. His house was attacked, his windows broke, when one of his children was sick, & a child of his went into distraction upon this treatment. His gristmill was broke, & persons prevented from grinding at it, & from having any connections with him.

II

Kearsley, John. Of Philadelphia. Physician. A man of ardent feelings; his zealous attachment to the Royal cause, and his impetuous temper, made him obnoxious to those whose acts he opposed. He was seized at his own house, in the summer or autumn of 1775, and carted through the streets to the tune of the "Rogue's March." In the affray, he was wounded in the hand by a bayonet. When mounted, the mob gave a loud huzza; and the Doctor, to show his contempt of "the people," took his wig in his injured hand, and swinging it around his head, huzzaed louder and longer than his persecutors. The ride over, it was determined to tar and feather him; but this was abandoned, to the disappointment of many. The doors and windows of his house were, however, broken by stones and brickbats. The same year he was put in prison, for writing letters abusive of the Whigs; and, while there, Stephen Bayard was allowed to attend to the settlement of his affairs. His sufferings caused insanity, which continued until his decease. He died in prison about fifteen months after his ride in the "Tory cart." He was attainted of treason, and his estate confiscated. His uncle, of the same Christian name, and a physician of Philadelphia, died there in 1772.

III

The account written on January 31 by Miss Ann Hulton, sister of Henry Hulton, Commissioner of Customs at Boston, in a letter sent home to England, adds further particulars:

> But the most shocking cruelty was exercised a few nights ago, upon a poor old man a tidesman one Malcolm he is reckond creasy, a quarrel was pickd with him, he was afterward taken, & tard, & featherd. Theres no law that knows a punishment for the greatest crimes beyond what this is, of cruel torture. And this instance exceeds any other before it, he was stript stark naked, one of the severest cold nights this winter, his body coverd all over with tar, then with feathers, his arm dislocated in tearing off his cloaths, he dragged in a cart with thousands attending, some beating him with clubs & knocking him out of the cart, then in again. They gave him several severe whipings, at different parts of the town. This spectacle of horror & sportive cruelty was exhibited for about five hours.
>
> The unhappy wretch they say behavd with the greatest intrepidity, & fortitude all the while, before he was taken, defended himself a long time against numbers, & afterwards when under torture they demanded of him to curse his masters the K: Gov., &c which they coud not make him do, but he still cried, "Curse all traitors." They brought him to the gallows & put a rope about his neck saying they woud hang him—he said he wished they woud, but that they coud not for God was above the Devil. The doctors say that it is impossible this poor creature can live. They say his flesh comes off his back in steaks.

IV

Owen Richards emigrated from Wales to Boston about 1750. He was in his Majesty's service by sea and land for nearly 30 years, mostly as a tidesman in the Customs at Boston. By his seizure of a cargo of sugar, etc., illegally imported in 1770, the disaffected inhabitants of Boston were so incensed that on the same night a tumultous mob of nearly 2,000 assembled outside his house and destroyed his furniture. He was dragged by the heels along the streets to the Custom House, and, after tearing off all his clothes, he was rolled in the channel and put in a cart, tarred and feathered, the feathers set on fire and a rope put around his neck. In this condition he was exposed round the town.

Whiskey Rebellion
1794

In March, 1791, the United States Congress, at the request of Secretary of the Treasury, Alexander Hamilton, levied a tax on distilled whiskey. The tax hit frontiersmen hard; because of poor transportation, the easiest and most profitable way for them to sell the grain they raised was to distill it into whiskey. Furthermore, those accused of evading the tax were required to stand trial in federal courts, which were far from the frontier. The federal court nearest to western Pennsylvania was hundreds of miles away, in Philadelphia. On June 6, 1794, the law was amended to allow state courts to hear cases, but this reform came too late to prevent the outbreak of an insurrection in the four western counties of the state.

On May 13, three weeks before the amendment of the law, the Philadelphia federal court issued subpoenas against thirty-seven distillers in western Pennsylvania. David Lenox, a federal marshal, and John Neville, the excise inspector of the territory, tried to serve the subpoenas but were forcibly prevented. Insurrectionists now began to terrorize excise collectors, rob mails, and suspend trials. On the 17th of July, a crowd of about 500 armed men under James McFarlane attacked the house of Inspector Neville, which was defended by a detachment of eleven federal soldiers. The crowd demanded that Neville surrender his commissions and official papers, a demand reminiscent of the riots against the stamp collectors in 1765. Learning that Neville had left, they asked the soldiers to surrender and allow them to search the house. The soldiers refused, and for an hour the two sides fought. McFarlane was killed and several on both sides were wounded. The rebels won, and burned the house, but allowed its defenders to go free. This fight and others like it alarmed federal officials, who feared that the rebellion might spread to the other frontier whiskey-producing areas—Kentucky, West Virginia, the Carolinas, and Georgia. On August 7 President Washington ordered the insurgents to return to their homes, and offered them amnesty if they would do so. When they did not accept his offer he called on the states to furnish 12,900 men to put down the insurrection. At the head of an army larger than the normal strength of the Continental forces during the Revolution, Washington, Henry Lee, and Hamilton marched into the rebel territory. But no fighting was necessary; the rebels simply dispersed. Twenty prisoners were taken, none of them influential leaders. Two were found guilty of high treason, but they were later pardoned by Washington.

The following account describes the attack on Neville's house. It is taken from a contemporary history by Hugh H. Breckenridge: *Incidents of the Insurrection in the Western Parts of Pennsylvania in the Year 1794* (1795), 18-19. On the insurrection, see Leland Baldwin: *Whiskey Rebels* (1939); Jacob E. Cooke: "The Whiskey Insurrection: A Re-Evaluation," *Pennsylvania History*, XXX (July 1963), 316-46.

McFarlane had been in Pittsburgh that day, and purchased a quantity of flints. He informed the people at the rendezvous that they might count upon a force from the town of Pittsburgh; that the sheriff was sent for to raise the posse; and that soldiers had gone out from the garrison to Neville's house. This information seemed to animate: They had no idea of an opposition that could be formidable.

In arranging the measures of the enterprise, a committee was appointed; with power like that of the national commissioners with the French armies. This committee offered the command to a Benjamin Parkison; who excused himself, as not being a man of military knowledge. James Mc-Farlane was then nominated, and accepted it. This was a major McFarlane of the militia, who had served with reputation, in the rank of a lieutenant, in the war with Great Britain, from the beginning to the end of it; and was a man of good private character; and had acquired a very handsome property, by industry in trade, after the expiration of the war.

The body having marched, and approached the house of the inspector, the horses were left with a guard; and arrangements made for an attack, should it be necessary. A flag was sent from the committee, with a demand of the inspector to deliver up his papers. This appears to have been the ultimate object of the rioters. The inspector had withdrawn from the house; having seen the force that was advancing; conceiving, I presume, that a demand might be made of his person: and that, in consequence of the encounter of the preceding morning, and the loss sustained by the assailants, his life would be in danger. In this case, he must have counted on their not being able to defend the house. Why then not have given direction to those whom he left in the house, not to attempt a defense? Perhaps he did it; but his brother-in-law, Kirkpatrick, a major in the service last war, judging less prudently, entertained the idea of being able to defend it.

It being communicated, on the return of the flag, that the inspector had left the house, a second flag was sent, and a demand made, that six persons should be admitted into the house, to search for his papers, and take them. This was refused; and notice was then given, by a third flag, for the lady of the inspector, and any other female part of the family to withdraw. They did withdraw; and the attack commenced. About fifteen minutes after the commencement, a flag was presented, or was thought to be presented, from the house; upon which, McFarlane stepped from a tree, behind which he stood, and commanding a cessation of the firing, received a ball in the inside of his thigh, near the groin, and instantly expired. The firing then continued; and a message was sent to the committee, who were sitting at some distance, to know whether the house should not be stormed: But, in the meantime, fire had been set to a barn, and to other buildings adjoining the mansion house; and in a short time, the intenseness of the heat, and the evident communicability of the flame to the house, had struck those in the house, with a sense of immediate danger of life; and they began to call for quarter: on which the firing ceased, and they were desired to come out, and surrender themselves. They came out; and the soldiers, three of whom are said to have been wounded, were suffered to pass by, and go where they thought proper. Major Kirkpatrick himself, had nearly passed through, when he was distinguished from the soldiers, and arrested; and ordered to deliver his musket. This he refused; when one presenting a gun to his breast, was about to fire; he dropped upon his knee, and asked quarter. The man took the major's hat from his head, and put it on the muzzle of his gun; but did him no other damage.—I depict these incidents, merely to give an intimate idea of the manners and spirit of the people.

Fire had been put to an end of the mansion house, before the fire communicated from the barn and other buildings. All were consumed; one small building excepted; to which fire was not put, but a guard set over it, at the suggestion of the negroes, that it contained their bacon.

Philadelphia Election Riot
1834

Sharp political antagonisms between the Democratic and Whig parties sometimes led to violence in the mid-1830's. The most incendiary issue was the Jacksonian attack on the Bank of the United States. When in 1834 there was a financial crisis, the level of violence rose sharply. In April, Jackson men fought with "the friends of the Bank" in the streets of New York City. In October, there was an even bloodier riot in Philadelphia, the home of the Bank. The Whigs were harassed at the polls of Moyamensing township by Jackson men, who hoped to win by scaring off the opposition. The Whigs counterattacked, the Jacksonians got reinforcements, and finally guns and bricks replaced fists. One man was killed, fifteen or twenty were wounded, and considerable property was destroyed.

The following account first appeared in the Philadelphia *Gazette*, October 15, 1834, and was reprinted in *Hazard's Register of Pennsylvania*, XIV (October 1834), 264-5.

Among the many disgraceful scenes of outrage which took place yesterday, that which occurred in the township of Moyamensing, at a late hour in the evening, appears to have been the most serious in its consequences. Besides the destruction of a block of five handsome and valuable houses, the property of our townsman Mr. Robb, it appears that several individuals were seriously injured, and perhaps one or more killed. The particulars of this dreadful scene of violence, as well as we could learn from the various contradictory statements made on the ground this morning, appear to be as follows:

The Whigs of Moyamensing had established their headquarters in the tavern at the corner of Christian and Ninth Street, opposite the District Hall, where the elections are held. The Jacksonmen established their headquarters on the opposite side of the way, by the erection of a booth on the pavement, having failed in the attempt to procure the use of an untenanted house in the same row with the Whigs. In the course of the evening, the Jackson party, being much stronger on the ground than their opponents, committed it is said many assaults upon peaceable Whig voters, by breaking their lanterns, tearing away their electioneering bills, and finally in knocking down and beating them. This course of conduct appears to have been pursued until human nature could submit to the aggravating insults no longer. The Whigs made a rally and to punish the insolence of the Jacksonmen, made a rush on them, and cut down their hickory pole. The ground then became quiet—the disturbance was considered as finally settled, and peace was fully restored. This state of things, however, continued but a short time; the opposing party, in the interim, had been collecting their forces from Southwark, the city, and upper districts, and suddenly and unexpectedly appeared on the ground in great numbers, and made a desperate attack upon the Whig headquarters, driving into the house, nearly every Whig on the ground. They deliberately set fire to the splendid Liberty Pole in front, and the watchbox at the corner, and then entered the tavern and adjoining houses in the row— destroyed the furniture in those which were tenanted—threw out the beds and bedding, &c. and piled them up in the street, and set the mass on fire!

Still unsatisfied with the work of destruction, the mob ransacked the lower rooms of the Whig tavern, threw out the furniture upon the blazing pile in the street, and grossly assaulted all upon whom they could lay their hands. The landlady and her shrieking children were driven with violence into the street, and severely maltreated. The persons in the upper rooms, now considering that the object of the mob was to murder them, procured fire arms and from the third story windows and the roof, fired into the street. Blank cartridges, it is said, were used first, but these were insufficient to intimidate the mob. Subsequently, we learn, several in the street were injured by buck shots, and it is said that one individual died while being conveyed to the hospital.

The crowd in front who stood their ground firmly, and replied to those inside by tremendous vollies of bricks, stones, and other missiles, at length made a desperate rush inside, and cleared the premises, not only of human beings, but of furniture, leaving not a particle untouched. Soon after, whether from accident or design we are unable to state, the tavern took fire, and the flames spread rapidly and fiercely in every direction. The situation of affairs was now awful and appalling.—The mob had entire possession of the whole place, not a solitary anti-Jackson man having the temerity to show his face. The alarm of fire was sounded, and the fire companies arrived on the spot, but the mob would not permit them to go into operation. Many were openly threatened that if they put a drop of water on the fire they would be beaten. One of two companies, however, persisted in their exertions, and one attachment was let out, but it was soon dragged away by main force, *and the whole block of buildings was permitted to burn down!*

These particulars embrace, we believe, all the facts of the case, without coloring or partiality. The scene altogether was most disgraceful to the country. The houses destroyed were the property of an unoffending citizen, who had acquired them by hard industry.—his loss will probably not fall short of $5,000.

Christiana Affair

1851

In the Compromise of 1850, Northern Congressmen reluctantly agreed to a harsh Fugitive Slave Act. Under its provisions, blacks accused of being runaway slaves were denied trial. Rather, when they were claimed, they were simply brought before federal commissioners, who were empowered to return them to slavery. The commissioners were paid ten dollars if they sent captives southward, five if they ordered a release. In addition, the federal marshals, whose job it was to capture alleged fugitives, could summon all citizens to their aid. No sooner had the law been passed than Negroes, many of whom were not fugitives, were arrested in Northern cities. But vigilance committees formed to challenge enforcement of the law, and crowds often gathered to rescue blacks. In February 1851 the slave Shadrach was rescued by a crowd of Bostonians, white and black. The following April, a crowd tried to free Thomas Sims, and was prevented by federal marshals. The first such rescue attempt in which a man was killed occurred in Christiana, Pennsylvania.

In September 1851 Edward Gorsuch of Maryland, learning that his escaped slaves had taken refuge in the black community of Christiana, went to Philadelphia to get a federal warrant to seize them. The warrant directed Deputy United States Marshal Henry Kline to arrest Nelson Ford and three other blacks. Gorsuch and Kline and their party went to the house of William Parker, a long-time leader of the free blacks of Christiana, where the slaves had taken refuge. Parker's wife summoned blacks from the surrounding countryside by blowing a horn; in they came, carrying guns, swords, corn cutters, and scythes. A few whites came as well, and Kline asked them to help him seize the slaves, but they refused. Gorsuch tried to claim his slaves, but the blacks refused to give them up. In the ensuing struggle, Gorsuch was killed, his sons and others of his party wounded, and the rest driven away.

By evening most of the blacks who had fought, including Parker and the slaves, were on the way to Canada, aided by Frederick Douglass. The next day, a contingent of United States Marines and a civilian posse arrived and arrested a large number of people, including the whites who had refused to help Kline. A total of thirty-eight were indicted for treason. Their trial was the first major test of the Fugitive Slave Act, but all were found not guilty on December 11. The South was furious: the Baltimore *Clipper*, for example, said that the slave owners were "honestly and lawfully endeavoring to repossess themselves of their property." The Southern fire-eaters said the affair showed the futility of laws and compromises. The Augusta *Constitu-*

tionalist said: "Our opponents are always pointing to the Fugitive Slave Law. We point you, people of Georgia, to the mangled corpses of your fellow citizens of the South. The Law will hereafter be a perfectly dead letter."

The following account was written by Parker: "The Freedman's Story," *Atlantic Monthly*, XVII (February-March 1866), 151-66, 276-95. See William V. Hensel: "The Christiana Riot and Treason Trials of 1851," Lancaster County Historical Society *Papers*, XV (1911); Roderick W. Nash: "The Christiana Riot: An Evaluation of Its National Significance," *Journal of the Lancaster County Historical Society*, LXV (Spring 1961), 65-91; Richard Grau: "The Christiana Riot of 1851: A Reappraisal," ibid., LXVIII (1964), 147-63.

The information brought by Mr. Williams spread through the vicinity like a fire in the prairies; and when I went home from my work in the evening, I found Pinckney (whom I should have said before was my brother-in-law), Abraham Johnson, Samuel Thompson and Joshua Kite at my house, all of them excited about the rumor. I laughed at them, and said it was all talk. This was the 10th of September, 1851. They stopped for the night with us, and we went to bed as usual. Before daylight, Joshua Kite rose, and started for his home. Directly, he ran back to the house, burst open the door, crying, "O William! kidnappers! kidnappers!"

He said that, when he was just beyond the yard, two men crossed before him, as if to stop him, and others came up on either side. As he said this, they had reached the door. Joshua ran up stairs (we slept up stairs), and they followed him; but I met them at the landing, as asked, "Who are you?"

The leader, Kline, replied, "I am the United States Marshal."

I then told him to take another step and I would break his neck.

He again said, "I am the United States Marshal."

I told him I did not care for him nor the United States. At that he turned and went down stairs.

Pinckney said, as he turned to go down,—"Where is the use in fighting? They will take us."

Kline heard him, and said, "Yes, give up, for we can and will take you anyhow."

I told them all not to be afraid, nor to give up to any slaveholder, but to fight until death.

"Yes," said Kline, "I have heard many a negro talk as big as you, and then have taken him; and I'll take you."

"You have not taken me yet," I replied; "and if you undertake it you will have your name recorded in history for this day's work."

Mr. Gorsuch then spoke, and said,—"Come, Mr. Kline, let's go up stairs and take them. We *can* take them. Come, follow me. I'll go up and get my property. What's in the way The law is in my favor, and the people are in my favor."

At that he began to ascend the stair; but I said to him,—"See here, old man, you can come up, but you can't go down again. Once up here, you are mine." . . .

Mr. Gorsuch then said, "You have my property."

To which I replied,—"Go in the room down there, and see if there is anything there belonging to you. There are beds and a bureau, chairs, and other things. Then go out to the barn; there you will find a cow and some hogs. See if any of them are yours."

He said,—"They are not mine; I want my men. They are here, and I am bound to have them." . . .

I denied that I had his property when he replied, "You have my men."

"Am I your man?" I asked.

"No."

I then called Pinckney forward.

"Is that your man?"

"No."

Abraham Johnson I called next, but Gorsuch said he was not his man.

The only plan left was to call both Pinckney and Johnson again; for had I called the others, he would have recognized them, for they were his slaves.

Abraham Johnson said, "Does such a shrivelled up old slaveholder as you own a nice, genteel young man as I am?"

At this Gorsuch took offence, and charged me with dictating his language. I then told him there were but five of us, which he denied, and still insisted that I had his property. One of the party then attacked the Abolitionists, affirming that, although they declared there could not be property in man, the Bible was conclusive authority in favor of property in human flesh.

"Yes," said Gorsuch, "does not the Bible Say, 'Servants, obey your masters'?"

I said that it did, but the same Bible said, "Give unto your servants that which is just and equal."

At this stage of the proceedings, we went into a mutual Scripture inquiry, and bandied views in the manner of garrulous old wives.

When I spoke of duty to servants, Gorsuch said, "Do you know that?"

"Where," I asked, "do you see it in Scripture that a man should traffic in his brother's blood?"

"Do you call a nigger my brother?" said Gorsuch.

"Yes," said I.

While I was talking to Gorsuch, his son said, "Father, will you take all this from a nigger?"

I answered him by saying that I respected old age; but that, if he would repeat that, I should knock his teeth down his throat. At this he fired upon me, and I ran up to him and knocked the pistol out of his hand, when he let the other one fall and ran in the field.

My brother-in-law, who was standing near, then said, "I can stop him" —and with his double-barrel gun he fired.

Young Gorsuch fell, but rose and ran on again. Pinckney fired a second time and again Gorsuch fell, but was soon up again and, running into the cornfield, lay down in the fence corner.

I returned to my men, and found Samuel Thompson talking to old Mr. Gorsuch, his master. They were both angry.

"Old man, you had better go home to Maryland," said Samuel.

"You had better give up, and come home with me," said the old man.

Thompson took Pinckney's gun from him, struck Gorsuch, and brought him to his knees. Gorsuch rose and signalled to his men. Thompson then knocked him down again, and he again rose. At this time all the white men opened fire, and we rushed upon them; when they turned, threw down their guns and ran away. We, being closely engaged, clubbed our rifles. We were too closely pressed to fire, but we found a good deal that could be done with empty guns.

Old Mr. Gorsuch was the bravest of his party; he held on to his pistols until the last, while all the others threw away their weapons. I saw as many as three at a time fighting with him. Sometimes he was on his knees, then on his back, and again his feet would be where his head should be. He was a fine soldier and a brave man. Whenever he saw the least opportunity, he would take aim. While in close quarters with the whites, we could load and fire but two or three times. Our guns got bent and out of order. So damaged did they become, that we could shoot with but two or three of them. Samuel Thompson bent his gun on old Mr. Gorsuch so badly, that it was of no use to us.

When the white men ran, they scattered. I ran after Nathan Nelson, but could not catch him. I never saw a man run faster. Returning, I saw Joshua Gorsuch coming, and Pinckney behind him. I reminded him that he would like "to take hold of a nigger," told him that now was his "chance," and struck him a blow on the side of the head which stopped him. Pinckney came up behind, and gave him a blow which brought him to the ground; as the others passed, they gave him a kick or jumped upon him, until the blood oozed out at his ears.

Nicholas Hutchings and Nathan Nelson of Baltimore County, Maryland, could outrun any men I ever saw. They and Kline were not brave, like the Gorsuches. Could our men have got them, they would have been satisfied.

One of our men ran after Dr. Pierce, as he richly deserved attention; but Pierce caught up with Castner Hanway, who rode between the fugitive and the Doctor, to shield him and some others. Hanway was told to get out of the way, or he would forfeit his life; he went aside quickly, and the man fired at the Marylander, but missed him,—he was too far off. I do not know whether he was wounded or not; but I do know that, if it had not been for Hanway, he would have been killed. . . .

The riot, so called, was now entirely ended. The elder Gorsuch was dead; his son and nephew were both wounded, and I have reason to believe others were,—how many, it would be difficult to say. Of our party, only two were wounded.

. . . Having driven the slavocrats off in every direction, our party now turned towards their several homes.

Bleeding Kansas
1854–1861

Congress in 1854 created two new territories, Kansas and Nebraska, and left the question of slavery to the future inhabitants. In the next decade, Kansas became the scene of a bloody struggle between pro-slavery and free-soil forces. On May 21, 1856, a large pro-slavery force "sacked" the free-soil stronghold, Lawrence, burning several houses. Apparently inflamed by the destruction in Lawrence and by several recent murders of free-soilers, John Brown, an ardent abolitionist, decided to retaliate. On May 24, 1856, in Potawatomie, together with six men, four of them his sons, he sought out, murdered, and mutilated the bodies of five pro-slavery men and boys, none guilty of any crime against the free-soilers. The Potawatomie massacre set off a guerilla war. Bands of pro-slavery Missourians attacked Brown and his men. At Osawatomie, over a half dozen men were killed, over twenty wounded, and the town was burned. At Marais de Cygnes in May, 1858, Southern guerillas lined up nine free-soilers and shot them, killing five. When Kansas was finally admitted as a free-soil state, on January 29, 1861, over 200 men had died. Violence continued almost until the end of the Civil War, as, for example, when Southerners on August 21, 1863, sacked Lawrence a second time and killed more than 150 persons.

The following confession of a member of Brown's band at Potawatomie, James Townsley, is taken from Charles Robinson: *The Kansas Conflict* (1892), 265-7. See also Alice Nichols: *Bleeding Kansas* (1954); James Malin: *John Brown and the Legend of '56* (1942); Oswald Garrison Villard: *John Brown: 1800-1859* (1911); and the essay on John Brown by C. Vann Woodward in Daniel Aaron, ed.: *America in Crisis* (1952).

"I joined the Potawatomie rifle company at its re-organization in May, 1856, at which time John Brown, Jr., was elected captain. On the 21st of the same month information was received that the Georgians were marching on Lawrence, threatening its destruction. The company was immediately called together, and about four o'clock P.M. we started on a forced march to aid in its defense. About two miles south of Middle Creek we were joined by the Osawatomie company under Captain Dayton, and proceeded to Mount Vernon, where we waited about two hours, until the moon rose. We then marched all night, camping the next morning, the 22nd, for breakfast, near Ottawa Jones's. Before we arrived at this point news had been received that Lawrence had been destroyed, and a question was raised whether we should return or go on. During the forenoon, however, we proceeded up Ottawa Creek to within about five miles of Palmyra, and went into camp near the residence of Captain Shore. Here we remained undecided over night. About noon the next day, the 23rd, Old John Brown came to me and said he had just received information that trouble was expected on the Potawatomie, and wanted to know if I would take my team and take him and his boys back, so they could keep watch of what was going on. I told him I would do so. The party, consisting of Old John Brown, Watson Brown, Oliver Brown, Henry Thompson (John Brown's son-in-law), and Mr. Winer, were soon ready for the trip, and we started, as near as I can remember, about two o'clock P.M. All of the party except Winer, who rode a pony, rode with me in my wagon. When within two or three miles of the Potawatomie Creek, we turned off the main road to the right, drove down to the edge of the timber between two deep ravines, and camped about one mile above Dutch Henry's crossing.

"After my team was fed and the party had taken supper, John Brown told me for the first time what he proposed to do. He said he wanted me to pilot the company up to the forks of the creek, some five or six miles above, into the neighborhood where I lived, and show them where all the pro-slavery men resided; that he proposed to sweep the creek as he came down of all the pro-slavery men living on it. I positively refused to do it. He insisted upon it, but when he found that I would not go, he decided to postpone the expedition until the following night. I then wanted to take my team and go home, but he would not let me do so, and said I should remain with them. We remained in camp that night and all the next day. Some time after dark we were ordered to march.

"We started, the whole company, in a northerly direction, crossing Mosquito Creek above the residence of the Doyles. Soon after crossing the creek some one of the party knocked at the door of the cabin, but received no reply—I have forgotten whose cabin it was, if I knew at the time. The next place we came to was the residence of the Doyles. John Brown, three of his sons, and son-in-law went to the door, leaving Frederick Brown, Winer, and myself a short distance from the house. About this time a large dog attacked us. Frederick Brown struck the dog a blow with his short two-edged sword, after which I dealt him a blow with my sabre, and heard no more of him. The old man Doyle and two sons were called out and marched some distance from the house towards Dutch Henry's, in the road, where a halt was made. Old John Brown drew his revolver and shot the old man Doyle in the forehead, and Brown's two youngest sons immediately fell upon the younger Doyles with their short two-edged swords.

"One of the young Doyles was stricken down in an instant, but the other attempted to escape, and was pursued a short distance by his assailant and cut down. The company then proceeded down Mosquito Creek, to the house of Allen Wilkinson. Here the old man Brown, three of his sons, and son-in-law, as at the Doyle residence, went to the door and ordered Wilkinson to come out, leaving Frederick Brown, Winer, and myself standing in the road east of the house. Wilkinson was taken and marched some distance south of his house and slain in the road, with a short sword, by one of the younger Browns. After he was killed his body was dragged out to one side and left.

"We then crossed the Potawatomie and came to the house of Henry Sherman, generally known as Dutch Henry. Here John Brown and the party, excepting Frederick Brown, Winer, and myself, who were left outside a short distance from the door, went into the house and brought out one or two persons, talked with them some, and then took them in again. They afterwards brought out William Sherman, Dutch Henry's brother, marched him down into the Potawatomie Creek, where he was slain with swords by Brown's two youngest sons, and left lying in the creek.

"It was the expressed intention of Brown to execute Dutch Henry also, but he was not found at home. He also hoped to find George Wilson, Probate Judge of Anderson County, there, and intended, if he did, to kill him too. Wilson had been notifying Free-State men to leave the Territory. I had received such a notice from him myself.

"Brown wanted me to pilot the party into the neighborhood where I lived, and point out all the pro-slavery men in it, whom he proposed to put to death. I positively refused to do it, and on account of my refusal I remained in camp all of the night upon which the first attack was to be made, and the next day. I told him I was willing to go with him to Lecompton and attack the leaders, or fight the enemy in open field anywhere, but I did not want to engage in killing these men. That night and the acts then perpetrated are vividly fixed in my memory, and I have thought of them many times since.

"I make this statement at the urgent request of my friends and neighbors, Judge James Hanway and Hon. Johnson Clarke, who have been present during all the time occupied in writing it out, and in whose hearing it has been several times read before signing."

JAMES TOWNSLEY

LANE, KAN., December 6, 1879

Baltimore Election Riot
1856

Violence at elections reached a peak in Baltimore in the 1850's. The city had a long history of election riots, but the rise of the Know-Nothing Party after 1854 sharply increased their severity. Innumerable street gangs—Plug-Uglies, Rough Skins, Rip-Raps, Blood Tubs, etc.—were used by the Know-Nothing Party to terrorize immigrants. The gangs developed several methods of eliminating opponents. The Blood Tubs, for example, got their name from their technique of intimidation: they took tubs of blood from local butchers, heaved Irishmen into them, then chased them down the street with knives. The sight of one blood-drenched victim was a powerful deterrent to other would-be voters. Another gang's strategy was to strap pointed shoemaker's awls to their knees; with these they would gouge persistent immigrant voters. Whenever Democratic clubs or immigrant groups retaliated, city-wide riots would begin.

From 1854 on, this was the pattern for elections in Baltimore. By these means, the Know-Nothings won local, state, and in 1856, Presidential contests. In many districts immigrants were stopped from voting entirely. In 1856 there were three riots—in September, October, and November—in which over a dozen were killed and hundreds injured. In 1857 and 1858 both the riots and the Know-Nothing victories were repeated. In 1859 a group of "respectable citizens regardless of party" organized a City Reform Association and promised to protect the polls. Undaunted, the political clubs held a monster rally, parading with huge awls and carrying banners depicting bleeding heads labeled "reformer." A blacksmith set up shop in the street and passed out hundreds of new-forged awls. Again the elections were marked by riots. But this time the state legislature intervened, invalidated the Know-Nothing victories, organized a new police force, and passed many reform bills. The gangs were disbanded, and the election of 1860 was peaceful.

The following description of one riot in 1856 in which five
were killed, and forty-five wounded, is taken from the Baltimore *American*, October 9, 1856. See Benjamin Tusca: *Know-
Nothingism in Baltimore, 1854-1860* (1925); and Laurence F.
Schmeckebier: *History of the Know Nothing Party in Maryland* (1899).

The order which generally characterized the polls in the earlier hours of
yesterday was not maintained throughout the day. Individual combats and
minor affrays occurred during the afternoon at a number of the polls;
and at two, the Twelfth and Eighteenth, serious riots, leading to loss of
life and serious injuries, resulted from the high state of excitement
originated between the aforesaid contesting parties.

The most serious riot was started in and around the Lexington market-
house. It commenced about three o'clock and continued for about two
hours. The parties engaged in the disturbance were numbers of the New-
Market Fire Company, and the "Rip Raps" and other political clubs. The
affair commenced at the Twelfth Ward polls, about the middle of the
day, when an effort was made by the Democrats to take possession. After
they had been repulsed, the aggressors retreated to the engine house, and
armed themselves with muskets and revolvers; they then took their position
in the market-house and began a heavy discharge of musketry directed
towards the polls. The firing attracted a large crowd, among whom were
the "Rip Raps," from the Fourteenth Ward polls. When these persons
had congregated, a fierce attack was made upon them, which continued
for a long time without intermission.

Several persons were killed, and a large number injured. Among those
killed was an Irishman, whose name could not be ascertained, who was
shot in the left breast, on the corner of Paca and Lexington Streets, whilst
stooping to pick up a brick. The ball entered the left breast and passed
downwards. A man by the name of Charles Brown was also killed whilst
peaceably walking along the street. He resided in Chase Street and leaves
a wife and three children. . . .

The combatants fought with the greatest determination and from
the free and desperate use they made of the fire-arms with which they
were provided, it is somewhat remarkable that a larger number were not
killed. The New Market party held possession of the market and would
rally from their engine-house after loading their pieces. Their opponents
rallied in Green Street, south of the market. Both parties, thus prepared,

would then carry on a guerilla warfare, firing at one another from the corners of the streets and from behind the pillars of the market, until their loads were exhausted, when they would retreat to their rallying points to prepare for another sally. All this was done with cool deliberation, and on the part of some of the combatants with an audacious courage which exhibited in a better cause would have merited praise. The stores and dwellings in the vicinity were all closed, and peaceably disposed people kept out of reach of danger; so that, as far as we can learn, with one exception, none but those who were parties to the conflict were either killed or wounded.

A desperate riot also occurred in the vicinity of the Eighth Ward. The foreign voters of the Ward took possession of the polls early in the day, and drove off several old residents who were holding Swann tickets. We saw a hundred of them chasing, with clubs and bricks, a man with slight make and small stature, who escaped into a grocery store on the corner of Forrest and Hillen Streets. His offense consisted in holding Swann tickets. Information of this condition of affairs having been received at the up-town Wards, a large party belonging to American clubs started over to that vicinity. One of them went along French Street and the other along Hillen Street; but they had scarcely reached the vicinity of the Eighth Ward polls, when they found themselves hemmed in by hundreds of infuriated opponents, a large number of whom were armed with muskets.

Both divisions of the "Rip Raps" were compelled to retreat before the superior arms of their assailants, and finally came to a stand on Calvert Street, near Monument, where a severe fight took place, which lasted for two hours, continuing up Monument Street to the vicinity of the Washington Monument, the tree-boxes along the square being greatly cut with bullets. The Irishmen then took a position behind the trees in the vacant space between Centre and Monument Streets, and a brisk firing was kept up for some time. . . .

The Democrats held complete possession of the Eighth Ward polls throughout the day, and used every exertion to prevent their opponents from voting. The result is seen in a decrease of the American vote and an immense increase in the Democratic, a large number being undoubtedly illegal. The vote is the largest by 300 ever polled in the ward, whilst at least two hundred Americans were prevented from voting.

In the Eighteenth Ward there was considerable disorder growing out of the immense number of voters in the ward and the limited time for voting. Each party struggled to make their way to the polls, but the

Americans being in superior strength generally prevailed. The passage of the bill dividing the wards, defeated by the recurrent Democratic members of the City Council, would have prevented this difficulty.

The other wards were generally quiet.

The city was in an uproar until a late hour last night, but no collisions, as far as we could learn, occurred.

Harper's Ferry
1859

John Brown arrived at Harper's Ferry in July, 1859. Posing as a cattle buyer he established a residence there, and by fall twenty-one of his followers had drifted in. He planned to seize the unguarded Federal Arsenal, rouse the slaves, and then, at the head of a liberated army, move southward along the Appalachians, spreading freedom as he went. To finance this scheme, he had raised $4,000 from Northern abolitionists, some of whom had very little idea of what he planned to do with the money.

Brown had long before concluded that only violence would overthrow slavery. He had studied the tactics of Toussaint L'Ouverture and Garibaldi, but his plan of action was poorly conceived. Frederick Douglass, one of Brown's backers, protested against his plan on tactical grounds, fearing correctly that Brown would be trapped in the town. The majority of Brown's followers also thought the plan a poor one, but agreed to follow him nonetheless.

On Sunday night, October 16, Brown and his men captured the Arsenal, and seized prominent citizens as hostages. Although they prevailed upon a few slaves to join them, the general uprising they had counted on did not occur. By mid-morning the local citizens began to attack Brown's forces in the Arsenal, forcing him to barricade himself in the building. In the firing, which continued throughout the day, two of Brown's sons were killed. A troop of Marines arrived under the command of Robert E. Lee and J. E. B. Stuart, and asked Brown to surrender. Although many of his men were dead or dying, he refused. Next morning the troops stormed the building. Brown was taken alive, tried and hanged. Twelve of his followers died at Harper's Ferry, as did five local residents and one Marine; more were wounded. The following account was written by John E. Daingerfield, one of the hostages: "John Brown at Harper's Ferry, the Fight at the Engine-House, as seen by one of his prisoners," *Century Illustrated Monthly Magazine*, XXX (June 1885), 265-7.

On Sunday night, Oct. 16, 1859, about twelve or one o'clock, the gate-keeper of the bridge over the Potomac leading into Maryland was startled by the steady tramp of many men approaching the gate, having with them wagons, who, upon reaching the gate, ordered it to be opened to them. This the gate-keeper refused to do, saying they were strangers. They, however, while parleying with him, seized him and, presenting a pistol at his head, compelled him to be silent. They then wrenched off the locks and came over, he thinks about sixty strong, though he was evidently frightened and could not speak with accuracy.

Upon getting over, the first building taken possession of was the depot of the Baltimore and Ohio Railroad, then in charge of a very trusty negro, who slept in the building. Upon Brown's men demanding admittance, he refused to let them come in, saying he was in charge, and his instructions were to let no one in at night. He was then shot down, a negro faithful to his trust being the first victim of those whose mission it was to free the African race from bondage.

Brown's party next proceeded to the hotel, rapped up the landlord, put him under arrest, and placed guards at the doors, so that no one could go out or come in. All this was in perfect quiet at dead of night. They went next to place guards at the arsenal and armories, and fix their pickets at all the streets, so that one one could come or go who was not at once picked up and placed with an armed guard over him and compelled to be silent.

Next they divided their force, sending Cook with some men to seize Colonel Washington and other slaveholders. These gentlemen Brown's party waked from sleep and compelled to go with them as prisoners, at the same time taking all the slaves they could find, carriages, horses, etc. . . .

About daylight one of my servants came to my room door and told me "there was war in the street." I, of course, got up at once, dressed, and went out, my dwelling being immediately on the street. Upon looking round I saw nothing exciting. The only person in view was a man from the country, who was riding rapidly, and I supposed he had lost some of his negroes, who had been stopped at the gate of the bridge and made fight.

I walked towards my office, then just within the armory inclosure, and not more than a hundred yards from my dwelling. As I proceeded I saw a man come out of an alley near me, then another, and another, all coming towards me. When they came up to me I inquired what all this meant; they said, nothing, only they had taken possession of the Government works.

I told them they talked like crazy men. They answered, "Not so crazy as you think, as you will soon see." Up to this time I had not seen any arms; presently, however, the men threw back the short cloaks they wore, and displayed Sharpes's rifles, pistols, and knives. Seeing these, and fearing something serious was going on, I told the men I believed I would return to my quarters. They at once cocked their guns, and told me I was a prisoner. . . .

They said I was in no personal danger; they only wanted to carry me to their captain, John Smith. . . .

Upon reaching the gate I saw what, indeed, looked like war—negroes armed with pikes, and sentinels with muskets all around. When I reached the gate I was turned over to "Captain Smith."

He called me by name, and asked if I knew Colonel Washington and others, mentioning familiar names. I said I did, and he then said, "Sir, you will find them there," motioning me towards the engine-room.

We were not kept closely confined, but were allowed to converse with him. I asked him what his object was; he replied, "To free the negroes of Virginia." He added that he was prepared to do it, and by twelve o'clock would have fifteen hundred men with him, ready armed.

Up to this time the citizens had hardly begun to move about, and knew nothing of the raid.

When they learned what was going on, some came out armed with old shot-guns, and were themselves shot by concealed men. All the stores, as well as the arsenal, were in the hands of Brown's men, and it was impossible to get either arms or ammunition, there being hardly any private arms owned by citizens. At last, however, a few weapons were obtained, and a body of citizens crossed the river and advanced from the Maryland side. They made a vigorous attack, and in a few minutes caused all the invaders who were not killed to retreat to Brown inside of the armory gate. Then he entered the engine-house, carrying his prisoners along, or rather part of them, as he made selections among them.

After getting into the engine-house with his men, he made this speech: "Gentlemen, perhaps you wonder why I have selected you from the others. It is because I believe you to be the most influential, and I have only to say now that you will have to share precisely the same fate that your friends extend to my men." He began at once to bar the doors and windows, and to cut port-holes through the brick wall.

Then commenced a terrible firing from without, from every point from which the windows could be seen, and in a few minutes every window was shattered, and hundreds of balls came through the doors. These shots were answered from within whenever the attacking party could be seen. This was kept up most of the day, and, strange to say, no prisoner was hurt, though thousands of balls were imbedded in the walls, and holes shot in the doors almost large enough for a man to creep through.

At night the firing ceased, for we were in total darkness, and nothing could be seen in the engine-house.

During the day and night I talked much with John Brown, and found him as brave as a man could be, and sensible upon all subjects except slavery. Upon that question he was a religious fanatic, and believed it was his duty to free the slaves, even if in doing so he lost his own life.

During a sharp fight one of Brown's sons was killed. He fell; then trying to raise himself, he said, "It is all over with me," and died instantly.

Brown did not leave his post at the port-hole, but when the fighting ceased he walked to his son's body, straightened out his limbs, took off his trappings, then turning to me, said, "This is the third son I have lost in this cause." Another son had been shot in the morning and was then dying, having been brought in from the street. While Brown was a murderer, yet I was constrained to think that he was not a vicious man, but was crazed upon the subject of slavery. Often during the affair in the engine-house, when his men would want to fire upon some one who might be seen passing, Brown would stop them, saying, "Don't shoot; that man is unarmed." The firing was kept up by our men all day and until late at night, and during this time several of his men were killed; but, as I said before, none of the prisoners were hurt though in great danger.

During the day and night many propositions *pro* and *con* were made, looking to Brown's surrender and the release of the prisoners, but without result.

When Colonel Lee came with the Government troops, at one o'clock at night, he at once sent a flag of truce by his aid, J. E. B. Stuart, to notify Brown of his arrival, and in the name of the United States to demand his surrender, advising him to throw himself upon the clemency of the Government.

Brown declined to accept Colonel Lee's terms, and determined to await the attack.

When Stuart was admitted, and a light brought, he exclaimed, "Why aren't you old Ossawatomie Brown, of Kansas, whom I once had there as my prisoner?" "Yes," was the answer, "but you did not keep me." This was the first intimation we had as to Brown's true name. . . .

Stuart told him he would return at early morning for his final reply and left him. . . .

When he had gone, Brown at once proceeded to barricade the doors, windows, etc., endeavoring to make the place as strong as possible.

During all this time no one of Brown's men showed the slightest fear, but calmly awaited the attack, selecting the best situations to fire from upon the attacking party, and arranging their guns and pistols so that a fresh one could be taken up as soon as one was discharged. During the night I had a long talk with Brown, and told him that he and his men were committing treason against the State and the United States. Two of his men, hearing the conversation, said to their leader, "Are we committing treason against our country by being here?" Brown answered, "Certainly." Both said. "If that is so, we don't want to fight any more. We thought we came to liberate the slaves, and did not know that was committing treason."

Both of these men were killed in the attack on the engine-house when Brown was taken.

When Lieutenant Stuart came in the morning for the final reply to the demand to surrender, I got up and went to Brown's side to hear his answer.

Stuart asked, "Are you ready to surrender, and trust to the mercy of the Government?"

Brown answered promptly, "No! I prefer to die here."

His manner did not betray the least fear.

Stuart stepped aside and made the signal for the attack, which was instantly begun with sledge-hammers to break down the door.

Finding it would not yield, the soldiers seized a long ladder for a battering-ram, and commenced beating the door with that, the party within firing incessantly. I had assisted in the barricading, fixing the fastenings so that I could remove them upon the first effort to get in. But I was not at the door when the battering began, and could not get to the fastenings until the ladder was used. I then quickly removed the fastenings, and after two or three strokes of the ladder the engine rolled partially back, making a small aperture, through which Lieutenant Green of the marines forced himself, jumped on top of the engine, and stood a second in the midst of a shower of balls, looking for John Brown. When he saw Brown he sprang about twelve feet at him, and gave an under-thrust of his sword, striking him about midway the body and raising him completely from the ground. Brown fell forward with his head between his knees, and Green struck him several times over the head, and, as I then supposed, split his skull at every stroke.

I was not two feet from Brown at that time. Of course I got out of the building as soon as possible, and did not know till some time later that Brown was not killed. It seems that in making the thrust Green's sword struck Brown's belt and did not penetrate the body. The sword was bent double. The reason that Brown was not killed when struck on the head was that Green was holding his sword in the middle, striking with the hilt and making only scalp wounds.

When Governor Wise came and was examining Brown, I heard the questions and answers; and no lawyer could have used more careful reserve, while at the same time he showed no disrespect. Governor Wise was astonished at the answers he received from Brown.

After some controversy between the United States and the State of Virginia as to which had jurisdiction over the prisoners, Brown was carried to the Charlestown jail, and, after a fair trial, was hanged.

New Orleans Coup d'État

1874

In the years following the New Orleans riot of 1866, armed bands roamed Louisiana. Brigadier-General Philip Sheridan, military governor of the district, estimated that in that decade over

3,500 persons, mostly black, were killed or wounded in frightful massacres in Bossier, Caddo, St. Landry, and Grant parishes.

In 1872, after the struggle for political control of the state reached a stalemate, violence began to be turned against the state itself. That year, the Republican candidate, William P. Kellog, was opposed by a coalition of dissident Republicans and Democrats backing John McEnery. The election was so muddled by fraud and coercion that it was impossible to determine who had won, and both sides claimed a victory. In January, 1873, as armed bands of whites and blacks paraded the streets, both candidates took oaths of office and set up rival legislatures. In March McEnery tried to assemble a militia force, but the New Orleans police, loyal to Kellog, dispersed the McEnery legislature. Kellog's faction then became the de facto government.

The whites of the state organized White Leagues, which were para-military organizations, dedicated to the recapture of power for whites. Their numbers, which eventually reached over 25,-000, included many reputable citizens and large property holders of the state. In September 1874 a shipment of rifles to the White League was confiscated by Governor Kellog's order. The leaders of the League called a mass meeting to protest this infringement of their right to bear arms. The White League military companies demanded that Kellog resign. He refused, ordered his Adjutant General, James A. Longstreet of Confederate Army fame, to rally the militia and join with General A. S. Badger's metropolitan police to defend his government, and then took refuge in the customs house.

The Canal Street meeting, numbering perhaps 5,000 or 6,000, then proclaimed McEnery Governor and D. B. Penn Lieutenant Governor. In McEnery's absence, Penn took command of the insurgent forces. He issued a proclamation calling on all Louisianans to get arms and support him in "driving the usurpers from power." At two p.m. on September 14 the White Leaguers captured the City Hall and the telegraph office. They next moved against the police and militia. In a short but bloody gun battle they routed the Kellog forces and effected a coup d'état. The White League lost 16 dead and 45 wounded, and the Longstreet-Kellog forces lost 11 dead and 60 wounded.

Kellog had, in the meantime, telegraphed President Grant, who ordered federal troops to put down the insurrection. This was done peacefully, since McEnery counselled against resisting federal force. Kellog resumed his functions on the 19th. But though the White League was temporarily defeated, the events of 1874 marked the beginning of the end of Reconstruction government. In 1876 the federal government refused to use force to support the Louisiana radical Republicans, the government collapsed and Reconstruction was at an end.

The following account of the White League battle was published in the New Orleans *Republican* and reprinted in Stuart Landry: *The Battle of Liberty Place* (1955). See Otis Singletary: *Negro Militia and Reconstruction* (1957); Ella Lonn: *Reconstruction in Louisiana after 1868* (1918); C. Vann Woodward: *Reunion and Reaction: The Compromise of 1877 and the End of Reconstruction* (1951); Frederick T. Wilson: *Federal Aid in Domestic Disturbances, 1787-1922*, Senate Document No. 263, 67th Congress, 2nd Session; and Alcee Fortier: *A History of Louisiana* (1904).

This condition of things was reported to General Badger at that time at the Jackson square station, with nearly all his force. He had a Gatling gun and three small brass howitzers for canister. The several police captains had charge of their commands, all apparently well armed and the men in good spirits.

Meantime, the various companies of the White League, armed with every variety of weapon, appeared in the streets, taking position in various portions of the city. Fully 3000 armed men were in their ranks. The corner of Poydras and St. Charles Streets was selected by General Ogden, the Grand Commander of the League, with his staff, from which point the movements of the organization were directed. About four o'clock a barricade of lumber, boxes, iron plates from the street crossings etc., was thrown up across Camp Street.

A few minutes before four o'clock General Badger issued an order for his command to march. They started up near the levee and met with no opposition until near the head of Canal Street. Arrived on the levee,— the artillery—three brass pieces and two Gatling guns—were deployed, and the infantry properly detailed to support them. No organized enemy appeared to oppose them. They were on open ground, near the iron building, but almost instantly a dropping fire from behind hay and cotton bales commenced on them. Loose and lively moving crowds of citizens were on Canal, Common, Gravier and the cross streets, and on hearing each shot they rushed one way or the other.

The police took their exposed position surrounded by apparently 600 men behind the bales of cotton and hay. Their attention was directed somewhat up the levee, where the greater strength of the enemy seemed to be, and sitting on his horse, General Badger raised his hat and gave the order to fire. At the first discharge every loose citizen sought cover, and there was a tremendous stampede for the side streets. The excitement spread to Camp Street, and men knew not which way to turn. Many called, "It's a false alarm; it is only done to keep carriages and cars away," but the fight of the day was going on with unparalleled vindictiveness. At the first discharge of the cannon every cotton and hay bale seemed to blaze with fire. Only heads and arms were presented as targets for the Winchesters of the police. Badger sat his horse, encouraging his men, and seemed to have a charmed life, for several men dropped every second. Not a man flinched while he had support, but the fire of their almost unseen enemy swept them away like wheat before the reaper.

A fifth of the force lay on the levee dead or so wounded as to be unable to move. Not enough men were left unhurt to support the artillery, and standing at the guns were not one-half enough to work them. Unable to see hardly a foe fall, but the crack and blaze coming uncreasingly from the bulwarks before them, a fire from roofs and windows behind and above them commencing and a man falling at each report, the majority who could walk sought the iron building, carrying their wounded. All but the commands of Rey and Joseph, which were somewhat out of the line of the main fight were demoralized. Every man in sight was blackened with powder and stained with his own blood. Sergeant John McCann, a conspicuous target, stood discharging his Winchester till the last shot was gone, and then, unarmed, received a disabling wound in the leg. Badger still sat his horse, cheering his men, and Captain Gray, with every man of the artillery killed or wounded, was loading a piece without assistance as coolly as he would have inspected it in the armory.

The contest lasted not more than ten minutes, and then the police were driven back from their charge. The fire from roofs and windows and vantage places redoubled, and of those who reached the Customhouse only two were without a mark.

As the last of his men melted away General Badger still sitting conspicuously on his horse was made the target of a hundred Belgian rifles and was seen to fall as Gray drove home a charge in his gun. Private Simons, slightly hit, called for one man to go and help him take him away, but the fire was unremitting. Nearly all were disabled and there was no one to help. A retreat was made by the main body to the Customhouse and in the hands of the enemy were left two Gatling and one twelve pound gun.

The rest of the force retreated to Jackson Square station with all the guns, picketed the streets and prepared for further resistance.

When shots were heard in the neighborhood of the Customhouse, the Leagues in reserve on Poydras Street barricaded Tchoupitoulas, Magazine, Camp and Carondelet Streets crossings. Bridges were torn up and horse cars were taken from the tracks and used to build the barricades.

By this time nearly every place of business was closed, and the central portion of our city in a state of fiery excitement. Non-combatants were seldom disturbed, and they generally passed to and fro as they pleased. Curiosity led many men into dangerous positions, especially on Canal Street, where several unarmed men were wounded and killed.

General Ogden, commanding the White League, had his horse shot under him, and he barely escaped serious injury.

Owing to the general confusion the report found it almost a matter of impossibility to make a correct list of the killed and wounded.

General A. S. Badger, beloved of all his command and the object of universal admiration for his cool self-reliance and unflinching courage, fell pierced with three musket shot, though the one in the leg is the only serious one, being a bad fracture of the bone below the knee.

After the fight was over the dead and wounded were removed to the Customhouse, where Drs. Ames and Schumaker attended to the wants of those who needed their services.

PART II

Economic Violence

Bread Riot in Boston
1713

In 1713, a severe food shortage in Boston led the town selectmen to petition the Massachusetts General Assembly for aid. The "threatening scarcity of provisions . . . in this great and populous town," they said, had led to such "extravagant prices that the necessities of the poor in the approaching winter must needs be very pressing," and they asked therefore that "speedy care be . . . taken to prevent the exportation thereof, which we fear too many will be encouraged to do by the prospect of the great markets abroad." On May 19, 1713, a crowd of Bostonians, angry because some of the larger merchants were exporting corn, rioted.

In response the government of the colony authorized the selectmen to appropriate grain and sell it at a fixed price. On December 10, a ship bearing 320 bushels of wheat was seized, and the ship captain was ordered "to deliver to the several bakers varying quantities of his cargo"; "the said bakers are likewise directed to bake the same into bread (and as prudently as they can) therewith to supply the necessities of the private families of this town with bread for their money."

This brief account of the riot itself comes from Samuel Sewell's *Diary*, printed in Massachusetts Historical Society Collections, Series 5, VI 384-5. See also Boston Registry Department: *Records Relating to the Early History of Boston*, XI, "A Report of the Record Commissioners of the City of Boston, Containing the Records of the Boston Selectmen, 1701-1715," 194-215.

Midweek, May 20. The rain hindered my return. . . . Got to Brother's at Salem about 7. and lodged there. By this means I was not entangled with the riot committed that night in Boston by 200 people or more, breaking open Arthur Mason's warehouse in the common, thinking to find corn there; wounded the Lieutenant Governor and Mr. Newton's son. . . . Were provoked by Captain Belchar's sending Indian Corn to Curacao. The select-men desired him not to send it; he told them, The hardest fend off! If they stopped his vessel, he would hinder the coming in of three times as much.

Mast Tree Riot
1734

Colonial lumber men resented the British law which required that the most valuable trees in the New England forests be marked with an arrow and reserved for masts for the Royal Navy. Many lumbermen ignored the rule and cut trees as they pleased. In 1734 the British Surveyor-General, Daniel Dunbar, investigated the area of the most blatant poaching, near Exeter, New Hampshire. Although townsmen refused to assist him he did discover royal trees in colonial mills. Returning to Portsmouth, Dunbar engaged ten men to help him confiscate the pilfered lumber, and by April 23, 1734, his small force arrived in Exeter. That evening the townspeople set upon Dunbar's men and beat them severely. The Surveyor-General arrived next day with more men, and broke up one of the larger mills. At this the townspeople drove off the intruders with small arms fire. Dunbar, who was also Lieutenant Governor of the Colony, appealed to the Legislature to punish the culprits, but as that body was largely composed of persons in the lumber trade, it did no more than to make a vague apology, and the local justices of the peace, many of whom were also mill owners, refused to prosecute the townspeople. The legislature's proclamation is from *Documents and Records Relating to the Province of New-Hampshire from 1722 to 1737*, IV, 678. See Joseph J. Malone: *Pine Trees and Politics* (1964); and Robert G. Albion: *Forests and Sea Power* (1926).

Whereas a great number of ill disposed persons assembled themselves together at Exeter in the Province of New Hampshire, on the 23d of April last past about 9 of the clock at night, and the and there in a riotous, tumultuous and most violent manner came into the house of Captain Samuel Gilman of said Exeter (who kept a public house in said town) and did then fall upon beat wound and terribly [sic] abuse a number of men hired and imployed by the Honorable David Dunbar, Esq. as Surveyor General of his Majesties woods, as assistants to him in the execution of said office, many of which were beat and so abused that they very narrowly escaped with their lives (as appears by examinations taken by power of his Majesties Justices of the Peace for said province) all of which is a very great dishonor to this his Majesties province and contrary to all laws and humanity, and ought to be detested and abhorred by all parts of the legislative power. In order therefore to the finding out and bringing to condign punishment the transgressors and abettors of so vile a piece of disobedience, and in order that so great an odium may not rest upon this province, and to convince his Majestie that such villainies are abhorred by the province in general, Therefore in the House of Representatives voted, that his Excellency the Governor and Council be earnestly desired to order a strict examination into that affaire that the utmost justice may be done to his Majestie and that the persons concerned therein may no longer escape the punishment they have by their actions so justly deserved.

New Jersey Tenant Riots
1745-1754

In 1664 James, Duke of York, granted the territory of New Jersey to Lords John Berkeley and George Carteret. The same year, unaware of the Duke's action, his appointed governor of the colony, Richard Nicholls, granted the same lands to groups of settlers. The rival claims led to eighty years of squabbling. The proprietors insisted on collecting rents, and the settlers, centered in Elizabeth Town and Newark, refused to pay. Legal battles were fought for decades, complicated by the settlers' practice of purchasing additional titles from the Indians, which the proprietors did not trouble to do. But most of the settlers' suits were unsuccessful and the proprietors were then enabled to press large numbers of eviction suits. By the 1740's the enraged settlers organized a committee to appeal to the King, but to no avail. In September 1745, Samuel Baldwin, holder of an Indian title and long in possession of his land, was arrested and taken to Newark jail. "The People in general," said a contemporary, "supposing the Design of the Proprietors was to ruin them (which they well knew, should they prosecute and succeed according to their Threats would be the consequence) . . . went to the Prison opened the Door, took out Baldwin, and returned peaceably. . . ." This action initiated a decade of riots and jail breaks, few of which were as peaceable as the first. In 1746 the governor called the riots "high treason," but only rarely did the Assembly furnish him with sufficient aid to keep the peace. In time, however, the riots became less frequent, and by 1754, after a series of accommodations had been made, they ceased entirely.

What follows is an account of a second jail break, January 15, 1746, to free men jailed for initiating the first one. This description was sent by the New Jersey Council to the Duke of Newcastle and the Lords of Trade: "State of the Facts about the Riots from September 19th, 1745, to December 8th, 1746," printed in the *Archives of the State of New Jersey*, First Series,

VI, 401-4. See Gary S. Horowitz: "The New Jersey Land Riots, 1745-1755," unpublished doctoral dissertation, Ohio State University, 1966; and Donald L. Kemmerer: *Path to Freedom: The Struggle for Self-Government in Colonial New Jersey, 1703-1776* (1968).

1745. January 15th. The Sheriff of Essex by virtue of the said warrant . . . arrested *Robert Young, Thomas Sarjeant & Nehemiah Baldwin* three of the persons named in the record aforesaid, and then proposed to them to enter into recognizance, as the said warrants and writts required;— the said Young & Baldwin pretended they had no friends in town to do it [i.e., post bail], but would send to their friends to come to do it with them;—Serjeant had a brother in Newark Town, who offered to be his surety, but Serjeant absolutely refused to enter into any recognizance; wherefore the said Sheriff committed them to Newark Gaol and he being, as well Collonel of the Militia, as Sheriff of the said County, ordered two of the officers, of each of the two company's of foot, belonging to Newark, to raise fifteen men each, to guard the prison that night, which, with a great deal of trouble, was, at last done,—And the Sheriff watched with them, himself, all that night.

1745. January 16th in the morning sundry of the guard, who watched, wanted to be discharged, but the Sheriff refused to discharge them till other men were got to relieve them, & sent the officers of the guard to bring others, but they could get none; wherefore the same persons continued on guard.

About ten in the morning of the 16th the said Sheriff ordered several persons present to assist him, in carrying Baldwin, one of the prisoners before a Judge of the Supream Court, as by the said warrant he was directed, most of them made frivolous pretences, as that they had no horses, and could not go, and perceiving their coolness to assist him, he with all he could get, which were only Major Johnson, Isaac Lyon, Daniel Harrison, and two or three more proceeded with the said Baldwin, but before he had gone two miles, they were assaulted by a great number of persons, with clubbs and other weapons, who, in a most violent manner, rescued, and carryed away, the prisoner, tho they had been beat off for near a mile distance, after the beginning of the assault.

The Sheriff and his assistants then returned to the gaol, to secure the *other two* persons there, and had, then, for that purpose two captains, three lieutenants, five justices of the peace, two constables, and about twenty six soldiers, well armed; but by two of the clock in the afternoon, the people gathered together in town, to the number of about two hundred, every one having a clubb, where upon two justices at the Sheriff's request, went to them, and asked the meaning of their meeting, together in such a manner, they answered they wanted the other two prisoners. The Justices used persuasions with them to disperse, but to no effect, wherefore, the said justices commanded silence, and one of them read the King's Proclamation appointed by the first of King George *against riots,* & acquainted the people with the bad consequences of such proceedings, but they paid no regard either to the Proclamation or to what was said to them.

Two of the new captains of the Newark Companies by the Sheriffs order went with their drumms, to the people, so met, and required all persons there, belonging to their companies, to follow the drums, and to defend the prison, but none followed, tho' many were there, upon which one *Amos Robards* of Newark, mounted his horse, and in words to this or the like effect, hollowed out, *Those who are upon my List, follow me;* which all, or the greatest part, did, their number then was esteemed to be about three hundred.

The said *Robards* and several others came from the multitude so met, to the Sheriff on guard at the gaol, and said they came to know upon what terms he would let the prisoners out. Who answered, on their giving surety for their appearance at the next Supream Court, and not otherwise and would send to Mr. Justice Bonnell, Second Judge of the Supream Court, to come and take the security, if they desired it.

Whereupon, they returned to the multitude, who, between four and five of the clock in the afternoon, lighted off their horses, and came up towards the gaol, huzzaing and swinging their clubbs.

The officers ordered the guard to face them, and when they came within ten yards, the soldiers were ordered to present and cock their firelocks, which were charged with powder & ball.

The multitude drove on, till they came within reach of the guard, & struck them with their clubbs, and the guard (having no orders to fire) returned the blows with their guns, and some were wounded on both sides, but none killed.—The multitude broke the ranks of the soldiers, and pressed on to the prison door, where the Sheriff stood with a drawn sword, and kept them off, till they gave him several blows, and forced him out from thence. They then, with axes and other instruments, broke open the prison door, and took out the two prisoners. As also one other prisoner, that was confined for debt, and went away; the rioters said that, if they had staid till the next day, they should have had three or four times that number, to their assistance.

New York Agrarian Rebellion
1766

Although the feudal system was never successfully established in America, efforts were made by some great landholders to acquire quasi-feudal privileges and powers. In New York particularly such a class emerged in the seventeenth century. By defrauding Indians and by using their influence in the colonial government to buy land at low prices, some families amassed huge landed estates: Philipsborough comprised 156,000 acres, the Highland Patent 205,000 and Rensselaerwyck, 1,000,000. The owners of these manors paid trifling quit rents to the crown, and in return were granted varying baronial rights and privileges, including criminal jurisdiction, the right to appoint magistrates and clergymen, and in some cases the right to name their own representatives to the Assembly of the colony. They seldom sold their land, preferring to rent it for short terms. Their tenants often paid rent in kind, occasionally in service. It was believed that this system, as Governor William Tryon remarked, was "a method which will ever create subordination."

New World tenants, however, chaffed against such a system, and some denied the justice of the great landholders' claim to rents. Tenants resisted in many ways. Some bought new titles from Indians, especially when the natives had been defrauded in the first sale, and then tried to contest their landlord's title in the courts. Invariably, however, they lost. Some invoked the uncertainty of colonial boundaries: when two colonies claimed the same area, tenants would side with the government that offered them the better terms. Many border disputes in fact masked struggles between landlords and tenants. But since the great holders usually controlled the judiciary, these legal tactics commonly proved fruitless. Increasingly, after 1750, the farmers used violence to assert their claims.

Tenant outbreaks in New York came to a climax in the agrarian rebellion of 1766. On June 26, 1766, the sheriff of Albany County, attempting to dispossess settlers on John Van Rensselaer's land, met an armed band of sixty men. They fought, and seven of the militia were wounded and one killed; three farmers were killed and many wounded. On another occasion a band of two hundred "marched to murther the Lord of the Manor and level his house, unless he would sign leases for 'em agreeable to their form, as these were now expired and that they would neither pay rent, taxes, etc., nor suffer other tenants." This band was dispersed by an armed posse led by Walter Livingston. In Poughkeepsie, 1,700 armed tenants closed courts and broke open jails. Another group marched to New York City, threatening to burn city homes of rural magnates, but were dispersed by the militia. The farmers were particularly disappointed that the Sons of Liberty refused to support them.

When the landowners appealed for help, the government declared the leaders of the insurrection guilty of high treason and sent soldiers to capture them. Afterwards, sporadic fighting continued, but superior force finally prevailed. The tenants were pillaged by the soldiers, the movement was broken, many tenants were evicted, and many fled to Vermont. The two differing accounts of the June 26 fight which follow are taken from the *Boston Gazetteer or Country Journal*, July 14, 1766, and the New York *Gazette*, July 7, 1766. See Irving Mark: *Agrarian Conflicts in Colonial New York, 1711-1775* (1940); and Staughton Lynd: "Tenant Rising at Livingston Manor," *New-York Historical Society Quarterly*, XLVII (1964), 163-77.

I

Wednesday an express came to town . . . by whom we had the following particulars. That the inhabitants of a place called Nobletown and a place called Spencer-Town lying west of Sheffield, Great Barrington, and Stockbridge, who had purchased of the Stockbridge Indians the lands they now possess; by virtue of an order of the General Court of this province, and settled about two hundred families; John Van Renselear Esq., pretending a right to said lands, had treated the inhabitants very cruelly, because they would not submit to him as tenants, he claiming a right to said lands by virtue of a patent from the Government of New York; that said Van Renselear some years ago raised a number of men and came upon the poor people, and pulled down some houses killed some people, imprisoned others, and has been contantly vexing and injuring the people. That on the 26th of last month said Renselear came down with between two and three hundred men, all armed with guns, pistols and swords; that upon intelligence that 500 men armed were coming against them, about forty or fifty of the inhabitants went out unarmed, except with sticks, and proceeded to a fence between them and the assailants, in order to compromise the matter between them. That the assailants came up to the fence, and Hermanus Schuyler the Sheriff of the County of Albany, fired his pistol down . . . upon them and three others fired their guns over them. The inhabitants thereupon desired to talk with them, and they would not harken; but the Sheriff, it was said by some who knew him, ordered the men to fire, who thereupon fired, and killed one of their own men, who had got over the fence and one of the inhabitants likewise within the fence. Upon this the chief of the inhabitants, unarmed as aforesaid, retreated most of them into the woods, but twelve betook themselves to the house from whence they set out and there defended themselves with six small arms and some ammunition that were therein. The two parties here fired upon each other. The assailants killed one man in the house, and the inhabitants wounded several of them, whom the rest carried off and retreated, to the number of seven, none of whom at the last accounts were dead. That the Sheriff shewed no paper, nor attempted to execute any warrant, and the inhabitants never offered any provocation at the fence, excepting their continuing there, nor had any one of them a gun, pistol or sword, till they retreated to the house. At the action at the fence one of the inhabitants had a leg broke, whereupon the assailants attempted to seize him and carry him off. He therefore begged they would consider the misery he was in, declaring he had rather die than be carried off, whereupon one of the assailants said "you shall die then" and discharging his pistol upon him as he lay on the ground, shot him to the body, as the wounded man told the informant; that the said wounded man was alive when he left him, but not like to continue long. The affray happened about sixteen miles distant from Hudson's River. It is feared the Dutch will pursue these poor people for thus defending themselves, as murderers; and keep them in great consternation.

II

(Extract of a letter from Claverack, near Albany, dated June 27.)

"For some months past a mob has frequently assembled and ranged the eastern parts of the manor of Renselaer. Last week they appeared at Mr. Livingston's with some proposals to him, but he being from home, they returned to Mr. Van Renselaer's son's, about two miles from Claverack, where not finding him at home, they used some insulting words and left a message for Mr. Renselaer that if he did not meet them next day at their rendezvous, they would come to him. On the 26th, the Sheriff of Albany, with 105 men under his command, went to disperse the rioters who were assembled it is supposed to the number of sixty, in a house on the Manor. On the Sheriff's advancing to the house, they fired upon him, and shot off his hat and wig, but he escaped unhurt. Many shots were exchanged on both sides. Of the militia, one man, Mr. Cornelius Ten-Broeck, of Claverack, was killed, and seven wounded; of the rioters, three were killed (two of whom were of the ringleaders) and many wounded, among whom was Capt. Noble (one of the chief instigators) in the back. The rioters retreated to Capt. Noble's house, where they formed a breast-work, and did not quit the house till the Sheriff's party left the place. Col. Renselaer's horse was killed under him. He afterwards went to Pough-keepsie to get assistance from the regulars to disperse the whole, but the regulars were gone to Pendergast's house, on Philipse patent."

Shays's Rebellion
1786–1787

A post-war depression, exacerbated by high taxes levied to pay off the Massachusetts Revolutionary war debt as rapidly as possible, hit the state's farmers hard. Mortgages were foreclosed, debtors were imprisoned, and some were even sold into servi-tude. In 1785-6, 4,000 suits for debt were filed in Worcester County alone. There 72 of 94 men in jail were debtors. When farmers began to organize to defend themselves against suits for debt, they followed the familiar Revolutionary pattern. First, they held local conventions which sent petitions of griev-

ances to the Massachusetts General Court in August 1786. When
their petitions failed to effect the legal closing of the courts, they
determined to close them by force. Under ex-officers of the
Continental army like Daniel Shays and Luke Day, hundreds
of farmers in western Massachusetts began to force courts to
suspend business. By October, Secretary of War Henry Knox
persuaded Congress to authorize the stationing of a contingent
of troops at the Springfield arsenal, ostensibly to fight the
Indians, actually to suppress the rebellion. By November the
movement had been defeated in eastern Massachusetts, but
the Shaysites still controlled the interior. On December 26 they
shut the Springfield courts, and Shays's army of 1,000 was threatening the arsenal there commanded by Major General William
Shepard. General Benjamin Lincoln moved in to assist Shepard,
and Luke Day, whom Shays expected to join the attack, failed
to appear. Shays's army was routed by artillery fire and shattered. To minimize the bloodshed, Shepard refrained from pursuit. The rebel remnant was reduced to guerilla action in the
winter snow. By March the fighting was over.

The several Shaysite leaders who had been captured (Shays
never was—he died over thirty years later in poverty in New
York) were threatened with hanging, but were eventually released. But the fears aroused by the insurrection lightened the
task of those who were trying to form a stronger national
government than the Confederation.

The account of the assault on the arsenal at Springfield is
from a contemporary account by George R. Minot: *The History
of the Insurrections, in Massachusetts, in the year MDCCLXXX-
VI, and the Rebellion Consequent Thereon* (1788), 108-12. On
the rebellion, see Richard Morris: "Insurrection in Massachusetts," in Daniel Aaron, ed.: *America in Crisis* (1952); Marion L.
Starkey: *A Little Rebellion* (1955); and Robert A. Feer:
"Shays's Rebellion," unpublished doctoral dissertation, Harvard
University, 1958.

The insurgents having collected these forces, which were respectable
from their numbers, and from the large proportion of old continental
soldiers which they contained, Shays, on the 24th of the month, sent a
message to Day, informing him that he proposed to attack the post at
Springfield the next day, on the east side; and desiring that Day's forces

might cooperate with him on the other. Whether Day found it really inconvenient to join in the attack on the 25th, or whether he was desirous of having the whole honour of General Shepard's surrender, which was anxiously expected by the insurgents, he was induced to delay the projected plan; and his reply to Shays's letter was that he could not assist in the attack on the day proposed, but would do it on the 26th. This answer, however, was luckily intercepted by General Shepard, and Shays took it for granted, that Day would cooperate with him at the time he had mentioned. But instead of this, Day only sent in an insolent summons to General Shepard, acquainting him, that the body of the people assembled in arms, adhering to the first principles in nature, self preservation, did in the most peremptory manner, demand

"1st. That the troops in Springfield should lay down their arms.

"2d. That their arms should be deposited in the publick stores, under the care of the proper officers, to be returned to the owners at the termination of the contest.

"3d. That the troops should return to their several homes upon parole."

On the same day, Shays sent a petition, as it was termed, from Wilbraham to General Lincoln, in which he observed, that from his unwillingness to be accessory to the shedding of blood, and from his desire of promoting peace, he was led to propose, that all the insurgents should be indemnified, until the next sitting of the General Court, and until an opportunity could be had for a hearing of their complaints; that the persons who had been taken by the government should be released, without punishment; that these conditions should be made sure by proclamation of the Governour: On which the insurgents should return to their homes, and wait for constitutional relief from the insupportable burdens under which they laboured. When this petition was written, General Lincoln was two days march from Springfield; and if the object of it had been really pacifick, some time would have been allowed for an answer.

The situation of General Shepard and his party, whom no one doubted the insurgents intended to attack with all their force, was truly alarming. His troops were decidedly inferiour in numbers to those of the enemy; and though he was possessed of artillery, yet he could derive little advantage from works thrown up on such a sudden emergency. So doubtful was the issue of an attack upon him, in the mind of General Lincoln, and so great was the chance of Shays's gaining importance and numbers from success, that on the 25th, General Brooks was called upon to march with the Middlesex militia to Springfield, as early as possible.

While affairs were in this critical state, General Shepard, about 4 o'clock in the afternoon of the 25th, perceived Shays advancing on the Boston road, towards the arsenal where the militia were posted, with his troops in open column. Possessed of the importance of that moment, in which the first blood should be drawn in the contest, the General sent one of his aids with two other gentlemen, several times, to know the intention of the enemy, and to warn them of their danger. The purport of their answer was, that they would have possession of the barracks; and they immediately marched onwards to within 250 yards of the arsenal. A message was again sent to inform them, that the militia was posted there by order of the Governour, and of Congress, and that if they approached nearer, they would be fired upon. To this, one of their leaders replied, that *that* was all they wanted; and they advanced one hundred yards further. Necessity now compelled General Shepard to fire, but his humanity did not desert him. He ordered the first shot to be directed over their heads; this however, instead of retarding, quickened their approach; and the artillery was at last, pointed at the centre of their column. This measure was not without its effect. A cry of murder arose from the rear of the insurgents, and their whole body was thrown into the utmost confusion. Shays attempted to display his column, but it was in vain. His troops retreated with precipitation to Ludlow, about ten miles from the place of action, leaving three of their men dead, and one wounded on the field.

The advantages which the militia had in their power, both from the disorder of this retreat, which was as injudicious as the mode of attack, and from the nature of the ground, would have enabled them to have killed the greater part of the insurgents, had a pursuit taken place. But the object of the commander was rather to terrify, than to destroy the deluded fugitives.

Anti-Bank Riot in Baltimore
1835

On March 24, 1834, the Bank of Maryland collapsed, and its depositors lost between two and three million dollars. Nevertheless, as *Niles Weekly Register* noted, the people of Baltimore "bore all this with astonishing meekness." The bank's affairs were put into the hands of trustees, but for seventeen months neither explanation nor accounting was made. During that time an intense pamphlet war was waged, and it became clear that a "stupendous fraud" had been committed. On August 6, 1835, three days after a particularly damning pamphlet had appeared, a crowd gathered to punish the defrauders. Their first attacks were made against the houses of the persons accused, and were limited to breaking windows; the crowd itself was not large and twice dispersed at the mayor's request. Still there were rumors of worse to come, and the mayor called a meeting of respectable citizens to consider how further disturbances should be dealt with. On August 8, the mayor organized a citizens' militia. That night, after the rioters destroyed one house, the militia confronted the rioters, and between ten and twenty were killed and about a hundred wounded. On August 9, the mayor deplored the "resort to deadly weapons" and released the prisoners who had been taken by the militia the previous night. That evening, with no opposition, many houses were sacked; still, when one bank director's wife told the crowd that she, not her husband, owned their house, they departed. For one day the rioters were unopposed. On the next, a counter-attack began. A meeting of "all such inhabitants as valued their rights and were disposed to protect them" elected the aged General Samuel Smith leader of a volunteer army, armed groups policed the city, and quiet was restored.

The account which follows is from *Niles Weekly Register* of August 15, 1835. See J. T. Scharf: *History of Maryland* (1879).

On Monday the 3d inst, as mentioned in the last Register, another weighty pamphlet appeared—and this, with certain comments upon it by Mr. Poultney, are put forward as the cause of the riots that followed—for a "feverish" state was soon visible: but still we had no idea that events would be pursued to the extremities which they reached. Nor would they, (as we still believe), had prudent and proper measures been adopted, as the emergency required, at the beginning of our troubles.

On Thursday evening, the 6th inst, a small number of persons assembled opposite to the splendid residence of Mr. Reverdy Johnson, on Monument Square. They dispersed, however, after breaking a few panes of glass, at the request of the mayor . . .

On Friday evening, the 7th, the mayor was on the ground, in Monument Square, attended by the city bailiffs, the watchmen, and many citizens, for his support. The crowd was much larger than on the preceding night, and more panes of glass were broken. They were addressed by the mayor, and by Gen. W. Jones, of Washington, who happened to be in the city. They were respectfully listened to, and the crowd dispersed at about 11 o'clock. But now the designs of the rioters began to develop themselves; and many of the citizens attached to the mayor's party, having mixed with the crowd to learn what they could, stated that it was intended, on the following night, to make a serious attack on Mr. Johnson's house, and then, to finish, for the present, by attacking that of Mr. John Glenn, in Charles Street. The events of that evening were, therefore, looked to with fearful anxiety. . . .

At about seven o'clock on Saturday night, the mayor, having previously called together a considerable number of citizens, it was agreed to station some hundreds of citizens, each provided with a staff or insignia of office, to guard every avenue leading to Reverdy Johnson's house in Monument Square. About thirty of this guard were mounted on horses. By dark, multitudes of people had assembled. The principal point of concentration, at this time, was in Baltimore Street at the intersection of North Calvert, which leads to the square. Here the crowds made frequent rushes upon the guard. Brickbats and stones were showered upon the guard like hail, and ultimately by the guard returned. A number of the latter were severely bruised and wounded. They however kept their posts. A large portion of the rioters, finding it impossible to get access to Johnson's house, started off to the house of John Glenn, in North Charles Street, which was not guarded, and commenced throwing stones and missiles at the windows and front door. The house was of brick, strongly built, and the door was barricaded in anticipation of an attack. For a brief space of time the assailants were diverted from their assaults upon the house by a number of the mounted guard rushing down and firing upon them. The assailants, however, soon renewed their attacks upon the house, and after a continued effort of near half an hour, it was taken possession of, and all the furniture it contained was broken up, and thrown into the street, and utterly destroyed.

The work of demolition was renewed sometime during yesterday, by numbers of young men and boys, who got in and continued through the afternoon to break up the woodwork, and to beat down the jams of the outer wall. A portion of the front wall of the second and third story has been thrown down, and the house exhibits the appearance of a wreck.

The guard stationed in different parts of the city, finding themselves so severely attacked, armed with muskets. At about one o'clock on Sunday morning, a company of some twenty-five, or perhaps thirty armed citizens, marched against the rioters, in Charles Street. They were received with a shower of stones, and in return fired into the crowd they opposed. They loaded and fired, we understand, there, several times. The police and guard also fired upon their assailants at their several stations, a number of times. It is supposed that in all there were eight or ten persons killed and dangerously wounded. A much larger number were less severely wounded. It is impossible to ascertain at this time, how many, and who, have been killed. Some of the mortally wounded have since died.

Last night (Sunday) at dark, the attack was renewed upon Reverdy Johnson's house. *There was now no opposition.* It was supposed, that several thousand people were spectators of the scene. The house was soon entered, and its furniture, a very extensive law library, and all its contents, were cast forth, and a bonfire made of them in front of the house. The whole interior of the house was torn out and cast upon the burning pile. The marble portico in front, and a great portion of the front wall were torn down by about 11 o'clock. Previous to this, however, an attack was commenced upon the house of John B. Morris, in South Street, one of the trustees of the bank of Maryland. His dwelling was entered and cleared—and the furniture and other contents piled up in the street and burnt. In the course of the proceedings, the house took fire inside, as R. Johnson's was also near doing, from the bonfire near it. In both instances, the engines were brought promptly to the spot, and the fire put out, so that the neighboring dwellings should not suffer.

From John R. Morris' house they proceeded to that of the mayor of the city, Jesse Hunt, esq. broke it open, took out the furniture, and burnt it before the door. They also destroyed the furniture of Evan T. Ellicott, and much injured his dwelling, in Pratt Street. They proceeded to the new house of Hugh McElderry in North Calvert Street, now finishing, broke the front windows, entered the door, and began to destroy the house, when the builder appeared and stated that as it was not finished, the key had not been given up, and that all the injury it might sustain would fall upon him, and thus complete his ruin. Upon this assurance, they desisted and retired. They were directors, it will be recollected, of the bank of Maryland.

They also attacked Capt. Willey's hardware store, in Franklin Street, and commenced destroying its contents, but desisted at the urgent solicitations of Mr. Lynch, who assured them that he and not Mr. W. was the owner, and that Capt. Willey had left town.

The house of Dr. Hintze was assailed; but his lady making her appearance, and declaring that the property was her own, she having received it from her father's estate—they listened to her appeal and departed without doing any injury.

Captain Bentzinger's house was also attacked, and all his furniture destroyed. This, as well as the attack on Capt. Willey and Dr. Hintze, was because of their opposition to the rioters; and, we are told, that more than 30 others were marked, on the same account. Among them the sheriff.

The very valuable libraries of Mr. Johnson and Mr. Glenn were destroyed, worth many thousand dollars, each. All their stock of wines, and many other valuable articles, fell a prey to the crowd, and were offered for sale, at small prices! . . .

On Sunday, the people, *without a head*, had nothing to do but to look on and tremble. No one felt himself safe—as everything was given up. Anarchy prevailed. The law and its officers were away!

But Monday morning changed the aspect of things.—It now appeared that the people were called upon to defend, not only their property, but also their lives—and it was manifest that there was a general, but gloomy, resolution entertained to do both. Things had reverted to their *original elements—there was no law*, and a head was wanted to bring order out of confusion. This was easily found in Gen. Samuel Smith—who being elected chairman by a great assemblage, at the Exchange, accepted the trust reposed in him, and, with the alacrity of youth, though in his 85th year, took his seat, and told the assembly that the time for resolving had passed away, and that for action had arrived. The flag of the union had been previously raised, and, with it at their head, the people marched to the Park, when being addressed briefly by General Smith and others, and told what they ought to do, they speedily retired to prepare themselves instantly to obey. The orders were *to arm*, and to repair to the City Hall. The fire companies were also called out, and appeared on the ground in great force. . . .

On Monday evening a large display of citizens, in arms, attended at the mayor's office; they were stationed in different parts of the city, with the firemen, ready also for action, and peace prevailed during the night. The streets were as quiet as the grave—except in the heavy tread of detachments of armed men to reconnoiter its different parts.

Flour Riot in New York
1837

The panic of 1837 brought widespread suffering, as prices of essential goods shot up to prohibitive highs. In New York City flour went from $5.62 a barrel in 1835 to $7.75 in 1836 to $12.00 in 1837. Prices of meat, coal, and rent rose in the same degree. One day in February 1837 a widely posted notice announced: "Bread, Meat, Rent and Fuel! Their prices must come down! . . . The people will meet in the Park, rain or shine, at 4 o'clock, P.M., on Monday afternoon. . . . All friends of humanity determined to resist monopolists and extortioners are invited to attend." The signatures of Locofoco Party leaders—Alexander Ming, Moses Jacques, and John Windt—appeared at the bottom. The Locofocos were an anti-monopoly faction of the Democratic Party. They argued that the depression had been caused by paper currency; to end it only hard money—specie— should be used as a medium of exchange. A crowd gathered on February 13 in response to the Locofoco call. But other speakers, not satisfied with the Locofoco analysis nor with their tactic of petitioning the State Legislature for aid, called for and led an assault on the local flour merchants, who, they said, were hoarding flour in order to drive up the price. One merchant, Eli Hart, whose warehouse was sacked, publicly denied the charge the next day, attributing the rise in prices to the "great scarcity of grain throughout the country."

This riot was one of the first in American history in which the poor attacked the property of the rich, and many conservatives saw it as the beginning of a revolution. The New York *Commercial Register* observed: 'Whoever will turn to the history of the French revolution of 1789, will find that the 'death dance' was commenced by mobs clamoring for bread, marching in procession, and committing outrages against the bakers." The description which follows is from the *Commercial Register*, a New York newspaper, as reprinted in *Niles Weekly Register*. Hezekiah Niles remarked that he was publishing the account "to enable the future historian to trace the downward course of this republic"; *Niles Weekly Register*, LI (February 25, 1837), 403.

At 4 o'clock, a concourse of several thousands had convened in front of the City Hall—composed, as we are assured, of the very *canaille* of the city—and combining within itself all the elements of outrage, riot and revolution. Moses Jacques was elected as the fitting chairman of such a meeting. But order was not the presiding genius on the occasion, and the meeting was divided into various groups, each of which was harangued by some chosen demagogue, after his own fashion, and on his own account.

Conspicuous among the orators was Alexander Ming, Jr. a patriot who has several times been honored as one of the candidates for the office of register of this city.—His discourse, on the present occasion, is represented as having been less exciting and inflammatory than were those of his fellow orators, as he confined himself to the currency question— enforcing the doctrines of his great colleague of reform colonel Benton— and advising people to discard bank notes, and receive nothing, but the precious metals. At the close of his harangue, Ming introduced a set of resolutions, of the character of which we are no further informed than that one of them proposed a memorial to the legislature, praying the prohibition of all bank notes under the denomination of one hundred dollars. The illustrious Bentonian patriot was then uplifted upon the shoulders of the sovereign mob, and borne proudly aloft over to Tammany Hall.

There were other speakers, however, who came directly to the business of the meeting, and in the most exciting manner, denounced the landlords, and the holders of flour, for the prices of rents and provisions. One of these orators, in the course of his address, after working upon the passions of his audience until they were fitted for the work of spoil and outrage, is reported to have expressly directed the popular vengeance against Mr. Eli Hart, who is one of our most extensive flour dealers on commission. "Fellow-citizens!" he exclaimed, "Mr. Hart has now 53,000 barrels of flour in his store; let us go and offer him eight dollars a barrel, and if he does not take it"—here some person touched the orator on the shoulder, and he suddenly lowered his voice, and finished his sentence by saying, "we shall depart from him in peace."

The hint was sufficient; and a large body of the meeting moved off in the direction of Mr. Hart's store, in Washington, between Dey and Courtlandt Streets. The store is a very large brick building, having three wide but strong iron doors upon the street. Being apprised of the approach of the mob, the clerks secured the doors and windows; but not until the middle door had been forced, and some twenty or thirty barrels of flour or more, rolled into the street, and the heads staved in. At this point of time Mr. Hart himself arrived on the ground, with a posse of officers from the police. The officers were assailed by a portion of the mob in Dey Street, their staves wrested from them, and shivered to pieces. The number of the mob not being large at this time, the officers succeeded in entering the store, and for a short time interrupted the work of destruction.

The mayor next arrived at the scene of waste and riot, and attempted to remonstrate with the infatuated multitude on the folly of their conduct—but to no purpose; their numbers were rapidly increasing, and his honor was assailed with missiles of all sorts at hand, and with such fury that he was compelled to retire. Large reinforcements of the rioters having arrived, the officers were driven from the field, and the store carried by assault—the first iron door torn from its hinges, being used as a battering ram against the others. The *destructives* at once rushed in, and the windows and doors of the lofts were broken open. And now again commenced the work of destruction.

Barrels of flour, by dozens, fifties and hundreds were tumbled into the street from the doors, and thrown in rapid succession from the windows, and the heads of those which did not break in falling, were instantly staved in. Intermingled with the flour, were sacks of wheat by the hundred, which were cast into the street, and their contents thrown upon the pavement. About one thousand bushels of wheat, and four or five hundred barrels of flour, were thus wantonly and foolishly as well as wickedly destroyed. The most active of the *destructionists* were foreigners—indeed the greater part of the assemblage was of exotic origin; but there were probably five hundred or a thousand others, standing by and abetting their incendiary labors.

Amidst the falling and bursting of the barrels and sacks of wheat, numbers of women were engaged, like the crones who strip the dead in battle, filling the boxes and baskets with which they were provided, and their aprons, with flour, and making off with it. One of the destructives, a boy named James Roach, was seen upon one of the upper window sills, throwing barrel after barrel into the street, and crying out with every throw— "here goes flour at eight dollars a barrel!" Early in the assault, Mr. Hart's counting room was entered, his books and papers seized and scattered to the winds. And herein, probably, consists his greatest loss.

Night had now closed upon the scene, but the work of destruction did not cease until strong bodies of police arrived, followed, soon afterward, by detachments of troops. The store was then cleared by justices Lownds and Bloodgood, and several of the rioters were arrested, and despatched to Bridewell, under charge of Bowyer, of the police. On his way to the prison, he and his assistants were assailed, his coat torn from his back, and several of the prisoners were rescued. Several more, however, were afterwards captured and secured.

Before the close of the proceedings at Hart's store, however, the cry of "Meech" was raised—whereupon a detachment of the rioters crossed over to Coenties slip, for the purpose of attacking the establishment of Meech & Co., but the store of S. H. Herrick & Co. coming first in their way, they commenced an attack upon that. The windows were first smashed in with a shower of brick-bats, and the doors immediately afterwards broken. Some twenty or thirty barrels of flour were then rolled into the street, and the heads of ten or a dozen knocked in.

The numbers of the rioters engaged in this work was comparatively small and they soon desisted from their labors—probably from an intimation that a strong body of the police were on the way thither. Another account is that they were induced to desist from the work of mischief, by an assurance from the owner, that if they would spare the flour, he would give it all to the poor today. Be this, however, as it may, the officers were promptly on the spot, and by the aid of the citizens who collected rapidly, the wretched rabble was dispersed—some thirty or forty of them having been taken and secured at the two points of action. Unfortunately, however, the ringleaders escaped almost, if not quite, to a man.

Squatters' Riots
1850

In the 1840's huge tracts of California land were purchased by speculators from Mexicans. The men who rushed to California after the discovery of gold, however, tended to ignore all legal titles, and settled where they chose. Some landholders succeeded in removing these squatters by lawsuits, but in 1850 the squatters formed an association to challenge the legitimacy of existing titles and, increasingly, to oppose absentee ownership of the land.

In May 1850, one squatter, John F. Madden, was successfully sued, and the court ordered that he be evicted. The Squatters' Association denounced the court order on the ground that an inalienable right to the soil had been given them by "country, nature and God," and issued a manifesto declaring that they had "deliberately resolved to appeal to arms and protect their sacred rights, if need be, with their lives." Heavily armed members of the Association guarded Madden's house, but the sheriff managed to dispossess him and arrested some of the squatters. On August 14 an armed and organized troop of squatters attempted to retake the contested property. The gun battle which followed is described in the first document below. The second account relates what happened the next day when the sheriff, having heard that the squatters were attempting to arouse the miners to march on Sacramento, tried to capture some of the squatters. Both accounts are from the Sacramento *Daily Times*, August 15 and 16, 1850, as reprinted in William J. Davis: *An Illustrated History of Sacramento County, California* (1890), 27-8, 30. See also Josiah Royce: "The Squatter Riot of –50 in Sacramento," *The Overland Monthly*, VI (September 1885), 225-46.

"At two o'clock a body of squatters, numbering about forty, proceeded to the foot of I street, on the levee, and undertook to regain possession of a lot of ground, which had been lately in the occupation of one of their party. They were fully armed, and a general understanding prevailed that their object included the liberation of the two men committed the day before to the prison ship, upon the charge of being concerned in a riotous assemblage on the morning of the 12th, for the purpose of forcibly resisting the process of law. After the displacement of some of the lumber upon the ground, the party of squatters were deterred from proceeding further in their intent. The Mayor, Hardin Biglow, had meantime requested all good citizens to aid in suppressing the threatened riot, and very large numbers had gathered about the spot—several citizens armed, proceeded also to the prison ship—but no demonstration was made in that direction.

"The squatters retreated in martial order, and passed up I street to Third, then to J and up to Fourth followed by a crowd of persons. They were here met by the mayor, who ordered them to deliver up their arms and disperse. This they refused to do, and immediately several shots were fired at him, four of which took effect. He fell from his horse, and was carried to his residence, dangerously if not mortally wounded. J. W. Woodland, who, unarmed, stood near the mayor at the time, received a shot in the groin which he survived but a few moments. A man, named Jesse Morgan, said to be from Millersville, Ohio, lately arrived, and who was seen to aim at the mayor, next fell dead, from the effects of a ball which passed through his neck. James Harper was very severely, but not dangerously, wounded in supporting the sheriff. It is difficult to give an exact detail of the terrible incidents which followed in such rapid succession. It appeared, from an examination before the coroner, that the party of squatters drew up in regular order, on arriving at the corner of Fourth Street, and that the sheriff was several times fired upon before he displayed any weapons. Testimony was also given as to the person who was seen to fire upon Woodland. The mounted leader of the squatters, an Irishman by the name of Maloney, had his horse shot under him; he endeavored to escape, was pursued a short distance up an alley and shot through the head, falling dead. Dr. Robinson, one of the armed party under his command, was wounded in the lower part of his body. Mr. Hale, of the firm of Crowell, Hale and Co., was slightly wounded in the leg. A young boy, son of Mr. Rogers, was also wounded. We have heard of several others, but are not assured of the correctness of the reports. Upon oath of several gentlemen that they saw Dr. Robinson deliberately aim at the mayor, he was arrested and placed in confinement. An Irishman, named Henry A. Caulfield, accused of a similar act with regard to both the mayor and Woodland, was arrested late in the afternoon.

"After these terrible scenes, which occupied less time than we have employed to describe them, had passed, a meeting of the council was held, the citizens gathered at the corner of Second and J Streets, and other places throughout the city, and proceeded to organize in parties to prevent further outrage. A body of mounted men under the command of the sheriff, hearing the report that the squatters were reinforcing at the fort, proceeded thither. The lawless mob was nowhere to be found; scouts were dispatched in all directions, but no trace of them could be discovered; meanwhile several other parties had formed into rank, and proceeded to different parts of the city, establishing rendezvous at various points. Brigadier-General A. M. Winn issued a proclamation, declaring the city under martial law, and ordering all law-abiding citizens to form themselves into volunteer companies, and report their organization at headquarters as soon as possible. At evening, quiet was fully restored throughout the city. Lieutenant-Governor McDougal, who left upon the Senator, and expects to meet the Gold Hunter, will bring up this morning a detachment of troops from Benicia. An extraordinary police force of 500 was summoned for duty during the night."

"Another day of gloom arrives in the dread succession which we are compelled to record. Scarcely had the funeral rites been rendered to one victim, ere a second is immolated upon the sacred altar of duty. The sheriff of this county, Joseph McKinney, was killed last evening. He had proceeded to Brighton in company with a party of about twenty, to make arrests of persons whom he has been advised were concerned in the riotous outrages of the 14th. On reaching Pavilion, and being assured that the parties sought for were at the hotel of one Allen in the neighborhood, it was arranged that Mr. McDowell, of Mormon Island, well known at the the house, should proceed there, make observations and return. They did not wait for him, however, but soon after rode up to the door, when the sheriff demanded of Allen that he and the others should surrender themselves. They refused to do this, and immediately several shots were fired, mortally wounding Mr. McKinney. He expired in a few moments. Meanwhile, several of those with him had entered the bar-room, where about a dozen squatters were assembled. Three of the latter were killed on the spot. Allen escaped, though wounded. Three prisoners were taken and brought into town. We have heard that a fourth and a negro squatter were also taken.

Railroad Strike

1877

The great strike of 1877 was the first large-scale protest against the new economic conditions brought about by industrialization. The most advanced sector of the rapidly developing economy was the railroads, and the severe depression of 1873 had hit railroad workers especially hard. In 1877, the railroads ordered a ten-percent cut in wages and planned, by doubling the number of cars per train, to cut the number of employees. A strike began on the Baltimore and Ohio line at Martinsburg, West Virginia, on July 17, 1877, and spread spontaneously down the line. The militia was called to clear the tracks at Cumberland, Maryland, but they refused. The state government in Baltimore was asked for militia, but Baltimore workers massed in large numbers to prevent the train carrying the militia from leaving. Twelve men were killed that day, and the crowd set the Baltimore and Ohio station on fire.

When the strike spread to the Pennsylvania Railroad, similar but even bloodier scenes were repeated in Pittsburgh. First the Pittsburgh militia refused to open the tracks blocked by their friends and relatives, then the railroad officials called for militia from Philadelphia. The strikers had a great deal of popular support, even among the city's businessmen, and thousands of men, women, and children met the Philadelphia troops at the station. When the militia advanced with fixed bayonets, they were stoned. They fired into the crowd, killing ten to twenty, wounding sixty or seventy. Thousands of enraged men then attacked the militia, who retreated to the railroad roundhouse, which the crowd then set on fire. The troops escaped from the burning building, but as they marched off they were shot at from windows, doorways, and rooftops. Then the crowd set fire to all the railroad property they could reach, destroying 104 locomotives, 2,152 cars, and the entire depot.

As the strike spread, President Hayes's cabinet narrowly

decided against declaring Pennsylvania in a state of insurrection and calling for 75,000 volunteers. Eventually all the railroads in the country, except in New England and the South, were struck. But without effective railroad unions, with only weak political organization and no central control or plan, strikers in city after city were shot down by militia and the United States Army. The strike collapsed.

Many people believed that the railroad strike was the result of a foreign conspiracy, the work of communists and socialists who hoped to reproduce the Paris Commune in American cities. The press and the business community demanded conspiracy laws against labor, and other legal safeguards against strikes, and above all increased armed forces. Armories were built in many of the nation's cities and militias were reorganized and strengthened. The *Independent*, a religious periodical, observed that if riots could not be prevented by ordinary police, "then bullets and bayonets, canister and grape . . . constitute the one remedy of the hour. . . . Rioters are worse than mad dogs."

The following account of the strike in Pittsburgh comes from the testimony of Major General Robert M. Brinton before an investigating committee of the Pennsylvania General Assembly: *Report of the Committee Appointed to Investigate the Railroad Riots in July, 1877*, 907-10. On the strike, see Robert V. Bruce: *1877: Year of Violence* (1959); Gerald M. Grob: "The Railroad Strikes of 1877," *Midwest Journal*, VI (Winter 1954-5), 16-34; and Philip Slaner: "The Railroad Strikes of 1877," *Marxist Quarterly*, I (April-June 1937), 214-36.

General Pearson ordered me to have the troops ready to move to Twenty-eighth Street. At that time, I told them in coming up, I had seen the hills covered with people, and I asked them in the event of their ordering me out, to go out with me, and look over the ground. I was an entire stranger there, and I thought they must be misinformed in regard to having cleared the hill, as they said General Brown's brigade had. I also met Mr. Cassatt at the depot, and I said in the event of our going down and clearing the tracks, can you move your trains. He said we can; we have crews already engaged to take out double-headers. General Pearson then ordered me down to Twenty-eighth Street. I ordered one brigade to go down Liberty Street. General Pearson then told me to go down the railroad, which I did, dragging the Gatling guns. We arrived at the crossing near Twenty-eighth

Street, going through rows of men, who were hooting and howling at us. Previous to this, while I was yet in the Union Depot, I had been approached by several parties, who wanted to know if I would fire on poor working-men. I didn't give any decided answer, not desiring any conversation with them. I called the brigade companies and several of the regimental companies together, and told them no matter what was done to us—even if they spit in our faces—I didn't want a shot fired, but if they attempted any personal violence, we had the right to defend ourselves, and we should do it. That was the order from which the firing commenced. We got down near to the Twenty-eighth Street crossing. There was a large concourse of people there, far back as you could see, back on the railroad, and we were stopped. Sheriff Fife and his posse were ahead of us, and I believe he attempted to read the riot act, at least I heard him saying something; but he disappeared, and I didn't see any more of him or his deputies. General Pearson was with us. We could not force our way through without using some force, and I asked General Pearson whether he had any instructions to give. He hesitated a moment, and then said that the tracks must be cleared. The crowd then had pressed in between the column of fours, and I ordered the fours put into lines backward, and face the rear rank, about to push the crowd back from either side, and form a hollow-square.

By Senator Yutzy:

Q. How did you march?

A. The right in front—the First regiment was in front. The crowd gave back. We had a little difficulty in getting them back to the line of the cars. Quite a number of cars were there—the Twenty-eighth Street crossing was blocked. The men standing there had evidently made up their minds to stay, saying that the railroad company had nothing to do with it, that they were not occupying anything but public ground. I then ordered two small companies, but finding them insufficient, I ordered up another command with arms aport, and attempted to push the crowd back but finding it impossible, I gave order to charge bayonets, which they did, and I saw one or two men bayoneted. The crowd at that time commenced firing on us, not only stones but pistol balls, and the men, acting on the orders already given to defend themselves, commenced firing—firing a few shots at first, which gradually went along the whole line. At that time, I had not over three hundred men. The second brigade had been left back, to guard the yard where the engines were to start from. . . . The firing lasted about a minute—not over that, and the crowd, the moment the firing commenced, or shortly afterwards, dispersed and went in every direction. I gave the order to cease firing, and my staff officers had the firing stopped, and the ranks, which were somewhat broken, were re-formed . . . I said to General Pearson at the time, that I thought we ought to continue to drive the crowd. I understood that they had gone to the arsenal. Several men came up to me and said that the crowd had gone to the United States arsenal to arm themselves, and I thought, when I found that they had gone away, that they would probably get arms and ammunition, and I proposed to General Pearson that we should follow the crowd. He hesitated some time about it, and finally I grew more imperative in my question, and I said, you must do something, I cannot allow my men to stand on the track with the crowd pushing around me, and not be allowed to fire. We will either have to move from there or attack the crowd. Finally, he said that the Second brigade had been moved into the round-house and machine shops, because he was afraid that they would be burned, and then he told me to move my whole force in, amounting to six hundred men, which I did just at dusk in the evening. We moved in there. They told me to occupy one round-house and the machine and upholstery shops and the lumber-yard, and that General Brown would move into the other round-house at Twenty-eighth Street, and I was not aware he was not there until I saw the flames. As soon as I went there, the crowd commenced trying to get into the yard, and I had a guard detailed and put out, and two of them were shot, one through the arm and one other through the leg, while on their beats. I then got down the Gatling guns and prepared to fire them, but thought it would be courtesy to communicate with General Pearson, and tell him what I was going to do; which I did, and he prohibited me from doing so. The crowd were firing pistol balls in at us, and a few rifle balls and a considerable number of stones. I went to General Pearson, and said, "I cannot stand it, we must defend ourselves." He said he would go to the mayor and see him, which would do more good than our bullets would, as he had a great deal of influence over the elements predominant then, and said that he did not want to take life unnecessarily, &c.; at the same time we were short of ammunition and rations, only having twenty rounds, and if we were going to be in a state of seige, I thought we ought to have a sufficient amount. General Pearson said he would go and see that we got provisions and also ammunition, and left, saying he would be back in an hour. He went through the lumber-yard, and left us. At the same time he told me to open any dispatches that came for him, and I asked if he had any new instructions. He said, "I want you to hold the place," and after he left I proposed to hold it in the way I thought proper, by firing into the mob at the gates, which drove them away from there, so that presently there were only pistol bullets and a few straggling musket balls. We continued to hold it in that way without receiving any communications from the other world. I expected General Pearson back every moment. I didn't want to take it on myself to move out there, or do anything. About two o'clock in the morning Colonel Snowden, of the Third regiment, called into the round-house, and directed my attention to what he considered a piece of artillery. It was quite dark at the time. We watched it for probably fifteen minutes, when a cloud cleared away, and we decided it was a piece of artillery, around which were quite a number of men who were training the piece. I immediately ordered Colonel Snowden to get fifty men out, and told him to lower their pieces and fire low, and I gave the order. They had got the piece finally into position to suit themselves, and a man had hold of the lanyard. I gave the order to fire, and when the smoke cleared away eleven of them were lying there.

Q. The mob had it?

A. Yes; it was a brass field-piece that they had captured from Hutchinson's battery, I believe. During the whole night we had a skirmish with those people. They ran cars down loaded with oil, and attempted to set fire to the building, but fortunately some jumped the track and blocked the others. The next morning they ran down cars from the Allegheny side, which came down with their own gravity, but we finally threw a pile of car wheels on the track, and upset the cars. They were burning. They were loaded with whisky, or the most of them with high wines. We put out those fires by fire extinguishers and also by a hose that we had there. We finally discovered that the building part of the Sixth division was on fire, and it communicated with the building we were in by the oil sheds. They got on fire, and the building we were in got on fire. During the night I had communication with General Latta, finding General Pearson did not return, and told him my situation, and received orders from him—or suggestions they were afterwards styled—in the first place to hold on vigorously, but in case I was obliged to leave there, to go out Penn Avenue east towards Torrens Station, and that there would be reinforcements sent to us not later than six o'clock in the morning; that part of the command—three hundred—who had failed to join, were at Walls Station, and would join Colonel Guthrie at Torrens, and that they would join us. We waited until ten minutes of eight o'clock, when the smoke got so great that the men could scarcely breathe, and we went through the machine shops. We couldn't go out of the gate, the regular gate, on account of the cars that had been upset there and were burning, and I went out, I think, Twenty-third Street—I am not very familiar with the streets—with the intention not to leave Pittsburgh, but to go to the Unted States arsenal, where I certainly could get ammunition and possibly something to eat, as we had nothing but a sandwich and a cup of coffee since leaving Philadelphia, and through the excitement and the loss of two nights' sleep, the men were very much fatigued and thoroughly worn out. We went out towards the arsenal, and probably had gone a quarter of a mile out Penn Avenue, when we were attacked. I was at the head of the column, and didn't see the force that was attacking us, but I sent a staff officer immediately to the rear. The firing was all at the rear, and I think four men were killed and some ten or twelve wounded.

Q. On your retreat from the round-house?

A. Yes; these men were shot from street cars, and from out of houses, and from behind chimneys. There was not any regular organized body, or a body sufficiently large to attack, until we got nearly to the arsenal, when—the Gatling guns I had placed between the two brigades, so that we could use them either in rear or at the front—when we opened with one of them, and dispersed the mob. We got to the arsenal, and I went ahead to see the commandant there, and went inside the gate, and went to his house and saw him, and told him who I was, and that my men were thoroughly worn out, and asked permission to form in the yard. The men were very thirsty, and the grounds were shady, and I thought we would wait there until I had orders from General Pearson. But we received positive orders from the commandant that we could not come in. I did not want any altercation with him, so I proceeded on eastward. I had received a communication from General Latta during the night, saying that he had made every attempt to feed us, and that it had been impossible, and I therefore thought that the best thing to do was to get something to eat. We had arrived within a short distance of Sharpsburg, when they told us if we came over there we could be fed. I concluded to do so, and went over there, and just as we got into the town, we were informed that two of the Fourteenth regiment, who had been on the hill, had been wounded seriously there by our shots, and that the people had no friendly feeling for us, and then I concluded we had better go on and wait for provisions, which I proceeded to do, when we were met by two gentlemen, who joined us, one belonging to the Pennsylvania Railroad, I believe, who said we could be fed a little lower down, at Claremont, where they gave us coffee and rations; but the rations they brought were berries—not very suitable things for soldiers to eat. We proceeded to Claremont, and there awaited orders.

Louisiana Sugar Strike
1887

The black rural laborers of the Louisiana sugar fields were among the most miserably exploited groups in the post-Reconstruction era. Wages, which had always been low, had been going steadily downwards since the depression of 1873. Three strikes had been crushed by the state militia. By 1887 the planters paid an average of $13 per month in scrip, exchangeable only at their own high-priced stores, or as rent for the twelve-by-fifteen foot cabins they owned. One local paper declared, "The laborers on these sugar plantations are, as is notoriously known, treated more like slaves than their fathers were in the days of slavery."

In 1887 the blacks formed a Knights of Labor local, and were quickly joined by many white sugar workers. On October 4 of that year they demanded $1 a day, payable in cash. The planters refused, and 9,000 blacks and 1,000 whites in four parishes walked out. The planters' response was swift. Although the strike was peaceful, they persuaded the Governor to send in the militia. At Pattersonville the militia shot into a crowd of strikers, killing four. Some prisoners were taken and turned over to local officials, who shot them the next day. At Thibodaux, the "most prominent citizens" organized an unofficial force of armed men who were strangers to the area, and martial law was declared. Blacks were forbidden to leave town by a court order, and violence was deliberately provoked. According to the report that follows, thirty-five unarmed blacks were killed. Elsewhere, two black strike leaders who had been imprisoned earlier in the strike were lynched. The strike was broken.

The following account is from a Negro newspaper, the New Orleans *Weekly Pelican*, of November 26, 1887. See also Sidney H. Kessler: "The Negro in Labor Strikes," *Midwest Journal*, VI (Winter 1954-5).

Murder, foul murder has been committed and the victims were inoffensive and law-abiding Negroes. Assassins more cruel, more desperate, more wanton than any who had hitherto practiced their nefarious business in Lousiana have been shooting down, like so many cattle, the Negroes in and around Thibodaux, Lafourche parish, La.

For three weeks past the public has been regaled, daily, with garbled reports of the troubles existing between the laborers and planters in the sugar district. Strange to say not one of these reports, excepting two, exculpated the Negroes from any desire, or any intention so far as their actions could be judged, of resorting to violence and bloodshed in order to secure the just and equable demand made by them for an increase of wages. Militia from different portions of the State have been on duty in the threatened section, and during all of this time the only acts and crimes of an outrageous character committed were so committed by either the troops, sugar planters or those in their hire. The Negroes during all of the time behaving peaceably, quietly and within the limits of the law, desiring only to secure what they asked and demanding what they had and have a perfect right to do—an increase of wages.

The planters refused to accede to their requests and at the same time ordered them from the plantations. At this juncture, and especially was it the case at both Thibodaux and Houma, the Knights of Labor, to which organization most of the laborers belong, hired all the empty houses in the above towns they could, and there quartered the homeless blacks. Such unexpected action maddened the planters and their followers, (some excepted) and as a sequence they resorted to arms and every other devilish device which the ingenuity of a few chosen spirits could devise in order to force the Negroes to work for the wages offered.

With an obstinacy worthy of the righteousness of their cause the Negroes quartered in Thibodaux refused to accede to the planters.

Such being the case, the planters determined to kill a number of them, thus endeavoring to force the balance into submission. The militia was withdrawn to better accomplish this purpose, and no sooner had they departed for home than the preparation for the killing of the Negroes began. Last Sunday night, about 11 o'clock, plantation wagons containing strange men fully armed were driven into Thibodaux and to Frost's restaurant and hotel and there the strangers were quartered. Who they were and where they came from, no one, with the exception of the planters and Judge Taylor Beattie, seemed to know; but it is a fact that next day, Monday, marshal law was declared and these cavalcades of armed men put on patrol duty and no Negro allowed to either leave or enter the town without shooters, insolent and overbearing toward the Negroes, doing all in their power to provoke a disturbance, walked around for two days, Monday and Tuesday. Finding that the Negroes could not be provoked from their usual quiet, it was resolved that some pretext or other should be given so that a massacre might ensue.

It came: Tuesday night the patrol shot two of their number, Gorman and Molaison, and the cry went forth "to arms, to arms! the Negroes are killing the whites!" This was enough. The unknown men who by this time had turned out to be Shreveport guerrillas, well versed in the Ouachita and Red River plan of killing "niggers," assisted by Lafourche's oldest and best, came forth and fired volley after volley, into the houses, the churches, and wherever a Negro could be found.

"Six killed and five wounded" is what the daily papers here say, but from an eye witness to the whole transaction we learn that no less than thirty-five Negroes were killed outright. Lame men and blind women shot; children and hoary-headed grandsires ruthlessly swept down! The Negroes offered no resistance; they could not, as the killing was unexpected. Those of them not killed took to the woods, a majority of them finding refuge in this city.

Such is a true tale of affairs as enacted at Thibodaux. To read it makes the blood of every man, black or white, tingle if his system is permeated with one spark of manhood. To even think that such disregard of human life is permitted in this portion of the United States makes one question whether or not the war was a failure?

Citizens of the United States killed by a mob directed by a State judge, and no redress for the same! Laboring men seeking an advance in wages, treated as if they were dogs! Black men whose equality before the law was secured at the point of the bayonet shown less consideration than serfs? This is what is being enacted in Louisiana to-day.

At such times and upon such occasions, words of condemnation fall like snow-flakes upon molten lead. The blacks should defend their lives, and if they needs must die, die with their faces toward their persecutors fighting for their homes, their children and their lawful rights.

Homestead
1892

Homestead is a classic example of the use of force in labor disputes. Although only 25% of the steel workers in Carnegie, Phipps and Company's Pennsylvania steel mills were union members, and although the union had agreed that the wage scale be pegged to the price of steel, Henry Clay Frick, the Company's General Manager, set out to crush the union. Frick proposed a new contract, cutting wages 22% and dispensing with many workers. The union rejected his offer. Frick then shut down the great steel plant at Homestead on June 29, 1892, and then hired 300 Pinkerton men armed with Winchesters to protect the steel mills, so that he could reopen with non-union labor. The workers, skilled and unskilled, union and non-union, native and foreign-born, answered the lockout with a strike, and prepared to prevent scabs from going into the mills. They hired a steam launch to patrol the river and formed picket lines to patrol the land approaches twenty-four hours a day.

The Pinkerton men came by special train, with coaches darkened, to a point five miles below Pittsburgh. There they were transferred to barges which moved up the Monongahela to Homestead. Forewarned, the strikers prepared to meet the barges with force, although it is not clear who fired the first shot. The ensuing river battle and the eventual surrender of the Pinkertons are described in the following account.

After the union victory on the river, the Governor sent in the National Guard, 8,000 strong. Protected by them, strikebreakers reopened the plant. Frick then fought the strikers in the courts, charging them with conspiracy, riot, and murder; about 185 indictments were made. To stay out of jail, the strikers had to raise over half a million dollars in bail. This financial drain, following their loss of wages, was fatal. In November, four and a half months after the strike began, it was crushed.

The following account of the battle of Homestead is taken

from testimony by a Pinkerton guard before a Congressional
Committee investigating corporate use of private armies. Senate
Report No. 1280, Fifty-Third Congress, Second Session, pp.
68-72. See also Leon Wolff: *Lockout* (1965); and Samuel
Yellen: *American Labor Struggles* (1936).

Q. Were you transported rather quietly and secretly from this point to
Homestead?

A. The trip was rather a quiet one, and very quickly and secretly
planned.

Q. Describe it, and give us the route you took?

A. We started out from the office on Fifth Avenue and we went along
the street to the Lake Shore Depot, where we entered the rear entrance
on the platform. Instead of going up to the regular passenger entrance
we took the one the employees take, so we went into the three rear cars
of the train very quickly. Directly we entered the rear of the cars, men
who seemed to be detectives and not patrolmen, stationed themselves at
the doors, and they prevented our exit, and they prevented the entrance of
any outside parties who might wish to enter. . . .

We ran rather slowly—it was not a scheduled train—on to Cleveland
. . . There we waited for an hour and our three cars were joined to seven
other cars of men from the east. We then, the whole train, went rapidly
on through Jefferson County to Youngstown, and from Youngstown to
Bellview, where we landed rapidly. We were told to prepare to land—
to leave the cars. During our trip we were not allowed to leave the cars
at all, we were kind of prisoners. We did not have any rights. That might
have been because they were afraid of union men, perhaps spies, who
would telegraph ahead to Homestead. They wanted to get inside the works
without bloodshed, but we had no rights whatever. Then we entered the
boats, some 300 of us. There was two covered barges, like these Mississippi
covered boats. . . .

We were told to fall in, and the roll of our names was called, and we
were told to secure our uniforms, which consisted of coat, hat, vest, and
pair of trowsers. When we had secured our uniforms we were some distance down the river, and we were told to keep quiet, and the lights were
turned out, and everything kept very quiet until we were given orders
softly to arise. I was lying down about an hour when the order was
sent around the boat for all the men to get ready to land. Then the captain
called out for men who could handle rifles. I did not want to handle a
rifle, and then he said we want two or three men here to guard the door

with clubs, so I said I would do that, and I got over the table and got a club like a policeman's club to guard the side door—that was to prevent men from coming in boats and jumping on to our barge from the river. I stayed there while the men who could handle rifles were marched down to the open end of the boat, and I did not see anything more of them until the firing commenced.

Q. Tell what further occurred as a matter of knowledge on your part?

A. I had a curiosity to see what was going on on the bank. I was stationed inside the boat at the side door, and as there were three or four other men afraid to carry rifles, they took upon themselves the duty of watching the door, and so I was told to go down to the other end of the boat to see what was going on, and I saw what appeared to be a lot of young men and boys on the bank, swearing and cursing and having large sticks. I did not see a gun or anything. They were swearing at our men. I did not see any more, but came back and resumed my position at the door. I had not been back more than two minutes when I heard a sharp pistol shot, and then there were 30, 40, or 100 of them, and our men came running and stampeding back as fast as they could and they got in the shelter of the door, and then they turned around and blazed away. It was so dark I could see the flames from the rifles easily. They fired about 50 shots —I was surprised to see them stand up, because the strikers were shooting also but they did not seem to be afraid of being hit. They had some shelter from the door. They fired in rather a professional manner I thought. The men inside the Chicago boat were rather afraid at hearing the rifles, and we all jumped for rifles that were laying on a table ready, and someone, I think a sergeant, opened a box of revolvers, and said, "all get revolvers," so I had now a Winchester rifle and a revolver. I called out to see if anybody had been hurt, and I saw a man there apparently strangling. He had been shot through the head and he died sometime afterwards, I think. His name was Kline, I believe. Of course it rather made us incensed to be shot at that way, but I kept out of danger as much as possible.

I was standing there when Nordrum came up, and he said to follow him, and I crossed over to the New York boat, where there were 40 men with rifles standing on the edge of the boat watching what was going on on shore. Nordrum spoke to the men on shore. He spoke in rather a loud manner—say a commanding manner. He said: "We are coming up that hill anyway, and we don't want any more trouble from you men." The men were in the mill windows. The mill is iron-clad. There were a few boys in sight, but the men were under shelter, all of them. I supposed I should have to go up the hill, and I didn't like the idea very well, because it was pretty nearly certain death, as I supposed. I thought it over in what little time I had, and I thought I would have to go anyway. While I was standing there, waiting for Nordrum to charge up the hill and we follow him, he went away, and he was gone quite a few minutes. I took advantage of that to look around the New York men's boat to see what was going on, and I saw about 150 of the New York men hiding in the aisle furthest from the shore. It was divided into bunks. They were hiding in the bunks —they were hiding under the mattresses; they didn't want to be told to shoulder a rifle and charge up the hill; they were naturally afraid of it. They were watchmen, and not detectives. Now the men who had the rifles were mostly detectives. There were 40 of the detectives, who I afterwards learned were regular employees of Pinkerton, but these other men were simply watchmen, and hired as watchmen, and told so, and nothing else. Seeing these men so afraid and cowering rather dispirited the rest of us, and those who had rifles—I noticed there seemed to be a fear among them all. I went to the end of the boat, and there I saw crowds on the bank, waving their hands, and all looking at the boat and appearing to be very frantic.

I judged we were going to have trouble and went back to the end where I had been placed and waited for Nordrum to come, but he did not turn up, and after I stood there about half an hour I concluded, as there was no one there to order us to do anything and as it was stated that the steam tug had pulled out, taking all those who had charge of us—I concluded I would look out for my life, and if anything was said about my leaving and not staying there I would say I did not intend to work for them any more; so I returned to the door I was told to guard, and in that place I stayed for the remainder of the day, during all the shooting and firing. I concluded if the boat was burned—we expected a thousand men would charge down the embankment and put us to massacre; that was what we expected all throughout the day—I concluded if the boat was burned I would defend my life with the other men. . . . During this firing there was a second battle. I was out of sight, but there were cracks of rifles, and our men replied with a regular fusilade. It kept up for ten minutes, bullets flying around as thick as hail, and men coming in shot and covered with blood. . . .

A good many of the men were thoroughly demoralized. They put on life-preservers and jumped under the tables and had no control over themselves whatever. Through the rest of the day there was this second battle when the strikers started the firing. There seemed to be sharpshooters picking us off. At first they fired straight at us, but after awhile they fired through the aisles on the side, and they would shoot men who thought they were safe. The bullets would come, zip, and you would hear some man yell, and you would know they were not cautious. There were sharpshooters picking us off all day, and about 12 o'clock barrels of burning oil were floating around the bank to burn us up, to compel us to go on the wharf and there shoot us down, but they didn't succeed because the oil was taken up by the water, and at about 1 o'clock a cannon was fired by the strikers.

Now, this cannon we supposed directly we heard it was fired to hit us below the water line and sink our boat, but the cannon did not hit us at all hardly. It was kept up all the afternoon. There was one shot came through the roof around me, through some cots, struck the wall and bounded out there, and one man picked it up. It was an iron ball, about two and a half inches in diameter. It tore a hole in the roof, but didn't do any harm except to make our men panicky, and there was an awful spirit of panic there, worse than the firing, because it demoralized the men. At about 3 o'clock we heard something; we thought was a cannon, but it was dynamite. Afterwards I learned it was worse than a cannon; sounded like a very large cannon. It partially wrecked the other boat. A stick of it fell near me. It broke open the door of the aisles, and it smashed open the door, and the sharpshooters were firing directly at any man in sight. That was about 3 o'clock. Most of the men were for surrender at this time, but the old detectives held out and said, "If you surrender you will be shot down like dogs; the best thing to do is to stay here." We could not cut our barges loose because there was a fall below, where we would be sunk. We were deserted by our captains and by our tug, and left there to be shot. We felt as though we had been betrayed and we did not understand it, and we did not know why the tug had pulled off and didn't know it had come back. About 4 o'clock some one or other authorized a surrender, effected by means of a medical student, who studies at the eclectic college over here, the most intelligent man on board for that matter, a Freemason. He secured a surrender. I don't know how he secured it by waving a flag. We secured a surrender. What he wanted was that our steam tug pull us away, but instead of that the strikers held that we should depart by way of the depot.

That surrender was effected, and I started up the embankment with the men who went out, and we were glad to get away and did not expect trouble; but I looked up the hill and there were our men being struck as they went up, and it looked rather disheartening. I had a telescope satchel in my hands and went about half way down to the mill yards without being hurt, when three fellows sprang at me and knocked me down twice and one said, 'You have killed two men this morning; I saw you." I dropped my satchel, and I think these men were probably thieves; I put them down for thieves. I supposed there was not going to be any more crowds, but in front of the miners' cottages there were crowds of miners, women, etc., and as we all went by they commenced to strike at us again, and a man picked up a stone and hit me upon the ear; I saw him throw it, and it glanced off, and right ahead I saw some thieves I judged to be from Pittsburgh. One had a sling shot, and he would hit a man upon the ear and if he had a satchel he would drop it. I got on further toward the depot and there were tremendous crowds on both sides and the men were just hauling and striking our men, and you would see them stumble as they passed by. I tried to get away from the crowd; I had no satchel, so I put my hat on and walked out of the line of Pinkerton men, but some one noticed me, and I started to run and about 100 got after me. I ran down a side street and ran through a yard. I ran about half a mile I suppose, but was rather weak and had had nothing to eat or drink and my legs gave out, could not run any further, and some man got hold of me by the back of my coat, and about 20 or 30 men came up and kicked me and pounded me with stones. I had no control of myself then. I thought I was about going and commenced to scream, and there were 2 or 3 strikers with rifles rushed up then and kept off the crowd and rushed me forward to a theater, and I was put in the theater and found about 150 of the Pinkerton men there, and that was the last violence offered me.

Coeur d'Alene

1892

Some of the most lethal incidents of industrial violence occurred in isolated mountain towns, where the absence of long-established communities and a substantial middle-class public led to stark confrontations across class lines. One ugly episode occurred in the lead and silver mining territory of Coeur d'Alene, Idaho.

The mine workers had organized a union, which forced a uniform wage in all the mines. In 1891, the mine owners organized a counter force, the Mine Owners Protective Association. In January 1892 the Association offered the union a new contract with a 25% cut in wages; when the miners refused it they were locked out. The employers' organization thereupon announced that "the Association has resolved never to hire another member of the miners' union."

The mine owners then imported hundreds of scabs and hired armed guards to protect them. At first the workers tried to meet entering trains and convince strikebreakers to join them, but with little success. On July 7, news arrived of the Homestead strike, which turned many toward more militant tactics. On July 11, a union miner was killed by Pinkerton guards; the miners then attacked the guards' barracks at the Frisco Mill with dynamite, killing one and wounding twenty. Next they attacked Gem Mine; after a long gun fight during which five miners were killed and fourteen wounded, they captured it. Hundreds of armed miners marched to other mines in the area and forced the immediate discharge of all non-union men. On July 13, the Governor declared a state of insurrection and sent the Idaho National Guard, reinforced by federal troops, into the area. The scabs were brought back; 600 miners were rounded up and put in bullpens (the mode of imprisonment became a national scandal), local officials sympathetic to the strikers were removed, and all active union men were fired. Yet most of those imprisoned were freed by the courts, and the strike was resumed. Since the mine owners were unable to work their mines without experienced labor, most eventually recognized the union. Only two companies, Bunker Hill and Sullivan, held out; a strike against them took place in 1899, which repeated the earlier pattern of violence. The following account is taken from the *Spokane Weekly Review*, July 14, 1892. See Robert Wayne Smith: *The Coeur d'Alene Mining War of 1892* (1961).

WALLACE, Idaho, July 11. [Special.]—This has been the most exciting day in the history of the Coeur d'Alene. The hitherto peaceful canyons of these mountains have echoed with the sharp and deadly report of the rifle, and the cliffs of Canyon Creek have reverberated with the detonations of bomb and dynamite used in the destruction of valuable property.

The long-dreaded conflict between the forces of the strikers and the non-union men who have taken their places has come at last. As a result five men are known to be dead and 16 are already in the hospital; the Frisco mill on Canyon Creek is in ruins; the Gem mine has surrendered to the strikers, the arms of its employees have been captured, and the employees themselves have been ordered out of the country. Flushed with the success of these victories the turbulent element among the strikers are preparing to move upon other strongholds of the non-union men and will probably show their hand at Wardner tomorrow.

About 6 o'clock this morning a non-union miner from the Gem mine, at the town of Gem, was fired upon at a point near the Frisco mine. He ran back to the Gem mine and afterward died of his wound.

This shot seemed to be the signal for the non-union forces, who quickly gathered in considerable numbers and marched upon the mine, a lively firing being kept up by both sides. The attacking forces, however, were too strong for the besieged forces, and to avoid further bloodshed the mine was surrendered, the arms given up and the non-union men were marched down the canyon and sent out of the district.

In the meantime a similar attack was made upon the property of the Helena and San Francisco company at the same place, and with a like result. The men in the mine and mill surrendered, and the besiegers then went up the hill and sent down a lot of dynamite on the tramway, expecting it to explode and wreck the mill. They did this in revenge for the severe manner in which Mr. Esler has spoken of their cause and themselves, but the first attempt failed. They then shot a bomb down the iron water flume, and when it struck the bottom there was a tremendous explosion that wrecked the mill and destroyed $125,000 worth of property.

After this a sort of truce was held and hostilities were suspended. The arms of the non-union men were stacked and placed in charge of one man, from each side, but they were afterward taken by the strikers, the mine owners claiming in violation of the agreement.

The dead, wounded, and prisoners were then placed aboard a special train and taken down to Wallace, and Canyon Creek is now in complete control of the strikers, and no one is permitted to invade the district.

The blackest feature of the direful conflict in the Coeur d'Alene was the tragedy enacted at the Old Mission on the Coeur d'Alene River and in Fourth of July Canyon. After driving many of the fugitive non-union men into the canyon and the river the desperate and impassioned strikers followed them up and shot them down like deer. Among those shot down was Foreman Monaghan of the Gem mine, who was coming out with his family. The family was spared, but Monaghan was run into the bush and shot through the back. He was picked up yesterday morning and taken back to the mines. It is thought he will die. It is reported that 12 bodies have already been recovered in Fourth of July Canyon. The non-union men had been entirely disarmed and were at the mercy of their pursuers. The boat that came down the lake yesterday picked up 30 more of the fugitives who had taken to the river and bush. They tell tales of frightful cruelty. Some of them were beaten with revolvers and many were robbed of all their valuables.

A middle-aged man who escaped the hands of the executioner at Mission had a doleful story to relate of his sufferings and privations after getting away from the strikers. He asked that his name be withheld, as he fears further acts of revenge.

"After the shooting began," said he, "we started and ran like so many sheep. We were taken completely by surprise and dumbfounded. I made for the railroad track and got into a car. The car was crowded with men and women, too. I saw Mrs. Monaghan crouching down between two seats. Pretty soon a big burly fellow made his appearance at the door of the car with a Winchester rifle. 'Git out of this car, you d————d s———————— ————————,' said he, and we all began scrambling for the door. I heard Mrs. Monaghan crying, 'For God's sake, don't take my life; I have two daughters here somewhere, and I've lost them.' The fellow told her she could stay. That's the last I heard in the car. The next moment I was crowded out of the door and made off as fast as I could run. There was a party of us together. Pretty soon shots began to whistle around our heads, but we kept on running, through fields and brush, the shots following us like a hail storm.

"Our party began to separate and then there were only two of us together. We came to a fence, and as we were both crowding through an opening a shot swished past my companion's ear, and he shouted: 'Oh, God, I'm shot!'

"After a bit I saw one of our men drop in the distance. I ran past where he was lying. He looked up at me and said: 'Tell Abbott I'm killed.' He was the son of Nightwatchman Abbott. I could do nothing for him.

"When night came we found ourselves in a swamp, with water up to our knees. We lost our bearing entirely and were afraid to move for fear of being discovered. As the night wore out we began to move, and when dawn appeared we saw a man with a dog. At first we were afraid to let him see us, but gradually our courage returned, and besides, we were starving to death. We went up to the man and told him our story. At first he refused to give us anything to eat, but after we promised him $3 he took us to his house, where we got a bowl of bread and milk, and he rowed us over the river on a raft. We wandered along a mile or two, and were finally picked up by the boat."

Pullman Strike
1894

The Pullman Palace Car Company built a model town for its workers, presumably for their comfort and uplift, but also for profit. Rents there were twenty to twenty-five percent higher than in surrounding communities, but many consented to live there, since it was subtly made clear that those who wanted jobs had better do so. During the depression of 1893, half Pullman's workers were laid off and the rest took a twenty percent wage cut, but no reduction in rents was made. Early in May 1894 a committee of employees asked for the restoration of their former wages, but were refused. On May 10 three of the committee were fired. On May 11 Pullman workers walked out and asked the American Railway Union, with which they were affiliated, to aid their strike. On June 26, the A.R.U. began to refuse to handle Pullman cars. Soon the railroad strike spread across two-thirds of the country. By June 28, all traffic on the twenty-four lines out of Chicago was halted; workers derailed freight cars, obstructed tracks, threw switches, pulled scab engineers off trains.

The railroad organization, the General Managers Association, persuaded the Chicago police to break up strikers' demonstrations and to assist them, got the United States Marshal to appoint 2,000 deputies, paid by the railroads, who were described by the Superintendent of Police as "thugs, thieves, and

ex-convicts." But the deputies were unable to start the trains
running again. Next the G.M.A. turned to the federal government. On July 2 Attorney-General Richard Olney, an ex-
railroad lawyer and a railroad director, obtained a federal injunction preventing the blocking of trains, issued on the grounds
that the federal mails were being interfered with. When the
injunction was defied, President Cleveland sent federal troops to
Chicago despite the objections of Illinois Governor Altgeld.
Large-scale street fights broke out, and crowds burned freight
cars and stoned trains. On July 6, hundreds of cars were burned
and the state militia was sent in. On July 7, four were killed and
twenty wounded in battles between the militia and the crowds.
By the next day there were 14,000 police, militia, troops, and the
federal marshals in Chicago, and the strike was put down.
Eugene Debs and other strike leaders were arrested for contempt and conspiracy, and Debs served six months in jail. In at
least seven other states violence took place, and thirty-four
were killed.

    The account of the fighting on July 7 is taken from the
Chicago *Times*, July 8, 1894. See Almont Lindsey: *Pullman
Strike* (1942); see also Stanley Buder: *Pullman: An Experiment
in Industrial Order and Community Planning, 1880-1930*
(1967).

Company C, Second Regiment, I. N. G. Capt. Mair, disciplined a mob of
rioters yesterday afternoon at Forty-ninth and Loomis Streets. The police
assisted, and taking up the work where the militia left off, finished the
job. There is no means of knowing how many rioters were killed or
wounded. The mob carried off many of its dying and injured. The returns, so far as the police, hospital, and physicians' reports give two dead,
eight fatally hurt, and 17 injured.

At 3 o'clock yesterday morning the troop, numbering forty men, went
out with the work train on the Wabash road as far as Sixty-ninth Street. On
account of the mobs encountered at every crossing, the wrecking crew
was unable to do any work and they started back over the Western Indiana
tracks. They were then transferred to the Grand Trunk tracks. While
the train was at work at Forty-ninth and Loomis Streets the crowd so
increased in numbers that it was seen a conflict was inevitable. With the
troops were eight police, who had been with the train during the entire

day. The wrecking crew had been clearing up overturned cars and drawing spikes near Frazer Street. Soon after 3 o'clock this work was completed. The soldiers and police were gathered about the crew, all of them being the center of a howling, hooting mob of thousands. The work at this point was just about completed at 3:30 P.M., when the crowd, worked to the highest pitch of excitement, began hurling rocks at the policemen and soldiers.

Attacks Leading Up to the Shooting

The wrecking train had been the target for hundreds of missiles of every sort since its work began. Several of the police officers and militia had been struck and the order was at last given to return the fire at the next serious volley of stones. It was not long coming. The engine and wreck car were moved slowly west along the track when a crowd was seen collecting at the crossing where a car had been fired and another derailed a short time before. Many women were seen in the front ranks of the gathering mobs. Their talk was vile in the extreme. They suddenly vanished as if by order of the leader of the rioters, and the small boy element fled. Some of the men retired to ambush.

Evidently an attack was planned. The engine stopped and preparations made toward the work of putting the derailed box car on the track. Several stones and sticks were thrown, but they fell short.

Then a missile struck the cab of the engine and rebounding struck a policeman. He fired instantly point blank at the mob. The rioters broke and ran to the cover of the sheds and stables in the alley between Loomis and Bishop Streets. Others ran into near-by saloons. The next instant a shot came from one of the sheds, and with it a shower of stones. The police answered with shots, which returned by the rioters in ambush.

Captain Mair, in command of the militia, formed his men and withstood the attack in silence. Suddenly one of the rocks struck Lieut. Harry Reed, and the blood flew from a gash in his temple. Satisfied that further delay would be folly, the militia waited but an instant for the fatal command to fire. It came:

"Make ready, aim, fire."

First Volley into the Insurrectionists

The first straggling volley fired in the Debs insurrection rang out. Some of the shots went wild. Others which followed were better aimed. A half dozen men were struck by bullets. Some ran screaming down the street. Three lay prostrate in the alley from which most of the stones came.

From 5,000 rioters a fierce yell went up. To say that the mob went wild is but a weak expression. The men acted like maniacs and demons. Fear was unknown in the moments that followed. Nothing but the second and third volleys promptly fired saved the little band of soldiers from total annihilation. Like wild animals the leaders of the mob left ambush and threw themselves on the soldiers even while the bullets were flying as fast as the men could load. The police had emptied their revolvers and were reloading.

The command to charge was given. A moment's hesitancy would have been fatal. Both the mob and the soldiers made a rush for the crossing and there they met and there the last shots were fired. From that moment only bayonets were used. Time and again the soldiers charged north on Loomis Street and east on Forty-ninth. The rioters gave ground slowly. Bayonets were too much for them. A dozen men in the front line of rioters received bayonet wounds. Stones and clubs were frequently used. A few more shots were fired and the mob fled. Again it rallied and charged the troops. Up and down the street they fought for several minutes. An occasional shot was fired either by policemen or officers. The soldiers used only their bayonets.

The Engineer Forced to Retreat

The fight was still on when the engineer on the wrecking engine was attacked by a mob which came from the south along Loomis. To save himself and his train he started it westward and the troops followed. Some of the rioters took this for a retreat and thought to score a victory by another attack. The company wheeled about with every man in line, column front. The last charge was made and the mob driven almost a block north on Loomis. The troops marched back amid a shower of stones thrown from between the houses on both sides of the street. The engine which they had been sent out to guard was half a mile away. They followed and overtook it at Ashland Avenue.

With Lieut. Reed partly unconscious and several of his men suffering from blows Capt. Mair gave the word to board the train and this was done. Before the police could reach the train, however, the engineer started ahead at full speed and, with the wounded Lieutenant, the troops were taken to the Dearborn Street Station.

POLICE HAVE A HARD FIGHT FOR LIFE
*After the Soldiers Leave the Mob Closes in
and Two Calls for Help Are Made*

When the train pulled away with the soldiers, leaving the police, the mob gave a yell of exultation and closed in on all sides. The shower of stones and railroad iron was terrific. The police backed up against each other and prepared to sell their lives dearly. Face to face with the muzzles of their revolvers, the crowd hesitated an instant. Officer Ryan, revolver and club in hand, fought his way to the nearest patrol box and called a patrol wagon. Lieut. Keleher of the Halsted Street Station responded with twelve men. While the wagon was on the way the rioters again closed in on the police. The little body of officers retreated slowly west on Forty-ninth Street under a shower of stones, holding the mob at bay with their revolvers. A part of the mob turned its attention to undoing the work done by the wrecking party. It set a car on fire, broke the switch, and tore up the rails. Then they again turned their attention to the police. In the meantime an alarm of fire was sent in, and with it a second call for police assistance. To this Capt. O'Neill and thirteen men responded.

By this time Lieut. Keleher had arrived. He found the situation serious. The mob was increasing every minute and bent on the destruction of the officers. He charged the mob with the patrol horses on the dead run. The crowd parted. When the railroad crossing was reached the eight policemen were being roughly handled. Keleher and his men jumped from the wagon and clubbed their way through to the band of officers. Then all started back against the crowd. Keleher was hit with a stone. Officer Lyons got hold of the man and put him under arrest. At this minute Capt. O'Neill and his men arrived. At the sight of further reinforcements the crowd fell back for a minute and at this instant up came Fire Marshal Fitzgerald, in response to the fire alarm. The strikers surrounded him, forced his horse into a ditch, upset the wagon and threw him out. Scrambling to his feet he drew his revolver and fought his way to the police line.

Police Fire and Break the Mob

But the presence of reinforcements held the mob in check only a moment. Tearing up cobble stones the mob made a determined charge. The situation was too dangerous for further temporizing. No command to fire was given, but the word was passed along the line for each officer to take care of himself. One by one, as occasion demanded, they fired point blank into the crowd. After a few shots the crowd wavered and then beat a retreat, after replying to the shots with a shower of stones. Several disabled rioters lay on the ground. The police followed with their clubs. A wire fence incloses the track. The rioters had forgotten it; when they turned to fly they were caught in a trap.

The police were not inclined to be merciful and driving the mob against the barbed wires clubbed it unmercifully. The crowd got away as best it could. Then O'Neill and his men went west on Forty-ninth Street and Keleher went east. As they went they knocked the rioters right and left. The crowd outside the fence rallied to the assistance of the rioters being driven by the police. The shower of stones was incessant.

At Fraizer and Forty-ninth Streets is a saloon kept by Max Preja. He is said to be an Anarchist. Flying strikers rushed into this saloon. O'Neill and his men followed them. As the police neared the saloon, windows in neighboring houses were thrown open and shots were fired. They flew too high. The police returned the fire and broke open the door of the saloon. They were greeted with a shower of stones and billiard balls. The officers forced the rioters up-stairs, sparing only old men and women. Rioters jumped from the windows. Everybody in the crowd except the bartender was driven into the street and for blocks in all directions.

Wounded Men Left on the Ground

The ground over which the fight had occurred was like a battlefield. The men shot by the troops and police lay about like logs. Hats knocked off and coats thrown off to lessen weight in the flight were scattered about, while on the Loomis Street crossing, where the eight police officers had made their stand, were fully 500 stones that had been thrown by the mob. In the alley between Bishop and Loomis Streets lay "Engine" Burke, dying from a wound in the left side. As the police lifted him up he was about breathing his last, and when they carried him into the drug store he died. The police say he was a character who gave them a world of trouble. Close by him was Thomas Jackman with a bullet wound in his stomach, from which he cannot recover. Henry Williams, who had been shot in the leg, was lying west of Loomis Street, and Tony Gagaski was near him with a bullet wound in his arm. The ambulances were called and the wounded that could be found were taken to the Union Hospital in Englewood.

Wheatland Riot
1913

Migrant agricultural workers have rarely been able to protect themselves against the exploitation to which they are vulnerable. In 1913, one attempt they made to organize themselves in California was brutally defeated.

E. B. Durst, a large-scale California grower, advertised widely for hop pickers, and recruited many more than he needed—2,800 men, women, and children of twenty-seven nationalities, among them Syrians, Mexicans, Hawaiians, Japanese, Lithuanians, Greeks, Poles, Hindus, Cubans, Puerto Ricans. Durst had facilities for half that number at best; there were nine toilets for 2,800 people and the fields surrounding the workers' camp were filthy in a few days; there was no provision for garbage removal nor was there drinking water closer than a mile from the camp, although lemonade was sold by a Durst relative. Also, Durst withheld 10¢ out of every dollar of wages, to be paid only at the end of the season. Many workers left early, forfeiting this part of their pay.

Led by a small number of I.W.W. members, the workers organized a mass meeting and sent a committee to demand that conditions be improved. After a heated argument, Durst slapped the leader of the committee, Blackie Ford, and fired all its members. A constable then tried to arrest Ford, but since he had no warrant, the pickers refused to allow the arrest. While the pickers were holding a mass meeting, the constable returned, bringing with him the sheriff and deputies and the district attorney of the county. The meeting was ordered to disperse. Again the sheriff tried to arrest Ford and was assaulted by angry pickers. A deputy fired into the air, and both sides began shooting. The district attorney, a deputy, and two pickers were killed.

When a posse of several hundred armed men and five companies of militia reached the farm the pickers fled. A roundup of pickers and Wobblies began all over the state. Private detectives were employed to augment the police forces. Many of those taken prisoner were beaten or starved. Two men, including Ford, were convicted of murder in the second degree on the ground that their agitation about labor conditions had created a climate conducive to violence. The I.W.W. in California organized a general strike to free the two men. It was unsuccessful, though the campaign did publicize the plight of the migrant workers.

The account which follows is from the San Francisco *Chronicle*, August 4, 1913. For further information on the migrant workers in California as well as on the Wheatland riot, see the Commission on Industrial Relations: *Testimony*, V, 4911-5026; and Carleton H. Parker: *The Casual Laborer and Other Essays* (1920).

WHEATLAND, August 3—Four men lie dead and an unknown number of foreign hop pickers are injured as a result of a riot near Wheatland at 5 o'clock tonight.

The dead are:

E. T. MANWELL, District Attorney of Yuba county.

S. REARDON, a deputy sheriff of Yuba county.

Unknown negro hop picker.

Unknown Puerto Rican hop picker.

The injured:

Sheriff George H. Voss, shot in leg and head; badly beaten.

Nels Nelson, wealthy farmer, arm shot away.

Constable L. B. Anderson, right arm shattered by bullets.

E. Bradshaw, onlooker, shot in elbow.

Two unknown women, shot and badly injured.

Two unknown men, injured.

The riot was the result of a wage controversy in which the laborers demanded $1.25 a day for hop picking instead of $1.00, the former scale.

A squad of ten deputies was rushed from Sacramento at the first report of trouble in an automobile. Sheriff Boss of Yuba county went in person at the head of the party and attempted to parley with the strikers. Some excitable person in the mob of Mexicans fired a shot at random. The result was a fusillade from both sides, in which hundreds of shots were exchanged. . . .

It is reported that I.W.W. members were leaders in the rioting. The trouble started when the Durst brothers, who employed 400 hop pickers of their ranch, refused to concede to the employees' demands for increased pay.

Durst and Constable Anderson attended a meeting of the strikers at noon today, and when Durst refused to grant the increase the men became abusive. Constable Anderson tried to arrest one. He was set upon and beaten and his revolver taken away. The constable then telephoned to Sheriff George H. Boss.

Boss swore in a posse of ten, and, accompanied by District Attorney Manwell, went to Wheatland in two automobiles. Boss and four of his deputies approached the mob concentrated near the ranch house. The Sheriff attempted to parley with the men, and urged them to cease the destruction of property.

It is reported that the ringleaders began to abuse the Sheriff and he threatened arrest. Boss seized one man more violent than his fellows and started to drag him to the automobile. His friends leaped upon the Sheriff and beat him unconscious. When the other deputies started to charge, those in the front rank fired.

Manwell, who was standing nearby, was instantly killed. So was E. Cunningham, a deputy, and father-in-law of Sheriff Boss. Several bullets were fired into Boss' body as he lay on the ground. Another deputy was also instantly killed.

Nels Nelson, a wealthy farmer, a member of the posse, had his arm shot away in the volley. Constable Anderson's right arm was badly shattered. Two women were also wounded, fatally it is reported.

The driver of the car in which the Sheriff was riding was the only one in that automobile to escape death or injury. He jumped into the car and fled. Firing ceased and those in the other automobile were permitted to pick up the dead and wounded and carry them back to Marysville.

The exchange of shots between the mob and the posse occurred at about 5 o'clock. The automobile carrying the dead and injured arrived in Marysville about an hour later.

Ludlow
1913–1914

The Ludlow strike in the Colorado mining fields in 1913-14 is one of the clearest examples of the use of armed force by employers to oppose labor organization. The Ludlow coal mine owners had long resisted unionization, but in 1913 the United Mine Workers decided to try again. The union asked the Governor to arrange a conference for them with the mine operators, but the operators refused. The union called a strike on September 25, 1913. Of the reforms demanded, five were simply that state laws which the owners ignored be put in force. Some of these, for example, dealt with safety regulations while others guaranteed workers' rights, such as the right to trade at stores of their own choosing. To break the strike, the Colorado Fuel and Iron Company imported agents from Texas, New Mexico, and West Virginia who were deputized by the local sheriff as soon as they arrived and thus given official powers. Spies were sent among the miners who had been evicted from company homes and now lived in tent colonies set up by the Union. Automobiles were fitted with armored plate and machine guns mounted on them. On October 7, 1913, guards attacked the Ludlow tent colony, killing a miner and wounding a small boy. At Walsenberg several days later they fired into a meeting, killing three. The next day one guard was killed, and the miners fired on the "Death Special," an armed locomotive, and forced its retreat.

At this point Governor Elias M. Ammons sent in the Colorado National Guard to prevent further violence. The strikers welcomed them, convinced that they would be preferable to a private army. But under pressure from the mine owners, the Governor reversed his policy. Under John Chase, the anti-union commander of the National Guard, the troops harassed and arrested the miners, and molested their wives and daughters. After a time, the private guards were allowed to join the

National Guard to replace those regular members who wanted
to return to their homes. Thirty-five of these newly recruited
guards, under the command of Lt. K. E. Linderfelt, drove to
Ludlow on April 20, 1914, and fired on the tent colony with
machine guns. Five men and a boy were killed. Linderfelt next
fired the tents with coal oil, and eleven children and two
women were smothered to death. Three prisoners, one of whom
was Louis Tikas, a Greek leader of the strike, were murdered.
Linderfelt broke a rifle over Tikas' head before the soldiers
shot him.

The massacre provoked a bloody counter attack by the
miners, who rampaged from mine to mine destroying and
killing. Seven hundred to one thousand armed strikers, organized
by union officials, soon gained control of large areas. By April
29, when President Wilson sent in federal troops, seventy-four
people had been killed.

Wilson tried to settle the strike, but the operators refused
to budge. On December 30, 1914, the miners gave up and called
off the strike.

The account which follows was written by George P. West
for the United States Commission on Industrial Relations' investigation into the Ludlow massacre: *Report on the Colorado
Strike* (1915), 101-38. See also Graham Adams: *Age of Industrial Violence* (1966).

. . . by April 20th the Colorado National Guard no longer offered even
a pretense of fairness or impartiality, and its units in the field had
degenerated into a force of professional gunmen and adventurers who
were economically dependent on and subservient to the will of the coal
operators. This force was dominated by an officer whose intense hatred
for the strikers had been demonstrated, and who did not lack the courage
and the belligerent spirit required to provoke hostilities. Although twelve
hundred men, women and children remained at the Ludlow Tent Colony
and Linderfelt's immediate force consisted of not more than thirty-five
men, the militiamen were equipped with machine guns and high powered
repeating rifles and could count on speedy reinforcement by the members
of Troop "A," which numbered about one hundred. The Ludlow Colony
had been repeatedly searched during the preceding weeks for arms and
ammunition, and Major Boughton's testimony before this Commission
indicates that Linderfelt believed the strikers to be unarmed. . . .

On April 20th militiamen destroyed the Ludlow Tent Colony, killing five men and one boy with rifle and machine gun fire and firing the tents with a torch.

Eleven children and two women of the colony who had taken refuge in a hole under one of the tents were burned to death or suffocated after the tents had been fired. During the firing of the tents, the militiamen became an uncontrolled mob and looted the tents of everything that appealed to their fancy or cupidity.

Hundreds of women and children were driven terror stricken into the hills or to shelter at near-by ranch houses. Others huddled for twelve hours in pits underneath their tents or in other places of shelter, while bullets from rifles and machine guns whistled overhead and kept them in constant terror.

The militiamen lost one man. He was shot through the neck early in the attack.

Three of the strikers killed at Ludlow were shot while under the guard of armed militiamen who had taken them prisoners. They included Louis Tikas, a leader of the Greek strikers, a man of high intelligence who had done his utmost that morning to maintain peace and prevent the attack and who had remained in or near the tent colony throughout the day to look after the women and children. Tikas was first seriously or mortally wounded by a blow on the head from the stock of a Springfield rifle in the hands of Lieutenant K. E. Linderfelt of the Colorado National Guard, and then shot three times in the back by militiamen and mine guards.

The assassination of Tikas and the death of thirteen women and children at Ludlow precipitated an armed and open rebellion against the authority of the State as represented by the militia. This rebellion constituted perhaps one of the nearest approaches to civil war and revolution ever known in this country in connection with an industrial conflict.

Strikers in the Trinidad and Walsenburg Districts of Southern Colorado, and in the Canyon City and Louisville Districts, armed themselves and swarmed over the hills, bent on avenging the death of their Ludlow comrades.

Two days after the Ludlow tragedy, on Wednesday, April 22, the responsible leaders of organized labor in Colorado telegraphed to President Wilson, notifying him that they had sent an appeal to every labor organization in Colorado urging them to gather arms and ammunition and organize themselves into companies.

By Wednesday, April 22, two days after the Ludlow killings, armed and enraged strikers were in possession of the field from Rouse, twelve miles south of Walsenburg, to Hastings and Delagua, southwest of Ludlow. Within this territory of eighteen miles north and south by four or five miles east and west were situated many mines manned by superintendents, foremen, mine guards and strikebreakers. Inflamed by what they considered the wanton slaughter of their women, children and comrades, the miners attacked mine after mine, driving off or killing the guards and setting fire to the buildings. At the Empire mine of the Southwestern Fuel Company near Aguilar the President of the company, J. W. Siple, with twenty men and eight women and children, took refuge in the mine stope after the shaft house and buildings had been burned and dynamited. The strikers besieged them for two days, Siple having declined to surrender on promise of safe conduct. The party was rescued on the arrival of fresh militiamen from Denver under Adjutant General Chase on Friday afternoon.

Mine buildings were burned by the strikers at the Southwestern, Hastings, Delagua, Empire, Green Canyon, Royal and Broadhead mines. . . .

On Saturday strikers attacked the Chandler mine near Canyon City, on the other side of a range of foot hills and many miles from any point where disorder had previously occurred. The mine was captured Sunday afternoon and some of the buildings were burned.

On Monday night strikers attacked the Hecla mine at Louisville, northwest of Denver, and about 250 miles north of Trinidad. They also surrounded the Vulcan mine at Lafayette, a camp near Louisville in the northern field. . . .

On Wednesday morning, or late in the preceding night, a party of about 200 armed strikers left the strikers' military colony near Trinidad and marched over the hills to Forbes, a mining camp which lies at the bottom of a canyon surrounded by steep hills. Most of the party were Greeks. Earlier in the strike, before the visit of the Congressional Committee, the strikers' tent colony at Forbes, situated on ground leased by them, had been twice destroyed by militiamen and mine guards, and on one occasion it had been swept by machine gun fire and a striker killed and a boy had been shot nine times through the legs. Bent on revenge for this earlier attack and for the killings at Ludlow, the strikers took up positions on the hills surrounding the mine buildings, and at daybreak poured a deadly fire into the camp. Nine mine guards and strikebreakers were shot to death and one striker was killed. The strikers fired the mine buildings, including a barn in which were thirty mules, and then withdrew to their camp near Trinidad.

Twenty-four hours later the federal troops arrived and all fighting ceased.

During the ten days of fighting at least fifty persons had lost their lives, including the twenty-one killed at Ludlow.

Steel Strike
1919

Freed from wartime restrictions and faced with rising prices and rising unemployment, labor unions launched vigorous organizing drives in 1919. Their chief targets were in the large-scale heavy industries which had long resisted unionization. Judge Elbert Gary of United States Steel, for example, refused to have anything to do with unions. Pressure from the rank and file in the steel mills led to a strike. On September 22, 1919, over 250,000 enthusiastic United States Steel workers walked out.

The steel company surrounded its plant with guards and imported droves of special "deputies"; on a 20-mile trip along the Monongahela River from Pittsburgh to Clairton there were perhaps as many as 25,000 men under arms. Strike meetings were broken up, mounted police rode down groups of strikers in mill towns, pickets were dispersed. In Farrell, Pa., one striker was killed and twenty injured. Much of the violence was set off by the steel company's policy of hiring black strike breakers. In Donora immigrant strikers fought blacks, and two men were killed. Corporation officials, taking advantage of national anticommunist feeling precipitated by the Bolshevik Revolution, stressed the syndicalist allegiance of one of the strike leaders, William Z. Foster. In Gary, Indiana, on October 4, riots were put down by eleven companies of state militia and 500 special police and 300 deputies; but the next day there was more fighting. Crowds of strikers stormed the Tyler Street gates of United States Steel, and other crowds assaulted Negro strike-breakers. Federal troops were called in and martial law declared. General Leonard Wood, the commanding officer, declared he would do his part "in rounding up of the Red element." Army intelligence men investigated radical influence among workers, raided radical headquarters, arrested scores of strikers, confiscated Bolshevist literature, and did their utmost to persuade the public that the strike was a Red plot. Most of the press came to agree that it was "an attempt at revolution, not a strike." The loss of public support and the direct use of force crushed the strike. Steel resisted organization until the rise of the C.I.O. in the 1930's.

The documents which follow are, first, some affidavits and extracts from affidavits describing police actions in small towns, printed in William Z. Foster: *The Great Steel Strike and its Lessons* (1920), 126-31; and second, an account of the rioting in Gary, Indiana, taken from the Chicago *Tribune*, October 5, 1919. See David Brody: *Steel Workers in Crisis* (1965); Interchurch World Movement: *Report on the Steel Strike of 1919* (1920); Marshall Olds: *Analysis of the Interchurch World Movement Report on the Steel Strike* (1922); and United States Senate Committee on Labor and Education: *Investigation of Strikes in the Steel Industry*, 66th Congress, 1st Session (1919).

I

The State Constabulary were sent, unasked for, into the quiet steel towns for the sole purpose of intimidating the strikers. . . .

A few affidavits, and extracts from affidavits, taken at random from among the hundreds in possession of the National Committee, will indicate the general conditions prevailing in the several districts:

Clairton, Pa.

John Doban, Andy Niski and Mike Hudak were walking home along the street when the State Police came and arrested the three, making ten holes in Mike Hudak's head. Were under arrest three days. Union bailed them out, $1,000.00 each

Butler, Pa., Oct. 3, 1919

I, *James Torok,*
Storekeeper,
103 Standard Ave.,
Lyndora, Pa.

On about August 15, 1919, I saw State Troopers chase a crippled man who could not run as fast as his horse, and run him down, the horse bumping him in the back with his head, knocked him down. Later three men were coming to my store to buy some things; the State Troopers ran their horses right on them and chased them home. One of the men stopped and said: "I have to go to the store," and the Trooper said: "Get to hell out of here, you sons — ——, or I will kill you," and started after them again, and the people ran home and stayed away from the store.

JAMES TOROK

Homestead, Pa.

. . . two State Policemen made a forcible entry into the home of deponent, Trachn Yenchenke, at 327 Third Ave., Homestead, Pa., and came to the place where deponent was asleep, kicked him and punched him, and handled him with extreme violence and took deponent without any explanation, without permitting deponent to dress, dragged him half naked from his home to waiting automobile and conveyed him against his will to the Homestead Police Station. . . . Fined $15.10.

TRACHN YENCHENKE

. . . in the steel strike the photographer secured a proof of State Police brutality which the most skilled Steel Trust apologists cannot explain away—a picture of the typically vicious assault upon Mr. R. Dressel, a hotel keeper of 532 Dickson St. (foreign quarter), Homestead, Pa. I quote from the latter's statement in connection therewith:

I, Rudolph Dressel, of the aforesaid address, do hereby make this statement of my own volition and without solicitation from any one. That on the 23rd day of September I was standing in front of my place of business at the aforesaid address and a friend of mine, namely, Adolph Kuehnemund, came to visit and consult me regarding personal matters. As I stood as shown in the picture above mentioned with my friend, the State Constabulary on duty in Homestead came down Dickson St. They had occasion to ride up and down the street several times and finally stopped directly in front of me and demanded that I move on. Before I had time to comply I was struck by the State Policeman. (The attitude of said Policeman is plainly shown in the aforesaid picture, and his threatening club is plainly seen descending towards me.)

My friend and I then entered my place of business and my friend a few minutes afterwards looked out on the street over the summer doors. The policeman immediately charged him and being unable to enter my place of business on horseback, dismounted and entered into my place of business on foot.

My friend being frightened at what had happened to me retired to a room in the rear of my place of business. The policeman entered this room, accompanied by another State Police, and without cause, reason or excuse, struck my friend and immediately thereafter arrested him. I was personally present at his hearing before Burgess P. H. McGuire of the above city, at which none of the aforesaid policemen were heard or even present. Burgess asked my friend what he was arrested for, and my friend referred to me inasmuch as he himself did not know. The Burgess immediately replied, "We have no time to hear your witnesses," and thereupon levied a fine of $10.00 and costs upon him. My friend having posted a forfeit of $25.00, the sum of $15.45 was deducted therefrom.

II

Eleven companies of Indiana state troops are being rushed to Gary and Indiana Harbor by Gov. James P. Goodrich. They are expected to reach the strike zone at 6 o'clock this morning.

They were ordered out last night after Gary had been swept for two hours by rioting strikers and sympathizers. It was the most serious outbreak since the strike was called on Sept. 22.

Scores were arrested and the hospitals were filled with wounded following a pitched battle between 5,000 strikers and several hundred policemen and special deputy sheriffs.

Riot Guns Quell Disorder

The disturbance was quelled only after two squads of policemen had been ordered out with riot guns and fire companies stood ready to charge the mobs with high pressure streams of water.

Not a shot was fired by either side during the fighting. Paving stones, bottles, bricks, and clubs were the weapons used by the strikers, and there was hardly a member of the Gary police force who escaped being struck. Missiles were rained down on their heads by strike sympathizers from second story windows.

The trouble was started by pickets returning from a mass meeting at which the strikers had been inflamed by the report that the steel mills would attempt to break the strike tomorrow. Plans also had been made at the meeting for a demonstration of strength by all strikers and their families in the streets of Gary at 10 o'clock tonight.

Race Question a Factor

Bitterness over the race question also developed and the strikers leaving the meeting made for a street car bearing strike breakers—most of them Negroes—to the mills of the United States Steel Corporation.

The motorman got the car started, but the throng surged in front of it and all around it, impeding progress. By the time Fourteenth Street was reached the crowd had swelled to 5,000. Some one jerked the trolly from the wire and twenty-five strikers climbed into the car to single out the strike breakers.

"Yank them off," shouted a striker from the crowd that was gathering around the car. One of the Negroes is said to have drawn a knife. Another urged him to use it, according to the pickets. The trolly pole of the car was jerked off and the Negroes thrown off the car. The motorman and conductor fled, one Negro was beaten into insensibility. The rest tried to escape. Each became the center of a hooting mob.

A Negro deputy worked his way into the jam and rescued the Negro, who had defended himself with the knife. Dragging him to safety, he took his knife from him and sent him home. This enraged the crowd and an attack was made on the deputy, while others chased the Negro.

In five minutes the mob numbered from 5,000 to 6,000. The police, headed by Capt. James McCartney, arrived on the double quick, followed by armed businessmen in automobiles. A large force of deputy sheriffs arrived at the same time. They organized with the police and charged the mob, which stood its ground. The police formed a wedge and bored in, swinging clubs and blackjacks. Gradually the mob was forced backward to Fifteenth Street.

Some construction is going on at this corner and piles of brick stood in a vacant lot. These were hurled into the lines of advancing police, several of whom were injured. Ordering his men not to fire, Capt. McCartney fought his way into the lot. Patrol wagons and automobiles were backed into the curb and scores of rioters were overpowered and thrown into the machines. They fought bitterly, several of them reaching out of the patrol wagons to hit whoever stood near.

Herrin Massacre

1922

The two major kinds of industrial violence in America are attacks by public authorities (army, militia, police, deputized private guards) on striking workers, and attacks by strikers on strike-breakers. The Herrin massacre is an example of the second. On April 1, 1922, soft-coal workers throughout the country struck. Despite the strike, the U.M.W. local in Herrin, Illinois, allowed William Lester, owner of a strip mine, to mine coal as long as he did not immediately ship it; this would give Lester a strong marketing position once the strike ended. By June 60,000 tons had been dug, and Lester, unable to wait, decided to sell. He fired the union miners, brought in fifty scabs from Chicago strike-breaking agencies, and hired armed guards. But the men in Herrin were fiercely loyal to the U.M.W., which, after twenty-five years of struggle, had greatly improved their lives. This attempt to employ non-union labor threatened all their gains. Emboldened by the refusal of the local sheriff to act against them, and bolstered by the denunciation of the scabs by John L. Lewis, President of the U.M.W., the union men looted local hardware stores to get guns, surrounded the mine, and started shooting. At dawn of June 22, the scabs surrendered when the Union promised that they would be escorted safely out of the county. But as the miners marched the scabs away from the site, they grew angry and ugly. "The only way," one shouted, "to free the country of strike-breakers is to kill them off and stop the breed." Shortly afterward the superintendent of the non-union men was shot, and a slaughter began. Men were told to run and then were shot at. Some were tied together and shot when they fell, some had their throats slit, some were hanged. In all, nineteen men were murdered.

There was a national uproar over the massacre, especially after the coroner's jury blamed the killing on Lester and two men tried for murder were found not guilty.

The following account is from the Chicago *Tribune*, June 23 and 24, 1922. See Paul M. Angle: *Bloody Williamson* (1952).

HERRIN, Ill., June 22—[By the Associated Press.]—Half a dozen wounded men, some of them lying on deathbeds, tonight gave an Associated Press correspondent the first actual eye witness accounts of the mine fight last night and this morning which brought dozens of casualties when 5,000 armed striking miners attacked the Lester Strip mine near here, which was being operated by imported workers and guards.

The substance of the statements by the wounded, who were among the beseiged, was that not a mine worker was injured during the fighting but that the numerous killed were shot down in cold blood after they had surrendered themselves and their arms.

There was nothing from the union miners to contradict these claims.

Several of the men imported to work the mine absolved the strikers from blame, saying that the ones responsible were those "who sent us here under false promises that there would be no trouble," and that "the miners would not object."

Chicagoan Tells of Battle

Joseph O'Rourke, 4147 Lake Park Avenue, Chicago, commissary clerk at the mine, gave the most vivid account of the fight. His story was related as he tossed in pain from half a dozen bullet holes through his body.

"I was sent down here by the Bertrand Commissary Company, on West Madison Street, in Chicago," he said.

"I had no idea what I was running into. I don't blame the miners much for attacking us, for we were unknowingly being used as dupes to keep them from their jobs. We were given arms when we arrived and a machine-gun was set up at one corner of the mine. Guards were with us all the time and most of the guards were tough fellows sent by a Chicago detective agency. I understand the miners sent us warnings to leave town or we would be run out. We never got them, perhaps the bosses did. When we saw the miners approaching yesterday afternoon, we did not know what to do. The guards prepared for fight, most of us workers wanted to surrender.

"Through the night the bullets rained in on us. We sought shelter as we could, the miners climbed upon the coal piles and earth embankments, and we were unable to see them. The guards kept firing, but most of us hid. Then the miners blew up our pumping station, we had no water and our food supplies were in a freight car in the hands of the miners. About sunrise we put up the white flag. The miners poured in and we surrendered our arms.

"Up to this time not one of us had been injured that I know of, although I understand that several of the miners had been shot. The miners spread around quickly and tied us together in groups of three and six. The tied men were rushed off in different directions. Some of them tried to run, but they were shot down as fast as they moved.

"One miner asked who was the machine gun operator. Some one pointed him out and he was shot in his tracks, and his body laid over the machine gun.

Men Tied Together, Shot

"They tied five men with me, took us out on the road and told us to run. We ran and hundreds of bullets followed us. We staggered on, but finally three of our group fell, pulling the others with us, tied down, several bullet holes being in me already.

"I laid there while men came up and fired more shots into us from three or four feet. Then everything went black. I woke up later and begged for water, but there was not any. I remember being dragged along the road, but I don't know by what. Then they brought us to the hospital."

Two TRIBUNE representatives . . . saw wild groups of the strikers, now completely transformed from reasonably legitimate guards of prisoners to man hunters, beating the brush for human quarry.

Then they saw two men, clothes torn and blood soaked, driven out from the timber. The prisoners, pleading, but with hope obviously abandoned, had their hands raised high.

Tied, Shot, and Knifed

Whether these were two of six men who were later walked out to the south side school and on to the cemetery at Herrin has not been established. It is known that at the cemetery these six had their shoes and stockings torn from their feet and were pounded forward.

An old woman stepped out in the roadway, with arms extended pleadingly. "O, what are you going to do?" she asked. A strong arm felled her and the marchers marched on.

But the elderly woman was an exception. Young matrons, and even maidens, encouraged their men folk.

"Let's make soap of them," one of them suggested as the six, banded together with a three-quarter inch rope, were shot down with one volley. An examination showed that one of the six still breathed. An executioner with ready knife, completed what the bullets had left unfinished.

One of the four men found under a tree in Harrison woods, where the body of a fifth was suspended from a branch, had offered a gold watch and $25 to his tormentors when he saw all was about over.

"You're a good scout," taunted one of his tormentors. "Make a run for it." The good fellow was shot down by the man who jeered at him.

"Be one of us, keep moving, and ask no questions," seemed to be the order of the day in the theater of operations which centered about Herrin.

Chicago Eviction Riot
1931

By 1931 the Great Depression had inflicted profound and general misery. The Illinois Board of Labor reported, for example, that 624,000 men in Chicago—over 40% of the labor force— were involuntarily unemployed. At least one-third of the city's population, over a million people, were in dire distress. For blacks the unemployment rate was three times that for whites. In the summer of 1931 over two hundred families a week were being evicted for non-payment of rent. Sometimes spontaneously, sometimes under the leadership of the Communist party, the unemployed slowly organized to resist evictions. Large crowds would gather to restore dispossessed families to their homes. Landlords responded by asking the Chicago police to enforce the evictions.

On August 3, 1931, about 5,000 people, mostly black, gathered as sympathizers moved the furniture of an aged Negro woman from the street back into her flat. Police arrived and arrested several men. The crowd angrily closed on the officers, and the police fired a shot in the air. In the ensuing clash, when several of the police were roughed up, they fired into the crowd point blank, killing three and wounding many more. The police claimed the blacks had been armed, but no weapons were found. Twenty thousand whites and forty thousand blacks marched in a mass funeral, and the anti-eviction movement spread to other northern cities. The following account is taken from the Chicago *Defender*, August 8, 1931. See also Mauritz Hallgren: *Seeds of Revolt* (1933).

Trouble that had been brewing for weeks came to a head Monday, as had been predicted by many, when a group of the alleged communists defied police officers and bailiffs and tried to return the furniture of Mrs. Diana Gross, 72 years old, 5016 S. Dearborn Street, to the flat from which it had been removed by the bailiff, armed with an eviction order from the municipal court.

For the past three weeks this same group of men, women and children, who are banded together in an organization known as the Unemployment Council, and headed by four or five fiery speakers, have been causing the police considerable trouble. They maintain headquarters at 3528 State St.

At 3638 Wabash Ave., a week ago, an assemblage of more than 2,000 grimly determined men and women caused a near riot when they refused to disperse on orders from the police. The crowd had marched to the Wabash Ave. address to aid Mrs. Leathia Jones, who with her four children had been evicted.

Police Aid Tenants

Deputy Commissioner of Police John Scanlon, Deputy Chief of Detectives Lawrence Rafferty and several others high in the police department were drawn to the scene, but serious trouble was averted when $25 was raised by the police and given to the landlord, Mrs. James Dailey, 3552 Vernon Ave. Mrs. Jones was permitted to return to the flat.

Urged on by this apparent victory, the same afternoon several hundred men and women assembled in front of 3744 Rhodes Ave., where another family had been evicted, and staged a demonstration. This affair never reached dangerous proportions and the crowd was soon scattered.

Last Wednesday afternoon another demonstration was staged at 29th St. and South Pkwy. A cordon of police was thrown around the vicinity and quiet was obtained. The crowd, in military formation, marched south to Washington Park, where meetings are held night and day.

Feeling ran high not only on the South side but throughout Chicago following Monday's revolt, and on every hand there were whispers of another race riot. . . .

Details of the rioting that resulted in the slaying of the Reds and the wounding of the officers and civilians were told by Patrolman Fred D. Graham, 430 E. 49th St., one of the injured policemen.

He explained to a Chicago *Defender* reporter that he and his partner, Charles Childress, with Lieut. John Hardy and Sergt. John Bush and other patrolmen went to the scene of the riot after a call had been received at the station that a group of communists had threatened to put Mrs. Gross' furniture back into the flat.

When they arrived they ordered the crowd to move away, the officer said. Like Coxey's army, it was said, another mob swung into Dearborn St. from 51st, singing as they marched, and joined their companions in front of the home of the evicted family. It became apparent at once, the officer said, that the situation was serious. More police were ordered when the communists continued to increase in numbers, and the police prepared to cope with conditions.

In an effort to prevent trouble three men, believed to be ringleaders of the group, were arrested by Graham and Childress and sent to the station. These officers, observing another patrol wagon coming to the scene, went back and mingled in the crowd. . . .

Shot Is Fired

Intent upon throwing a scare into the crowd, Childress said he fired a shot into the air. Turning to look for his partner, the officer said, he saw Graham lying on the ground and blood flowing from a wound on his head. He had been struck with a blunt instrument. While Graham was down, Childress declared, several members of the rioting clan kicked him in the sides and in the stomach.

He ran to his partner's rescue and succeeded in pulling the angry battlers off the wounded policeman. A few feet away Officers Martin Ernst and John McFadden, both severely beaten, were lying on the ground, groaning. They and Graham were rushed to Mercy Hospital, McFadden and Ernst are still in the hospital in a serious condition.

Gray attempted to grab Officer Henry Lyons' revolver and was killed by Patrolman William Jordan. Lyons said he killed Paige. O'Neil was killed by Officer Graham.

William Boyden, 43 years old, 4937 St. Lawrence Ave., who had stopped at the corner to watch the rioting, was hit in the chest by a stray bullet. He was taken to the Bridewell Hospital. He will recover.

Temporary suspension of evictions on the South side was ordered by Assistant Bailiff J. M. Lee at the direction of Bailiff Horan. The service of eviction notices, however, will go on, it was said.

Southern Tenant Farmers' Union
1935

The New Deal's primary solution to agricultural crisis was retrenchment in agricultural production, supplemented by subsidies to cooperating farmers. The program succeeded in raising agricultural prices, but in the South it was disastrous for many tenant farmers, sharecroppers, and laborers. Many landlords appropriated to themselves acreage reduction benefits that were supposed to be paid to tenants. Worse, in many places where acreage was cut back, landowners simply dispossessed tenants and sharecroppers, who were then reduced to the status of casual laborers and had to be fed from relief funds. Together, blacks and whites organized tenant farmers' unions. Those formed in the New Deal era were not the first of such experiments. During the earlier years of the Depression a Sharecroppers' Union in Alabama was violently broken up. But the most effective organizational efforts were made in Arkansas, where two young socialists, H. L. Mitchell and Clay East, with the advice and backing of Norman Thomas and the Socialist party, organized the Southern Tenant Farmers' Union. Earlier organizational attempts by sharecroppers and tenants had been made in Arkansas, but had been violently suppressed: in 1919, for example, a union of blacks in Phillips County had been massacred. This new movement was inter-racial. Socialists and ministers were prominent among its organizers, and by 1935 there were 10,000 members in 80 local units. They stressed peaceful action, and spent much time arguing that the New Deal's agricultural program hurt the small farmers. In 1935 local whites and absentee corporations began to try to break the union by violence. Although some of its members were killed, and numbers of other harassed, attacked, and jailed, the Southern Tenant Farmers' Union persisted. One large strike led by its members was moderately successful, but they were never able to change the economic structure of the area.

The following account is taken from a contemporary pamphlet written by Howard Kester, a minister and S.T.F.U. organizer: *Revolt Among the Sharecroppers* (1936), 82-5. See Stuart Jamieson: *Labor Unionism in American Agriculture* (1945); and David Eugene Conrad: *Forgotten Farmers: The Story of Sharecroppers in the New Deal* (1965).

While violence of one type or another had been continuously poured out upon the membership of the union from its early beginning, it was in March 1935 that a "reign of terror" ripped into the country like a hurricane. For two and a half months violence raged throughout northeastern Arkansas and in neighboring states until it looked at times as if the union would be completely smashed. Meetings were banned and broken up, members were falsely accused, arrested and jailed, convicted on trumped up charges and thrown into prison; relief was shut off; union members were evicted from the land by the hundreds; homes were riddled with bullets from machine guns; churches were burned and schoolhouses stuffed with hay and the floors removed; highways were patrolled night and day by armed vigilantes looking for the leaders; organizers were beaten, mobbed and murdered until the entire country was terrorized. Some idea of the extent and character of the terror may be gained by citing a few instances which occurred in the space of ten days from the 21st of March to the 1st of April. All of these incidents were reported by either the Associated Press, the United Press, the Federated Press or by special correspondents assigned to the fields, and may be checked by those who wish to do so.

March 21st

A mob of approximately forty men, led by the manager of one of the largest plantations in Poinsett County, a town constable, a deputy sheriff, and composed of planters and riding bosses, attempted to lynch the Rev. A. B. Brookins, seventy-year-old Negro minister, chaplain of the union and a member of the National Executive Council.

After the mob had failed on four different occasions to lure Brookins from his cabin in Marked Tree, the mob turned their guns upon his home and riddled it with bullets. Brookins escaped in his night clothes while his daughter was shot through the head and his wife escaped death by lying prone upon the floor.

March 21st

W. H. Stultz, president of the Southern Tenant Farmers' Union, found a note on his doorsteps warning him to leave Poinsett County within twenty-four hours. This note, written on a typewriter, was signed with ten X's and said, "We have decided to give you twenty-four hours to get out of Poinsett County."

On the following day Stultz was taken into the office of the Chapman-Dewey Land Company by A. C. Spellings, Fred Bradsher and Bob Frazier on a pretext that Chief of Police Shannabery wanted to see him. While in the offices guns were laid upon a nearby barrel by the vigilantes and efforts were made by them to get Stultz to give them a pretext whereby to kill him. After being detained for three hours he was told by one of the men that he would "personally see to it that if you don't leave town that your brains are blown out and your body thrown in the St. Francis River." Stultz, the father of six small children, had been a sharecropper until driven from the land because of union activities. Night riders terrorized his family and attempted to blow up his home, and in order to save them from almost certain death he and his family were moved to Memphis by the union.

March 21st

The Rev. T. A. Allen, Negro preacher and organizer of the union, was found shot through the heart and his body weighted with chains and rocks in the waters of the Coldwater River near Hernando, Mississippi. The sheriff informed the reporter of the United Press that Allen was probably killed by enraged planters and that there would be no investigation.

March 22nd

Mrs. Mary Green, wife of a member of the union in Mississippi County, died of fright when armed vigilantes came to her home to lynch her husband who was active in organizing the sharecroppers in that county.

March 22nd

After threatening Clay East, former President of the Southern Tenant Farmers' Union, and Miss Mary Hillyer, of New York, with violence if they addressed a meeting of the union in Marked Tree, a mob drove the two into the office of C. T. Carpenter, the union attorney, surrounded the building and blocked all exits. After requesting protection from the mayor, East agreed to talk with the mob. He was told that if he ever returned to Poinsett County that he would be shot on sight. Mayor Fox finally interceded with the mob, which allowed Mr. East and Miss Hillyer to leave town but formed an armed band to escort them out of the county.

March 23rd
An armed band of twenty or thirty men attempted to kill C. T. Carpenter of Marked Tree, attorney for the union, at his home shortly before midnight. The leaders of the mob demanded that Carpenter give himself up, but this he refused to do. With gun in hand, Carpenter prevented the mob from breaking into his home. The presence of his wife probably prevented the mob from shooting directly at Carpenter, but as they departed they poured bullets into the porch and sides of the house, breaking out the lights.

On the following night a committee from the vigilantes called upon Mr. Carpenter in his office and threatened to shoot him there if he did not sever his connections with the union. This he refused to do.

An item in the *New York Times* reads "A band of forty-odd night riders fired upon the home of C. T. Carpenter, southern Democrat, whose father fought with General Lee in the Army of the Confederacy. The raid was a climax to a similar attack upon the homes of Negro members of the union."

March 27th
John Allen, secretary of the union on the Twist plantation in Cross County, escaped a mob of riding bosses and deputies, who were trying to lynch him, by hiding in the swamps around the St. Francis River.

During the frantic search for Allen numerous beatings occurred. When a Negro woman refused to reveal Allen's whereabouts her ear was severed from her head by a lick from the gun of a riding boss.

March 30th
An armed band of vigilantes mobbed a group of Negro men and women who were returning home from church near Marked Tree. Both men and women were severely beaten by pistols and flashlights and scores of children were trampled underfoot by the members of the mob.

March 30th
A Negro church near Hitchiecoon, in which the union had been holding meetings, was burned to the ground by vigilantes.

March 30th
Walter Moskop, a member of the trio which toured the East in behalf of the union narrowly escaped a mob which had gathered about his home to lynch him. Moskop's eleven-year-old son overheard the conversation

between the vigilantes and informed his father of the mob's intention just in time for him to be smuggled out of his home by friends.

April 2nd
The home of the Rev. E. B. McKinney, vice-president of the union, was riddled with more than two hundred and fifty bullets from machine guns by vigilantes. McKinney's family and a number of friends were inside. Two occupants of the home were severely wounded and the family given until sunrise to get out of the county. The mob was looking for H. L. Mitchell and the author who were reported to be holding a meeting in McKinney's home at the time.

Shortly after Norman Thomas returned to New York he spoke over a coast-to-coast hook-up of the NBC. He opened his address with these words: "There is a reign of terror in the cotton country of eastern Arkansas. It will end either in the establishment of complete and slavish submission to the vilest exploitation in America or in bloodshed, or in both. . . . The plantation system involves the most stark serfdom and exploitation that is left in the Western world."

Memorial Day Massacre
1937

During the thirties the C.I.O., aided by the New Deal's labor policy, launched a forceful organizing drive. By 1937 some employers, notably General Motors and United States Steel, had come to accept unions, but many had not. The Little Steel companies, Bethlehem, Republic, Youngstown Sheet and Tube, and Inland, led the opposition to the C.I.O. In 1937, when the Steel Workers Organizing Committee called the Little Steel strike, Republic decided to keep its South Chicago plant open by housing non-strikers within the mills and hiring armed guards.

The Chicago police protected the strike-breakers and broke up union picket lines. On Memorial Day 1,500 strikers—largely Slavs, Italians, Jews, and Mexicans—meeting in a field near their strike headquarters, voted to march to the Republic plant and picket en masse. A column of 2,000 to 3,000 strikers, singing union songs and chanting "C.I.O." was stopped by the police as it neared the mill. What happened next is not known—either some strikers threw stones or some police fired in the air—but the police then opened fire on the crowd. Five were killed on the spot and five died later. Six of these ten men were shot in the back. Fifty-eight strikers and sixteen policemen were injured.

Although none of the marchers was found with guns, the police insisted that they had fired to defend themselves from a blood-thirsty armed mob led by "outside agitators" and "Communists." The Chicago press praised their suppression of a "murderous mob" and their stemming of a "revolutionary tide." Paramount Pictures, which had filmed most of the riot, suppressed the film because they felt it might "incite local riot and perhaps riotous demonstrations." Senator Robert LaFollette, then investigating violations of free speech and the rights of labor, thought the public interest required its release. He subpoenaed the film, which graphically refuted the Chicago Police Department's testimony. The following description of the film was written by a reporter who attended the Congressional screening for the St. Louis *Post Dispatch*, June 16, 1937. See Donald G. Sofchalk: "The Chicago Memorial Day Incident: An Episode of Mass Action," *Labor History*, VI (Winter 1965), 3-43.

WASHINGTON, June 16—Five agents of the La Follette Civil Liberties Committee, headed by Robert Wohlforth, the committee's secretary, arrived in Chicago yesterday to begin an investigation of the tragic events of Memorial Day, when nine persons were killed or fatally wounded by city police in smashing an attempt by steel strike demonstrators to march past the Republic Steel Co. plant in South Chicago.

Appearance of the committee's agents on the scene coincided with the death of the ninth victim, a 17-year-old boy reported to have joined the pickets in the hope of getting a job in the mill after settlement of the strike.

It was learned today that the committee's decision to proceed with the inquiry was hastened by the private showing here last week of a suppressed newsreel, in which the police attack on the demonstrators is graphically recorded. The committee obtained possession of the film in New York, after its maker, the Paramount Co., had announced that it would not be exhibited publicly, for fear of inciting riots throughout the country.

Senators Shocked by Scenes

The showing of the film here was conducted with the utmost secrecy. The audience was almost limited to Senators La Follette (Prog.), Wisconsin, and Thomas (Dem.), Utah, who compose the committee, and members of the staff. Those who saw it were shocked and amazed by scenes showing scores of uniformed policemen firing their revolvers pointblank into a dense crowd of men, women, and children, and then pursuing and clubbing the survivors unmercifully as they made frantic efforts to escape.

The impression produced by these fearful scenes was heightened by the sound record which accompanies the picture, reproducing the roar of police fire and the screams of the victims. It was run off several times for the scrutiny of the investigators, and at each showing they detected additional instances of "frightfulness." It is expected to be of extraordinary value in identifying individual policemen and their victims. The film itself evidently is an outstanding example of camera reporting under difficult conditions.

Description of Picture

The following description of the picture comes from a person who saw it several times, and had a particular interest in studying it closely for detail. Its accuracy is beyond question.

The first scenes show police drawn up in a long line across a dirt road which runs diagonally through a large open field before turning into a street which is parallel to, and some 200 yards distant from, the high fence surrounding the Republic mill. The police line extends to 40 or 50 yards on each side of the dirt road. Behind the line, and in the street beyond, nearer the mill, are several patrol wagons and numerous reserve squads of police.

Straggling across the field, in a long irregular line, headed by two men carrying American flags, the demonstrators are shown approaching. Many carry placards. They appear to number about 300—approximately the same as the police—although it is known that some 2,000 strike sympathizers were watching the march from a distance.

Marchers Halted by Police

A vivid close-up shows the head of the parade being halted at the police line. The flag-bearers are in front. Behind them the placards are massed. They bear such devices as: "Come on Out—Help Win the Strike"; "Republic vs. the People," and "C.I.O." Between the flag-bearers is the marchers' spokesman, a muscular young man in shirtsleeves, with a C.I.O. button on the band of his felt hat.

He is arguing earnestly with a police officer who appears to be in command. His vigorous gestures indicate that he is insisting on permission to continue through the police line, but in the general din of yelling and talking his words cannot be distinguished. His expression is serious, but no suggestion of threat or violence is apparent. The police officer, whose back is to the camera, makes one impatient gesture of refusal, and says something which cannot be understood.

Then suddenly, without apparent warning, there is a terrific roar of pistol shots, and men in the front ranks of the marchers go down like grass before a scythe. The camera catches approximately a dozen falling simultaneously in a heap. The massive, sustained roar of the police pistols lasts perhaps two or three seconds.

Police Charge with Sticks

Instantly the police charge on the marchers with riot sticks flying. At the same time tear gas grenades are seen sailing into the mass of demonstrators, and clouds of gas rise over them. Most of the crowd is now in flight. The only discernible case of resistance is that of a marcher with a placard on a stick, which he uses in an attempt to fend off a charging policeman. He is successful for only an instant. Then he goes down under a shower of blows.

The scenes which follow are among the most harrowing of the picture. Although the ground is strewn with dead and wounded, and the mass of the marchers are in precipitate flight down the dirt road and across the field, a number of individuals, either through foolish hardihood, or because they have not yet realized what grim and deadly business is in progress around them, have remained behind, caught in the midst of the charging police.

In a manner which is appallingly businesslike, groups of policemen close in on these isolated individuals, and go to work on them with their clubs. In several instances, from two to four policemen are seen beating one man. One strikes him horizontally across the face, using his club as he would wield a baseball bat. Another crashes it down on top of his head, and still another is whipping him across the back.

These men try to protect their heads with their arms, but it is only a matter of a second or two until they go down. In one such scene, directly in the foreground, a policemen gives the fallen man a final smash on the head, before moving on to the next job.

In the front line during the parley with the police is a girl, not more than five feet tall, who can hardly weigh more than 100 pounds. Under one arm she is carrying a purse and some newspapers. After the first deafening volley of shots she turns, to find that her path to flight is blocked by a heap of fallen men. She stumbles over them, apparently dazed.

The scene shifts for a moment, then she is seen going down under a quick blow from a policeman's club, delivered from behind. She gets up, and staggers around. A few moments later she is shown being shoved into a patrol wagon, as blood cascades down her face and spreads over her clothing.

Straggler's Futile Flight

Preceding this episode, however, is a scene which, for sheer horror, outdoes the rest. A husky, middle-aged, bare-headed man has found himself caught far behind the rear ranks of the fleeing marchers. Between him and the others, policemen are as thick as flies, but he elects to run the gantlet. Astonishingly agile for one of his age and build, he runs like a deer, leaping a ditch, dodging as he goes. Surprised policemen take hasty swings as he passes them. Some get him on the back, some on the back of the head, but he keeps his feet, and keeps going.

The scene is bursting with a frightful sort of drama. Will he make it? The suspense is almost intolerable to those who watch. It begins to look as if he will get through. But no! The police in front have turned around now, and are waiting for him. Still trying desperately, he swings to the right. He has put his hands up, and is holding them high above his head as he runs.

It is no use. There are police on the right. He is cornered. He turns, still holding high his hands. Quickly the bluecoats close in, and the night sticks fly—above his head, from the sides, from the rear. His upraised arms fall limply under the flailing blows, and he slumps to the ground in a twisting fall, as the clubs continue to rain on him.

C.I.O. officers report that when one of the victims was delivered at an undertaking establishment, it was found this his brains literally had been beaten out, his skull crushed by blows.

Man Paralyzed by Bullet

Ensuing scenes are hardly less poignant. A man shot through the back is paralyzed from the waist. Two policemen try to make him stand up, to get into a patrol wagon, but when they let him go his legs crumple, and he falls with his face in the dirt, almost under the rear step of the wagon. He moves his head and arms, but his legs are limp. He raises his head like a turtle, and claws the ground.

A man over whose white shirt front the blood is spreading, perceptibly, is dragged to the side of the road. Two or three policemen bend over and look at him closely. One of them shakes his head, and slips a newspaper under the wounded man's head. There is a plain intimation that he is dying. A man in civilian clothing comes up, feels his pulse a moment then drops the hand, and walks away. Another, in a uniform which might be that of a company policeman, stops an instant, looks at the prostrate figure, and continues on his way.

Loading Wounded in Wagons

The scene shifts to the patrol wagons in the rear. Men with bloody heads, bloody faces, bloody shirts, are being loaded in. One who apparently has been shot in the leg, drags himself painfully into the picture with the aid of two policemen. An elderly man, bent almost double, holding one hand on the back of his head, clambers painfully up the steps and slumps onto the seat, burying his face in both hands. The shoulders of his white shirt are drenched with blood.

There is continuous talking, but it is difficult to distinguish anything with one exception—out of the babble there rises this clear and distinct ejaculation:

"God Almighty!"

The camera shifts back to the central scene. Here and there is a body sprawled in what appears to be the grotesque indifference of death. Far off toward the corner of the field, whence they had come originally, the routed marchers are still in flight, with an irregular line of policemen in close pursuit. It is impossible to discern, at this distance, whether violence has ended.

A policeman, somewhat disheveled, his coat open, a scowl on his face, approaches another who is standing in front of the camera. He is sweaty and tired. He says something indistinguishable. Then his face breaks into a sudden grin, he makes a motion of dusting off his hands, and strides away. The film ends.

PART III

Racial Violence

Slave Revolts and Their Suppression

New York Slave Revolt
1712

American slavery was always marked by violence, most of it by masters against slaves. Slaves also used violence, ranging from full-scale revolts to individual breaks for freedom, but compared to some other slave societies, slave-initiated violence was relatively slight, in part because whites were so quick to put down real or imagined threats with extraordinary and intimidating violence, formal or informal, legal or illegal. In the eighteenth century, suppression of rebellious blacks was harsh in the extreme.

An example of violence on the part of both slaves and masters is the revolt of 1712 in New York City. A number of blacks, along with some Indians, planned to revolt against their enslavement. They bound themselves to secrecy with a blood oath and rubbed their bodies with a supposedly invulnerable powder given them by a free black "sorcerer." On the night of April 6, they set fire to the outhouse of their masters, and lay in ambush to slay those who came to put the fire out. They managed to kill nine whites and wound others before the Governor sent troops to end the revolt. The slaves fled, but most were captured, and several committed suicide rather than be taken. After a trial, twenty-four were sentenced to death, but the Governor reprieved six. Of the remaining eighteen who were tried, some were hanged, some were tortured, some burned to death. One sentence read that the rebel was to be "burned with a slow fire that he may continue in torment for eight or ten hours and continue burning in the said fire until he be dead and consumed to ashes." In 1741 thirteen blacks were sentenced to be burned to death when an alleged slave conspiracy was reported.

The following account is taken from a letter by Governor Robert Hunter to the Lords of Trade, June 23, 1712, in E. B. O'Callaghan, ed.: *Documents Relative to the Colonial History of the State of New-York* (1855), V, 341. See Kenneth Scott: "The Slave Insurrection in New York in 1712," *New-York Historical Society Quarterly*, XLV (January 1961), 43-74; T. Wood Clarke: "The Negro Plot of 1741," *New York History*, XXV (April 1944), 167-81; and Winthrop D. Jordan: *White over Black: American Attitudes Toward the Negro, 1550-1812* (1968).

I must now give your Lordships an account of a bloody conspiracy of some of the slaves of this place, to destroy as many of the inhabitants as they could. It was put in execution in this manner, when they had resolved to revenge themselves, for some hard usage, they apprehended to have received from their masters (for I can find no other cause) they agreed to meet in the orchard of Mr. Crook in the middle of the town, some provided with fire arms, some with swords and others with knives and hatchets. This was the sixth day of April, the time of meeting was about twelve or one o'clock in the night, when about three and twenty of them were got together. One coffee and negroe slave to one Vantilburgh set fire to an out house of his masters, and then repairing to his place where the rest were they all sallyed out together with their arms and marched to the fire. By this time the noise of fire spreading through the town, the people began to flock to it. Upon the approach of several the slaves fired and killed them. The noise of the guns gave the alarm, and some escaping their shot soon published the cause of the fire, which was the reason that not above nine Christians were killed, and about five or six wounded. Upon the first notice which was very soon after the mischief was begun, I order'd a detachment from the fort under a proper officer to march against them, but the slaves made their retreat into the woods, by the favour of the night. Having ordered sentries the next day in the most proper places on the Island to prevent their escape, I caused the day following the militia of this town and of the county of West Chester to drive [to] the Island, and by this means and strict searches in the town, we found all that put the design in execution. Six of these having first laid violent hands upon themselves, the rest were forthwith brought to their tryal before the Justices of this place, who are authorized by Act of Assembly to hold a court in such cases. In that court were twenty-seven condemned, whereof twenty-one were executed, one being a woman with child, her execution by that means suspended. Some were burnt, others hanged, one broke on the wheel, and one hung alive in chains in the town, so that there has been the most exemplary punishment inflicted that could be possibly thought of.

Louisiana Uprising
1811

The sanguinary triumph of the blacks of Haiti in 1791 terrified slaveholders and Southern whites, who took every precaution to prevent insurrection from spreading to the United States. There were indeed some slave reactions to the West Indian ferment, but with two exceptions they were small, spontaneous outbursts. One exception was Gabriel's abortive uprising of 1800, after which thirty or forty blacks were killed in retaliation; the second was the Louisiana uprising of 1811.

Louisiana had had several insurrection scares in the 1790's and early 1800's. In 1795 a planned revolt in the parish of Pointe Coupee was stopped when a quarrel among the leaders led to its discovery. Troops sent by the Spanish authorities killed twenty-five slaves, and others were captured and tried. Of those found guilty, "sixteen . . . were hung in different parts of the parish; the nine remaining were put on board of a galley, which floated down to New Orleans. On her way one of them was landed near the church of each parish along the river, and left hanging on a tree."

In 1811 a major revolt broke out in the parish of St. John the Baptist, about thirty-six miles north of New Orleans. An estimated 500 slaves on the André sugar plantation wounded the owner, killed his son, and forming into companies, "each under an officer, with beat of drums and flags displayed," marched on New Orleans. Recruiting more slaves as they went, they attacked and burned four or five plantations before they were met by hundreds of militia and United States troops, and, on January 10, defeated. Sixteen leaders were tried and executed. As a warning to others, their heads were mounted on poles at intervals along the Mississippi above New Orleans.

The following account appeared first in the Louisiana *Gazette,* and was reprinted in the Richmond *Enquirer,* February 22, 1811. See Herbert Aptheker: *American Negro Slave Revolts* (1943); Francois-Xavier Martin: *History of Louisiana from the Earliest Period* (1882); Erwin Adams Davis: *The Story of Louisiana* (1960); and John S. Kendall: "Shadow over the City," *Louisiana Historical Quarterly,* XXII (1939).

NEW ORLEANS, *January 11*

The militia on the west side of the river crossed above the banditti yesterday about ten o'clock, and attacked them; killed several, took some prisoners, and dispersed the whole body; the fugitives retreated to the swamp, several of whom after returned and surrendered, among which is *Charles,* a yellow fellow, the property of Mr. Andre, who was leader of the miscreants.

From every account we have received, the danger appears to be at an end. No mature plan had been arranged by the brigands, and measures now adopted will ensure tranquillity. Gen. Hampton is on the coast with a respectable force—Major Milton, who was on his march to Baton Rouge with about 150 regular troops, we are informed, was above where the ravages commenced, and was moving down; so that there is little doubt, but before this, the whole of the banditti are completely routed.

January 12

The accounts from the coast corroborate that of yesterday. The troops continue to kill and capture the fugitives, ten or twelve of whom were brought to town this morning; and in a few days the planters can with safety return to their farms. We expect soon (perhaps on Monday) to give a detailed account of the damage done by the brigands.

. . .

Extract of a letter from Gen. Hampton to Governor Claiborne bearing date on this day, the 12th of Jan. 1811, from the plantation of Mr. Destrehan. "Having yesterday formed a junction with Maj. Milton's command, which has descended far beyond the commencement of this shocking insurrection, and having posted him in this neighborhood, to protect and give countenance to the various companies of the citizens, that are scouring the country in every direction, I shall permit the detachments that came with me from the city to return. But I have judged it expedient to order a company of Light Artillery and one of Dragoons to descend from Baton Rouge, and to touch at every settlement of consequence, and to crush any disturbances that may have taken place higher up.—The chiefs of the party are taken."

January 17

It is very difficult to obtain anything like a correct statement of the damages done by the banditti on the coast. They commenced their depredations on the night of the 8th inst. at Mr. Andry's, killed young Mr. Andry, and wounded the old gentleman. After seizing some public arms that were in one of Mr. Andry's stores, and breaking open sideboards and liquor stores, and getting half *drunk* they marched down the coast from plantation to plantation, plundering and destroying property on their way; the inhabitants generally made their escape and the banditti continued on their march until 4 o'clock in the afternoon of Wednesday, when they arrived at the plantation of Mr. Cadit Fortier, there they halted, (having marched upwards of five leagues) and commenced killing poultry, cooking, eating, drinking and rioting.

When the alarm reached the city, much confusion was manifested. The most active citizens armed themselves, and in about an hour after the alarm (although the weather was extremely bad) commenced their march, their force not exceeding thirty men, mounted on tolerable horses, but were continually reinforcing as they progressed up the coast. The road for two or three leagues was crowded with carriages and carts full of people, making their escape from the ravages of the banditti—negroes, half naked, up to their knees in the mud, with large packages on their heads driving along towards the city. The accounts we received were various.

When we had arrived within a league of Mr. Fortier's, where the banditti were feasting, our numbers had increased to near one hundred, but badly armed and accoutered. Major Durrington, of the United States Infantry, was named as our commandant—but indeed it was but a name; for he was decidedly of the opinion, that we ought not to attack the enemy with the small force we had until day-light; in this opinion he was supported by the best informed characters in the detachment, but without avail, for some of those who were for attacking had advanced.—The Major gave orders to prepare for action (this was about eight o'clock at night) and at the moment when every disposition was making for the attack, General Hampton arrived, and decided against attacking them until the infantry could be brought up; this he was not able to effect, although every exertion was made, until 4 o'clock in the morning. The clouds had dispersed, the moon shone clear, and it was excessively cold; the arms of the United States troops glittered in the moonbeam, and must have been the cause of the brigands discovering us; for soon after the foot filed off to take them in the rear, they rang the alarm bell, and with a degree of extraordinary silence for such a rabble, commenced and affected their retreat up the river.

When we took position of the ground where the brigands had been committing their ravages all night, our troops and horses were so exhausted that they were unable to pursue the fugitives; however, by the activity of the militia above and the promptness of Major Milton, and the regular force under his command, that day and the next, the whole of the banditti were routed, killed, wounded and dispersed, and everything was tranquil.

In this melancholy affair, but two citizens have fell by the hands of these brigands, and three dwelling houses burned; not a single sugar house nor sugar works were molested. The poor wretches who were concerned in the depredations, have paid for their crimes—upwards of 100, it is generally supposed, have been killed and hung, and more will be executed.

January 22
An accurate enumeration was taken on Thursday last, of the Negroes killed and missing, from Mr. Fortier's to Mr. Andry's, and is as follows, viz.

Killed and executed,	66
Missing,	17
Sent to N. Orleans for trial	16
	99

From this statement the loss is not so great as was at first calculated. Those reported missing are supposed generally to be dead in the woods, as many bodies have been seen by the patrol.

Vesey Uprising
1822

In late May 1822, Devany Prioleau, a Charleston slave, told his owner of a supposed slave insurrection plot. He said that another slave, William Paul, had divulged the secret. The two men were promptly arrested, and Paul implicated several others. Slave after slave, brought in and questioned, denied knowledge of any plot. Then on June 14, another slave corroborated Paul's testimony and declared that the uprising was set for the 16th. Although it did not occur, ten slaves were arrested, and a quickly invoked court heard secret testimony against them, and also against Denmark Vesey, a free Negro, arrested on the 21st. On July 2, after having been found guilty of "crimes of the blackest hue," Vesey and five others were hung, all protesting their innocence. By now Charleston was in a panic; all blacks seemed potential assassins. The slaves themselves were terrified of vigilante reprisals, though some courageously donned black armbands in mourning for those executed. Rumors of an impending rebellion were heard anew, the court was reassembled, and a second roundup of slaves and free blacks was made. Twenty-two blacks were hung on one day, and their bodies left to dangle for hours. After thirty-five had been hung, the court satisfied itself by deporting thirty-seven more. As the judges explained to the Governor, "The terror of example we thought would be sufficiently operative by the number of criminals sentenced to death."

Doubts have recently been raised by scholars as to whether or not an insurrection was actually planned. Richard C. Wade has noted that most of the essential testimony was obtained by torture, and that no corroborative circumstantial evidence was produced—for example, the hundreds of pikes that were supposed to have been stored.

The following account is taken from a pamphlet describing and reflecting on the affair by A Colored American: *The Late*

Contemplated Insurrection in Charleston, S.C., with the Ex-
ecution of Thirty-Six of the Patriots . . . (1850). See John
Lofton: *Insurrection in South Carolina: The Turbulent World*
of Denmark Vesey (1964); and Richard C. Wade: "The Vesey
Plot: A Reconsideration," *Journal of Southern History*, XXX
(May 1964), 143-61. See also the same author's *Slavery in the*
Cities (1964); and Vincent Harding: "Religion and Resistance
Among Ante-Bellum Negroes, 1800-1860," in August Meier
and Elliot Rudwick, eds.: *The Making of Black America*
(1969), I, 179-200.

Several years after the enactment of laws to cut off entirely all hopes, and
to prevent the slaves from acquiring their liberty by purchase, as the
sequel of this sad narrative will tell, it is probable that a party of the·
disappointed slaves, justly incensed with the cruel passage of such un-
civilized laws, which were a great and intolerable hinderance to their
peace and happiness, had conspired to free themselves from the yoke of
the most unholy bondage ever invented by man in that liberty-loving
country—to become owners of their own sacred persons, over the bodies
of their masters. In this matter, however, they failed owing to one of the
party who was found to be a traitor to their supposed righteous cause,
who communed with a free colored man on the subject of their intention
to make an attempt to liberate themselves, who in turn communicated
the whole subject matter to the constituted authorities of the city of
Charleston; which timely information saved the city from a bloody servile
contest. But it resulted in the capture of the entire band of patriots, and
in their subsequent execution—the most barbarous on record in that
day—notwithstanding the sanctity of their cause, made holy by the
American Revolution.

The mock and summary trial of those brave men, after the alleged
plot was discovered and the party taken prisoners, exceeds credence, and
will ever blight the escutcheon of the Palmetto State. A Court was summoned for the express purpose of trying the contemplated conspirators,
composed of gentlemen slaveholders, upon the plan of Judge Lynch, for
which the South is peculiarly celebrated. The proceedings were, as usual
when slave interests are supposed to be interfered with, a solemn farce;
and in this form the business was conducted. Freeholders were readily
selected, pre-disposed to condemn and hang every prisoner brought before
them on the charge of insurrection ("as a terror to the slaves, to keep
them in awe for a quarter of a century," as one of the prosecutors said,

and that there was "nothing too bad for the slaves to contemplate doing, but the masters had the ability to punish them for it") without sufficient lawful evidence that was necessary to convict anybody except in the Slave States. The prisoners were arraigned in the most despotic form of the darkest gone-by age, where they were truly forlorn. No lawyer dared to defend them fairly or professionally. I think the Governor and one of the Judges of the Supreme Court were threatened with violence for expressing an opinion adverse to the ruling party of the city at that time.

Under such charges as were brought the accused, one of the prisoners, whose name was Pharo, acted as States-evidence on the promise of rewards, with security for his life; which promise the honorable Court failed to keep, and Pharo was condemned and hung with twenty-one others of the so-called conspirators, at the lines of Charleston, after every information was extracted from him, and, as it was alleged, he proved himself to be a false witness. All the arrangements having been prepared and ready for the accommodation and sitting of the Court, the prisoner was brought out of his dungeon and securely fixed in the hall of the prison house, without a friend to support him in this dreadful emergency, where accusation against him was pronounced by the Court, charging the individual prisoner with a criminal meeting with one or more other slaves who contemplated to raise an insurrection, with an intent to overthrow the present form of Government in Charleston—to establish a rule of their own. The accused, after his arrest, was cut off from all communication whatever with his acquaintances, and was not allowed to see nor to have an interview, nor to consult with a friend on any occasion; neither was he allowed to see or confront his accuser face to face. O how cruelly this part of the arrangement was carried out with unchristian ferocity! Indeed all the condemnation of culprits that did occur on that awful and melancholy occasion, in sending thirty-six brave men to a premature, but honorable, grave (Colonel Isaac Hayne, of Revolutionary memory, died on the scaffold), was cowardly and shamefully done in secret, and upon very slight circumstantial and secret evidence alone. The accused was tried, not by a jury, oh, no! He was condemned to die, and none but slaveholders, who would taunt him, were permitted to speak with the prisoner on any consideration.

In this horrible situation he was led out of prison to be executed, without friend or relative to assuage or console the culprit in his overwhelming calamity. Nay, the endearing ties of nature were ruthlessly sundered by the demon "office-hunter," neither wife nor children, ah, no! no colored persons whatever were allowed to manifest the slightest grief for affliction in their family. Even the affliction of death, which comes of the power of

God, in his Divine Providence, was treated with disregard; nor were the free colored people allowed to wear a bit of crape to mourn the loss of father, mother, brother, sister, daughter or son, but the act was construed into sympathy for the contemplated conspirators (such was the rage of leading young men, who were looking forward to political advancement, and who knew that oppressing the colored people was the sure road in which to obtain that end), and punished accordingly.

The matter of hanging the contemplated conspirators, and whipping and stripping the peaceable colored people of their black dress, crape, &c., continued for several weeks, and would perhaps have continued much longer. There was a very large number of persons already imprisoned, waiting their turn for the scaffold; but some of the citizens who had already suffered great loss in having their slaves hung without full remuneration for their value, and the fears of others who were surfeited in seeing, and having their property in human flesh sacrificed in order to gratify and pave the way of a few young men to office, without sufficient pay for this loss of property in the condemned slaves (Governor Ben—tt, the then executive of the State, perhaps would have hesitated to take $10,000 for two of his slaves that were executed for being declared leaders of the contemplated conspiracy. They were men above the ordinary standing of first-rate slaves, of deep piety and experience—ingenious engineers and millwrights; indeed, it was said of them they were above mediocrity); when one of the freeholders, as I have been informed, devised the following plan to rid themselves of the measures:—

A rash youth had, by his advice and zealous counsel, put the city under. He sent into the interior of the country, beyond the residence of any of the reported contemplated conspirators, and had two of his slaves brought before the august assembled Court, to discover what effect their appearance would have on the secret evidence, dressed as they were in their country rags. The secret witnesses, after reviewing carefully the persons brought before them for inspection, declared that there was no accusation against them, and they were discharged free from blame into the hands of their owners: the identical slaves were washed and dressed fashionably, and again presented before the Court for examination, on charges pretended to be preferred against them, when the same disinterested, pure witness, who had previously declared these men innocent of any criminal charge against the State, without hesitation, on their second and improved appearance before the Court, pronounced these very men participants in the scheme of the contemplated conspiracy.

The success of this method on the part of the Court to detect false witness was complete, for they had become surfeited of their own abominable work; and stayed the execution of more than a hundred valiant victims prepared by their order for the scaffold, as the Court themselves declared in a publication issued by authority from one of the public presses in Charleston, the contents of which has escaped my memory. I recollect this much of their statement, however, viz., "that many others, including a blind man formerly from St. Domingo, were fit subjects for the gallows; but motives of humanity prevented their execution." The motives of humanity alleged by the Court, I apprehend were not praiseworthy motives to discover false witness or arrest the execution of the patrician band; ah, no! but after a gluttonous destruction of the lives of thirty-six honorable and brave men, for their own self-protection against prospective loss. Some of the honorable members of the Court owned slaves who were implicated in the affair of the contemplated insurrection. That circumstance, perhaps was one of the chief motives of humanity that influenced the Court to stay their hand and authority.

This disgraceful, wholesale murder of thirty-six remarkably upright and worthy men, principally to make sure a popular platform for office-hunters to be elevated upon, is without parallel, even in Charleston. The day on which twenty-two of the patriots were hung, or rather sacrificed to the wicked principles of slavery, at one time, owing to some bad arrangement in preparing the ropes—some of which were too long, others not properly adjusted so as to choke effectually the sufferers to death, but so as to give them the power of utterance, whilst their feet could touch the ground—they, in their agony of strangulation, begged earnestly to be despatched; which was done with pistol-shot by the Captain of the City Guard, who was always prepared for such an emergency; i.e. shooting slaves.

Nat Turner
1831

The slave uprising in which the greatest number of whites were killed was Nat Turner's revolt in Southampton county in Southeastern Virginia. Turner, born in 1800, learned to read and immersed himself in the Bible; there he found sanction for his opposition to slavery and knowledge enough to make himself a religious leader among his fellows. In the spring of 1828 he became convinced that he had a mission to lead a rebellion. As he related, he "heard a loud noise in the heavens, and the Spirit instantly appeared to me and said that the Serpent was loosened, and Christ had laid down the yoke he had borne for the sins of men, and that I should take it on and fight against the Serpent, for the time was fast approaching when the first should be last and the last should be first." He awaited the divine signal, which came to him in the form of a solar eclipse on February 12, 1831. By August 21, he had organized his forces and was able to begin. Starting with the murder of Turner's master, Joseph Travis, and his family, the slaves marched from plantation to plantation, gathering adherents and slaughtering whites. By August 23, they had gone twenty miles and killed at least fifty-seven whites. They were headed toward the town of Jerusalem, where arms were stored, but one group went off to recruit more followers from a nearby plantation and then stayed to get drunk. The rest were attacked by a band of whites, were temporarily relieved when the second group of slaves returned, but scattered when a company of militia arrived. Turner tried to regroup his forces, but could not. The massacre of whites was followed by a massacre of blacks. Bands of militia and vigilante groups murdered blacks indiscriminately throughout the surrounding territory. It is estimated that at least one hundred blacks were killed. Turner escaped capture until October 30, when he was caught, tried, and hung, the twentieth of his band to be legally executed.

The following account of the uprising is Turner's confession, made before he was executed: *The Confessions of Nat Turner, The Leader of the Late Insurrection in Southampton, Virginia as Fully and Voluntarily made to Thomas R. Gray, in the Prison where he was Confined . . .* (1831), reprinted as an appendix to Herbert Aptheker: *Nat Turner's Slave Rebellion* (1937; 1968). See also Aptheker: *American Negro Slave Revolts* (1943); William S. Drewry: *The Southampton Insurrection* (1900); and Marion D. deB. Kilson: "Towards Freedom: An Analysis of the Slave Revolts in the United States," *Phylon*, XXV (1964), 175-87.

. . . It was quickly agreed we should commence at home (Mr. J. Travis') on that night, and until we had armed and equipped ourselves, and gathered sufficient force, neither age nor sex was to be spared (which was invariably adhered to). We remained at the feast, until about two hours in the night, when we went to the house and found Austin; they all went to the cider press and drank, except myself. On returning to the house, Hark went to the door with an axe, for the purpose of breaking it open, as we knew we were strong enough to murder the family, if they were awaked by the noise; but reflecting that it might create an alarm in the neighborhood, we determined to enter the house secretly, and murder them whilst sleeping. Hark got a ladder and set it against the chimney, on which I ascended, and hoisting a window, entered and came downstairs, unbarred the door, and removed the guns from their places. It was then observed that I must spill the first blood. On which, armed with a hatchet, and accompanied by Will, I entered my master's chamber. It being dark, I could not give a death blow, the hatchet glanced from his head, he sprang from the bed and called his wife, it was his last word; Will laid him dead, with a blow of his axe, and Mrs. Travis shared the same fate, as she lay in bed. The murder of this family, five in number, was the work of a moment, not one of them awoke; there was a little infant sleeping in a cradle, that was forgotten, until we had left the house and gone some distance, when Henry and Will returned and killed it; we got here, four guns that would shoot, and several old muskets, with a pound or two of powder. We remained some time at the barn, where we paraded; I formed them in a line as soldiers, and after carrying them through all the manoeuvres I was master of marched them off to Mr. Salathul Francis', about six hundred yards distant. Sam and Will went to the door and knocked. Mr. Francis asked who was there, Sam replied it was him, and he had a letter for him, on which he got up and came to the door; they immediately seized him, and dragging him out a little from the door, he was dispatched by repeated blows on the head; there was no other white person in the family. We started from there for Mrs. Reese's, maintaining the most perfect silence on our march, where finding the door unlocked, we entered, and murdered Mrs. Reese in her bed, while sleeping; her son awoke, but it was only to sleep the sleep of death, he had only time to say who is that, and he was no more. From Mrs. Reese's we went to Mrs. Turner's, a mile distant, which we reached about sunrise, on Monday morning. Henry, Austin, and Sam went to the still, where, finding Mr. Peebles, Austin shot him, and the rest of us went to the house; as we approached, the family discovered us, and shut the door. Vain hope! Will, with one stroke of his axe, opened it, and we entered and found Mrs. Turner and Mrs. Newsome in the middle of a room almost frightened to death. Will immediately killed Mrs. Turner, with one blow of his axe. I took Mrs. Newsome by the hand, and with the sword I had when I was apprehended, I struct her several blows over the head, but not being able to kill her, as the sword was dull. Will turning around and discovering it, despatched her also. A general destruction of property and search for money and ammunition, always succeeded the murders. By this time my company amounted to fifteen, and nine men mounted, who started for Mrs. Whitehead's. . . .

Our number amounted now to fifty or sixty, all mounted and armed with guns, axes, swords and clubs.—On reaching Mr. James W. Parker's gate, immediately on the road leading to Jerusalem, and about three miles distant, it was proposed to me to call there, but I objected, as I knew he was gone to Jerusalem, and my object was to reach there as soon as possible; but some of the men having relations at Mr. Parker's it was agreed that they might call and get his people. I remained at the gate on the road, with seven or eight; the others going across the field to the house, about half a mile off. After waiting some time for them, I became impatient, and started to the house for them, and on our return we were met by a party of white men who had pursued our blood-stained track. . . . Immediately on discovering the whites, I ordered my men to halt and form, as they appeared to be alarmed.—The white men, eighteen in number, approached us about one hundred yards, when one of them fired. . . . And I discovered about half of them retreating, I then ordered my men to fire and rush on them; the few remaining stood their ground until we approached within fifty yards, when they fired and retreated. We pursued and overtook some of them who we thought we left dead; (they were not killed) after pursuing them about two hundred yards, and rising a little hill, I discovered they were met by another party, and had halted, and were re-loading their guns. . . .

As I saw them re-loading their guns, and more coming up than I saw at first, and several of my bravest men being wounded, the others became panick struck and squandered over the field; the white men pursued and fired on us several times. Hark had his horse shot under him, and I caught another for him as it was running by me; five or six of my men were wounded, but none left on the field. . . .

Texas Slave Insurrection
1860

On July 8, 1860, most of the business section of Dallas was burned to the ground, and fires were kindled in seven other Texas towns; more followed in the next several days. Rumor reported the fires to be part of an abolition plot to free the slaves and massacre the whites. Slaves were tortured and "confessed" to complicity in a Northern plot. An abolitionist's letter was found, outlining a master plan for freeing slaves in Texas. Some incendiaries were caught and arrested. Early in August, another great fire decimated the town of Henderson, destroying 43 buildings at a loss of $220,000.

Hysteria then swept across Texas. Following a well-established tradition, vigilante committees were organized to expose conspirators and to suppress every trace of dissent. Fort Worth, for example, passed resolutions calling for the preparation of two lists of "black Republicans, abolitionists or higher-law men of every class; List No. 1, all suspected persons; No. 2, black list, to be exterminated by immediate hanging." "Trials" and executions followed. Estimates of the number of men killed run from 75 to 100. Most of them were blacks, though some were Northern whites. The vigilante terror continued throughout the summer.

So harsh a response must be understood in the light of the long-standing Southern fear of servile revolt. The Harper's Ferry raid had occurred the year before, and the election campaign of 1860 heightened anxiety for Southern institutions. Texas had had a similar panic during the election of 1856. The revolt, real or imagined, was magnified for political ends by the secessionists and the Breckinridge party, who used it to discredit the moderates Bell and Douglas, to reinforce anti-Republican sentiment, and to silence Unionist critics.

The following account, a letter to the editor of a Northern paper written by a Southern white, is taken from an anti-abolition pamphlet by John Townsend: *The Doom of Slavery in the Union; its Safety out of it* (1860). For additional information see William W. White: "The Texas Slave Insurrection of 1860," *Southwestern Historical Quarterly*, LII (January 1949), 259-85; and Ollinger Crenshaw: "The Psychological Background of the Election of 1860 in the South," *North Carolina Historical Review*, XIX (July 1942), 260-79.

Marshall, Texas, Aug. 12, 1860

Editors of the Evening Day Book:

The wildest excitement prevails throughout the north-western, north-eastern, and the central portions of Texas, in consequence of *Abolition incendiarism*. I have no doubt but you have seen, ere this reaches you, the burning of Dallas, Denton, Black Jack Grove, and quite a large number of stores and mills. Loss estimated at between $1,500,000 and $2,000,000. Since then the *Abolitionists* have been detected in attempts to fire a number of other towns South of the above, and in an extensive plan of insurrection among the negros, headed by these demons of hell. On some plantations the negros have been examined, and arms and ammunition in considearble amount have been found in their possession; they all admit they were given to them by these *Lincolnites*. Every day we hear of the burning of some town, mill, store, or farmhouse. Henderson was burnt to ashes on the 6th instant, being the general election day for State and county officers. We hear of two or three other towns burnt on the same day. *Women and children* have been so frightened by these burnings and threatened rebellion of the negros, that in several instances they have *left their homes in their fright, and when found were almost confirmed maniacs!* Military companies are organized all over the state, and one-half of our citizens do constant patrol duty. But unfortunately up to this time Judge Lynch has had the honor to preside only in ten cases of whites (northern Lincolnites) and about sixty-five of negros, all of whom were hung or burnt, as to the degree of their implication in the rebellion and burning. The plan was to burn all of the towns, thereby destroy the arms and ammunition, also country stores, mills, farms, and corn cribs, &c. Then on election day they were to be headed by John Browns, and march south for Houston and Galveston city, where they would all unite, and after pillaging and burning those two cities, the negros were promised by these devils incarnate, that they would have in readiness a number of vessels, and would take them forthwith to Mexico, where they would be free. The *credulity of the negro* is so great, that he can be *induced to believe almost anything*, no matter how impossible it may be, particularly when he is informed by a shrewd white man that the thing can be done, and that he will lead them on and accomplish the object. But the end is not yet. I believe that the northern churches are at the bottom of this whole affair—in fact the fanatics have already acknowledged it. They say that this Texas raid is in revenge for the expulsion of some of their brethren of the Methodist church from Texas, about twelve or eighteen months ago, for preaching and teaching Abolition incendiarism to the negros in northern Texas. Unless the churches send out new recruits of John Browns, I fear the boys will have nothing to do this winter (as they have hung all that can be found), the school boys have become so excited by the sport in hanging Abolitionists, that the schools are completely deserted, they having formed companies, and will go seventy-five or one hundred miles on horseback to participate in a single execution of the sentence of Judge Lynch's Court. It has now become a settled conviction in the South *that this Union cannot subsist one day after Abe Lincoln has been declared President*, if God, in his infinite wisdom, should permit him to live that long, for they (the people of the South) have made up their minds that they had rather die, sword in hand, in defence of their homes, their wives, their children and slaves, in defence of the Constitution, the laws, and their sacred honor, than *tamely submit to an organized system of robbery*, a *degraded and loathsome scheme of amalgamation*, a breaking up of the compromises of the Constitution, and a total exclusion of the South from the common territories of the country won by their blood and treasure.

W.R.D.W.

Race Riots

Providence
1831

Rhode Island began emancipating slaves in 1784; by 1825 there were 1,400 free Negroes and but four elderly slaves in the state. Race prejudice, however, remained. Blacks were restricted to menial labor, exploited by employers, segregated in religion and education, and subject to frequent physical harassment and humiliation. Much racial violence occurred, including the "Hard Scrabble" riot of 1824, when a small black hamlet near Providence was demolished and after which many blacks left the state.

A new black district, Snow Town, grew up in Providence, which was also frequented by sailors. The mingling of blacks and lower-class whites affronted the rest of the citizens. In September 1831 a fight between the blacks and sailors of Snow Town drew large crowds from Providence, and a riot began. After two days of destruction and the death of several men while the civil authorities tried in vain to keep the peace, the militia was called out—much of the property of Snow Town belonged to influential whites—and the riot was forcibly put down with a toll of four dead and fourteen wounded.

The following account is taken from the Providence *Journal*, as reprinted in the New York *American*, September 27, 1831. See also Irving H. Bartlett: "The Free Negro in Providence, Rhode Island," *Negro History Bulletin*, XIV (December 1950), 51 *ff.*

FATAL RIOTS IN PROVIDENCE, R.I.—For several evenings of last week this usually orderly and quiet town was disturbed by riots, which, we lament to state, were only quelled on Saturday at the price of the death of several citizens.

The origin of the difficulties was on Wednesday night, when some sailors belonging to the ship Lyon from Göttenburg got into a row in Olney's lane with some colored people of dissolute characters. The result was that the blacks fired upon the white assailants; and a young man of 22 years of age, who had just shipped as second mate of an Indiaman; and, as is alleged, was accidentally passing, without mingling in the affray, in company with three of his shipmates, in search of the cook, was shot dead, thirty or forty buckshot having entered his breast and stomach, and his companions were more or less wounded. A black named Richard Johnson was arrested on suspicion. When the death of the white man was made known throughout the town, a mob immediately assembled, and in spite of the authorities, demolished the furniture and part of the suspected houses in Olney's lane.

To prevent a recurrence of similar outrages, and to preserve the peace and quiet of the town, the Town Council doubled the usual number of watchmen, and called out constables, ordering them to arrest all persons committing open outrages upon private property. The Sheriff with his officers, and the Governor of the State with the members of the Town Council and many of the most respectable citizens assembled also at the same place. The utmost exertions of the civil authorites to maintain order proved inadequate. The mob assembled and carried on their attacks systematically, with implements of various kinds. Several of the riotous persons arrested by the Sheriff were openly rescued by their companions and taken forcibly from the custody of this officer. In this situation, with all the power of the civil authorities set at defiance, the Governor of the State at the request of the Sheriff of the county, called out one of the military companies to aid in suppressing the tumult. The order having been issued at a late hour of the evening, only about thirty-five members of the company could be collected. Under the orders of the Sheriff these few spirited men proceeded to the spot, where they were assailed by various sorts of missiles, and several of them were wounded by large stones. One individual of the company was so severely injured as to falter and leave the ranks, and another was bathed in blood, from a wound cut in his head, which was the blood first drawn by the offensive attacks of the mob.—Thus assailed, they continued firm in their ranks, under a shower of stones, until it became evident that no alternative remained but instant resistance or retreat. Unwilling to resort to fire arms, although exposed to being maimed, or even to the loss of life from the weight and impetuosity of stones discharged at them whilst standing forth openly, to sustain the laws of the land, they patiently bore their attacks and finally retreated by order of the Governor. The mob went on steadily until nearly morning with their work of destruction, in open defiance and derision of all the constituted authorities of the town and of the state. A few of the rioters were, however, seized and securely lodged in jail. . . .

As had been contemplated, the mob again assembled at the approach of evening; but intimidated by the vigilant and energetic measures that had been taken, after some ineffectual attempts to excite to open outrages on the part of the leaders of the mob, one of whom was armed with a sword, they dispersed; not, however, as it was openly expressed, without a determination of mustering an overpowering force to complete their purposes on the ensuing evening.

To again defeat these renewed systematic attacks to be repeated for the fourth night in succession, orders were again issued to the bands of armed citizens to hold themselves in readiness.

According to the proposed plan the attack was recommenced for the fourth time by the mob at an early hour of the evening, and the work of destruction of buildings and other private property went on as usual. The noise of the crash of falling materials, mingled with shouts and imprecations, were on this calm night distinctly to be heard even in the distant parts of the town to interrupt the quiet and excite the alarm of every peaceable citizen, and of every man capable of reflecting on the consequences of living in a land in which lawless rioters continued unchecked and triumphant. The alarm bell having been sounded, the citizens repaired to the scene of riot, with their muskets in martial array, passed through the mob, accompanied with their hisses and derision, and took post on the hill above. Proclamation was then made by a magistrate under the riot act, the mob ordered to disperse, and notice audibly given, that otherwise in five minutes they would be fired upon. They came down to do so. Instead of dispersing, a part retired to ground west of that held by the authorities, and another portion in open resistance to the laws and of those who were present to support those laws, attacked a house within a stone's throw, with great violence. Upon this, the Sheriff with a part of the force, proceeded with an intention to disperse this assailing multitude; but were compelled to halt before leaving the hill, by showers of stones thrown from the mob on the west. Two vollies were now fired over their heads without any other effect than producing repeated vollies of stones in return. Another portion of the military were despatched as a reinforcement, and the Sheriff with the first then proceeded down the road to protect the buildings, the mob partly separating on each side, and partly retiring before them.

After effecting a passage over the adjacent bridge, amidst shouts and insults, the mob closed in their rear, separating them from the main body, and threw stones so unremittingly, that many of the soldiers were severely wounded. An order was now distinctly to be heard directing the mob to leave the street, or it would become necessary to fire upon them. Renewed discharges of stones were the only result. Thus assailed, they were now compelled to turn and face the rioters, and, as a last resort, it having become absolutely necessary for the preservation of the lives of those under arms, orders were at length given to fire, which were obeyed. Until this moment, all entreaties, all orders, all force had proved ineffectual. In a few minutes afterwards the mob dispersed and quiet was again restored.

Cincinnati
1841

Although the Northwest was anti-slavery, it was even more anti-black. For example, in 1804 blacks and mulattos in Ohio were required to obtain a certificate of freedom or leave the state. They had to register officially, and no one was allowed to employ a black unless his papers were in order. In 1807 potential Negro newcomers to Ohio were forbidden entrance unless they posted a bond of $500 guaranteeing their good behavior.

At first, when there were few blacks in Ohio, these laws were not strictly enforced, but by the mid-1820's their numbers had much increased, particularly in Cincinnati, just across the river from Kentucky, and agitation for their eviction began, fed by the prejudices of a large number of Southern white migrants. In addition, Cincinnati businessmen feared that their trade with the South might suffer if free Ohio Negroes were able to harbor fugitive slaves. In 1829, blacks were given sixty days to post the bond required by the 1807 law or leave town. Before the time was up white mobs attacked a Negro district, killing and burning. Afterwards over 1,000 Negroes left Cincinnati for Canada and founded the town of Wilberforce, Ontario.

Still, in the next decade, blacks continued to come to Cincinnati, and much to the distress of the Irish workers, with whom they competed for jobs, they prospered. In 1841 after a series of small racial clashes, another major riot, described in this document, broke out. The following account from the Cincinnati *Daily Gazette*, September 6, 1841, was reprinted in Wendell P. Dabney's *Cincinnati's Colored Citizens* (1926), 49-54. See also Carter Woodson: "The Negroes of Cincinnati Prior to the Civil War," *Journal of Negro History*, I (January 1916), 1-22.

This city has been in a most alarming condition for several days, and from about eight o'clock on Friday evening until about three o'clock yesterday morning, almost entirely at the mercy of a lawless mob, ranging in number from two to fifteen hundred.

On Tuesday evening last, a quarrel took place near the corner of Sixth Street and Broadway, between a party of Irishmen and some Negroes, in which blows were exchanged and other weapons, if not firearms, used. Some two or three of each party were wounded.

On Wednesday night the quarrel was renewed in some way, and some time after midnight a party of excited men, armed with clubs, etc., attacked a house occupied as a negro boarding house, on McAllister Street, demanding the surrender of a Negro who they said had fled into the house and was there secreted, and uttering the most violent threats against the house and the Negroes in general. Several of the adjoining houses were occupied by Negro families, including women and children. The violence increased and was resisted by those in or about the houses. An engagement took place, several were wounded on each side, and some say guns and pistols were discharged from the house. The interference of some gentlemen in the neighborhood succeeded in restoring quiet. . . .

On Friday, during the day, there was considerable excitement, threats of violence and lawless outbreaking were indicated in various ways, and came to the ears of the police and of the Negroes. Attacks were expected upon the Negro residences in McAllister, Sixth and New Streets. The Negroes armed themselves, and the knowledge of this increased the excite-

ment. But we do not know that it produced any known measure of precaution on the part of the police to preserve the peace of the city.

Before eight o'clock in the evening, a mob, the principal organization of which, we understand, was arranged in Kentucky, openly assembled in Fifth Street Market, unmolested by the police or citizens. The
number of this mob, as they deliberately marched from their rendezvous
toward Broadway and Sixth Street, is variously estimated, but the number increased as they progressed. They were armed with clubs, stones,
etc. Reaching the scene of operations, with shouts and blasphemous
imprecations, they attacked a negro confectionery on Broadway, and
demolished the doors and windows. This attracted an immense crowd.
Savage yells were uttered to encourage the mob onward to the general
attack upon the Negroes. About this time the Mayor came up and
addressed the people, exhorting them to peace and obedience to law. The
savage yell was instantly raised, "Down with him." "Run him off," was
shouted, intermixed with horrid imprecations, and exhortations to the
mob to move onward.

They advanced to the attack with stones, etc., and were repeatedly
fired upon by the Negroes. The mob scattered, but immediately rallied
again, and again were in like manner, repulsed. Men were wounded on
both sides and carried off, and many reported dead. The Negroes rallied
several times, advanced upon the crowd, and most unjustifiably fired
down the street into it, causing a great rush in various directions. These
things were repeated until past one o'clock, when a party procured an
iron six-pounder from near the river, loaded it with boiler punchings,
etc., and hauled it to the ground, against the exhorations of the Mayor
and others. It was posted on Broadway, and pointed down Sixth Street.
The yells continued, but there was a partial cessation of firing. Many of
the Negroes had fled to the hills. The attack upon houses was recommenced with firing of guns on both sides, which continued during most
of the night, and exaggerated rumors of the killed and wounded filled
the streets. The cannon was discharged several times. About two o'clock
a portion of the military, upon the call of the Mayor, proceeded to the
scene of disorder and succeeded in keeping the mob at bay. In the morning, and throughout the day, several blocks, including the battle-ground,
were surrounded by sentinels, and kept under martial law—keeping within
the Negroes there, and adding to them such as were brought during the
day, seized without particular charge, by parties who scoured the city,
assuming the authority of the law. . . .

It was resolved to embody the male Negroes and march them to jail for security, under the protection of the military and civil authorities.

From two hundred and fifty to three hundred Negroes, including sound and maimed, were with some difficulty marched off to jail, surrounded by the military and officers; and a dense mass of men, women and boys, confounding all distinction between the orderly and disorderly, accompanied with deafening yells.

They were safely lodged, and still remained in prison, separated from their families. The crowd was in that way dispersed. Some then supposed that we should have a quiet night, but others, more observing, discovered that the lawless mob had determined on further violence, to be enacted immediately after nightfall. Citizens disposed to aid the authorities were invited to assemble, enroll themselves, and organize for action. The military were ordered out, firemen were out, clothed with authority as a police band. About eighty citizens enrolled themselves as assistants of the marshal, and acted during the night under his direction, in connection with Judge Torrence, who was selected by themselves. A portion of this force was mounted, and a troop of horse and several companies of volunteer infantry continued on duty till near midnight. Some were then discharged to sleep upon their arms; other remained on duty till morning, guarding the jail, etc. As was anticipated, the mob, efficiently organized, early commenced operations, dividing their force and making attacks at different points, thus distracting the attention of the police. The first successful onset was made upon the printing establishment of the "Philanthropist." They succeeded in entering the establishment, breaking up the press, and running with it, amid savage yells, down through Main Street to the river, into which it was thrown.

The military appeared in the alley near the office, interrupting the mob for a short time. They escaped through by-ways, and, when the military retired, returned to their work of destruction in the office, which they completed. Several houses were broken open in different parts of the city, occupied by Negroes, and the windows, doors and furniture totally destroyed. From this work they were driven by the police, and finally dispersed from mere exhaustion. . . .

New York Draft Riot
1863

The New York Draft Riot of July 1863 was in large measure a race riot, magnified by labor unrest, unfair draft laws, an unpopular war, religious and ethnic tensions, class antagonisms, and exacerbated by the violence of street gangs and volunteer firemen. This most brutal of all civil upheavals cost a greater number of lives than any other incident of domestic violence in American history.

Racial and economic tensions had been closely linked since the 1840's. Before then Negroes had virtually controlled some occupations: longshoremen, hod carriers, brick makers, barbers, waiters, and domestic servants. The Irish influx, particularly after 1846, led to a sharp struggle between the blacks and the newcomers, which the Irish won. Many blacks could find no employment but strike breaking, which often led, particularly on the docks, to violence. Existing animosities were made more severe by the Emancipation Proclamation. Anti-war Democrats told white workers that the freed slaves would all come north and take their jobs. In 1863, when the Conscription Act was passed, Democrats like mayoral candidate Fernando Wood predicted that Republicans would bring in freedmen to take draftees' jobs while they were away fighting to end slavery. Yet the same men also predicted that the blacks would live lazily on public relief for which the whites would pay taxes.

Class antagonisms were deepened by a provision of the Conscription Act which allowed men to escape conscription by paying $300. In fact, it was resentment over this injustice that started the riot, which began as an assault on draft headquarters. The violence then quickly became directed to an attack on wealthy homes. The role played by ethnic hatreds is made clear by the fact that many of the rioters were Irish laborers, whereas many native American workers had no part in the riot.

The riot lasted three days. Rioters first destroyed the building in which draft headquarters were located, and then marched through the streets, forcing factories and shops to close and recruiting their workers. They cut telegraph lines and tore up railroad tracks. They defeated the first forces sent to oppose them, and mauled the Superintendent of Police almost to death. Now numbering in the thousands, the mob split into several groups. Some burned mansions, some were repulsed in an attack on the Mayor's house, some burned the colored orphan asylum. An armory on Second Avenue was captured, but many died there when it caught fire. The mob then launched an assault against the city officials, attacking Police Headquarters and fighting pitched battles with the police. As night fell, the mob increasingly turned its fury against blacks, burning, stomping, clubbing, hanging, shooting. On the second day, the mob fought militia armed with cannon. Barricades went up on Ninth Avenue. The Union Steam Works, with a large store of carbines, was seized by the mob, and burning and looting continued throughout the city. More army units were brought in on the third day, and howitzers filled with cannister and grapeshot cut down scores of rioters. Other mobs defeated militia detachments defending shipyards where navy ships were being built. By the fourth day, Union troops returning from Gettysburg were brought in and the riot was finally stopped. The number of casualties is uncertain: estimates have varied widely, from less than a score to as many as 1,000 or 1,200 persons killed or wounded. Numerous deaths were unreported or were attributed to causes other than riots. There were an unknown number of secret burials. The coroner's office stopped holding inquests, and the burial permit bureau was closed. Undetermined numbers of victims were thrown into the rivers and drowned. The number of victims was probably not less than 300, and may have been much higher. The black population of the city declined 20% between 1860 and 1865, from 12,472 to 9,945, because so many blacks left the city in terror.

There were riots in many Northern cities—Newark, Jersey City, Troy, Boston, Toledo, Evansville, among others—during the war, often stirred up by the draft and by racial issues, though none was as bloody as New York's.

Three accounts of the New York riot follow. The first is taken from the official army record written by Captain H. R. Putnam of the Twelfth U.S. Infantry; the second is an account by B. Franklin Ryer of the New York City Police; both are printed in the appendix of Joel Tyler Headley: *The Great Riots of New York* (1873); third is a contemporary account of the fate of some of the rioters' black victims in David Barnes: *The Draft Riots in New York, July, 1863* (1863). See James McCague: *The Second Rebellion* (1968); Albon P. Man: "Labor Competition and the New York Draft Riots of 1863," *Journal of Negro History*, XXXVI (October 1951), 375-405; and *The Bloody Week! Riot, Murder and Arson* (1863).

I — PUTNAM
Operations on Thursday evening

About six o'clock P.M., General Dodge and Colonel Mott informed General Brown, that the troops at Grammercy Park had marched down Twenty-second Street, and been attacked by an armed mob; that they had been driven back, leaving their dead in the street. The general ordered me to take my company, and a portion of the Twentieth and Twenty-eighth New York volunteer batteries, about eighty men, armed as infantry, commanded by Lieutenant B. F. Ryer. Lieutenant Ryer had with him Lieutenant Robert F. Joyce and Lieutenant F. M. Chase, Twenty-eighth New York battery. My whole command amounted to one hundred and sixty men.

With this force I marched to the Grammercy Hotel. At a short distance from the hotel, I saw some of the rioters fire from a house on some of Colonel Mott's command. I immediately sent Lieutenant Joyce with a few men to search the house. The search was fruitless, the men having escaped to the rear. I then told the women in the house that the artillery would open on the house, if any more shots were fired from it. We then marched down Twenty-second Street, between Second and Third Avenues, found the body of a sergeant of Davis' Cavalry, who had been killed two hours before. I ordered a livery-stable keeper to put his horses to a carriage, and accompany me, for the purpose of carrying the dead and wounded. He replied that the mob would kill him if he did, and that he dare not do it. He was informed that he would be protected if he went, but if he refused he would be instantly shot. The horses were speedily harnessed, and the body put into the carriage. The mob at this time commenced firing on us from the houses. We at once commenced searching the houses, while my skirmishers drove the rioters back from every window and from the roofs. The houses were searched from cellar to the roof. The mob made a desperate fight, and evidently seemed to think they could whip us. Every house that was used to conceal these rioters was cleared. A large number was killed, and several prisoners taken. We then marched to Second Avenue, where we found the mob in great force and concealed in houses. They fired on us from house-tops, and from windows, and also from cross streets. We soon cleared the streets, and then commenced searching the houses. We searched thirteen houses, killed those within that resisted, and took the remainder prisoners. Some of them fought like incarnate fiends, and would not surrender. All such were shot on the spot. The soldiers captured a large number of revolvers of large size, which I allowed them to keep. The mob at this place were well armed; nearly every one had some kind of fire-arms, and had one blunderbuss which they fired on us.

If they had been cool and steady, they might have done us great harm. As it was, they fired wildly, running to a window and firing, and then retreating back out of danger.

When my soldiers once got into a house they made short work of it. The fight lasted about forty minutes and was more severe than all the rest in which my company was engaged. There were none of my men killed. Sergeant Cadro, of company F, Twelfth Infantry (my own), was slightly wounded in the hand; private Krouse was also slightly wounded.

The mob being entirely dispersed, we returned to head-quarters.

II—RYDER

Sir:—I have the honor to transmit herewith, a report of the operations of my command during the period of the late riots in New York City.

Pursuant to orders from General Brown, I reported to him with my command, which comprised parts of the Twenty-sixth and Twenty-eighth batteries (numbering one hundred men, well armed and equipped, with rifles), on Tuesday, the 14th inst., at about 6 P.M. Immediately on report-ing, I received orders to march to Thirty-sixth Street and Second and Third Avenues, to recover the body of Colonel O'Brien, who had been killed in that neighborhood. On arriving there we found that the body had been removed, and no sign of the mob remaining. I immediately marched back to head-quarters in Mulberry Street, and reported the fact about twelve o'clock. I then marched my men through Grand Street, nearly to the ferry, and then backward and forward, through the various narrow streets in that part of the city, without being able to discover any disorderly persons. In this way I marched for four hours, and returned again to head-quarters, at four o'clock A.M., the 15th inst.

About seven o'clock, I again received orders to proceed to Thirty-second Street and Seventh Avenue, and quell the disturbance there at all hazards. I marched there through a heavy rain, and found a crowd of some two hundred or three hundred rioters, who had been engaged in hanging a negro. They immediately dispersed, without my having to fire a shot; I then repaired to the arsenal, Seventh Avenue, to obtain information where I could next meet the mob. I was ordered by General Sandford to march my command inside the lines of his "videttes" and outer pickets. I was then ordered to march to Thirty-second Street and Seventh Avenue, and quell the disturbance, which had broken out anew—the mob trying to break into a house in which a number of negro families had taken refuge. I dispersed the mob, and brought the negroes, some fourteen in number, into the arsenal. I then placed one half of my command across Seventh Avenue and Thirty-second Street, and while in this position, the mob made a rush up the avenue, but were promptly met by two volleys of musketry from my command, when they retired with considerable loss. Soon after one of the rioters endeavored to wrest the musket from the hands of one of my sentries, but received the contents instead. During the time I was engaged with the rioters in Seventh Avenue, Lieutenant Robert F. Joyce, in command of the second platoon, received information that a large number of muskets were concealed in a house on Thirty-second Street, near Broadway, and taking fifteen men from his command, proceeded to the house, and overcoming all the obstacles that were thrown in his way, succeeded in taking seventy-three Enfield rifles with accoutrements; and placing them on a cart brought them to the arsenal, although he was threatened by 500 men in the streets. About four o'clock, information reached me that a large mob had collected in Forty-second Street, between Tenth and Eleventh Avenues, and were endeavoring to burn the buildings in that neighborhood. I immediately marched my command, numbering about fifty men (the remainder being on guard near the arsenal), to the scene of the disturbance; on arriving in Forty-second Street, between Ninth and Tenth Avenues, we were saluted with groans, hisses, etc., and when at the corner of Tenth Avenue, received a storm of bricks, and missiles of every description, and shots from the roofs and windows of the buildings.

Wheeling the platoons right and left, I formed them so as to sweep the streets and avenue in all directions. I advised the mob to disperse in one minute, or I would fire, there being 2,000 men at least. A few of them moved away, but the greater part remained, when I ordered my troops to fire, and had to fire at least five volleys before I could disperse the mob; when they again commenced firing on us from the windows, and house-tops; one shot fired on us from the windows came near depriving us of a man, as the ball grazed his head, but terminated in nothing serious. I then ordered Lieutenant F. M. Chase to take ten men, and search the houses from top to bottom, which he immediately did, and captured two prisoners. I succeeded finally in clearing the streets and closing the houses, and I remained on the ground as long as there was any necessity for a force there. I then started for the arsenal, but had not progressed more than half a block, when the mob, who had been joined by another crowd of rioters, made a rush up the street, as if to overpower my force. I allowed them to approach very close, with the impression that I was falling back, when I suddenly halted my command, and faced the second platoon to the rear, and fired two more volleys into them. They immediately dispersed, and I was informed it was their last gathering in that locality. There were at least fifty killed, and a large number wounded, and I marched off with my command, without hardly a scratch. Having delivered our prisoners over to the authorities at the Twentieth Precinct station-house, I again returned to the arsenal, and after a slight disturbance there, in which I arrested two of the rioters, I had the privilege of a few minutes rest.

III—BARNES

James Costello (colored).—James Costello, No. 97 West Thirty-third Street, killed on Tuesday morning, July 14th. Costello was a shoemaker, an active man in his business, industrious and sober. He went out early in the morning upon an errand, was accosted, and finally was pursued by a powerful man. He ran down the street; endeavored to make his escape; was nearly overtaken by his pursuer; in self-defence he turned and shot the rioter with a revolver. The shot proved to be mortal; he died two days after. Costello was immediately set upon by the mob. They first mangled his body, then hanged it. They then cut down his body and dragged it through the gutters, smashing it with stones, and finally burnt it. The mob then attempted to kill Mrs. Costello and her children, but she escaped by climbing fences and taking refuge in a police station-house.

Abraham Franklin (colored).—This young man, who was murdered by the mob on the corner of Twenty-seventh Street and Seventh Avenue, was a quiet, inoffensive man, of unexceptionable character. He was a cripple, but supported himself and his mother, being employed as a coachman. A short time previous to the assault, he called upon his mother to see if anything could be done by him for her safety. The old lady said she considered herself perfectly safe; but if her time to die had come, she was ready to die. Her son then knelt down by her side, and implored the protection of Heaven in behalf of his mother. The old lady said that it seemed to her that good angels were present in the room. Scarcely had the supplicant risen from his knees, when the mob broke down the door, seized him, beat him over the head and face with fists and clubs, and then hanged him in the presence of his parent. While they were thus engaged the military came and drove them away, cutting down the body of Franklin, who raised his arm once slightly and gave a few signs of life. The military then moved on to quell other riots, when the mob returned and again suspended the now probably lifeless body of Franklin, cutting out pieces of flesh, and otherwise shockingly mutilating it. . . .

William Jones (colored).—A crowd of rioters in Clarkson Street, in pursuit of a negro, who in self-defence had fired on some rowdies, met an inoffensive colored man returning from a bakery with a loaf of bread under his arm. They instantly set upon and beat him and, after nearly killing him, hung him to a lamp-post. His body was left suspended for several hours. A fire was made underneath him, and he was literally roasted as he hung, the mob reveling in their demoniac act. . . .

———— Williams (colored).—He was attacked on the corner of Le Roy and Washington Streets, on Tuesday morning, July 14th, knocked down, a number of men jumped upon, kicked, and stamped upon him until insensible. One of the murderers knelt on the body and drove a knife into it; the blade being too small he threw it away and resorted to his fists. Another seized a huge stone, weighing near twenty pounds, and deliberately crushed it again and again on to the victim. A force of police, under Captain Dickson, arrived and rescued the man, who was conveyed to the New York Hospital. He was only able to articulate "Williams" in response to a question as to his name, and remained insensible thereafter, dying in a few days.

New Orleans
1866

Southern whites were not prepared to accept the revolutionary social changes implicit in emancipation. With the concurrence of Andrew Johnson's administration, they tried to restore, in whatever form they could, the pre-war economic, social, and racial order. In Louisiana, the Constitutional Convention of 1864 allowed only whites to vote, so that ex-Confederates won the state elections of 1865 on a platform of suppression of the blacks. As the Democrats avowed in their 1865 platform, "We hold this to be a Government of the White People, made and to be perpetuated for the exclusive political benefit of the White Race." After taking control, the Democrats enacted the Black Codes, which reduced the black man to virtual peonage. Radicals realized that to remain politically viable they must enfranchise the Negroes and disfranchise the ex-Confederates. By a process of dubious legality, they reconvened the 1864 Convention in the Mechanics Institute in New Orelans, on July 30, 1866. Crowds of bitter whites and jubilant blacks gathered outside. In the course of the hot afternoon, a white newsboy baited a black into shooting at him. Instead of arresting the Negro, the police began shooting at all the assmbled blacks. The whites then furiously assaulted the Hall; what happened there is described in the following account by a radical who was there. By the time federal troops arrived, 38 men were dead and 146 wounded. The event was among those exploited by Northern radicals to gain control of Congress in the 1866 elections, and take over the direction of Reconstruction in 1867.

The following testimony of J. D. O'Connell, a state Senator of Louisiana in 1864 and 1865 was given to a Congressional Committee investigating the riot (printed as H.R. No. 16, Thirty-Ninth Congress, Second Session, 77-9). See also Donald

E. Reynolds: "The New Orleans Riot of 1866 Reconsidered,"
Louisiana History, V (1964), 5–27.

As I entered the hall I found the convention, in accordance with the proclamation of the president *pro tem.*, Judge Howell, had assembled, or rather a portion of them had assembled. As I entered I found the Rev. Mr. Horton offering prayer. There was a large number of spectators. I was invited within the bar by some of my acquaintances, members of the convention. I remained until a resolution was presented by Mr. Cutler, I think, that the sergeant-at-arms be despatched to notify absent members to come in. Subsequently he introduced another resolution to take a recess for half an hour or an hour—my recollection does not serve me which—until the sergeant-at-arms could notify members to appear. Immediately after this I heard what appeared to be music on the street. I went to one of the windows, looked out, and saw a crowd of people advancing towards the hall. It appeared to be a small procession. They had a United States flag at their head and a few brass instruments, pieces of music. When I first saw this I understood there was considerable excitement. I heard considerable noise in the street. Immediately afterwards the head of the procession entered the hall where the convention was to meet, and deposited their flag and instruments in the hall. I asked some gentlemen in regard to the nature of the procession, and was informed by the sergeant-at-arms that at a mass meeting held on the 27th—three days previous—the flag belonging to the hall had been taken away, and he supposed they were returning that flag. I heard some shots fired in the direction of Canal Street about that time, and saw people retreating towards Common Street. As the mass of people were retreating towards Common Street they came in view from the windows of the hall. I saw a policeman follow the crowd and discharge his revolver towards them. The people on the street were principally colored, and they took possession of a pile of brickbats on the street, quite close to the hall, and commenced firing them at the police and citizens acting with them, who were shooting their revolvers towards the negroes. As the crowds were driven further back towards Common Street I saw two colored men have long pistols, which appeared to be horse-pistols, and discharge them towards the police. These were the only arms I saw discharged toward the police. The police became very numerous about this time. I suppose there were no less than 2,000 police and citizens who assembled to attack this crowd of colored people. The colored people defended themselves until they were driven on towards

Common Street. They then rallied again, and drove the police towards Canal Street. I believe they drove each other first towards Common and then towards Canal Street twice or three times, when the colored people were dispersed. During this time some shots were fired at the hall from the street by people coming from the direction of Canal Street. I saw there was danger that they would enter the building; I called upon Mr. Mollere, and asked him to assist me in closing the windows. The windows on both sides of the hall are so located (the building standing alone) that persons standing on Dryades Street could fire obliquely through them. The crowd outside became very threatening, and commenced firing into the windows. It consisted of police in uniform and others with badges; some having white handkerchiefs around their necks, some with blue ribbons in their button-holes, and some with a sleeve tied up. I recognized these marks distinctly. It is usual at large fires, and other places where difficulties are likely to occur, for persons to identify each other in this way, by buttoning up their coats, and tying a white handkerchief round their neck or round the arm. Mr. Mollere assisted me in putting the windows down. By this time the firing became so dangerous that I found that for my own safety I had to quit the windows. The crowd of negroes was driven up to Common Street, and then the mob driving them returned in the direction of the hall, placing themselves in front, on the steps of the Medical College, which is situated on the Common Street side of the hall, some on sheds, in the yard of that building, and on the fence, while others took position on the fences, sheds, and door steps of the houses in that vicinity on Canal Street. The only protection for the people within the hall was to get in the shade of the masonry between the windows, and to lie flat on the floor, which some did to avoid the firing, which came through the windows. At times I could see where bullets entering the hall would knock against the wall on the opposite side. The crowd continued firing on both sides into the hall in this way for perhaps ten or fifteen minutes before they attempted entering the building. Those who at first attempted to defend the building rushed terror-stricken up stairs. The first rush up stairs was made by the police and citizens, who fired upon the occupants of the hall without asking them to surrender or giving them any opportunity to. Some went into the middle of the hall and fired at the men who lay on the floor, which was very thick with men who had found it necessary to their safety to lie down. Persons lying right alongside me were shot by the police, and I saw that it was no more safe there than to stand. I got up, and advanced upon the door. About the same time Mr. Fish and Mr. Horton advanced to the door. At this time a policeman levelled his pistol at me and fired, but the ball did not hit me. I asked Mr. Horton not to come to the door. He was holding a white handkerchief, and asking the men for God's sake not to murder them, saying they were not armed. I lost sight of Mr. Fish about this time, and I presume he went out. Mr. Horton returned, and showed me where he had been wounded in the arm. I advised him to find Dr. Hire, and have the blood stanched, or the ball extracted if necessary. I remained until the third attack. During this time the crowd of people in the room advanced upon the platform, and attempted to get out through the president's room, a small ante-room situated at the side of the stage, but the entire space at the side of the building had been taken possession of by this crowd, and they found there was no exit. Several who were fool-hardy enough to jump fell among this crowd, and of course were killed before they could get over the fence. I looked through the windows, and saw the people on the fences with their revolvers, waiting to shoot anybody who would show themselves, and I saw the police shoot many colored people who attempted to escape. The second attack they entered again, and the police came up to negroes and white men, indiscriminately taking no prisoners, but shooting them as rapidly as possible. I saw one policeman, while a negro was kneeling before him and begging for mercy, shoot into his side. I saw another discharge his revolver into a negro lying flat on the floor. All this time I was anxiously hoping the military would arrive and quell the riot, and allow those in the hall to get away, either as prisoners taken to jail or otherwise. I had no choice. I would as soon have gone to jail, protected, as anywhere, although I was simply a spectator. There was no hope, however, that the military would arrive soon, and I suggested that we barricade the hall, and hold it until the military should come. It was the only chance we had. I succeeded in getting the chairs placed against the doors. The doors, however, opened into the lobby, and the fastenings outside were very soon torn off. We had no protection except the chairs, and they constituted very little, as it was easy to fire through between them. The police made another attack, and entered the hall, when those inside took the chairs and drove them out, and this they did two distinct times. On the fifth attack they entered again, headed by an officer who seemed to be a sergeant, from his uniform. He came to the door with a white handkerchief, opened it suddenly and waved his handkerchief. I supposed they had become human again, and that this meant that they were willing to give us protection. I went to the door and found Mr. S. S. Fish in the hall close by the door. I asked him to assist us in taking the chairs away. I spoke to this policeman and asked him if they meant to give us protection against the mob, who would kill us. He said "Yes, we'll protect you." I asked him if he was serious about it to let me have his hand, which he did. I, of course, had confidence then that he would do as he said, and afford us protection. I pulled the chairs down and drove the colored people from the door, so that their presence should not provoke the police to any further acts of violence. They very submissively went toward the other end of the hall. As the police entered the hall, one in the rear of the one I had spoken to advanced, calling out, "Yes, you G—d d——d sons of bitches, we'll protect you." I had no confidence that they would protect us, but when they entered the hall, even this man who had tendered me his hand rushed forward with the others, discharging their pistols indiscriminately. One of the police, pointing his pistol towards me, said, "So you will surrender, you G—d d——d son of a bitch," and discharging his revolver towards my head, said, "Take that and go to hell, will you?" I was standing close to him, and had the presence of mind to throw up his hand, and the ball passed through my hat both in front and rear. I retired towards the door, and another policeman approached me with a long knife and struck at me. I defended myself against him with the leg of a chair and got back into the room. Those inside again rallied with broken chairs and whatever they could get hold of, and drove the police out. I suppose this was about twenty-five minutes of three o'clock. The fight had gone on continuously up to this time. I assisted in driving them out, and followed them to the top of the stairs. As I returned to the room again, the stairs being from ten to twenty feet distant, I found the doors shut and held against me, so that I had to remain in the lobby. If any of you have visited the buidling, you will recollect that the stairs are so situated that a person coming up them could not perceive a man standing in the lobby until nearly at the top. I thought it best to make as good an effort as possible to get down stairs, though I had no hope of escaping. When I found the crowd had again nearly reached the top of the stairs, seeing a vacancy near the foot of them, I jumped, and I suppose those persons below, not understanding what it meant, or thinking I was one of themselves, became panic-stricken. They went out and carried me along with them without knowing who I was. As I got on to the street I saw a line of police standing like soldiers across Dryades Street, towards Canal Street. Parties would leave their positions, go to the sides of the building and fire their revolvers into the hall. I went to two of them and tried to get their numbers, so that I could know who they were, but their hat-bands, on which they wore the letters "police" and the number, were turned wrong side out. I then spoke to them, and told them if they wanted anything of the people in the hall why not enter the room like men; that it was cowardly to shoot into a building that way. Two of them left, but eight or ten of them kept on discharging their revolvers. I then left and went down Canal and St. Charles Streets to General Baird's headquarters. I informed him that I had just left the hall and of the position of affairs there, and asked him, for God's sake, to send the military. He said he would as soon as they arrived. I tried to impress upon him the necessity of immediate action. He told me he could do nothing until the military should come, and told me very sharply that he understood his business. I of course left his headquarters. I went home, changed my clothes, and in the course of half or three quarters of an hour went down Canal Street again and found the military just coming out and taking position in the streets. That was about all that I saw.

Vicksburg
1874

The Reconstruction era was the bloodiest period of American civil violence, as whites acted to reverse their military defeat by multiple acts of civil violence directed against blacks and their allies, the so-called carpetbaggers and scalawags. Almost immediately after Appomattox, violence began. Defeated Confederates engaged in sporadic guerilla activities, lynching, and terrorism, and sometimes in riots. One of the first big riots was in May 1866, when Memphis whites shot, beat, robbed, and raped blacks and burned Negro schools, churches, and homes. At Laurens, South Carolina, in October 1870, thirteen people were killed and several hundred wounded. In Arkansas there was outright rebellion in 1868, as whites closed down the courts, overpowered and assassinated civil authorities, and shot hundreds of blacks. In Texas, according to a United States attorney, a thousand blacks a year were killed from 1868 to 1870, "mostly from political hatred of the race." In Louisiana, General Philip Sheridan estimated that from 1866 to 1875, thirty-five hundred people, mostly blacks, were killed or wounded. In 1868 alone,

1,884 were killed and wounded. In addition to numerous riots in New Orleans, there were frightful massacres in rural areas. In 1873, in Colfax, at least sixty, possibly as many as two hundred, blacks were butchered. In a "nigger hunt" in Bossier parish in 1868, a hundred and sixty-two blacks died. Twenty-five to thirty were killed in Meridian, Mississippi, in 1871, and eighty were estimated to have been killed in the 1875 riots in and around Yazoo City, Mississippi.

Blacks did not suffer these attacks in silence. At the behest of Reconstruction governors, they formed militia companies in some areas, and in others organized informally to defend themselves. On numerous occasions armed bands of blacks fought whites. Indeed, it was these signs of resistance that stimulated the worst white violence. The Vicksburg riot of 1874 is one instance of black resistance and white retaliation. Trouble began when whites forced the black Republican sheriff, Peter Crosby, to surrender his office at gunpoint. Crosby rallied blacks to his defense, and on Monday, December 7, about 125 armed blacks marched into town. The terrified whites organized themselves into a militia and jailed Crosby. After a period of indecision, the blacks decided to return home, but as they were leaving the whites began chasing and shooting at them. After killing some of the blacks and scattering the rest, whites roamed the countryside lynching or shooting at least thirty blacks.

The following account is taken from a majority report of a Congressional Committee investigation, "Vicksburg Troubles," House of Representatives Report No. 265, 43rd Congress, 2nd Session, pages vii-ix. See Vernon Lane Wharton: *The Negro in Mississippi, 1865–1890* (1947); Joel Williamson: *After Slavery: The Negro in South Carolina During Reconstruction, 1861–1877* (1965); Kenneth M. Stampp: *The Era of Reconstruction, 1865–1877* (1965); Otis A. Singletary: *Negro Militia and Reconstruction* (1957); and W. E. B. DuBois: *Black Reconstruction* (1935).

About 3 o'clock in the morning of Monday, the 7th, the alarm was struck by the watchman on the court-house cupola, but it proved to be a false alarm. Between 7 and 8 the same watchman, E. D. Richardson, struck the alarm again, reporting that a considerably body of men were approaching on the Cherry Street road, information of whose approach was given by

Dr. Hunt. In a very short time the court-house square was filled by a large number of excited men, armed with all sorts of weapons.

Dr. O'Leary, the mayor of the city, put the city under martial law, and delegated supreme command over the armed citizens to Horace H. Miller, an officer of some experience on the confederate side in the late war. Why he did not give this command to some of the many State militia officers on the ground, such as Brigadier-General Furlong, Colonel Beaird, Colonel French, and others, it is impossible to say, further than that it is a just inference that it was given to Colonel Miller from his known and declared position in the white line.

On assuming command, Colonel Miller first seized upon Crosby as the probable chief of the movement, and placed him under guard at the court-house. He then detailed parties of mounted men to patrol Vicksburgh and drive all colored people off the streets—orders which were executed with extreme brutality, as will appear. Having thus secured his rear, this skillful officer moved out with a force of about eighty to one hundred well-armed men on Cherry Street, and soon confronted a body of colored men under Andrew Owens. Miller rode up where they had halted in a deep cut, on the brow of a hill, within the city limits, having first disposed his own force on the slope of the opposite hill, with a ravine and bridge between the two, and having advanced in due form a line of skirmishers to cover the bridge.

Owens, the leader of the blacks, informed Colonel Miller that they were coming in in obedience to an order from Crosby as sheriff. Miller stated that Crosby was captured and the party could do no good, but might receive much harm. Owens then demanded to see Crosby and take orders from him, and stated that he was willing to withdraw if Crosby said so. This request was granted by Miller, and Owens was escorted under guard to the court-house, where he saw Crosby and was told by him to go home.

On returning to his people, he informed Colonel Miller that he should take his men home, and they immediately proceeded to return by the way they came.

The Fleeing Negroes Fired Upon

It is clearly in testimony that they did so, and that no shot was fired by them. They retired, not in any military order, but in a confused and noisy group, about half a mile, when suddenly, and without any orders from any officer, fire was opened upon them by the whites. This fire appears to have commenced from some mounted men, who during the time of the parley had gained the flank of the colored people, but immediately became general, and was followed by a rush of all the whites who had proper arms, upon these unresisting and retreating men, who in good faith were carrying out the agreement.

There could not have been, at the outside, more than one hundred and twenty-five colored men in Owens's party, and of these, certainly not one-half armed with any weapon but a pistol, and many wholly unarmed, and none of them armed with weapons of effectiveness. It was no battle; it was a simple massacre, unutterably disgraceful to all engaged in it. The attack began without orders; your committee do not believe that Colonel Miller ever would have given such an order, but when it began, his undisciplined mob ran on entirely beyond his control.

In the language of one of the heroes of that day who fought in that bloody field, Mr. Cratcher, "There wasn't any danger, for we were firing with long-range gun at long range, and they with shot-guns or short-range guns."

The testimony of Richardson, their own watchman, who saw it all from the cupola of the court-house; the testimony of Franciola and Owens, and of Cratcher, proves that the body of colored people had left the ground with no intention of a fight when the carnage commenced, wholly and unnecessarily on the part of the whites.

To read the reports of the newspapers, or even to take the testimony of some of the participants, the passage of the bridge of Lodi was nothing to the fight on Cherry Street. To lead eighty or one hundred men under heavy fire down an exposed hill, to cross a bridge and storm the opposing height in the presence of a foe superior in numbers, is an exploit worthy of the heroic days of the republic, but the truth of history compels your committee to say that there was no enemy in sight or reach during the wonderful evolution, and, further, that no white man was killed or wounded, or in any danger except from the careless shooting of his own comrades. The black people on being fired upon scattered in all directions, singly or in groups of two or three, and occasionally returned an ineffectual fire.

The killing of these men, thus retiring in good faith, was murder, willful, cowardly, and in violation of all laws of peace or of war.

Eight or nine colored men were killed here, and about twenty rescued by Colonel Miller, and sent as prisoners, under escort, to the court-house.

The Affair at Pemberton Monument

Meanwhile, another alarm of approaching forces had been given. This time they came by the Jackson road. From the best judgment your committee can form, this affair occurred in this way: A portion of the men attacked and driven as before mentioned, on Cherry Street, crossed over to a point near the Pemberton monument. A mounted company of whites, known as Captain Hogin's, from the Yazoo River country, were coming in to help defend the city. With that curious inconsistency which seems to be part of their nature, they had left their wives, children, and property unprotected in a heavy black settlement, and gone to defend Vicksburgh, which was already armed to the teeth, against an imaginary invasion. This phenomenon can only be understood by the light of actual events as proof that no man believed in any actual danger to wife, children, or property, but was fully determined to use this outbreak as a means to political success, for these men who left their families and property unprotected to go to Vicksburgh were members of the people's club or white line. In carelessly approaching the city, one man, named Olli Brown, was shot from ambush, probably by some of the men so crully attacked a short time before on the Cherry-Street road. A rush was at once made on the spot, the actual murderers of Brown fled, and the mixed force of whites, part from the city and part of Hogin's command, fell upon another party, under command of Asberry, fired upon and routed them, killing several in the skirmish, but losing no men except Brown. . . .

But scenes far worse, far more painful, remain. . .

It is in evidence that the aids deputed by Colonel Miller ordered every colored man they met off the street, and that in so doing they shot three unresisting and unarmed men. And yet these men, who murdered these American citizens in cold blood on the streets of Vicksburgh, are men who by birth, education, and family relations stand high in society as now constituted in that city. Exaggerated statements of the peril of the city are telegraphed to all parts of the country; the Associated Press receives and distributes these false dispatches; and the whole country is ablaze with excitement over the "insurrection at Vicksburgh." Offers of aid to the people of the beleaguered city come back from all quarters, and on the same night of the seventh of December, one hundred and sixty armed men from Louisiana pour in to the rescue. We quote one telegram from Texas:

[*Telegram dated Trinity, Tex., December 12, 1874.
Received at Vicksburgh, December 12, 1874.*]

To President Board of Supervisors:

Do you want any men? Can raise good crowd within twenty-four hours to kill out your negroes.

J. G. GATES and
A. H. MASON

No longer law; no longer order. The city filled with men drunken with excitement, or worse; full of violence; full of unrestrained passion; that night of December 7 is a perfect carnival of released rascality. Decent people shut their doors and bar their windows, while the bad and dangerous element which exists in all cities, but especially in river towns, is thoroughly master of the situation.

Unauthorized searches by self-constituted authority into private houses; searches for arms converted, as is unusual, into robbery and thieving; insolent abuse of quiet people—all these wrongs are to be justly apprehended where neither the form nor the substance of law remains.

One poor old man, half crazed, but harmless, sitting quietly in a neighbor's house, is brutally shot to death in the presence of terrified women and shrieking children. He gained his wretched living by hunting and fishing, and had a shot-gun. No one pretended that Tom Bidderman had anything to do with the fight, but he was black, and had a gun in his house, and so they murdered him for amusement as they were going from the city to restore order in the country.

Patrols of mounted men, members of the people's clubs, traversed the settlements and executed their own hellish ideas of justice.

On that same Monday, after the sham fight was over, about noon, a party of five mounted men rode down to the house of Robert Banks, about two miles from Vicksburgh and off from the road. They dismounted and bade the old man hold their horses and went into the house. There were Mrs. Banks and five or six other frightened women, and young Robert Banks, a boy of eighteen. They asked the boy if he had any weapons, and he gave them a pistol which was in the house. Then they struck him, and, as he fled, pursued him through the house, and shot him to death. Returning, they came where the father still stood, holding their horses, ordered him to walk out to the front, and, in the presence of his family, deaf to the entreaties of the wife and mother, these cold-blooded assassins of the son, murdered the father also.

A poor old man, Mingo Green, very old and so decrepit that he was compelled to support his steps with a cane, a local exhorter of some note, chanced to meet a party of these patrols, and was put to death, and left lying in the road with the top of his head cut smooth off, or, as the witness expressed it, "the whole inside of his head showed white like a china bowl."

A man named Buck Worrell, peaceable and unoffending, living some eight miles from Vicksburgh, not accused, even, of any complicity in the difficulty, was on the Tuesday after chased by these patrols from his own house up to the house of Mr. Edwards, a white man for whom he worked, where he prayed protection of the ladies there present. Miss Martha Edwards, to whom he appealed, merely said that she did not want him killed in her yard. They respected the young lady's wishes, and took him into the road and shot him dead in the presence of his wife. This was done by Hebron's company, one of the people's clubs.

Handy Hilliard, in no way connected with the troubles, living quietly at home with his wife and children, near Vicksburgh, was murdered in cold blood.

Buck Ward was murdered on Tuesday, the 8th of December, at Mr. Wallis's plantation.

In the Yazoo beat, which is patrolled by Captain Hogin's company, of which Olli Brown is a member, when the funeral-procession was forming at the house, some negroes were seen at the bend of the road. Captain Hogin ordered two of his men to charge them. In so doing, one of the white men, William Vaughn, was killed. In revenge, as the committee suppose, for these two deaths of Brown and Vaughn, but some days after, three negro men, George Shephard, Joe Cook, and Emanuel Toales, were taken from their homes and families; they were shot, their throats cut, and their ears cut off, and their unburied bodies left to rot.

Other cases equally shocking to humanity were told to the committee, for which we must refer to the evidence, and your committee are forced to believe that a large part yet remains untold.

The case of Anthony Mack deserves some notice. This man was charged with commanding the party that killed Vaughn. A warrant was issued for him; he was arrested in Yazoo County, and delivered to two men, one of whom was Hogin, to be brought to Vicksburgh for trial. One the way these worthy officers of the law killed their prisoner, but the place and manner of his death are not known.

The Bodies of Murdered Negroes Neglected, etc.

From all the information before us, the committee find that in the whole affair two white men—Brown and Vaughn—appear to have been killed, and twenty-nine blacks more than half of whom were deliberately put to death in cold blood. How many more are missing and unaccounted for, lying in the cane, it is impossible to ascertain. One of the witnesses stated that we (the committee) never could find out; "but *we* watch where the buzzards hover, and there we find the dead men."

Wilmington
1898

In 1894 a fusion of Populists and Republicans ousted the Democrats from power in North Carolina. Increasing political activity among Negroes was a major source of Republican strength. In 1896 Republican Daniel Russell was elected Governor. Blacks began to receive some federal and state patronage: one was made Collector of Customs in Wilmington, some were made postmasters, others justices of the peace, school committeemen, and aldermen. In 1897, five were elected to the 165-member North Carolina House of Representatives.

In the campaign of 1898 the Democrats used quantities of inflammatory propaganda against "Negro domination." A vigilante group, the Red Shirts, which was organized that October, intimidated and killed blacks and threatened more violence on election day. Alfred M. Waddell, a noted Democrat, told whites: "Go to the polls tomorrow and if you find the negro out voting, tell him to leave the polls and if he refuses, kill him, shoot him down in his tracks. We shall win tomorrow if we have to do it with guns." On November 8, the Democrats won a decisive victory.

Two days later, on November 10, white citizens of Wilmington initiated a riot, first burning down the office of a Negro newspaper, then launching a general massacre of blacks. Estimates of the number killed range widely from 20 to over 100. The whites then deposed the Mayor, forced all Negro officials to resign, expelled all black political leaders, and instituted a new government at gun point. The state Assembly, now controlled by Democrats, completed the process of depriving Negroes of political power by such devises as a poll tax and a grandfather clause. The following reminiscence by Gunner Jessie Blake, a participant in the riot, affords an insight into the mentality of the white mobs. His account was recorded by a sympathetic listener, Harry Hayden, in *The Wilmington Rebellion* (1936),

1-21. See also Helen G. Edmonds: *The Negro and Fusion Politics in North Carolina, 1894–1901* (1951).

Smoke was curling languidly from the old pipe Gunner Jessie Blake puffed upon as he reclined in an easy chair in the dimly lit drawing room of his mansion amid the pines, "Woodley-on-the-Sound," where the aged Confederate veteran, survivor of both bombardments of nearby Fort Fisher in the North-South war, was entertaining two young veterans of the late World War. . . .

"You boys were too young to remember much about the Wilmington Rebellion, November 10, 1898," began Mr. Blake, an unreconstructed Rebel who to this day *holds that the South fought for Independence, not Slavery,* and who continues to use the ante- and post-bellum by-word, damnedyank, as a single word without even dignifying the appellation with a capital "D."

"So, I am going to give you the inside story of this insurrection," he proceeded, "wherein the white people of Wilmington overthrew the constituted municipal authority overnight and substituted a reform rule, doing all this legally and with some needless bloodshed, to be sure, but at the same time they eliminated the Negroes from the political life of the city and the state. This Rebellion was the very beginning of Negro disfranchisement in the South and an important step in the establishment of 'White Supremacy' in the Southland. . . .

"The Rebellion was an organized resistance," Mr. Blake said, "on the part of the white citizens of this community to the established government, which had long irked them because it was dominated by 'Carpet Baggers' and Negroes, and also because the better element here wished to establish 'White Supremacy' in the city, the state and throughout the South, and thereby remove the then stupid and ignorant Negroes from their numerically dominating position in the government. . . .

"The older generation of Southern born men were at their wits' end. They had passed through the rigors of the North-South war and through the tyrannies of Reconstruction when Confiscation (the latter the most hated word in the conquered Confederacy next to damnedyankee) of properties without due process of law, was the rule rather than the exception. They had seen 'Forty Acres and a Mule' buy many a Negro's vote.

"Black rapists were attacking Southern girls and women, those pure and lovely creatures who graced the homes in Dixie Land, and the brutes were committing this dastardly crime with more frequency while the majority of them were escaping punishment through the influence of the powers that be.

"These old Southern gentlemen had calculated that time and time only would remove the terrors of Reconstruction, a condition that was imposed upon the conquered Southerners by the victorious Northerners, but they were not willing to sit supinely by and see their girls and women assaulted by beastly brutes.

"The better element among the Northerners in the North could not want them and their little friends to grow up amid such conditions. . . .

" 'I do not want Southern girls growing into womanhood in fear of the Negro rapist.' "

"A group of nine citizens met at the home of Mr. Hugh MacRae and there decided that the attitude and actions of the Negroes made it necessary for them to take some steps towards protecting their families and homes in their immediate neighborhood, Seventh and Market Streets. . . .

"This group of citizens, who will hereafter be referred to as the 'Secret Nine,' divided the city into sections, placing a responsible citizen as captain in charge of each area, and they named Messrs. Lathrop and Manning as their contact men, who were the only ones of the 'Secret Nine' known to the divisional captains. . . .

"The better element planned to gain relief from Negro impudence and domination, from grafting and from immoral conditions; the 'Secret Nine' and the white leaders marked time, hoping something would happen to arouse the citizenry to concerted action.

"But the 'watch-and-wait policy' of the 'Secret Nine' did not obtain for long, as during the latter part of October (1898) there appeared in the columns of The Wilmington (Negro) Daily Record an editorial, written by the Negro editor, Alex Manly, which aroused a state-wide revulsion to the city and state administrations then in the hands of the Republicans and Fusionists. The editorial attempted to justify the Negro rape fiends at the expense of the virtue of Southern womanhood."

Mr. Blake walked over to the library table, stooped and picked up an old scrap book that was reposing on the table's shelf, and then he read the following obnoxious editorial from The Wilmington Record:

> Poor whites are careless in the matter of protecting their women, especially on the farm. They are careless of their conduct towards them, and our experience among the poor white people in the county teaches us that women of that race are not more particular in the matter of clandestine meetings with colored men, than are the white man and colored women.
>
> Meetings of this kind go on for some time until the woman's infatuation, or the man's boldness, bring attention to them, and the man is lynched for rape.

Every Negro lynched is called a "big, burly, black brute," when in fact, many of those who have been thus dealt with had white men for their fathers, and were not only not "black" and "burly," but were sufficiently attractive for white girls of culture and refinement to fall in love with them, as is very well known to all.

"That editorial," Mr. Blake declared with some vehemence as he banged the closed scrap book with his fist, "is the straw that broke Mister Nigger's political back in the Southland." . . .

"Excitement reigned supreme on election day and the day following," Mr. Blake said, adding that "the tension between the races was at the breaking point, as two Pinkerton detectives, Negroes, had reported to their white employers that the Negro women, servants in the homes of white citizens, had agreed to set fire to the dwellings of their employers, and the Negro men had openly threatened to 'burn the town down' if the 'White Supremacy' issue was carried in the political contest. The very atmosphere was surcharged with tinder, and only a spark, a misstep by individuals of either race, was needed to set the whites and the blacks at each other's throats.

"When Mr. Hugh MacRae was sitting on his porch on Market Street on the afternoon of the election, he saw a band of 'Red Shirts,' fifty in number, with blood in their eyes, mounted upon fiery and well caparisoned steeds and led by Mike Dowling, an Irishman, who had organized this band of vigilantes. The hot headed 'Red Shirts' paused in front of Mr. MacRae's home and the level headed Scotsman walked toward the group to learn what was amiss.

"Dowling told Mr. MacRae that they were headed for 'The Record' building to lynch Editor Manly and burn the structure. Mr. MacRae pleaded with Dowling and his 'Red Shirts' to desist in their plans. Messrs. MacRae, Dowling and other leaders of the 'Red Shirts' repaired across the street to Sasser's Drug store and there he, Mr. MacRae, showed them a 'Declaration of White Independence' that he had drawn up for presentation at a mass meeting of white citizens the next day.

"The 'Red Shirts' were finally persuaded by Mr. MacRae to abandon their plans for the lynching, but only after Mr. MacRae had called up the newspapers on the telephone and dictated a call for a mass meeting of the citizens for the next morning. . . .

"A thousand or more white citizens, representative of all walks of life from the minister to the merchant, the mariner to the mendicant, attended the mass meeting in the New Hanover county court house the next morning, November 10, at 11 o'clock.

"Colonel Alfred Moore Waddell, a mild mannered Southern gentleman, noted for his extremely conservative tendencies, was called upon to preside over the gathering. In addressing this meeting, Colonel Waddell said: . . . 'We will not live under these intolerable conditions. No society can stand it. We intend to change it, if we have to choke the current of Cape Fear River with (Negro) carcasses!' "

"*That* declaration," Mr. Blake said, "brought forth tremendous applause from the large gathering of white men at the mass meeting. His speech, other than the two paragraphs I have just quoted, was largely a statement of facts, but he was a silver tongued orator and the crowd cheered this distinguished white haired and bearded Southern gentleman throughout the course of his address." (He was as much respected by the Negroes as he was admired by the whites; his character was unimpeachable.)

"Colonel Waddel, in concluding his address, announced that he heartily approved the set of resolutions which had been prepared by Mr. Hugh MacRae and which included the latter's 'Declaration of White Independence.'

"These resolutions were unanimously approved by the meeting, followed by a wonderful demonstration, the assemblage rising to its feet and cheering: 'Right! Right! Right!' and there were cries of 'Fumigate' the city with 'The Record' and 'Lynch Manly.' "

Mr. Blake then read the resolutions from the scrap book, as follows:

Believing that the Constitution of the United States contemplated a government to be carried on by an enlightened people; believing that its framers did not anticipate the enfranchisement of an ignorant population of African origin, and believing that those men of the state of North Carolina, who joined in framing the union, did not contemplate for their descendants subjection to an inferior race.

We, the undersigned citizens of the city of Wilmington and county of New Hanover, do hereby declare that we will no longer be ruled and will never again be ruled, by men of African origin.

This condition we have in part endured because we felt that the consequences of the war of secession were such as to deprive us of the fair consideration of many of our countrymen. . . .

"Armed with a Winchester rifle, Colonel Waddell ordered the citizens to form in front of the Armory for an orderly procession out to 'The Record' plant, which was located in 'Free Love Hall,' on Seventh between Nun and Church Streets.

"As this band of silent yet determined men marched up Market Street it passed the beautiful colonial columned mansion, the Bellamy home. From the balcony of this mansion, a Chief Justice of the United States Supreme Court, Salmon P. Chase, delivered an address shortly after Lincoln's tragic assassination, advocating Negro suffrage and thereby sowing the seeds that were now blossoming forth into a white rebellion.

"The printing press of 'The Record' was wrecked by the maddened white men, who also destroyed other equipment, and the type that had been used in producing the editorial that had reflected upon the virtue and character of Southern womanhood was scattered to the four winds by these men, who stood four-square for the virtue of their women and for the supremacy of the white race over the African.

"Some lamps that had been hanging from the ceiling of the plant were torn down and thrown upon the floor, which then became saturated with kerosene oil; and then a member of the band struck a match, with the result that the two-story frame building was soon in flames.

"The leaders and most of the citizens had designed only to destroy the press," Mr. Blake averred, adding philosophically: "all of which proves that a mob, no matter how well disciplined, is no stronger than its weakest link.

"The crowd of armed men, which had destroyed the plant and building of the nefarious Wilmington (Negro) Daily Record, dispersed, repairing peacefully to their respective homes," Mr. Blake said, continuing his narrative:

"But in about an hour the tension between the two races broke with the shooting of William H. (Bill) Mayo, a white citizen, who was wounded by the first shot that was fired in the Wilmington Rebellion as he was standing on the sidewalk near his home, Third and Harnett Streets. Mayo's assailant, Dan Wright, was captured by members of the Wilmington Light Infantry and the Naval Reserves after he had been riddled by 13 bullets. Wright died next day in a hospital.

"Then the 'Red Shirts' began to ride and the Negroes began to run. . . . The Africans, or at least those Negroes who had foolishly believed in the remote possibility of social equality with the former masters of their parents, began to slink before the Caucasians. They, the Negroes, appeared to turn primal, slinking away like tigers at bay, snarling as they retreated before the bristling bayonets, barking guns and flaming 'Red Shirts.'

"Six Negroes were shot down near the corner of Fourth and Brunswick Streets, the Negro casualties for the day—November 11, 1898—totaling nine. One of these, who had fired at the whites from a Negro dance hall, 'Manhattan,' over in 'Brooklyn,' was shot 15 or 20 times. A member of this shooting party later exclaimed:

" 'When we tu'nd him ovah, Misto Niggah had a look o' s'prise on his face, I ashure ye!'

"One 'Red Shirt' said he had seen six Negroes shot down near the Cape Fear Lumber Company's plant and that their bodies were buried in a ditch. . . . Another 'Red Shirt' described the killing of nine Negroes by a lone white man, who killed them one at a time with his Winchester rifle as they filed out of a shanty door in 'Brooklyn' and after they had fired on him. . . . Another told of how a Negro had been killed and his body thrown in Cape Fear River after he had approached two white men on the wharf. . . .

"Other military units came to Wilmington to assist the white citizens in establishing 'White Supremacy' here, as follows: The Fayetteville (N.C.) Light Infantry, the Kinston division, Naval Reserves, Lieut. W. D. Pollock in command; the Maxton Guards, Captain G. B. Patterson, and the Sampson Light Infantry, Captain H. W. Hines commanding. Military organizations from as far South as New Orleans telegraphed offering to come here if their services were needed in the contest.

"When the Rebellion was in full blast 'The Committee of Twenty-five' appointed Frank H. Stedman and Charles W. Worth as a committee to call upon Mayor Silas P. Wright and the Board of Aldermen and demand that these officials resign. The mayor had expressed a willingness to quit, but not during the crisis. He changed his mind, however, when he saw white citizens walking the streets with revolvers in their hands. The Negroes, too, had suddenly turned submissive, they were carrying their hats in their hands. . . .

"African continued to cringe before Caucasian as the troops paraded the streets, as the guns barked and the bayonets flared, for a new municipal administration of the 'White Supremacy' persuasion had been established in a day! The old order of Negro domination over the white citizenry had ended."

Atlanta
1906

In the 1890's, the Populist movement divided Southern whites. Since both Populists and Democrats could at times use blacks against their opponents, the minimal political rights of blacks were maintained. When Populism declined, the reunited whites combined to eliminate the political power of blacks. Many states followed Mississippi, which in 1890 disfranchised Negroes. Leaders like Benjamin Tillman in South Carolina, Charles Aycock in North Carolina, and Hoke Smith in Georgia led movements against black voting rights. Racial feeling was intensified by such books as Charles Carroll's *The Negro a Beast*, Robert W. Shufeldt's *The Negro, A Menace to American Civilization*, and by the former Populist Tom Watson, who preached in Atlanta the superiority of the Aryan and the menace of Negro domination.

At the same time, the white press was treating black crime, especially assault and rape, in an inflammatory fashion and in 1906 this problem touched off a riot in Atlanta, Georgia. On Saturday, September 22, the papers printed extras about new assaults on white women. The Atlanta *News* ran five such editions with huge type proclaiming "Third Assault" and "Fourth Assault." In fact, of the twelve assaults alleged during the week before the riot, Ray Stannard Baker's investigation showed that two did occur and three were attempted, but the other seven were merely rumors. But the press was believed, and there was a wave of beatings and shootings of blacks. A peaceful Sunday was followed by a second outbreak on Monday when police in the suburb of Brownsville arrested Negroes who had armed themselves against further attack. At least twelve blacks were killed and over seventy wounded.

The following account is taken from the Atlanta *Constitution*, September 23, 1906. See Ray Stannard Baker: *Following* the *Color Line* (1908); W. E. B. DuBois: "The Atlanta Massacre," *The Independent*, LXI (October 4, 1906), 799-800; "The Atlanta Riots," *Outlook*, LXXXIV (November 3, 1906), 555-66; and Charles Crowe: "Racial Massacre in Atlanta, September 22, 1906," *Journal of Negro History*, LIV (April 1969), 150-73.

At 10 o'clock there were at least ten thousand men on the streets, and they were becoming more and more turbulent and bent on mischief.

It was about this hour when Mayor Woodward again begged the crowd to disperse and go home. They cheered him and returned to their business of chasing and beating negroes.

Will Drown Them Out

"I will drown them out," said the mayor.

He ran to the fire alarm box at the corner of Ivy and Decatur Streets and turned in the general alarm.

Soon the entire fire department, headed by Chief Joyner, was on the scene. The mayor explained to the chief what was up, and instructed him to lay hose all along Decatur Street from Ivy to Peachtree and to force the crowd back at the mouth of the nozzles.

In a few minutes the pipes were laid and the downpour of water caused the crowds to make a hasty retreat. They did this with a cheer and turned into the side streets.

In five minutes the mob had again formed at the corner of Edgewood avenue and Pryor Street, out of the reach of the water. Once more the chasing of negroes began.

Negroes were often advised by well intending white people not to force their way where the mob was holding sway, but many of them seemingly defiant kept on their way and they soon found that they would have fared better had they taken advice.

The mob, making a run from Edgewood Avenue into Peachtree, collected at the corner of Marietta, where they were again out of reach of water.

By this time there were no negroes in sight of the mob and it was passing the time away with yelling.

Then the trolley cars began to come in with Negroes on them. Had this but been foreseen and policemen sent out to meet the incoming cars to get the negroes off of them, the riot might have been checked in time. But this could not be foreseen, and when car No. 207, bound for Grant Park via Georgia Avenue, came down Edgewood Avenue and stopped at the corner of Marietta Street, the mob saw that it was half filled with negroes.

"Take them off. Kill them. Lynch them," came in shouts from the mob.

. . . The motor man put on speed, and for a moment it looked as though the negroes on the car would escape, and it could be seen that they looked less frightened. However, there was a delay of a second, and the next moment someone wrung the trolley off the wire and in the next instant the car windows were being smashed and white men were striking through the windows with sticks.

Someone gave an order for the trolley to be put on to furnish light, and when this flashed on a fierce battle was on between the whites and the blacks, some half dozen whites having entered the car with sticks. The negroes, incited by a negro woman who smiled while the fight was in progress, fought until overpowered and dragged off. Some were pulled through the windows, and the negro women were almost disrobed. The women were given a few cuffs on the head and allowed to escape, but each of the negro men received fearful beatings from sticks handled by the whites, some of whom were boys from 12 to 15 years old.

Five Negroes Escaped

After being severely beaten, five of the negroes escaped up side streets, but one, an 18-year-old negro named Evans, made a show of resistance, and time and again he was knocked down. With blood streaming from his head, he rose to his feet and made an effort to draw a knife, having struggled on and reached a point midway between Broad and Forsyth Streets at this time. That sealed his fate.

"He's trying to cut a white man," was the cry that went up, and as he broke away the crowd pursued him hotly. Once more he went down just at the corner of Forsyth and Marietta Streets, but again struggled to his feet and ran south down Forsyth Street. Just between Bluthenthal & Bickerts' side-door entrance and the barber shop he was overtaken, and this was his final stand. He was beaten again, and while he was struggling, surrounded by about twenty, he gave a groan and sank to the sidewalk. Before the crowd scattered the blood was running down the inclined sidewalk and he was dead within three minutes after he fell. . . .

A few seconds later a negro was dragged from a Marietta car, beaten, allowed to escape for a moment and then given chase as he entered on a wild run, leaving a bloody trail behind him, toward Forsyth Street. Just on the opposite side of the street from the main entrance to the post office, he was again surrounded on the pavement, and was thrown down.

"For God's sake have mercy on me, white folks," was the negro's despairing cry.

"We'll give you the same kind of mercy your kind gave white women," was the answer, and but a few moments elapsed before no sound was heard from that negro. . . .

One of the worst battles of the night was that which took place around the post office. Here the mob, yelling for blood, rushed upon a negro barber shop just across from the federal building.

"Get 'em, Get 'em all." With this for their slogan, the crowd, armed with heavy clubs, canes, revolvers, several rifles, stones and weapons of every description made a rush upon the negro barber shop. Those in the first line of the crowd made known their coming by throwing bricks and stones that went crashing through the windows and glass doors.

Hard upon these missiles rushed such a sea of angry men and boys as swept everything before them.

The two negro barbers working at their chairs made no effort to meet the mob. One man held up both his hands. A brick caught him in the face, and at the same time shots were fired. Both men fell to the floor. Still unsatisfied, the mob rushed into the barber shop, leaving the place a mass of ruins.

The bodies of both barbers were first kicked and then dragged from the place. Grabbing at their clothing, this was soon torn from them, many of the crowd taking these rags of shirts and clothing home as souvenirs or waving them above their heads to invite to further riot.

When dragged into the street, the faces of both barbers were terribly mutilated, while the floor of the shop was wet with puddles of blood. On and on these bodies were dragged across the street to where the new building of the electric and gas company stands. In the alleyway leading by the side of the building the bodies were thrown together and left there.

At about the same time another portion of the mob busied itself with one negro caught upon the streets. He was summarily treated. Felled with a single blow, shots were fired at the body until the crowd for its own safety called for a halt on this method and yelled, "Beat 'em up. Beat 'em up. You'll kill good white men by shooting."

By way of reply, the mob began beating the body of the negro, which was already beyond the possibility of struggle or pain. Satisfied that the negro was dead, his body was thrown by the side of the two negro barbers and left there, the pile of three of them making a ghastly monument to the work of the night, and almost within the shadow of the monument of Henry W. Grady.

East St. Louis
1917

The East St. Louis race riot was touched off by an influx of Southern blacks into what was already an industrial slum, short of housing, transit, and recreation facilities. But the pivotal issue was jobs. Many blacks had been imported by employers eager to drive down labor costs and to break strikes. A strike was called in April at an aluminum plant when union whites were fired and blacks hired in their places. Although the strike was crushed by a combination of militia, injunctions, and both black and white strikebreakers, the union blamed its defeat on the blacks. A union meeting in May demanded that "East St. Louis must remain a white man's town." A riot followed during which buildings were demolished and solitary blacks were attacked and beaten. Harassments and beatings continued through June.

On July 1, in the late evening, a group of whites in a Ford drove through the black district, shooting into homes. When the car made a second foray, the blacks fired back. The police sent a squad car, unfortunately also a Ford, to investigate. Thinking it was the same car, some Negroes fired on it again, killing two policemen. The next day, as reports of the shooting spread, a new riot began. Streetcars were stopped, blacks were pulled off, stoned, clubbed, kicked, and shot. Mobs thousands strong roamed the streets chanting: "Get a Nigger, get another." Most blacks were terrified into passivity, though at one point about a hundred armed men barricaded themselves in a building and defended themselves. In this instance, when the whites demanded that the militia protect them, the militia refused, instead gave safe-conduct out of the city to the embattled blacks. The official casualty figures were 9 whites and 39 blacks killed, hundreds wounded, but police estimated black deaths at 100. Over 300 buildings were destroyed. Four whites and eleven blacks were charged with homicide. All charges against the police (some of whom had abetted the riot) were dropped on condition that three policemen plead guilty to rioting. The officers drew lots to decide who would make the pleas, and the others paid the fines, a total of $150.

The account below was written by W. E. B. DuBois and Martha Gruening, who were commissioned by the NAACP to investigate. "Massacre at East St. Louis," *Crisis*, XIV (1917), 222-38. Many of the incidents they reported, and others as well, are included in the testimony taken by a Congressional Committee which investigated the riot: Report of the Special Committee authorized by Congress to Investigate the East St. Louis Riots, H. R. Doc. No. 1231, 65th Congress, 2nd Session (July 15, 1918). See Elliot M. Rudwick: *Race Riot at East St. Louis, July 2, 1917* (1964).

A Negro, his head laid open by a great stone-cut, had been dragged to the mouth of the alley on Fourth Street and a small rope was being put about his neck. There was joking comment on the weakness of the rope, and everyone was prepared for what happened when it was pulled over a projecting cable box, a short distance up the pole. It broke, letting the Negro tumble back to his knees, and causing one of the men who was pulling on it to sprawl on the pavement.

An old man, with a cap like those worn by street car conductors, but showing no badge of car service, came out of his house to protest. "Don't you hang that man on this street," he shouted. "I dare you to." He was pushed angrily away, and a rope, obviously strong enough for its purpose, was brought.

Right here I saw the most sickening incident of the evening. To put the rope around the Negro's neck, one of the lynchers stuck his fingers inside the gaping scalp and lifted the Negro's head by it, literally bathing his hand in the man's blood.

"Get hold, and pull for East St. Louis!" called a man with a black coat and a new straw hat, as he seized the other end of the rope. The rope was long, but not too long for the number of hands that grasped it, and this time the Negro was lifted to a height of about seven feet from the ground. The body was left hanging there. . . .

A Negro weighing 300 pounds came out of the burning line of dwellings just north and east of the Southern freight house. His hands were elevated and his yellow face was speckled with the awful fear of death.

"Get him!" they cried. Here was a chance to see suffering, something that bullets didn't always make.

So a man in the crowd clubbed his revolver and struck the Negro in the face with it. Another dashed an iron bolt between the Negro's eyes. Still another stood near and battered him with a rock.

Then the giant Negro toppled to the ground. "This is the way," cried one. He ran back a few paces, then ran at the prostrate black at full speed and made a flying leap.

His heels struck right in the middle of the battered face. A girl stepped up and struck the bleeding man with her foot. The blood spurted onto her stockings and men laughed and grunted.

No amount of suffering awakened pity in the hearts of the rioters. Mr. Wood tells us that . . . A few Negroes, caught on the street, were kicked and shot to death. As flies settled on their terrible wounds, the gaping-mouthed mobsmen forbade the dying blacks to brush them off. Girls with blood on their stockings helped to kick in what had been black faces of the corpses on the street.

The first houses were fired shortly after 5 o'clock. These were back of Main Street, between Broadway and Railroad Avenue. Negroes were "flushed" from the burning houses, and ran for their lives, screaming and begging for mercy. A Negro crawled into a shed and fired on the white men. Guardsmen started after him, but when they saw he was armed, turned to the mob and said:

"He's armed, boys. You can have him. A white man's life is worth the lives of a thousand Negroes."

A few minutes later matches were applied to hastily gathered debris piled about the corner of one of three small houses 100 feet from the first fired. These were back of the International Harvester Company's plant. Eight Negroes fled into the last of the houses and hid in the basement. When roof and walls were about to fall in, an aged Negro woman came out. She was permitted to walk to safety. Three Negro women followed and were not fired upon. Then came four Negro men, and 100 shots were fired at them. They fell. No one ventured out to see if they were dead, as the place had come to resemble No Man's Land, with bullets flying back and forth and sparks from the fires falling everywhere.

A Negro who crawled on hands and knees through the weeds was a target for a volley. The mob then burned back to Main Street and another Negro was spied on a Main Street car. He was dragged to the street and a rioter stood over him, shooting.

The crowd then turned to Black Valley. Here the greatest fire damage was caused. Flames soon were raging and the shrieking rioters stood about in the streets, made lurid by the flames, and shot and beat Negroes as they fled from their burning homes.

They pursued the women who were driven out of the burning homes, with the idea, not of extinguishing their burning clothing, but of inflicting added pain, if possible. They stood around in groups, laughing and jeering, while they witnessed the final writhings of the terror and pain wracked wretches who crawled to the streets to die after their flesh had been cooked in their own homes.

Mrs. Cox saw a Negro beheaded with a butcher's knife by someone in a crowd standing near the Free Bridge. The crowd had to have its jest. So its members laughingly threw the head over one side of the bridge and the body over the other.

A trolley-car came along. The crowd forced its inmates to put their hands out the window. Colored people thus recognized were hauled out of the car to be beaten, trampled on, shot. A little twelve-year-old colored girl fainted—her mother knelt beside her. The crowd surged in on her. When its ranks opened up again Mrs. Cox saw the mother prostrate with a hole as large as one's fist in her head. . . .

It was Mrs. Cox, too, who saw the baby snatched from its mother's arms and thrown into the flames, to be followed afterwards by the mother. This last act was the only merciful one on the part of the crowd.

Lulu Suggs is twenty-four years old, and has lived in East St. Louis since April. She tells of seeing children thrown into the fire. She says: "My house was burned and all the contents. My husband was at Swift's the night of the riot. I, with about one hundred women and children, stayed in a cellar all night, Monday night. The School for Negroes on Winstanly Avenue was burned to the ground. When there was a big fire the rioters would stop to amuse themselves, and at such time I would peep out and actually saw children thrown into the fire. Tuesday came and with that the protection of the soldiers. We escaped to St. Louis."

Testimony of Beatrice Deshong, age 26 years:

"I saw the mob robbing the homes of Negroes and then set fire to them. The soldiers stood with folded arms and looked on as the houses burned. I saw a Negro man killed instantly by a member of the mob, men, small boys, and women and little girls all were trying to do something to injure the Negroes. I saw a colored woman stripped of all of her clothes except her waist. I don't know what became of her. The police and the soldiers were assisting the mob to kill Negroes and to destroy their homes. I saw the mob hang a colored man to a telegraph pole and riddle him with bullets. I saw the mob chasing a colored man who had a baby in his arms. The mob was shooting at him all of the time as long as I saw him. I ran for my life. I was nearly exhausted when a white man in the block opened the door of his warehouse and told me to go in there and hide. I went in and stayed there all night. The mob bombarded the house during the night, but I was not discovered nor hurt. The mob stole the jewelry of Negroes and used axes and hatchets to chop up pianos and furniture that belonged to them. The mob was seemingly well arranged to do their desperate work. I recognized some of the wealthy people's sons and some of the bank officials in the mob. They were as vile as they could be."

Chicago
1919

During World War I Southern blacks moved in great numbers to Northern cities, in part because of the wartime demand for labor. Between 1916 and 1919 Chicago's black population doubled, and the ghetto district pushed toward white territory. Whites, many of them also recent Southern migrants, resented this "intrusion" on their living space and their jobs. While the war boom lasted, the races lived in uneasy peace, clashing only occasionally at the boundary line between their districts. But the end of the war brought a decline in jobs, a rash of strikes, and the frequent use of blacks as strike-breakers. It also brought a new Negro militancy, particularly among returning veterans who had been treated as equals in European cities. The day before the riot, the last of the returning black troops paraded down Michigan Avenue. Tension in Chicago rose during the summer of 1919, during which many blacks were molested, attacked, or killed. Twenty-four black houses were bombed in June and July. At best the Chicago police were of no help to the blacks, and they soon lost confidence in the protection of the law.

On July 27th a Negro youth swimming in Lake Michigan floated past the imaginary boundary line which separated a "white" from a "black" beach. He was stoned, and drowned, but the police refused to arrest his white assailants—indeed, they arrested a Negro on a white complaint. A bloody riot was then touched off which ended seven days later; 23 blacks and 15 whites died, over 500 were injured, and about 1,000 left homeless. Major race riots also occurred that year in Charleston, South Carolina, Long View, Texas, Washington, D.C., Knoxville, Tennessee, and Omaha, Nebraska.

The following account appeared in the Chicago *Defender*, a Negro paper, on August 2, 1919. On the Chicago Riot, see Chicago Commission on Race Relations: *The Negro in Chicago* (1922); Arthur Waskow: *From Race Riot to Sit-In* (1966); and William M. Tuttle, "Labor Conflict and Racial Violence: The Black Worker in Chicago, 1894–1919," *Labor History*, X (Fall 1969).

For fully four days this old city has been rocked in a quake of racial antagonism, seared in a blaze of red hate flaming as fiercely as the heat of day—each hour ushering in new stories of slaying, looting, arson, rapine, sending the awful roll of casualties to a grand total of 40 dead and more than 500 wounded, many of them perhaps fatally. A certain madness distinctly indicated in reports of shootings, stabbings, and burning of buildings which literally pour in every minute. Women and children have not been spared. Traffic has been stopped. Phone wires have been cut. Victims lay in every street and vacant lots. Hospitals are filled: 4,000 troops rest in arms, among which are companies of the old Eighth Regiment, while the inadequate force of police battle vainly to save the city's honor.

Undertakers on the South Side refused to accept bodies of white victims. White undertakers refused to accept black victims. Both for the same reason. They feared the vengeance of the mobs without.

Every little while bodies were found in some street, alley, or vacant lot—and no one sought to care for them. Patrols were unable to accommodate them because they were being used in rushing live victims to hospitals. Some victims were dragged to a mob's "No Man's Land" and dropped.

The telephone wires in the raging districts were cut in many places by the rioters and it became difficult to estimate the number of dead victims.

Hospitals Filled with Maimed

Provident Hospital, 36th and Dearborn Streets, situated in the heart of the "black belt," as well as other hospitals in the surrounding districts, are filled with the maimed and dying. Every hour, every minute, every second, finds patrols backed up and unloading their human freight branded with the red symbol of this orgy of hate. Many victims have reached the hospitals, only to die before kind hands could attend to them. So pressing has the situation become that schools, drug stores and private houses are being used. Trucks, drays and hearses are being used for ambulances.

Monday Sees Reign of Terror

Following the Sunday affray, the red tongues had blabbed their fill, and Monday morning found the thoroughfares in the white neighborhoods throated with a sea of humananity—everywhere—some armed with guns, bricks, clubs and an oath. The presence of a black face in their vicinity was the signal for a carnival of death, and before any aid could reach the poor, unfortunate one his body reposed in some kindly gutter, his brains spilled over a dirty pavement. Some of the victims were chased, caught and dragged into alleys and lots, where they were left for dead. In all parts of the city, white mobs dragged from surface cars, black passengers, wholly ignorant of any trouble, and set upon them. An unidentified young woman and a 3 month old baby were found dead on the street at the intersection of 47th Street and Wentworth avenue. She had attempted to board a car there when the mob seized her, beat her, slashed her body into ribbons and beat the baby's brains out against against a telegraph pole. Not satisfied with this, one rioter severed her breasts, and a white youngster bore them aloft on a pole, triumphantly, while a crowd hooted gleefully. All the time this was happening, several policemen were in the crowd, but did not make any attempt to make rescue until too late.

Rioters operating in the vicinity of the stockyards, which lies in the heart of white residences west of Halsted Street, attacked scores of workers—women and men alike returning from work. Stories of these outrages began to flutter into the black vicinities and hysterical men harangued their fellows to avenge the killings—and soon they, infected with the insanity of the mob, rushed through the streets, drove high powered motor cars or waited for street cars, which they attacked with gunfire and stones. Shortly after noon the traffic south of 22d Street and north of 65th Street, west of Cottage Grove Avenue and east of Wentworth Avenue, was stopped with the exception of trolley cars. Whites who entered this zone were set upon with unmeasurable fury.

Policemen employed in the disturbed sections were wholly unable to handle the situation. When one did attempt to carry out his duty he was beaten and his gun taken from him. The fury of the mob could not be abated. Mounted police were employed, but to no avail.

35th Vortex of Night's Rioting

With the approach of darkness the rioting gave prospects of being continued throughout the night. Whites boarded the platforms and shot through the windows of the trains at passengers. Some of the passengers alighting from cars were thrown from the elevated structure, suffering broken legs, fractured skulls, and death.

The block between State Street and Wabash Avenue on East 35th Street was the scene of probably the most shooting and rioting of the evening and a pitched battle ensued between the police, whites and blacks.

The trouble climaxed when white occupants of the Angelus apartments began firing shots and throwing missiles from their windows. One man was shot through the head, but before his name could be secured he was spirited away. The attack developed a hysterical battling fervor and the mob charged the building and the battle was on.

Police were shot. Whites were seen to tumble out of automobiles, from doorways and other places, wounded or suffering from bruises inflicted by gunshot, stones or bricks. A reign of terror literally ensued. Automobiles were stopped, occupants beaten and machines wrecked. Streetcars operating in 35th Street were wrecked at will and north and south bound State Street cars' windows were shattered and white occupants beaten.

Trolley cars operating east and west on 35th Street were stopped, since they always left the vicinity in a perforated state. Shortly after 3 o'clock all service was dincontinued on 43rd, 47th and 51st streets.

Stores Looted; Homes Burned

Tiring of street fights, rioters turned to burning and looting. This was truly a sleepless night, and a resume of the day's happenings nourished an inclination for renewed hostilities from another angle. The homes of blacks isolated in white neighborhoods were burned to the ground and the owners and occupants beaten and thrown unconscious in the smouldering embers. Meanwhile rioters in the "black belt" smashed windows and looted shops of white merchants on State Street.

Other rioters, manning high powered cars and armed, flitted up and down the darkened streets, chancing shots at fleeting whites on the street and those riding in street cars.

Toward midnight quiet reigned along State Street under the vigilance of 400 policemen and scores of uniformed men of the 8th Regiment.

Tuesday dawned sorrowing with a death toll of 20 dead and 300 injured. In the early morning a thirteen-year-old lad standing on his porch at 51st and Wabash Avenue was shot to death by a white man who, in an attempt to get away, encountered a mob and his existence became history. A mounted policeman, unknown, fatally wounded a small boy in the 49th block of Dearborn Street and was shot to death by some unknown rioter.

Workers thronging the loop district to their work were set upon by mobs of sailors and marines roving the streets and several fatal casualties have been reported. Infuriated white rioters attempted to storm the Palmer house and the post office where there are large numbers of employees, but an adequate police force dispersed them and later the men were spirited away to their homes in closed government mail trucks and other conveyances. White clerks have replaced our clerks in the main post office temporarily and our men have been shifted to outlying post offices. The loop violence came as a surprise to the police. Police and reserves had been scattered over the South Side rioting district, as no outbreaks had been expected in this quarter. Toward noon stations therein were overwhelmed with calls.

Tulsa

1921

On May 31, 1921, a Tulsa Negro was accused of rape and arrested. Rumors of plans to lynch him raced through the city, but a group of armed blacks appeared at the jail to defend the would-be victim. When a gun fight broke out between them and the police, many whites went berserk. The blacks retreated to the ghetto district to defend themselves, while a small army of whites assaulted black neighborhoods. Held off at first by snipers, the whites, led by American Legionnaires, slowly gained ground. They set many fires, and repeatedly shot down blacks who attempted to escape the flames. Finally, martial law was declared, and black survivors were taken to detention camps for their safety. Almost the entire black district, one mile square, had been burned to the ground. Official counts list 85 men killed, 60 of them black, but O. T. Johnson, head of the Salvation Army, and director of a squad of black grave-diggers who buried the corpses and charred remains, declared that 150 had died.

The following account is taken from *The New York Times*, June 2, 1921. See Allen Grimshaw: "A Study in Social Violence: Urban Race Riots in the United States," unpublished doctoral dissertation, University of Pennsylvania, 1959; Loren L. Gill: "The Tulsa Race Riot," unpublished Master's essay, University of Tulsa, 1946; and Walter F. White: "Eruption of Tulsa," *Nation*, CXII (June 29, 1921), 909-10.

After twenty-four hours of one of the most disastrous race wars ever visited upon an American city, during which time eighty-five or more persons were killed and the Negro quarter of Tulsa comprising upward of thirty densely populated blocks, was wiped out by fire, the State militia had gained virtual control tonight and the rioting seems to have come to an end.

An official estimate early tonight was eighty-five of whom it was said twenty-five might be whites and sixty negroes. This followed a statement issued by Police Chief Daly, saying that he believed the probable ultimate to be 175, and that many persons lost their lives in the fires.

Events Developed Fast in the City's Day of Tragedy

Dick Rowland, a Negro, was arrested late yesterday afternoon, accused of assault upon a orphan white girl. He was taken to the Court House and lodged in jail on the upper floor.

Apparently rumors of an attempt to lynch him got about, for about 7 o'clock motor cars containing armed negroes appeared on the principal streets, headed for the Court House.

Thereupon armed white men also began to gather in the same neighborhood. Soon the streets were filled with shouting, gesticulating men.

The first shooting affray came soon after dark, when a negro was stopped by a police officer and his gun taken away. He attempted to resist, according to the officer, and was shot dead.

Meanwhile a great crowd of whites gathered about the Court House steps, nearly all of them being unarmed.

As the minutes passed, the white men obtained more guns and began to assume a belligerent attitude themselves. Finally a verbal altercation between the factions began. E. S. MacQueen, detective, attempted to intervene.

Suddenly a shot rang out and instantly the firing became general and the crowd scattered in haste, while armed negroes began training their guns on the fleeing forms. At least one white man was killed in this affray.

The negroes finally retreated slowly up Boulder Street, the alley back of the Court House, which is on Boston Street, firing as they went. When they emerged on Fourth Street hot skirmishes ensued.

A second white man was killed about this time, according to the police, when a party of whites, passing in a motor car mistook him for a negro, and shot him. He died almost instantly.

Guardsmen Rushed to Scene

Soon after the Court House outbreak the authorities realized their inability to control the mobs with police alone and at 11 o'clock a call was sent to Governor Robertson for troops.

The Governor promptly directed Adjt. Gen. Charles I. Barrett to take any steps necessary to handle the trouble. The Adjutant General ordered out three companies of guardsmen here and sent instructions to commanding officers in several nearby towns to be prepared to rush men here on immediate notice. The local guardsmen were thrown about the Court House to prevent the crowd from breaking through.

The mob in this vicinity was finally dispersed early in the morning without any shooting. Rowland, the negro prisoner, was spirited away from the jail early in the day by deputies from the office of Sheriff McCullough, who refused to divulge his whereabouts.

Armed Forces Face Each Other

Throughout the early morning hours 500 white men and a thousand negroes faced each other across the railroad tracks. It was reported early to Police Headquarters that the bodies of six to ten negroes could be seen lying in a space described as "no man's land." The police also had a report that three railway switchmen and a brakeman had been shot to death. The trainmen were killed, it was ·said, because they refused to permit members of the opposing crowds to ride upon a switch engine passing between the lines. The engineer was reported to have escaped.

Attempts by white rioters to burn the negro quarter began early and were persistent.

Incendiarism and a New Battle

As the dawn broke sixty or seventy motor cars filled with armed white men formed a circle around the negro section. Half a dozen airplanes circled overhead. There was much shouting and shooting. About this hour (6:30 o'clock) incendiarism by wholesale was resumed. Almost simultaneously fire began to burst forth from the doors and windows of frame shacks along Archer Street. Soon dense clouds of black smoke enveloped the location.

The invaders were apparently supplied with inflammables. According to the police they set off altogether more than 25 separate fires.

As the fire enveloped houses, negroes would dart out with upraised hands, shouting "Don't shoot!" As they dashed through the smoke they were ordered to surrender and were quickly removed to detention camps.

In an outbreak at 7:30 o'clock in the Stand Pipe Hill district in the extreme northern end of the negro quarters, Mrs. S. A. Gilmore, a white woman, was shot in the left arm and side. She was standing on the front porch of her home when she was shot by a negro. The heaviest fighting was in the northern section, where hundreds of negroes were concentrated in a valley. Fifty barricaded in a church.

Several massed attacks were launched against the church, but each time the attackers had to fall back on the fire of the negro defenders. Finally a torch was applied to the building and the occupants began to pour out, firing as they ran. Several of the negroes were killed.

Apparently the negroes were either expecting or preparing for trouble with the whites. In almost every second house burned there were explosions of boxes of shells. The police say that the I.W.W. and other malcontents had, been stirring up animosity between the blacks and whites for months. . . .

It was found necessary very early to establish detention camps for the negroes who had fled from the blazing section where they had been living.

Convention Hall was thrown open to accommodate the terrorstriken fugitives. Throughout the early morning long lines of negroes streamed westward along the streets leading to the hall. Many wore their night clothes and were barefooted. Their sunken eyes told of a sleepless night and their ashen faces bespoke gripping fear.

Men, women and children carried bundles of clothing on their heads and backs. The articles they saved were varied and in many cases would have been ludicrous but for the gravity of the situation. Here an old woman clung to a Bible, there a girl with dishevelled hair carried a wooly white dog under her arm and behind trotted a little girl with a big wax doll.

By 9 o'clock 2,000 negroes had been gathered at Convention Hall, all being under guard. Soon the edifice was filled, as was also the police station. The rest of those gathered up as fugitives or combatants were taken to the baseball park.

Detroit
1943

In 1941 the United States went to war with a segregated army and a white navy and air corps. Many Negroes seized upon wartime conditions and wartime ideology to launch their own campaign against discrimination: the black press and black organizations promoted a "Double V" campaign, victory abroad and at home. Numerous protests against discrimination climaxed in the threat of a Negro March on Washington, which was called off only when one of the primary objectives was attained in Roosevelt's Executive Order 8802, which banned discrimination in defense industries. In Detroit, where blacks had long been barred from the automobile unions, the UAW–CIO saw the need for changing this policy, particularly if the Ford plants were to be unionized. In April, 1941, many Negroes supported a strike against Ford, the only remaining open shop, and when the strike succeeded they were taken into the UAW by thousands.

These black advances produced a powerful reaction among whites. Housing, jobs, job seniority, and police conduct had long been serious issues in Detroit. They were now exacerbated by the activities of right wing agitators like Gerald L. K. Smith and Father Charles Coughlin and the quasi-fascist Black Legion, which engaged in a violent campaign of terrorism. On Sunday evening, June 20, 1943, a fight between a black and a white in an amusement park was followed by a series of rumors of atrocities against both white and black women. Then Detroit erupted. Blacks smashed, looted, and burned white stores, and were shot down by the police. Whites attacked blacks with iron pipes, clubs, rocks, and knives. When the riot was over, 34 people were dead, 25 of them blacks.

The account is from Thurgood Marshall: "The Gestapo in Detroit," *The Crisis*, L (August 1943), 232–3. See Alfred McClung Lee and Norman D. Humphrey: *Race Riot* (1943); Robert Shogan and Tom Craig: *The Detroit Race Riot: A Study in Violence* (1964); Harvard Sitkoff: "The Detroit Race Riot of 1943," *Michigan History*, LIII (Fall 1969); and Bernard Sternsher, ed.: *The Negro Depression and War* (1969).

Belle Isle is a municipal recreation park where thousands of white and Negro war workers and their families go on Sundays for their outings. There had been isolated instances of racial friction in the past. On Sunday night, June 20, there was trouble between a group of white and Negro people. The disturbance was under control by midnight. During the time of the disturbance and after it was under control, the police searched the automobiles of all Negroes and searched the Negroes as well. They did not search the white people. One Negro who was to be inducted into the army the following week was arrested because another person in the car had a small pen knife. This youth was later sentenced to 90 days in jail before his family could locate him. Many Negroes were arrested during this period and rushed to local police stations. At the very beginning the police demonstrated that they would continue to handle racial disorders by searching, beating and arresting Negroes while using mere persuasion on white people.

The Riot Spreads

A short time after midnight disorder broke out in a white neighborhood near the Roxy theatre on Woodward Avenue. The Roxy is an all night theatre attended by white and Negro patrons. Several Negroes were beaten and others were forced to remain in the theatre for lack of police protection. The rumor spread among the white people that a Negro had raped a white woman on Belle Island and that the Negroes were rioting.

At about the same time a rumor spread around Hastings and Adams Streets in the Negro area that white sailors had thrown a Negro woman and her baby into the lake at Belle Isle and that the police were beating Negroes. This rumor was also repeated by an unidentified Negro at one of the night spots. Some Negroes began to attack white persons in the area. The police immediately began to use their sticks and revolvers against them. The Negroes began to break out the windows of stores of white merchants on Hastings Street.

The interesting thing is that when the windows in the stores on Hastings Street were first broken, there was no looting. An officer of the Merchants' Association walked the length of Hastings Street, starting 7 o'clock Monday morning and noticed that none of the stores with broken windows had been looted. It is thus clear that the original breaking of windows was not for the purpose of looting.

Throughout Monday the police, instead of placing men in front of the stores to protect them from looting, contented themselves with driving up and down Hastings Street from time to time, stopping in front of the stores. The usual procedure was to jump out of the squad cars with drawn revolvers and riot guns to shoot whoever might be in the store. The policemen would then tell the Negro bystanders to "run and not look back." On several occasions, persons running were shot in the back. In other instances, bystanders were clubbed by police. To the police, all Negroes on Hastings Street were "looters." This included war workers returning from work. There is no question that many Negroes were guilty of looting, just as there is always looting during earthquakes or as there was when English towns were bombed by the Germans.

Cars Detoured into Mobs

Woodward Avenue is one of the main thoroughfares of the city of Detroit. Small groups of white people began to rove up and down Woodward beating Negroes, stoning cars containing Negroes, stopping street cars and yanking Negroes from them, and stabbing and shooting Negroes. In no case did the police do more than try to "reason" with these mobs, many of which were, at this stage, quite small. The police did not draw their revolvers or riot guns, and never used any force to disperse these mobs. As a result of this, the mobs got larger and bolder and even attacked Negroes on the pavement of the City Hall in demonstration not only of their contempt for Negroes, but of their contempt for law and order as represented by the municipal government. . . .

While investigating the riot, we obtained many affidavits from Negroes concerning police brutality during the riot. It is impossible to include the facts of all of these affidavits. However, typical instances may be cited. A Negro soldier in uniform who had recently been released from the army with a medical discharge, was on his way down Brush Street Monday morning, toward a theatre on Woodward Avenue. This soldier was not aware of the fact that the riot was still going on. While in the Negro neighborhood on Brush Street, he reached a corner where a squad car drove up and discharged several policemen with drawn revolvers who announced to a small group on the corner to run and not look back. Several of the Negroes who did not move quite fast enough for the police were struck with night sticks and revolvers. The soldier was yanked from behind by one policeman and struck in the head with a blunt instrument and knocked to the ground, where he remained in a stupor. The police then returned to their squad car and drove off. A Negro woman in the block noticed the entire incident from her window, and she rushed out with a cold, damp towel to bind the soldier's head. She then hailed two Negro postal employees who carried the soldier to a hospital where his life was saved.

There are many additional affidavits of similar occurrences involving obviously innocent civilians throughout many Negro sections in Detroit where there had been no rioting at all. It was characteristic of these cases that the policemen would drive up to a corner, jump out with drawn revolvers, striking at Negroes indiscriminately, oft times shooting at them, and in all cases forcing them to run. At the same time on Woodward Avenue, white civilians were seizing Negroes and telling them to "run, nigger, run." At least two Negroes, "shot while looting," were innocent persons who happened to be in the area at that time.

One Negro who had been an employee of a bank in Detroit for the past eighteen years was on his way to work on a Woodward Avenue street car when he was seized by one of the white mobs. In the presence of at least four policemen, he was beaten and stabbed in the side. He also heard several shots fired from the back of the mob. He managed to run to two of the policemen who proceeded to "protect" him from the mob. The two policemen, followed by two mounted policemen, proceeded down Woodward Avenue. While he was being escorted by these policemen, the man was struck in the face by at least eight of the mob, and at no time was any effort made to prevent him from being struck. After a short distance this man noticed a squad car parked on the other side of the street. In sheer desperation, he broke away from the two policemen who claimed to be protecting him and ran to the squad car, begging for protection. The officer in the squad car put him in the back seat and drove off, thereby saving his life.

During all this time, the fact that the man was either shot or stabbed was evident because of the fact that blood was spurting from his side. Despite this obvious felony, committed in the presence of at least four policemen, no effort was made at that time either to protect the victim or to arrest the persons guilty of the felony.

In addition to the many cases of one-sided enforcement of the law by the police, there are two glaring examples of criminal aggression against innocent Negro citizens and workers by members of the Michigan state police and Detroit police.

Shooting in YMCA

On the night of June 22 at about 10 o'clock, some of the residents of the St. Antoine Branch of the Y.M.C.A. were returning to the dormitory. Several were on their way home from the Y.W.C.A. across the street. State police were searching some other Negroes on the pavement of the Y.M.C.A. when two of the Y.M.C.A. residents were stopped and searched for weapons. After none was found they were allowed to proceed to the building. Just as the last of the Y.M.C.A. men was about to enter the building, he heard someone behind him yell what sounded to him like, "Hi, Ridley" (Ridley is also a resident of the Y). Another resident said he heard someone yell what sounded to him like "Heil, Hitler."

A state policeman, Ted Anders, jumped from his car with his revolver drawn, ran to the steps of the Y.M.C.A., put one foot on the bottom step and fired through the outside door. Immediately after firing the shot he entered the building. Other officers followed. Julian Witherspoon, who had just entered the building, was lying on the floor, shot in the side by the bullet that was fired through the outside door. There had been no show of violence or weapons of any kind by anyone in or around the Y.M.C.A.

The officers with drawn revolvers ordered all those residents of the

Y.M.C.A. who were in the lobby of their building to raise their hands in the air and line up against the wall like criminals. During all this time these men were called "black b—— and monkeys," and other vile names by the officers. At least one man was struck, another was forced to throw his lunch on the floor. All the men in the lobby were searched.

The desk clerk was also forced to line up. The officers then went behind the desk and into the private offices and searched everything. The officers also made the clerk open all locked drawers, threatening to shoot him if he did not do so.

Witherspoon was later removed to the hospital and has subsequently been released.

Ghetto Riots

Harlem
1935

The Harlem riot of 1935 marked a turning point in racial violence. Previous race riots had almost always been initiated by whites, and whites fought blacks. In this riot there was no fighting between the two races: instead blacks attacked white property and the police who were trying to protect it.

During the depression, Harlem was a world of poverty and hopelessness, and its miseries were embittered by discrimination and exclusion. Conditions in Northern ghettos, never very good, became appalling as the national economy broke down. Men could find no work, and women competed desperately for jobs as maids at pathetic wages. Local businesses which profited from Harlem trade refused to hire black labor—for example, the public utility company employed three Negro maids and two Negro inspectors. At Harlem Hospital the few black nurses ate in segregated dining rooms. Harlem streets were repaved by white crews, and most labor unions refused to admit Negroes. When Negro activists launched a Jobs for Negroes campaign, and picketed and boycotted the 125th Street stores that remained lily-white, their effort was eventually quashed by anti-picketing injunctions.

The week before the riot of March 19, 1935, a black man was battered by policemen and his eye was gouged out; then the man was charged with felonious assault, although a grand jury refused to indict him. Then on March 19, Lino Rivera, a sixteen-year old Negro, stole a knife from a Kress store (one of the staunchest holdouts against hiring blacks) and was seen being taken to the basement by a police officer. Negro spectators assumed he was going to be beaten up. Crowds formed, and speakers began denouncing the police. When the speakers were then beaten up and arrested, Harlem erupted. Rioters smashed and gutted over two hundred stores, including many that had been picketed unsuccessfully. Looting was widespread, particularly of food and clothing stores. Police shot and killed one Negro, and snipers shot back. More than one hundred people were injured. More than $2,000,000 in property was destroyed.

After the riot, Mayor LaGuardia appointed a commission to investigate its causes, including E. Franklin Frazier, the distinguished Negro sociologist from Howard University. The Commission rejected the widespread idea that Communists or outside agitators were responsible for the riot, and blamed it on discrimination, unemployment, and police brutality. They predicted that if these conditions continued, the events of March 19 would be repeated. Mayor LaGuardia refused to release the report, but it was finally made public by the New York *Amsterdam News*, the city's leading Negro newspaper.

The following account of the beginning of the riot is from the Mayor's Commission on Conditions in Harlem: *The Negro in Harlem; A Report on the Social and Economic Conditions Responsible for the Outbreak* (1935). See Roi Ottley: *New World a-Coming: Inside Black America* (1943; 1968); and Robert M. Fogelson: "Violence as Protest," in Robert H. Connery: *Urban Riots: Violence and Social Change* (1969).

At about 2:30 on the afternoon of March 19, 1935, Lino Rivera, a 16-year-old colored boy, stole a knife from a counter in the rear of E. H.

Kress and Company on 125th Street. He was seen by the manager of the store, Jackson Smith, and an assistant, Charles Hurley, who were on the balcony at the time. Mr. Hurley and another employee overtook the boy before he was able to make his escape through the front door. When the two men took the knife from Rivera's pocket and threatened him with punishment, the boy in his fright tried to cling to a pillar and bit the hands of his captors. Rivera was finally taken to the front entrance, where Mounted Patrolman Donahue was called. The boy was then taken back into the store by the officer, who asked the manager if an arrest was desired. While Mr. Smith, the manager, instructed the officer to let the culprit go free—as he had done in many cases before —an officer from the Crime Prevention Bureau was sent to the store.

This relatively unimportant case of juvenile pilfering would never have acquired the significance which it later took on had not a fortuitous combination of subsequent events made it the spark that set aflame the smouldering resentments of the people of Harlem against racial discrimination and poverty in the midst of plenty. Patrolman Donahue, in order to avoid the curious and excited spectators, took the boy through the basement to the rear entrance on 124th Street. But his act only confirmed the outcry of a hysterical Negro woman that they had taken "the boy to the basement to beat him up." Likewise, the appearance of the ambulance which had been summoned to dress the wounded hands of the boy's captors not only seemed to substantiate her charge, but, when it left empty, gave color to another rumor that that the boy was dead. By an odd trick of fate, still another incident furnished the final confirmation of the rumor of the boy's death to the excited throng of shoppers. A hearse which was usually kept in a garage opposite the store on 124th Street was parked in front of the store entrance while the driver entered the store to see his brother-in-law. The rumor of the death of the boy, which became now to the aroused Negro shoppers an established fact, awakened the deep-seated sense of wrongs and denials and even memories of injustices in the South. One woman was heard to cry out that the treatment was "just like down South where they lynch us." The deep sense of wrong expressed in this remark was echoed in the rising resentment which turned the hundred or more shoppers into an indignant crowd.

The sporadic attempts on the part of the police to assure the crowd within the store that no harm had been done the boy fell upon unbelieving ears, partly because no systematic attempt was made to let representatives of the crowd determine the truth for themselves, and partly because of the attitude of the policemen. According to the testimony of one policeman, a committee of women from among the shoppers was permitted to search the basement, but these women have never been located. On the other hand, when the crowd became too insistent about learning the fate of the boy, the police told them that it was none of their business and attempted to shove them towards the door. This only tended to infuriate the crowd and was interpreted by them as further evidence of the suppression of a wronged race. At 5:30 it became necessary to close the store.

The closing of the store did not stay the rumors that were current inside. With incredible swiftness the feelings and attitude of the outraged crowd of 'shoppers was communicated to those on 125th Street and soon all of Harlem was repeating the rumor that a Negro boy had been murdered in the basement of Kress' store. The first sign of the reaction of the community appeared when a group of men attempted to start a public meeting at a nearby corner. When the police ordered the group to move from the corner, they set up a stand in front of Kress' store. A Negro who acted as chairman introduced a white speaker. Scarcely had the speaker uttered the first words of his address to the crowd when someone threw a missile through the window of Kress' store. This was the signal for the police to drag the speaker from the stand and disperse the crowd. Immediately, the crowd reassembled across the street and another speaker attempted to address the crowd from a porch on a lamp-post. He was pulled down from his post and arrested along with the other speaker on a charge of "unlawful assemblage." . . . the extreme barbarity which was shown towards at least one of these speakers was seemingly motivated by the fact that these policemen who made derogatory and threatening remarks concerning Negroes were outraged because white men dared to take the part of Negroes. . . . These actions on the part of the police only tended to arouse resentment in the crowd which was increasing all the time along 125th Street. From 125th Street the crowds spread to Seventh Avenue and Lenox Avenue and the smashing of windows and looting of shops gathered momentum as the evening and the night came on. . . .

From its inception, as we have pointed out, the outbreak was a spontaneous and unpremeditated action on the part, first, of women shoppers in Kress' store and, later, of the crowds on 125th Street that had been formed as the result of the rumor of a boy's death in the store. As the fever of excitement based upon this rumor spread to other sections of the community, other crowds, formed by many unemployed standing about the streets and other on-lookers, sprang up spontaneously. At no time does it seem that these crowds were under the direction of any single individual or that they acted as a part of a conspiracy against law and order. The very susceptibility which the people in the community showed towards this rumor—which was more or less vague, depending upon the circumstances under which it was communicated —was due to the feeling of insecurity produced by years of unemployment and deep-seated resentment against the many forms of discrimination which they had suffered as a racial minority.

While it is difficult to estimate the actual number of persons who participated in the outburst, it does not seem, from available sources of information, that more than a few thousand were involved. These were not concentrated at any time in one place. Crowds formed here and there as the rumors spread. When a crowd was dispersed by the police, it often re-formed again. These crowds constantly changed their make-up. When bricks thrown through store windows brought the police, the crowds would often dissolve, only to gather again and continue their assaults upon property. Looting often followed the smashing of store windows. The screaming of sirens, the sound of pistol shots and the cracking of glass created in many a need for destruction and excitement. Rubbish, flower pots, or any object at hand were tossed from windows into the street. People seized property when there was no possible use which it would serve. They acted as if there were a chance to seize what rightfully belonged to them, but had long been withheld. The crowds showed various needs and changed their mood from time to time. Some of the destruction was carried on in a playful spirit. Even the looting, which has furnished many an amusing tale, was sometimes done in the spirit of children taking preserves from a closet to which they have accidentally found the key. The mood of these crowds was determined in many cases by the attitude of the police towards their unruly conduct. But, in the end, neither the threats nor the reassurances of the police could restrain these spontaneous outbursts until the crowds had spent themselves in giving release to their pent-up emotions. . . .

Watts
1965

The background of the uprising in the Watts district of Los Angeles in August 1965 is by no means unusual in the history of blacks in cities: it includes huge relief rolls, declining or stationary incomes in a period of inflationary prosperity, poor housing, and unfair treatment by the police. On August 11, an incident of alleged police brutality was being talked about in Watts: it was said that while arresting a drunken Negro driver the police had used excessive force. A further rumor spread that police had clubbed a pregnant woman. These rumors sparked a violent outburst of resentment and fury: blacks stoned police cars, then white passersby, then looted and burned white-owned stores. However, no one was killed until riot police and the National Guard were called in. In the six days of rioting, 34 persons were killed and 1,032 injured. Forty million dollars in property was destroyed, 600 buildings damaged or demolished. Over 3,400 adults and over 500 juveniles were arrested. Perhaps as many as 7,000–10,000 blacks took part in the riot.

A commission to study the Los Angeles riot, appointed by Governor Pat Brown and headed by John McCone, called the riots "an insensate rage of destruction," and intimated that the violence was chargeable to a small number of criminals, unemployed, delinquents, and social misfits. But students of the riot data reported that the rioters were given widespread support. Following is an excerpt from a 200-page chronology of events compiled by the McCone Commission's staff: California Governor's Commission on the Los Angeles Riots: *Transcripts, Depositions, Consultants' Reports, and Selected Documents*, II, Chronology of Los Angeles Riots, 28, 32–3, 43–4, 86, 173–4, 188–9. See Paul Jacobs: *Prelude to Riot: A View of Urban America from the Bottom* (1966); Robert Fogelson: "White on Black: A Critique of the McCone Commission Report on the Los Angeles Riots," *Political Science Quarterly*, LXXXII

(September 1967); Robert Conot: *Rivers of Blood, Years of Darkness* (1967); and Jerry Cohen and William S. Murphy: *Burn Baby Burn* (1966).

EVENTS OF AUGUST 12, 1965

By 12:20 A.M. approximately 50 to 75 youths were on either side of Avalon Blvd. at Imperial Highway, throwing missiles at passing cars and the police used vehicles with red lights and sirens within the riot area perimeter in an effort to disperse the crowd. As they did so, the rock throwing crowd dispersed, only to return as the police left the scene. Some of the older citizens in the area were inquiring, "What are those crazy kids doing?" A number of adult Negroes expressed the opinion that the police should open fire on the rock throwers to stop their activities. The police did not discharge firearms at rioters. It was estimated that by 12:30 A.M. 70% of the rioters were children and the remainder were young adults and adults. Their major activity was throwing missiles at passing vehicles driven by Caucasians. One rioter stationed himself a block from the intersection of Avalon Blvd. and Imperial Highway, where the major group of rioters were centered, and signaled to this group, whenever a vehicle driven by a Caucasian approached the intersection, so that it could be stoned. . . .

Witnesses stated at this time, young Negro rioters said: "I'm throwing rocks because I'm tired of a white man misusing me." "Man this is the part of town they have given us, and if they don't want to be killed they had better keep their —— out of here." "The cops think we are scared of them because they got guns, but you can only die once; if I get a few of them I don't mind dying."

. . . Sunrise disclosed five burned automobiles, amidst a large amount of rubble, broken bricks, stones, and shattered glass, in the vicinity of the intersection of Imperial Highway and Avalon Blvd.

As an indication of the mood of the crowd of approximately 400 persons who had gathered . . . on Thursday morning, the following comments of the youths in the crowd are quoted:

"Like why, man, should I got home? These —— cops have been pushin' me 'round all my life. Kickin' my —— and things like that. Whitey ain't no good. He talked 'bout law and order, its his law and his order it ain't mine . . ."

"——, if I've got to die, I ain't dyin' in Vietnam, I'm going to die here . . ."

"I don't have no job. I ain't worked for two years. —He, the white man, got everything, I ain't got nothin. What you expect me to do? I get my kicks when I see Whitey running —If they come in here tonight I'm going to kill me one."

"They always —— with the Blood—beatin' them with stocks, hand-cuffing women, I saw one of them —— go up side a cat's head and split it wide open. They treat the Blood like dirt—They've been doing it for years. Look how they treated us when we were slaves—We still slaves . . ."

"Whitey use his cops to keep us here. We are like hogs in a pen— then they come in with those silly helmets sticks and guns and things —Who the —— Parker [i.e., Police Chief Parker] think he is, God?"

AUGUST 13

At 1:57 A.M. the Los Angeles Sheriff's deputies on perimeter control, refused entry into the riot area to fire department units for the safety of the firemen.

Three cars were on fire as well as a building, in the 1200 block of Imperial Highway, and when fire department vehicles appeared in the area they were struck by thrown projectiles.

By 2:00 A.M. the perimeter established around the riot area was dissolved according to Deputy Chief Murdock, because of outbreaks of rioting beyond the original perimeter lines.

The owner of a liquor store in the 2000 block at East 103rd Street was reported to have barricaded himself in his store and to have shot persons attempting to break in.

At 2:16 A.M. a group of rioters proceding north on Central Avenue, on 120 St. overturned and burned automobiles in the street.

At 2:00 P.M. District Attorney investigators at Broadway and Manchester Avenue observed cars containing young men between the ages of 18 and 20 years. The youths were not stopped nor detained and it appeared that these youth had some type of communication system, because teen-agers and adults could be spotted using telephone booths. After making phone calls, the youngsters would get in their cars and head for other locations.

Business buildings on 103rd St. in Watts were burned completely for two blocks and firemen were driven off by uncontrolled rioters. Rioters completely overran law enforcement personnel and the number of fire alarms became so numerous that fire control was mainly by visual patrol.

At 2:08 P.M. a police officer was injured at 108th St. and Central Avenue as a result of the heavy stoning of police vehicles. The intersection became impassable.

. . . Between 6:00 P.M. and 6:15 P.M. police were requested at 49th St. and Avalon Blvd. as two hundred rioters were looting and overturning vehicles. Numerous shots were fired in the vicinity of Broadway and 88th St. Two vehicles were on fire at 51st St. and Avalon Blvd. and 200 rioters were throwing rocks and bottles in that area. Looters had completely taken over the Safeway market. . . .

The LAPD officers swept 103rd St., posting fixed positions. The area was in flames. The fire department had been driven from the area by rioters but was now able to return under police protection. Police swept Broadway and also established fixed posts on that thoroughfare. At 89th St. and Broadway the police formed a skirmish line in order to break up rioters. Warning shots were fired by police over the heads of rioters and Leon Posey Jr., who was standing on the sidewalk was struck in the head by a 38 caliber bullet. (A coroner's inquest subsequently held the death of Posey was accidental.)

AUGUST 14

At 5:15 A.M. Paul E. Harbin was shot and killed by police . . . as a looter. (Coroner's inquest held this a justifiable homicide.) At 5:15 A.M. George Fentroy was killed by police at 62nd St. and South Broadway, as a looter. Police had observed two looters leaving the buildings with their arms full of clothing and ordered them to halt. The persons refused to heed the command. One suspect escaped. (Coroner's inquest held the killing of Fentroy was justifiable homicide.) At 5:30 A.M. Miller C. Burroughs was shot and killed by police . . . as a looter. (Coroner's inquest held this a justifiable homicide.) At 5:30 A.M. Leon Cauley was shot and killed . . . by police, as a looter. (Coroner's inquest held this a justifiable homicide.)

Detroit
1967

In 1967 ghetto uprisings erupted throughout the country. The National Advisory Commission on Civil Disorders counted 164 disorders and 83 deaths in the first nine months of the year, capped by major outbreaks in Newark and Detroit in July. The Commission repeated the findings of many of its predecessors about the background of rioting, but it went beyond them in saying: "White racism is essentially responsible for the explosive mixture which has been accumulating in our cities since the end of World War I." It also cited as causes "white terrorism against non-violent protest" and called the police agents of "white racism and white repression." The Commission noted that the rioters were better educated than non-rioters, were unemployed or underemployed, were racially proud, extremely hostile to whites and middle-class blacks, and highly distrustful of the American political system.

The Detroit uprising, the largest of the year, began with a police raid on five "blind pigs," drinking and gambling clubs originally set up during prohibition, at 3:45 on Sunday morning, July 23. Eighty-two people were hauled away in police cars, which were stoned by a crowd of onlookers. By morning the crowds had grown to thousands, and window smashing and looting began. When the police proved unable to control the outbreak, the National Guard and then federal paratroopers were called in. The inexperienced, frightened Guardsmen sprayed bullets wildly at real or imagined snipers. The police rounded up blacks and beat some of them to extract confessions. Many men were brought to police stations uninjured and were taken from them to hospitals, bleeding severely; one woman was forced to strip while police snapped pictures and molested her. Although there was sniping at police and firemen from rooftops, of the 27 who were arrested for sniping, 24 were dismissed.

Forty-three persons were killed in the riot, thirty-three of them blacks. The police killed twenty or twenty-one, the National Guard perhaps as many as nine, and the rioters two or three. Arrests totaled 7,200.

The following interview with a young black who claimed to be one of those sniping at the police during the riot was written by Ray Rogers, the New York *Post*, July 29, 1967. See *Report of the National Advisory Commission on Civil Disorders* (1968); and on the Detroit situation, John Hersey: *The Algiers Motel Incident* (1968).

A teenage Negro who identified himself as one of the elusive Detroit snipers says "the war" will not be over until "they kill all of us."

But, he insisted yesterday, his activities were not organized.

"When the thing broke out me and my main man [best friend] were out there helping. We threw some cocktails. But after a while we got tired of that so we decided to go home and get our pieces [guns]," he explained.

"We knew they were going to try and step on this thing before it got out of hand so we figured we would give them something to think about," he giggled.

"Got One or Two"

"We had them —— cops so scared that first night they were shooting at one another. I know I got one or two of them, but I don't think I killed them. I wish I had, the dirty ——."

The young man explained that he went and got his "piece" after he and his buddy had looted a liquor store.

"We drank a little. And after a while—boom, just like that we decided to do some shootin'."

Did he realize he could be killed?

"I'm not crazy—I'm not crazy to be killed. I'm just gettin' even for what they did to us. Really. That's where it's at.

"Man, they killed Malcolm X just like that. So I'm gonna take a few of them with me. They may get me later on, but somebody else will take my place—just like that."

He explained that he avoided the area patrolled by the airborne troops because of the intensity with which they returned fire.

"They got a lot of soul brothers in their outfit too and I'm not trying to waste my own kind. I am after them honkies . . ." he said.

Mother Died

His mother had died years ago leaving him and his sister in a dilapidated apartment, he said.

"Man, that place was so bad that I hated to come home at night. My sister became a hustler for a guy I grew up with." He said he had heard that she had been shot Wednesday night while looting a store.

"That makes me mad. Why they have to shoot somebody for takin' something out of a store during a riot? These white mothers are something else," he said angrily as he rubbed his long, powerful fingers together.

He said he wished he had a better weapon than the U.S. M-1-automatic carbine because it lacked range and fire power. Thus he could not fire more than one or two rounds at most before National Guardsmen laid down a heavy barrage.

"But I know I got two of them. I saw them mothers fall.

"One was a honky-tonk cop with a big belly and he couldn't run too fast. And when I hit him he hollered and hit the pavement.

"And them stupid mothers fired all over the place except the place where I was—I was laying among some bricks in a burnt-out store. It was beautiful, baby, so beautiful I almost cried with joy."

He said he never carried the carbine with him and he hid it in a different place after each time he used it.

He laughed and said:

"Twice they had their hands on me and searched me but they let me go. That's why I say that the war ain't over until they put all of us in jail or kill us. . . . I mean all of us soul brothers. But they can't do that because there's too many of us."

Suddenly he began talking about his early life.

"I went to school just like you did. I believed in all that oakie-doak and then I woke up one day and said later for that stuff because that stuff would just mess up my mind, just mess up my mind. I hustled and did a little bit of everything to stay alive.

"I got a couple of kids by some sister on the other side of town but I never see them. What can I say to them?"

He said that he and his buddy paid his 10-year old cousin to watch for National Guard patrols while they were staked out on roofs. They communicated with him by a toy walkie-talkie.

"It was funny for a while because all they could do was lay there and holler at one another. Man, it was beautiful. We controlled the scene.

"We were just like guerrillas—real ones."

Some Casualties of Conquest

The Paxton Riots
1763-1764

Paxton, a small frontier town on the east bank of the Susque-
hanna River, was in an exposed situation during the hostilities
of the French and Indian War. Its men had fought bitterly
against Indian raids and its population had suffered casualties
and atrocities, along with many nearby towns. Like the other
settlers of Western Pennsylvania, they resented the domination
of provincial politics by the easterners, who were over-repre-
sented in the Assembly, and they were enraged by the non-
resistant philosophy of the influential Quakers. The legislature's
reluctance to wage war and support frontier defense was regarded by frontiersmen, who were chiefly Scotch-Irish Presby-
terians, as evidence of a callous indifference to their interests.
The first sufferers from this rage of the men of Paxton were
the Indians of Conestoga, a pathetic and harmless remnant of a
tribe quite friendly to the whites, who lived chiefly by selling
brooms and baskets and by begging. On December 14 the "Paxton Boys" descended upon Conestoga and killed the six Indians
—three men, two women and a boy—whom they found there.
By proclamation of Governor John Penn, the surviving fourteen Conestoga Indians were placed under the protection of the
province, but the Paxton Boys swept into Lancaster, where the
Conestogas had been housed in the jail for their protection, and
swiftly slaughtered them. Learning that another much larger
group of Indians, who had been converted to Christianity by
the Moravians, were being sheltered and fed in Philadelphia, the
Paxton Boys mustered their forces and marched upon the city
with the announced intention of killing the Indians. Many Phila-
delphians, outraged at the news of the massacres and alarmed
at the prospect of hostilities, prepared to meet the rioters with

arms. Even Quakers were seen carrying muskets. Benjamin Franklin and other civic leaders were dispatched to meet the Paxton men at Germantown, where the would-be rioters were persuaded to draft a statement of their grievances for the governor and the Assembly and to return home. The issues that came to a head in the Paxton massacres shook the entire province and stirred a voluminous pamphlet debate. In the tragedy of the Conestogas the imperial wars, the struggles between whites and Indians, the sectional politics of the colony, and the preliminaries of the Revolution all converged.

The following account is from an indignant pamphlet by Benjamin Franklin: *A Narrative of the Late Massacres in Lancaster County....* (1764) in his *Writings* (Smythe edn., 1905–7), IV, 289 ff. The pamphlet literature has been edited, with a valuable introduction by J. R. Dunbar: *The Paxton Papers* (1957); for the affair see Brooke Hindle: "The March of the Paxton Boys," *William and Mary Quarterly*, III (October 1946), 461–86.

These Indians were the remains of a tribe of the Six Nations, settled at Conestogoe, and thence called Conestogoe Indians. On the first arrival of the English in Pennsylvania, messengers from this tribe came to welcome them, with presents of venison, corn, and skins; and the whole tribe entered into a treaty of friendship with the first Proprietor, William Penn, which was to last "as long as the sun should shine, or the waters run in the rivers."

This treaty has been since frequently renewed, and the chain brightened, as they express it, from time to time. It has never been violated, on their part or ours, till now. . . .

On Wednesday, the 14th of December, 1763, fifty-seven men, from some of our frontier townships, who had projected the destruction of this little commonwealth, came, all well mounted, and armed with forelocks, hangers and hatchets, having travelled through the country in the night to Conestogoe Manor. There they surrounded the small village of Indian huts, and just at break of day broke into them all at once. Only three men, two women, and a young boy, were found at home, the rest being out among the neighboring white people, some to sell the baskets, brooms and bowls they manufactured, and others on other occasions. These poor defenceless creatures were immediately fired upon, stabbed, and hatcheted to death! The good Shehaes, among the rest, cut to pieces in his bed. All of them were scalped and otherwise horribly mangled. Then their huts were set on fire, and most of them burnt down. When the troop, pleased with their own conduct and bravery, but enraged that any of the poor Indians had escaped the massacre, rode off, and in small parties, by different roads, went home.

The universal concern of the neighbouring white people on hearing of this event, and the lamentations of the younger Indians, when they returned and saw the desolation, and the butchered half-burnt bodies of their murdered parents and other relations, cannot well be expressed.

The Magistrates of Lancaster sent out to collect the remaining Indians, brought them into the town for their better security against any farther attempt; and it is said condoled with them on the misfortune that had happened, took them by the hand, comforted and *promised them protection*. They were all put into the workhouse, a strong building, as the place of greatest safety. . . .

Notwithstanding [the Governor's] proclamation, those cruel men again assembled themselves, and hearing that the remaining fourteen Indians were in the workhouse at Lancaster, they suddenly appeared in that town, on the 27th of December. Fifty of them, armed as before, dismounting, went directly to the workhouse, and by violence broke open the door, and entered with the utmost fury in their countenances. When the poor wretches saw they had no protection nigh, nor could possibly escape, and being without the least weapon for defence, they divided into their little families, the children clinging to the parents; they fell on their knees, protested their innocence, declared their love to the English, and that, in their whole lives, they had never done them injury; and in this posture they all received the hatchet! Men, women and little children were every one inhumanly murdered!—in cold blood!

The barbarous men who committed the atrocious act, in defiance of government, of all laws human and divine, and to the eternal disgrace of their country and colour, then mounted their horses, huzza'd in triumph, as if they had gained a victory, and rode off—*unmolested!*

The bodies of the murdered were then brought out and exposed in the street, till a hole could be made in the earth to receive and cover them.

But the wickedness cannot be covered, the guilt will lie on the whole land, till justice is done on the murderers. THE BLOOD OF THE INNOCENT WILL CRY TO HEAVEN FOR VENGEANCE.

It is said that, Shehaes being before told, that it was to be feared some English might come from the frontier into the country, and murder him and his people; he replied, "It is impossible: there are Indians, indeed, in the woods, who would kill me and mine, if they could get at us, for my friendship to the English; but the English will wrap me in their match-coat, and secure me from all danger." How unfortunately was he mistaken! . . .

Cheyenne Massacre
1864

The story of the Sand Creek massacre is one of the bloodiest and most disgraceful episodes in the American Indian wars. The territory from Central Kansas to the Rocky Mountains, between the Platte and Arkansas Rivers, had been the domain of the Southern Cheyenne and Arapaho Indians before the 1850's. The gold rush to Pike's Peak brought many settlers to the territory and put great pressure on the Indian tribes. By 1859 the Indians were compressed into a small circle of territory which straddled a main line of white emigration. In 1861 the Indians were persuaded by government officials to sell that land to the United States and move to a gameless, arid section of the southeastern Colorado Territory. The Indians claimed they had been cheated and had misunderstood the treaty; in 1864 some tribes in Colorado were goaded into a war and killed many settlers. The Cheyenne, who were then at peace under Chief Black Kettle, gave up their arms and camped where they were promised protection by federal troops against the Colorado militia. Those promises were not kept. A contingent of Colorado militia under the command of Colonel J. M. Chivington, a Methodist pastor in civil life, fell upon the unsuspecting camp, refused to acknowledge a white flag of surrender, and slaughtered and mutilated perhaps as many as 450 men, women, and children. The soldiers scalped the dead and dying, then cut out the genitals of the women and stuck them on poles or wore them in their hats. Chivington later remarked that the children had to be killed because "nits make lice."

A local newspaper called this episode "a brilliant feat of arms," and said that the soldiers "had covered themselves with glory." A Congressional Committee, however, said Chivington had "deliberately planned and executed a foul and dastardly massacre which would have disgraced the veriest savage among those who were the victims of his cruelty." Chief Black Kettle, who survived, sorrowfully confessed that "my shame is as big as the earth." "It is hard," he mildly added, "for me to believe the white man any more." He was killed in 1868 during the Washita war, when his winter camp was raided by a force under Colonel George A. Custer.

The following account is from the testimony of John S. Smith, an Indian agent well known to the Cheyenne and present during the raid, before the Joint Committee on the Conduct of the War: "Massacre of the Cheyenne Indians," 38th Congress, 2nd Session, III (1865). See also Stan Hoig: *The Sand Creek Massacre* (1961); and Ralph K. Andrist: *The Long Death: The Last Days of the Plains Indians* (1964).

I left to go to this village of Indians on the 26th of November last. I arrived there on the 27th and remained there the 28th. On the morning of the 29th, between daylight and sunrise—nearer sunrise than daybreak— a large number of troops were discovered from three-quarters of a mile to a mile below the village. The Indians, who discovered them, ran to my camp, called me out, and wanted me to go and see what troops they were, and what they wanted. The head chief of the nation, Black Kettle, and head chief of the Cheyennes, was encamped there with us. Some years previous he had been presented with a fine American flag by Colonel Greenwood, a commissioner, who had been sent out there. Black Kettle ran this American flag up to the top of his lodge, with a small white flag tied right under it, as he had been advised to do in case he should meet with any troops out on the prairies. I then left my own camp and started for that portion of the troops that was nearest the village, supposing I could go up to them. I did not know but they might be strange troops, and thought my presence and explanations could reconcile matters. Lieutenant Wilson was in command of the detachment to which I tried to make my approach; but they fired several volleys at me, and I returned back to my camp and entered my lodge.

After I had left my lodge to go out and see what was going on, Colonel Chivington rode up to within fifty or sixty yards of where I was camped; he recognized me at once. They all call me Uncle John in that country. He said, "Run here, Uncle John; you are all right." I went to him as fast as I could. He told me to get in between him and his troops, who were then coming up very fast; I did so; directly another officer who knew me—Lieutenant Baldwin, in command of a battery—tried to assist me to get a horse; but there was no loose horse there at the time. He said, "Catch hold of the caisson, and keep up with us."

By this time the Indians had fled; had scattered in every direction. The troops were some on one side of the river and some on the other, following up the Indians. We had been encamped on the north side of the river; I followed along, holding on the caisson, sometimes running, sometimes walking. Finally, about a mile above the village, the troops had got a parcel of the Indians hemmed in under the bank of the river; as soon as the troops overtook them, they commenced firing on them; some troops had got above them, so that they were completely surrounded. There were probably a hundred Indians hemmed in there, men, women, and children; the most of the men in the village escaped.

By the time I got up with the battery to the place where these Indians were surrounded there had been some considerable firing. Four or five soldiers had been killed, some with arrows and some with bullets. The soldiers continued firing on these Indians, who numbered about a hundred, until they had almost completely destroyed them. I think I saw altogether some seventy dead bodies lying there; the greater portion women and children. There may have been thirty warriors, old and young; the rest were women and small children of different ages and sizes.

The troops at that time were very much scattered. There were not over two hundred troops in the main fight, engaged in killing this body of Indians under the bank. The balance of the troops were scattered in different directions, running after small parties of Indians who were trying to make their escape. I did not go to see how many they might have killed outside of this party under the bank of the river. Being still quite weak from my last sickness, I returned with the first body of troops that went back to the camp.

. . .

QUESTION. Were the women and children slaughtered indiscriminately, or only so far as they were with the warriors?

ANSWER. Indiscriminately.

QUESTION. Were there any acts of barbarity perpetrated there that came under your own observation?

ANSWER. Yes, sir; I saw the bodies of those lying there cut all to pieces, worse mutilated than any I ever saw before; the women cut all to pieces.

By Mr. Buckalew:

QUESTION. How cut?

ANSWER. With knives; scalped; their brains knocked out; children two or three months old; all ages lying there, from sucking infants up to warriors. . . . They were terribly mutilated, lying there in the water and sand; most of them in the bed of the creek, dead and dying, making many struggles. They were so badly mutilated and covered with sand and water that it was very hard for me to tell one from another. . . .

By Mr. Gooch:

QUESTION. Did you see it done?

ANSWER. Yes, sir; I saw them fall.

QUESTION. Fall when they were killed?

ANSWER. Yes, sir.

QUESTION. Did you see them when they were mutilated?

ANSWER. Yes, sir.

QUESTION. By whom were they mutilated?

ANSWER. By the United States troops.

QUESTION. Do you know whether or not it was done by the direction or consent of any of the officers?

ANSWER. I do not; I hardly think it was. . . .

QUESTION. Were there any other barbarities or atrocities committed there other than those you have mentioned, that you saw?

ANSWER. Yes, sir; I had a half-breed son there, who gave himself up. He started at the time the Indians fled; being a half-breed he had but little hope of being spared, and seeing them fire at me, he ran away with the Indians for the distance of about a mile. During the fight up there he walked back to my camp and went into the lodge. It was surrounded by soldiers at the time. He came in quietly and sat down; he remainded there that day, that night, and the next day in the afternoon; about four o'clock in the evening, as I was sitting inside the camp, a soldier came up outside of the lodge and called me by name. I got up and went out; he took me by the arm and walked towards Colonel Chivington's camp, which was about sixty yards from my camp. Said he, "I am sorry to tell you, but they are going to kill your son Jack." I knew the feeling towards the whole camp of Indians, and that there was no use to make any resistance. I said, "I can't help it." I then walked on towards where Colonel Chivington was standing by his camp-fire; when I had got within a few feet of him I heard a gun fired, and saw a crowd run to my lodge, and they told me that Jack was dead.

QUESTION. What action did Colonel Chivington take in regard to that matter?

ANSWER. Major Anthony, who was present, told Colonel Chivington that he had heard some remarks made, indicating that they were desirous of killing Jack; and that he (Colonel Chivington) had it in his power to save him, and that by saving him he might make him a very useful man, as he was well acquainted with all the Cheyenne and Arapahoe country, and he could be used as a guide or interpreter. Colonel Chivington replied to Major Anthony, as the Major himself told me, that he had no orders to receive and no advice to give.

Wounded Knee Massacre
1890

The Plains Indians were the last stumbling blocks to white control of the West. When an effort was launched to confine them to reservations in the 1870's, the Sioux and Northern Cheyenne refused and the Army was sent to corral them. At first the Oglala Sioux under Crazy Horse repulsed General George Crook's forces at Rosebud Creek, Montana, and when Lt. Col. George Custer and the Seventh Cavalry rashly attacked an Indian camp at Little Big Horn on June 25, 1876, he and 225 of his men were killed by the combined forces of Crazy Horse, Sitting Bull, Gall and other chiefs. But during the next winter the Army hounded the bands until, driven by hunger, they sought the food and shelter of the reservations.

The seven tribes of the Teton Sioux, numbering about 16,000 in 1880, were placed on a reservation in South Dakota. There they faced a more deadly enemy than the military: the "civilizing" methods of the Indian Agents. "To allow them to drag along," said the Commissioner of Indian Affairs in 1881, "in their old superstitions, laziness and filth, when we have the power to elevate them in the scale of humanity, would be a lasting disgrace to our government." They were forced to give up customs related to war and to sacrifice their traditional economy based on the buffalo hunt in favor of goverment doles; their political and religious structures, thus far largely intact, were destroyed. The power of the chiefs was undermined. Children were put in schools run by whites, and parents who balked found their food rations cut off. Sioux religious customs, particularly the Sun Dance, were outlawed as "demoralizing and barbarous," and missionaries flocked to the reservation. This situation was worsened by governmental chicanery over the land question. Settlers were demanding the further restriction of reservation territory, and in 1889, Congress passed the Sioux Act, which when ratified by the Indians would take half their land in return for some cash payment, continued rations, and various other promises. It was bitterly resisted by many Sioux, but in the end, faced with the certainty of ultimate expropriation, they agreed. Two weeks afterwards, the promised ration levels were cut back, and numerous other promises soon proved empty. As one Indian remarked: "They made us many promises, more than I can remember, but they never kept but one: they promised to take our land and they took it."

Thus crushed, the Indians succumbed to an overwhelming despair and turned to messianic religion. An Indian Messiah had appeared who preached that all Indians would be soon free, dead Indians would be reborn, the whites would leave the continent, the buffalo would be plentiful again, and the old way of life would be restored. All that Indians need do was to follow the tenets of the new faith and dance a prescribed Ghost Dance. The Ghost Dance, which spread throughout the western coun-

try before it eventually wore itself out, took on for the Sioux
a particularly militant form. The people danced till they
dropped, and then danced again, and when the Agents tried to
forbid the practice, they were warned away at gunpoint. The
Sioux believed that all who wore the Ghost Shirts were invulnerable to bullets. Although the Sioux made no hostile moves,
the Agents were so alarmed that they called in the army to
suppress the dance and, supposedly, to prevent an outbreak.

When the troops arrived, a large body of Indians fled to the
Badlands where they began to dance in relays almost continuously. Some chiefs were persuaded to defect from the new
religion, others were arrested. When Indian police attempted
to take Sitting Bull into custody, his tribe resisted and the great
chief was killed. Eventually all tribes but those in Pine Ridge
Reservation were under control. General Nelson A. Miles, who
commanded the troops, was particularly worried about the Mini-
conjou Sioux, led by Chief Big Foot, who was presumed hostile,
but who was actually suffering from pneumonia and was heading his band toward an agency to surrender. The Indians were
intercepted first by troops of the Seventh Cavalry (Custer's
old command), under the command of Col. James W. Forsyth.
The Indians surrendered immediately, raising a white flag. On
December 29, 1890, the camp was surrounded. The Indians were
disarmed. Forsyth suspected that the braves were concealing
more weapons under their blankets. They were being inspected
when one Indian pulled out a rifle and it discharged. Some
claimed he was placing it on the pile of confiscated weapons and
it went off accidentally, others that he deliberately shot at the
troops. Immediately the soldiers fired a volley point blank into
the Indians, and then wholesale fighting began. The artillery
had been trained on the camp and was now discharged amidst
the women and children, and fleeing Indians were shot down.
It is estimated that 200 to 250 Indians were killed. General Miles,
who has been followed by most historians, termed it a "massacre,"
and relieved Forsyth of his command for "reprehensible" behavior. But Forsyth was restored by the Secretary of War,
who blamed the incident entirely on the Indians, and eighteen
soldiers received Congressional Medals of Honor. The massacre
marked the psychic as well as physical crushing of the Sioux,
the end of the Indian wars, and the completion of the white
man's conquest of the Indians.

The two accounts by survivors were taken down by James MacGregor in 1940: *The Wounded Knee Massacre from the Viewpoint of the Sioux* (1940), 103–7, 127–8. See James Mooney: *The Ghost-Dance Religion and the Sioux Outbreak of 1890*, 14th Annual Report of the Bureau of American Ethnology, 1892–3, Pt. II (1896); Robert M. Utley: *The Last Days of the Sioux Nation* (1963); Elaine Goodale Eastman: "The Ghost Dance War and Wounded Knee Massacre of 1890–1," *Nebraska History*, XXVI (1945), 26–42; Merril J. Mattes: "The Enigma of Wounded Knee," *Plains Anthropologist*, V (1960), 1–11; and Alvin M. Josephy, Jr.: *The Indian Heritage of America* (1968).

DEWEY BEARD

William Bergen, Interpreter

I was a member of the band that was killed here. Just a little beyond Porcupine Butte we were coming this way when we were met by the soldiers. Big Foot, who was sick and had been sick then for four days, had a hemorrhage, came up with a flag of truce tied to a stick. We were traveling in a peaceful manner, no intention of any trouble. I was told that this was an officer that came around to where Big Foot was laying, so I followed him up possibly a yard right behind him. I wanted to know what his intentions were. This officer asked Big Foot—"Are you the man that is named Big Foot and can you talk?" He asked him where he was going. I am going to my people who are camped down here. The officer then stated that he had heard that they had left Cheyenne River and the Army was on the lookout for him. "I have seen you and I am very glad to have met you. I want you to turn over your guns." Big Foot answered, "Yes, I am a man of that kind." The officer wanted to know what he meant by that, so the interpreter told him that he was a peaceful man. He says, "You have requested that I give you my guns, but I am going to a certain place and when I get there I will lay down my arms."

"Now, you meet us out here on the prairie and expect me to give you my guns out here. I am a little bit afraid that there might be something crooked about it, something that may occur that wouldn't be fair. There are a lot of children here." The officer then said they are bringing a wagon and I want you to get in that and they will take you down to where we are camped. Shortly a wagon drew up and they wrapped a blanket around him and placed him in the wagon and started to camp, so we followed.

This side of the store, where you see these houses, is where we were camped and right this way is where the soldiers were camped. In the evening they unloaded some bacon, sugar and hardtack in the center and stated that someone should issue this out, so the women all came into the center and I am the one that issued it out to them. We heard a mule braying over this way and also heard the soldiers making a complete circle from the south to the north direction. I forgot something too that I wanted to repeat. That evening I noticed that they were erecting cannons up here, also hauling up quite a lot of ammunition for it. I could see them doing it. Shortly after we erected our camp, guards were stationed around. They were walking their beat. I also noticed that night besides the store there was some fires built there and we knew that they were the Indian Scouts. The following morning there was a bugle call shortly after that another bugle call, then I saw the soldiers mounting the horses and surrounding us. Even though they had surrounded us and we noticed all these peculiar actions, I never thought there was anything wrong. I thought it wouldn't be no time until we could be starting towards the Agency. It was announced that all men should come to the center for a talk and that after the talk they were to move on to Pine Ridge Agency. So they all came to the center. Shortly after that I also followed and came to the center where they all were gathered. After I got there and looked around and the men were just sitting around unconcerned. Big Foot was brought out of his tepee and sat in front of his tent and the older men were gathered around him and sitting right near him in the center. The interpreter said that the officer said that yesterday we promised some guns and that he was going to collect them now. I don't remember how many soldiers there were, but these soldiers were climbing on top of wagons, unpacking things, taking axes and other things, and they were taking them to where the guns were already laid down. Some of the Indians were further east that had guns in their arms but were not seen for some time. They were out over where the soldiers were so finally they called to them to bring their arms to the center and put them down. One of them started towards the center with his gun. This fellow that started said: "Now it was understood yesterday that we were to put down our guns after we reached the Agency, but here you are calling for our guns so he took the gun and showed it to them." He started towards the guns where they were laid down and one soldier started from the east side towards him and another from the west side towards this Indian. Even so, he was still unconcerned. He was not scared about it. If they had left him alone he was going to put his gun down where he should. They grabbed him and spinned him in the east direction. He was still unconcerned even then. He hadn't his gun pointed at anyone.

His intention was to put that gun down. They came on and grabbed the gun that he was going to put down. Right after they spun him around there was the report of a gun, was quite loud. I couldn't say that anybody was shot but following that was a crash. The flag of truce that we had was stuck in the ground right there where we were sitting. They fired on us anyhow. Right after that crash, that is when all the people were falling over. I remained standing there for some little time and a man came up to me and I recognized him as a man known as High Hawk. He said, come on they have started this way, so let's go. So we started up this little hill; coming up this way, the soldiers started to shoot at us and as they did High Hawk was shot and fell down. I wasn't so started back and then they knocked me down. I was alone so I was trying to look out for myself. They had killed my wife and baby. I saw men lying around, shot down. I went around them the best I could, got down in the ravine, then I fell down again. I was shot and wounded at the first time I told you that I fell. I went up this ravine and could see that they were traveling in that direction. I saw women and children lying all over there. They got up to a cut bank up the ravine and there I found a great many that were in there hiding. We were going to try and go on through the ravine but it was surrounded by the soldiers, so we just had to stay in that cut bank. Right near there was a butte with a ridge on it. They placed a cannon on it pointing in our direction and fired on us right along. I saw one man that was shot with one of these cannons. That man's name was Hawk Feather Shooter.

MRS. ROUGH FEATHER
Ben American Horse, Interpreter

I started from Cherry Creek with Big Foot's band. We were going to Pine Ridge to visit relatives. I am now 73 years old but I remember lots of things that happened. I was a widow and was with my parents. The soldiers met us near the Porcupine Butte, and after they talked to Big Foot we went on to Wounded Knee Creek, where the soldiers were camped and we camped there too. The next morning we were getting ready to break camp when the Indian men were ordered by the soldiers to come to the center of the camp and bring all their guns. After they did this, the soldiers came to where the Indian women were and searched the tents and the wagons for arms. They made us give up axes, crowbars, knives, awls, etc. About this time an awful noise was heard and I was paralyzed for a time. Then my head cleared and I saw nearly all the people on the ground bleeding. I could move some now, so I ran to a cut bank and lay down there. I saw some of the other Indians running up the coulee so I ran with them, but the soldiers kept shooting at us and the bullets flew all around us, and a bullet went between my leg but I was not hit one time. My father, my mother, my grandmother, my older brother and my younger brother were all killed. My son who was two years old was shot in the mouth that later caused his death.

We had ten horses, harness, wagon, tent, buffalo robes, and I had a good Navajo blanket. All this property was lost or taken by the Government or other people. I had a hard time in my life and you can see that I am having a hard time now. It is cold weather and this is an old house and I suffer from cold. It is hard to get wood as we have to go a long way to get it.

I was in Montana, where they had a big battle with Custer, and the Indians won and then lots of soldiers came and we escaped to Canada. I was only about ten years old then and don't know much about that, but remember hearing lots of guns and hearing lots of war-whoops. After a while we went to Standing Rock Reservation for four years, then I went to Rosebud for a short time and then to Cherry Creek, where Big Foot was camping.

Rough Feather, whom I married two years after the Massacre, was there too, and he gave his statement at the meeting you had at Wounded Knee. He saw lots of wounded Indians; so he got a team and a wagon and picked up some of his wounded relatives and took them to Pine Ridge and put them in the church that they were using for a hospital. Is the Government going to pay us for what they did to us?

Brutalities in the Philippines

1897–1902

In 1898 the United States went to war with Spain ostensibly to free Cuba and put an end to the atrocities that the Spaniards were committing there. It ended by annexing the Philippines and by committing some atrocities of its own. In August 1898, after Admiral George Dewey's Asiatic Squadron destroyed the Spanish fleet in Manila Bay, the Spanish garrison surrendered and the town was occupied. The surrender was hastened by the Spaniards' fear of the Filipino guerillas under young General Emilio Aguinaldo, who had been brought back out of exile with Dewey's approval and help. The American occupation was hastened by the prospect that Aguinaldo's men would themselves take Manila. In June of that year Aguinaldo had set up a provincial government and had proclaimed the independence of the Philippines from Spain. When he and his followers learned in January 1899 that the Treaty of Paris concluded between the United States and Spain the month before had included the cession of the Philippines to the United States, they felt betrayed and they soon engaged in an armed revolt against the United States. But, as William H. Taft, the President of the Philippine Commission put it, "We propose to stay there indefinitely in working out this good that we propose to do them." In the ensuing guerilla warfare which raged until the summer of 1901 and was not formally ended until a year later, the United States eventually had to use a force of 70,000 men, and to endure considerably higher casualties, including 4,300 deaths, than had been sustained in the Spanish War itself. On both sides the war was fought with extraordinary ferocity, and Filipino fighters and civilians suffered staggering losses. Particularly disturbing to anti-imperialist critics of the war in the United States were reports of atrocities and tortures on the part of the American forces. To the generation that has lived through the war in Vietnam some of these charges, persuasively documented despite military censorship and in many cases sustained by Congressional investigations, seem depressingly familiar, beginning with an attitude of arrogance and condescension toward Asiatic peoples and ending in the use of torture, the creation of concentration camps, the burning of villages, and the wanton execution of prisoners of war and civilians. After Aguinaldo was captured through a ruse on March 23, 1901, the war tapered off, although sporadic uprisings against American authority continued for years. In 1906, Moro tribesman rebelled. American troops under General Leonard Wood surrounded their stronghold and killed them all: 600 men, women, and children died; the Americans lost 15. President Theodore Roosevelt congratulated Wood and his men "upon the brilliant feat of arms wherein you and they so well upheld the honor of the American flag."

The following testimony was given by three American soldiers at "Hearings Before the Senate Committee on the Philippines," Senate Doc., 331, 57th Congress, 1st Session (1902), 1539–41, 2061–2, 2550–1. On the problem of atrocities see Moorfield Storey and Marcial P. Lichauco: *The Conquest of the Philippines by the United States* (1926); James H. Blount: *American Occupation of the Philippines* (1913); Leon Wolff: *Little Brown Brother* (1961); Henry F. Graff, ed.: *American Imperialism and the Philippine Insurrection* (1969); and Mark Twain: *Mark Twain's Autobiography* (1924), II, 186–200.

TESTIMONY OF D. J. EVANS

Q. The committee would like to hear from you in regard to the conduct of the war, and whether you were the witness of any cruelties inflicted upon the natives in the Philippine Islands; and if so, under what circumstances.—A. The case had reference to was where they gave the water cure to a native in the Ilicano Province at Ilocos Norte.

Q. That is in the extreme northern part of Luzon?—A. Yes, sir. There were two native scouts that were with the American forces. They went out and brought back in a couple of insurgents. They were known to be insurgents by their own confession, and besides that, they had the mark that most insurgents in that part of the country carry; it is a little brand on the left breast, generally inflicted with a nail or head of a cartridge, heated. They tried to find out from this native—

Q. What kind of a brand did you say it was?—A. A small brand put on with a nail head or cartridge.

Senator Beveridge. A scar on the flesh?

The Witness. Yes, sir.

They tried to get him to tell where the rest of the insurgents were at that time. We knew about where they were, but we did not know how to get at them. They were in the hills, and it happened that there was only one path that could get to them, and we did not get to them that time. They refused to tell this one path and they commenced this so-called "water cure." The first thing one of the Americans—I mean one of the scouts for the Americans—grabbed one of the men by the head and jerked his head back, and then they took a tomato can and poured water down his throat until he could hold no more, and during this time one of the natives had a rattan whip, about as large as my finger, and he struck him on the face and on the bare back, and every time they would strike him it would raise a large welt, and some blood would come. And when this native could hold no more water, then they forced a gag into his mouth; they stood him up and tied his hands behind him; they stood him up against a post and fastened him so he could not move. Then one man, an American soldier, who was over six feet tall, and who was very strong, too, struck this native in the pit of the stomach as hard as he could strike him, just as rapidly as he could. It seemed as if he didn't get tired of striking him.

By Senator Allison:

Q. With his hand?—A. With his clenched fist. He struck him right in the pit of the stomach and it made the native very sick. They kept that operation up for quite a time, and finally I thought the fellow was about to die, but I don't believe he was as bad as that, because finally he told them he would tell, and from that on he was taken away, and I saw no more of him.

Q. Did he tell?—A. I believe he did, because I didn't hear of any more water cure inflicted on him.

TESTIMONY OF WILLIAM LEWIS SMITH

Q. You may state whether or not you witnessed what is known as the water cure.—A. I did, sir.

Q. And where did you see it?—A. At the town of Igbaras.

Q. On what day?—A. November 27, 1900.

Q. Upon whom was it inflicted?—A. Upon the presidente of the town and two native police.

Q. Did you observe it inflicted more than once?—A. I saw part of it at one time and the whole of it the second time.

Q. Describe what you saw on the first occasion.—A. We arrived at the town about daylight in the morning. It was just breaking day. There was an outpost put all over the town, so that no people could leave town by the gates, and we proceeded to quarters. A detachment of our company was stationed there. The company that we joined was commanded by Lieutenant Conger, of the Eighteenth Infantry, known as Gordon's Scouts. We proceeded to quarters, and I was one of a detail that was sent out to ask the presidente to come over to the quarters. On the way we met him and proceeded to the house of the padre, the priest of the town, to get him. He was not at home.

The presidente went along over to the quarters. When I got back to the quarters, the boys were sitting around, and I went upstairs, and the first that I saw of the presidente was that he was stripped. He had nothing on but his pants. His shirt and coat were off, and his hands were tied behind him, and Lieutenant Conger stood over him, and also a contract doctor by the name of Dr. Lyons, and as we stopped there they proceeded to give him what is known as the water cure. It was given from a large tank. I should say the tank held—well—a hundred gallons, anyway. I do not know whether it was full at the time, but the tank would hold about that—two barrels of water I should think, surely. He was thrown on his back, and these four or five men, known as the water detail of these Gordon Scouts, held him down. Water was administered by the opening of the faucet. We could not get close enough to see exactly how it was done, because if we would congregate there at all the officers would tell us to pass on. We had to go upstairs to get into our squad room, and if we would congregate there they would tell us to pass on. We would go back and forth and see it at times.

The second time I saw it after he had confessed what they wanted— I do not know whether he confessed or not, I only saw a part of that—but downstairs they asked him through an interpreter, they all stood over him at the time, and they asked him if he sent any word out to the insurgents when the troops arrived in town. One of the native police in the meantime disclosed that he had, that he had sent him personally, so in order to get that from him Lieutenant Conger called for the water detail. This time it was given by means of a syringe. Two men went out to their saddlebags and obtained two syringes, large bulbs, a common syringe, about 2 feet of common hose pipe, I should think, on either end. One was inserted in his mouth and the other up his nose. We could all stand by there and see that. When this doctor said to get a pail of water, and they started into the building with him, Captain Glenn was there, and he said, "No, this is good enough right here on the outside." So we all had a chance to witness it that time; and as the water did not seem to have the desired effect, the doctor stood over him and said to get a cup of salt. One of the men went upstairs and procured a cup of salt and it was thrown into the water, and the interpreter stood there all the time, and after he had had it some time he did disclose what they wanted, and he said he was willing to guide us out there. We went out and stayed the greater part of the day, but did not see anything of the insurgents. That is what I saw of the water cure.

Q. What became of that town?—A. It was burned about 8 o'clock, under orders of Captain Glenn. Lieutenant Conger started out with his men—that is, the Eighteenth Infantry—to burn part of the town. Captain

McDonald, of the Twenty-sixth, took his men and went to the lower end of the town. We started burning after they started burning at the other end, in order to give the natives time to get out before their buildings were burned.

Senator Dubois. Did you personally do any of the burning?

The Witness. Yes; I did set fire to some buildings.

By Senator Rawlins:

Q. How were those occupied?—A. By native men, women, and children alike. Nearly all of the buildings were bamboo and nipa, and all you have to do is to light this nipa roof and it is gone in a short time.

Q. What became of the furniture and household effects?—A. They do not have a great deal of furniture or household effects. They sleep on the floor. Only the better class there have beds. They sleep on the floor as a rule. Of course, what few tables and benches they had were destroyed. They only had time to save the clothes that they wore at the time.

Q. Was any discrimination made as to whose buildings should be burned, and whose not?—A. The church was to be saved and the quarters occupied by our men, and five large buildings that were not made of this bamboo construction, but were made of wood—good buildings. They were to be saved for the occupancy of the women and children after the rest of the town was burned.

Q. You have already stated, I think, that this water cure was inflicted by Lieutenant Conger of the regulars, by scouts under his command?—A. Yes, sir. The way he had of ordering it done was, "Water detail"; that is all I heard him say. The men went on then and did the rest of it. The men stood over, as did Captain Glenn and Dr. Lyons, and witnessed it both times.

Q. After the town was burned and after you returned the presidente what became of him?—A. He was taken to Iloilo for trial; I don't know what his sentence was.

Q. How old a man was he?—A. He was a man 45 or 50 years old, I should think; 45 years old anyway.

By Senator Dietrich:

Q. You say that the presidente, after having received the water cure the second time, acted as guide to show you where the insurgents were?—A. In the mountains, yes.

Q. How did he go, afoot or horseback?—A. Horseback.

Q. He seemed to be in good condition, did he?—A. Yes, sir.

Q. And the water cure did not seem to injure him very much?—A. No;

it does not seem to injure anyone very much after forcing the water out of him. They forced it out by placing a foot on the stomach.

By Senator Beveridge:

Q. The chief effect is fright, is it not?—A. Yes, sir.

  Q. This was two years ago?—A. Yes, sir.

  Senator Culberson. The chief effect of what?

  Senator Beveridge. The chief effect of the water cure.

By Senator Beveridge:

Q. Do you know of many outrages by the natives upon the American troops?

  Senator Rawlins. I object to the question.

  The Witness. No, sir; I do not know.

  The Chairman. Did you ever see any other cases of water cure?

  The Witness. No, sir.

TESTIMONY OF RICHARD T. O'BRIEN

By Senator Beveridge:

Q. Are you a pretty good shot?—A. No, sir.

  Q. Are any of our soldiers good shots?—A. Yes, sir.

  Q. Were any in that squad good shots?—A. Yes, sir. They were all snap shots, most all of them.

  Q. They did not shoot but once?—A. No, sir.

  Q. You had more than one cartridge?—A. Yes, sir.

  Q. You just fired a volley at the boy and quit?—A. Yes, sir. That brought the people in the houses out, brought them to the doors and out into the street, and how the order started and who gave it I don't know, but the town was fired on. I saw an old fellow come to the door, and he looked out; he got a shot in the abdomen and fell to his knees and turned around and died.

  Q. Were you shooting then, too?—A. Yes, sir.

  Q. And had you any orders to shoot?—A. Yes, sir.

  Q. Who ordered you to shoot?—A. I don't know, sir.

  Q. You were shooting a good deal like you shot at the boy?—A. No, sir.

  Senator Carmack. The orders were given to fire. Go ahead and tell the whole story.

  The Witness. After that two old men came out, hand in hand. I should think they were over 50 years old, probably between 50 and 70 years old. They had a white flag. They were shot down. At the other end of the town we heard screams, and there was a woman there; she was burned up, and in her arms was a baby, and on the floor was another child. The baby was at her breast, the one in her arms, and this child on the floor was, I should judge, about 3 years of age. They were burned. Whether she was demoralized or driven insane I don't know. She stayed in the house.

The Chairman. What troops were those?

The Witness. M Company, the Twenty-sixth.

By Senator Patterson:

Q. How many men were there in M Company at that time?—A. I don't know, sir.

Q. About how many?—A. There were very nearly a hundred.

Senator Dubois. Excuse me a moment. I did not catch the name of the town.

The Witness. La Nog.

By Senator Beveridge:

Q. Where is that?—A. About 16 miles—

Q. On what island?—A. Panay. It is northeast of Igbarras about 16 miles. . . .

Senator Carmack. Were any orders given when you entered the town about prisoners or anything of that sort?—A. No, sir. In regard to that order being issued, as he would go along in Indian file, the word would pass along "take no prisoners." Nobody would know where it emanated from.

By Senator Beveridge:

Q. Where would you get that order?—A. It would start at the head of the line and come down.

Q. Did you think that unusual?—A. No; we did not then.

Q. Did you inquire where the order came from?—A. No, sir.

Q. Did your sergeant give you the order?—A. I don't know, sir.

Q. It came down the line?—A. It came down the line; yes.

Q. And you obeyed it?—A. Yes.

Senator Patterson. What was the result of that order or those orders at any time?

The Witness. Well, if there was any fighting the fighting was continued until everybody had fled or everybody was killed. . . .

By Senator Dietrich:

Q. A while ago, while you were stating about one of the battles, you stated it was very difficult to make close observations while you were in the heat of battle. It is pretty hard to observe things in battle, is it not?—A. Yes, sir.

Q. Where was this fight or battle where these two old men were killed?—A. At La Nog.

Q. How many insurgents were there there?—A. No insurgents, so far as I know, because there were no shots fired by the Filipinos.

Q. How many American soldiers were there?—A. I cannot say, because there were some men stationed at Guimbal.

Q. Were you there?—A. I was at La Nog; yes, sir.

Q. Did you see these men killed?—A. Yes, sir.

Q. You say that they raised the flag of truce?—A. They had a white flag; some sort of a piece of white cloth on a bamboo stick. They came out hand in hand; they had their hands clasped.

Q. Did you shoot at them?—A. No, sir; I did not.

Q. Did you see anybody else shoot at them?—A. Yes, sir.

Q. Who?—A. Well, I saw people shooting in that direction; I don't know whether they were shooting directly at those people or not.

Senator Beveridge. Could you give the names of those whom you saw shoot?—A. No, sir. I know Sergeant Conway . . . reported to Captain McDonald that he had killed two more niggers.

PART IV

Religious and Ethnic Violence

Persecution of Quakers
1656–1661

Although the Puritans had fled from religious persecution, they had no intention of setting up a regime of religious freedom in the New World. Those who lived among them were expected to worship in the Puritan way alone. At first, in the open spaces of America, the Puritan fathers conceived of banishment after warning as the way to deal with heretics and nonconformists, and this was the penalty meted out to Roger Williams and Anne Hutchinson.

The Quakers, with their fanatical persistence, proved more difficult. They came to stay, and if ejected would often return. Persecution seemed only to attract more of them, and they kept trickling in. The first Quakers, two women from Barbados, were clapped into jail in 1656, stripped, and searched for signs of witchcraft; their books were seized and burned in the market-place. At length they were shipped off to Barbados again. As Quakers continued to come, more severe punishments were resorted to—whipping, ear cropping, branding, and tongue boring. In 1658 the General Court resolved to use the death penalty, but this only attracted more volunteers for martyrdom. In 1659 three Quakers were sentenced to death. One, Mary Dyer, was spared at the last minute and banished, though she returned once again and was finally hanged in 1660. In 1661 a fourth Quaker was hanged. By this time, with twenty-eight Quakers in prison, some of the Puritan leaders gagged at the thought of an unlimited number of executions—and that even without assured success against the Quaker invasions. Several judges now balked at a death verdict. In the meantime, the monarchy had been restored in England, and the English Quaker, Edward Burrough, won an audience with Charles II to tell him of the Massachusetts persecutions. The king listened with sympathy, summoned his lords to hear, and remarked: "Lo, these are my good subjects of New England. I will put a stop to them and grant appeals to England." Executions, but not all lesser persecutions, were stopped. Only in 1674 did Boston Quakers begin to worship in peace; in 1697 they were able to build their first meetinghouse there.

The following petition by Quakers to Charles, begging his intervention in their behalf against the Massachusetts laws, was reprinted and introduced in Joseph Besse: *A Collection of the Sufferings of the People Called Quakers* (London, 1753), I, xxvi–xxxii. For a suggestive discussion of the Quaker persecutions from a sociological standpoint, see Kai Erikson: *Wayward Puritans: A Study in the Sociology of Deviants* (1966). See also George Bishop: *New England Judged by the Spirit of the Lord* (1703); and Brooks Adams: *The Emancipation of Massachusetts* (1887).

During the continuance under so rigorous a persecution here in England, the popular prejudice against them spread itself also into foreign countries, especially the English Plantations in America, where falsehood and calumny had anticipated their arrival, and prepossessed the minds of those in Authority against them: hence it came to pass that in New-England a set of fiery zealots, who, through impatience under sufferings from the Bishops in Old-England, had fled from thence, being invested with power, and placed at the helm of government, exceeded all others in their cruelty towards this people, the barbarity of whose reception soon after their first arrival there, is well described in a summary account thereof drawn up by some of the sufferers, and presented to King Charles the Second after his Restoration, by Edward Burrough, being as follows, viz.

"A DECLARATION OF SOME PART OF THE SUFFERINGS OF THE PEOPLE OF GOD IN SCORN CALLED QUAKERS, FROM THE PROFESSORS IN NEW-ENGLAND, ONLY FOR THE EXERCISE OF THEIR CONSCIENCES TO THE LORD, AND OBEYING AND CONFESSING TO THE TRUTH, AS IN HIS LIGHT HE HAD DISCOVERED IT TO THEM.

"1. Two honest and innocent women stripped stark naked, and searched after such an inhuman manner, as modesty will not permit particularly to mention.

"2. Twelve strangers in that country, but free-born of this nation, received twenty-three whippings, the most of them being with a whip of three cords with knots at the ends, and laid on with as much strength as could be by the arm of their executioner, the stripes amounting to three hundred and seventy.

"3. Eighteen inhabitants of the country, being free-born English, received twenty-three whippings, the stripes amounting to two hundred and fifty. . . .

"5. Two beaten with pitched ropes, the blows amounting to an hundred and thirty-nine, by which one of them brought near unto death, much of his body being beaten like unto a jelly, and one of their doctors, a member of their church, who saw him, said, *it would be a miracle if ever he recovered, he expecting the flesh should rot off the bones*, who afterwards was banished upon pain of death. There are many witnesses of this there. . . .

"10. One laid neck and heels in irons for sixteen hours.

"11. One very deeply burnt in the right hand with the letter H after he had been whipt with above thirty stripes.

"12. One chained to a log of wood the most part of twenty days, in an open prison, in the winter-time. . . .

"14. Three had their right ears cut by the hangman in the prison, the door being barred, and not a Friend suffered to be present while it was doing, though some much desired. . . .

"18. Also three of the servants of the lord they put to death, all of them for obedience to the truth, in the testimony of it, against the WICKED RULERS and LAWS at Boston. . . .

"These things, O King! from time to time have we patiently suffered, and not for the transgression of any just or righteous law, either pertaining to the worship of God, or the civil government of England, but simply and barely for our consciences to God. . . .

"And this, O King! we are assured of, that in time to come it will not repent thee, if by a close rebuke thou stoppest the BLOODY PROCEEDINGS of these BLOODY PERSECUTORS, for in so doing thou wilt engage the heart of many honest people unto thee both there and here, and for such works of mercy the blessing is obtained; and shewing it is the way to prosper: we are witnesses of these things, who

"Besides many long imprisonments, and many cruel whippings, had our ears cut,

JOHN ROUSE   JOHN COPELAND."

Burning of Ursuline Convent
1834

In the late 1820's large numbers of Irish immigrants arrived in the Eastern seaboard cities, and slums began to grow. The Irish had no choice but to accept the wages offered them, however low, but native workers resented the threat this posed to their wage level. The Protestant tradition had long equated Catholicism, and despotism, and had denounced Catholics for their subservience to Rome; now some writers began to say that the Catholicism of the Irish made them a threat to American democratic institutions. By the early 1830's some groups began to organize against the supposed menace. The Protestant Association was founded in 1831 in New York to propagandize against Catholicism. In Massachusetts the General Association of Congregational Churches urged pastors to save the country "from the degrading influence of popery."

Religious, ethnic, and class tensions came to a head, particularly in Boston, over the issue of Catholic schools. The unfamiliar nature of convent schools in particular gave rise to all sorts of speculation about immoral behavior and to sensational rumors about secret passageways from priests' homes to nunneries, the sexual abuse of female students by confessors, and the burial of illegitimate babies in convent crypts.

In 1834, Elizabeth Harrison, an unstable nun at the Ursuline Convent in Charlestown, Massachusetts, ran away and asked local citizens to help her. Soon after she reconsidered, asked to be readmitted, and was taken back. Even though Charlestown selectmen visited her and satisfied themselves that she wanted to stay, rumors persisted that she had been forced to go back. One public notice read: "To Arms!! To Arms!! Ye brave and free. The avenging sword unshield!! Leave not one stone upon another of that curst Nunnery that prostitutes female virtue and liberty under the garb of holy Religion. When Bonaparte opened the Nunneries in Europe he found cords of infant skulls!!!!!"

On August 11, a mob led by Charlestown truckmen and New Hampshire brickmakers sacked and burned the convent, as described in the following document: *Documents Relating to the Ursuline Convent in Charlestown . . .* (1842), 13–14. See Ephraim Tucker: "The Burning of the Ursuline Convent," Worcester Society of Antiquity *Collections*, IX, 40–1; Oscar Handlin: *Boston's Immigrants* (1941); and Ray Alan Billington: *The Protestant Crusade, 1800–1860* (1938).

Soon after 9 o'clock, the rioters began to assemble in considerable numbers, arriving on foot and in wagons from different quarters; and a party of about forty or fifty proceeded to the front of the building, using violent and threatening language. They were addressed by the lady at the head of the establishment, who, desiring to know their wishes, was replied to that they wanted to enter and see the person alleged to be secreted. She answered, that their selectmen had that day visited the house, and could give them satisfactory information, and that any of them on calling the next day at a suitable hour, might see for themselves; at the same time remonstrating against such violation of the peace and of the repose of so many children of their most reputable citizens.

Shortly afterwards, the same, or another party, with increased numbers, approached the convent, using still more threatening and much gross and indecent language. The lady above referred to again addressed them in terms of remonstrance and reproach, and desired to know whether none of their selectmen were present. Some of them replied that one was there, mentioning his name. He then came forward and announced his presence, stating that he was there for the purpose of defending her. She inquired whether he had procured the attendance of any others of the Board; and upon being answered in the negative, replied that she would not trust the establishment to his protection, and that if he came there to protect them, he should show it by taking measures to disperse the mob.

It appears from various testimony that he did attempt to dissuade the rioters from their design, by assurances that the selectmen had seen the nun who was supposed to have been secreted, and that the stories reported concerning her were untrue. But his assertions drew forth only expressions of distrust and insult. The mob continued upon the ground with much noise and tumult, and were in that state left by this magistrate, who returned home and retired to bed.

At about eleven o'clock, a bonfire was kindled on the land of Alvah

Kelly, adjoining that of the eastern boundary of the convent, and distant about two hundred and seventy yards from the building, the fences of which were taken for the purpose. This is believed to have been a concerted signal for the assembling of all concerned in the plot.

The bells were then rung as for an alarm of fire, in Charlestown and in this city, and great multitudes arrived from all quarters. . . . The attack was instantly commenced by the breaking of fences, and the hurling of stones and clubs against the windows and doors. . . .

At the time of this attack upon the convent, there were within its walls, about sixty female children and ten adults; one of whom was in the last stages of pulmonary consumption, another suffering under convulsion fits, and the unhappy female, who had been the immediate cause of the excitement, was by the agitations of the night in raving delirium.

No warning was given of the intended assault, nor could the miscreants, by whom it was made, have known whether their missiles might not kill or wound the helpless inmates of this devoted dwelling. Fortunately for them, cowardice prompted what mercy and manhood denied: after the first attack, the assailants paused awhile from the fear that some secret force was concealed in the convent or in ambush to surprise them; and in this interval the governess was enabled to secure the retreat of her little flock and terrified sisters into the garden. But before this was fully effected, the rioters, finding they had nothing but women and children to contend against, regained their courage, and ere all the inmates could escape, entered the building. . . . The mob had now full possession of the house, and loud cries were heard for torches or lights. . . .

Three or four torches which were, or precisely resembled engine torches, were then brought up from the road; and immediately upon their arrival, the rioters proceeded into every room in the building, rifling every drawer, desk and trunk which they found, and breaking up and destroying all the furniture, and casting much of it from the windows; sacrificing in their brutal fury, costly piano fortes and harps, and other valuable instruments; the little treasures of children, abandoned in their hasty flight; and even the vessels and symbols of christian worship.

After having thus ransacked every room in the building, they proceeded with great deliberation, about one o'clock, to make preparation for setting fire to it. For this purpose, broken furniture, books, curtains and other combustible materials, were placed in the centre of several of the rooms; and, as if in mockery of God as well as of man, the Bible was cast, with shouts of exultation, upon the pile first kindled; and as upon this were subsequently thrown the vestments used in religious service, and the ornaments of the altar, these shouts and yells were repeated. Nor did they cease until the Cross was wrenched from its place, and cast into the flames, as the final triumph of this fiend-like enterprise.

But the work of destruction did not end here. Soon after the convent was in flames, the rioters passed to the library, or bishop's lodge, which stood near, and after throwing the books and pictures from the windows, a prey to those without, fired that also.

Some time afterwards they proceeded to the farm-house, formerly occupied as the convent, and first making a similar assault with stones and clubs upon the doors and windows, in order to ascertain whether they had any thing to fear from persons within, the torches were deliberately applied to that building; and, unwilling to leave one object connected with the establishment to escape their fury, although the day had broken, and three buildings were then in flames or reduced to ashes, the extensive barn, with its contents, was in like manner devoted to destruction. And not content with all this, they burst open the tomb of the establishment, rifled it of the sacred vessels there deposited, wrested the plates from the coffins, and exposed to view the mouldering remains of their tenants.

Nor is it the least humiliating feature in this scene of cowardly and audacious violation of all that man ought to hold sacred and dear, that it was perpetrated in the presence of men vested with authority, and of the multitudes of our fellow citizens, while not one arm was lifted in the defence of helpless women and children, or in vindication of the violated laws of God and man. The spirit of violence, sacrilege, and plunder, reigned triumphant.

Anti-Mormon Riot

1838

The early history of the Mormon Church from its founding by Joseph Smith in Western New York in 1830 is a tale of persecution and flight. The Mormons moved first to Ohio in search of peace, but there, in 1832 and 1833, they were tarred and feathered, beaten and shot, and their homes were destroyed. They moved again in 1838, this time to Missouri, but soon they were attacked once again. The governor of Missouri declared that "the Mormons must be treated as enemies and must be exterminated or driven from the state, if necessary, for the public good." On October 30, 1838, a mob led by three state militia captains fell upon a small colony of Mormons at Haun's Mill and killed or wounded most of them.

The Mormons next fled to Carthage, Illinois, but there persecution continued. On June 27, 1844, after Smith had imperiously ordered the Mormons to destroy a local newspaper which criticized him, Smith and his brother were jailed on the charge of inciting a riot. There they were killed by a mob. Afterwards, Mormons took their last long trek to Utah under the leadership of Brigham Young.

The following account of the Haun's Mill massacre, written by Joseph Young, Brigham Young's elder brother, is taken from John P. Greene: *Facts Relative to the Expulsion of the Mormons or Latter Day Saints, from the State of Missouri under the "Exterminating Order"* (1939). See Fawn Brodie: *No Man Knows My History* (1945).

It was about 4 o'clock, while sitting in my cabin with my babe in my arms, and my wife standing by my side, the door being open, I cast my eyes on the opposite bank of Shoal-creek, and saw a large company of armed men, on horses, directing their course towards the mills with all possible speed. As they advanced through the scattering trees that stood on the edge of the prairie, they seemed to form themselves into a three-square position, forming a van-guard in front. At this moment, David Evans, seeing the superiority of their numbers, (there being 240 of them, according to their own account,) swung his hat, and cried for peace. This not being heeded, they continued to advance, and their leader, Mr. Comstock, fired a gun, which was followed by a solemn pause of ten or twelve seconds, when, all at once, they discharged about 100 rifles, aiming at a blacksmith shop into which our friends had fled for safety; and charging up to the shop, the cracks of which between the logs were sufficiently large to enable them to aim directly at the bodies of those who had there fled for refuge from the fire of their murderers. There were several families tented in rear of the shop, whose lives were exposed, and amidst a shower of bullets fled to the woods in different directions.

After standing and gazing on this bloody scene for a few minutes, and finding myself in the uttermost danger, the bullets having reached the house where I was living, I committed my family to the protection of Heaven, and leaving the house on the opposite side, I took a path which led up the hill, following the trail of three of my brethren that had fled from the shop. While ascending the hill we were discovered by the mob, who immediately fired at us, and continued to do so till we reached the summit. In descending the hill I secreted myself in a thicket of bushes where I lay till eight o'clock in the evening, at which time I heard a female voice calling my name in an undertone, telling me that the mob had gone, and there was no danger. I immediately left the thicket, and went to the house of Benjamin Lewis, where I found my family, (who had fled there,) in safety, and two of my friends, mortally wounded, one of whom died before morning.

Here we passed the painful night in deep and awful reflections on the scenes of the preceding evening. After day-light appeared, some four or five men, with myself, who had escaped with our lives from the horrid massacre, repaired as soon as possible to the mills, to learn the condition of our friends, whose fate we had but too truly anticipated.

When we arrived at the house of Mr. Honn, we found Mr. Merrick's body lying in rear of the house;—Mr. McBride's in front, literally mangled from head to foot. We were informed by Miss Rebecca Judd, who was an eye witness, that he was shot with his own gun, after he had given it up, and then cut to pieces with a corn cutter, by a Mr. Rogers, of Davies county, who keeps a ferry on Grand River, and who has since repeatedly boasted of this act of savage barbarity. Mr. York's body we found in the house, and after viewing these corpses, we immediately went to the blacksmith shop, where we found nine of our friends, eight of whom were already dead; the other, Mr. Cox, of Indiana, struggling in the agonies of death, who expired. We immediately prepared and carried them to the place of interment. This last office of kindness due to the relics of departed friends, was not attended with the customary ceremonies, nor decency, for we were in jeopardy, every moment expecting to be fired upon by the mob, who, we supposed, were lying in ambush, waiting for the first opportunity to despatch the remaining few who were providentially preserved from the slaughter of the preceding day. However, we accomplished, without molestation, this painful task. The place of burying was a vault in the ground, formerly intended for a well, into which we threw the bodies of our friends promiscuously.

Among those slain I will mention Sardius Smith, son of Warren Smith, about 9 years old, who, through fear, had crawled under the bellows in the shop, where he remained till the massacre was over, when he was discovered by a Mr. Glaze of Carroll county, who presented his rifle near the boy's head and literally blowed off the upper part of it. Mr. Stanley of Carroll told me afterwards that Glaze boasted of this fiendlike murder and heroic deed all over the country.

The number killed and mortally wounded in this wanton slaughter was 18 or 19. . . .

To finish their work of destruction this band of murderers composed of men from Davies, Livingston, Ray, Carroll and Chariton counties, led by some of the principal men of that section of the upper country . . . proceeded to rob houses, wagons and tents, of bedding and clothing, drove off horses and wagons, leaving widows and orphans destitute of the necessaries of life, and even stripped the clothing from the bodies of the slain!

Philadelphia Nativist Riots
1844

Central Philadelphia was peopled mainly by native American Protestants, its industrial suburbs by many immigrant Catholic workers. In the 1820's and '30's the two groups had often clashed in election riots, fights between volunteer fire companies, and ethnic and religious quarrels. In the early 1840's the use of the Protestant Bible in the public schools became a source of contention. When the Catholic Bishop of Philadelphia persuaded the school authorities to allow the Catholic Bible as well, many Protestants were incensed.

In 1844 in the suburb of Kensington, a group of American Protestants announced that they would hold a meeting in the Third Ward, an Irish stronghold. On May 3 and again on May

6 the Irish repelled their unwanted visitors. After the second incident the city was in an uproar. Street speakers denounced Catholics; one nativist journal announced: "The bloody hand of the Pope has stretched itself forth to our destruction," and urged Protestants to arm themselves. On May 7, a Protestant mob shrieking: "Kill them. Kill them. Blood for Blood!" marched to the Irish section, burned down over thirty homes and tenements, and two churches. Fourteen or more persons were killed or injured.

On July 5, rumors spread that weapons had been collected in the Church of St. Philip de Neri in Southwark, another suburb, and a mob formed outside. A committee discovered guns and ammunition in the church, and tried to keep the discovery a secret, but the news spread. For a time the mob was prevented from assaulting the church by the state militia. Then on July 7 the crowd heard that armed Irish volunteers—the Hibernia Greens—were inside the church, and demanded their removal. As the volunteers left, they were taunted by the mob and fired back. Both sides later returned to the church with augmented forces, the Irish volunteers and the rioters both armed with cannon. The mob shot their cannon, the Irish replied with theirs. In this riot, at least thirteen persons were killed and more than fifty wounded. Two grand juries placed all the blame on the Irish, but many people throughout the nation condemned the nativists for their violence and their destruction of property.

The following account was written by a Catholic who witnessed the events as a young boy and wrote about them thirty years later. It was published as "The Anti-Catholic Riots in Philadelphia in 1844," in *American Catholic Historical Researches*, XIII (April 1896), 60–4. See also Ray A. Billington: *The Protestant Crusade, 1800–1860* (1938); and Elizabeth M. Geffen: "Violence in Philadelphia in the 1840's & 50's," *Pennsylvania History*, XXXVI (October 1969).

Instead of longing for the glorious 4th of July we dreaded its approach— many feared a renewal of the fearful scenes of violence May had brought us. What, then, was our surprise when early on the morrow we learned that the pastor of the adjoining parish of St. Philip's, whose church was situated in the most bigoted part of Southwark, surrounded with the most ignorant and reckless sort of Nativists, had, the day before, openly, in broad daylight, had arms and ammunition carried into the church, and that a company of volunteers, called the "Hibernia Greens," were in possession of the sacred edifice. It was a day of fearful, yea, truly awful, anxiety. During the evening, rumor, busy jade, caused many a heart to beat in dread, and many a head to bow in prayer.

On the Festival of the Most Precious Blood, my sisters and I offered our holy communion that God might protect our churches and our homes. During this season of terror our first thoughts were always not for ourselves or homes but for our churches. Judging of others by ourselves, there were few Catholics who would not have gratefully looked on the ashes of their homes, if the House of God were only spared. After the eight and half o'clock Mass we walked down to the fortified temple. The excited crowd of the previous night was all dispersed, and, except by ourselves, and a few other of the curious descendants of an unhappily curious mother, the street was deserted. Had the authorities of the municipality of Southwark, whose office was "round the corner," posted a dozen constables in the neighborhood, no mob had assembled on the 6th day of July 1844.

Our apprehensions having been allayed by the peaceful surroundings of the church, we took our usual seats in St. Mary's for the late Mass. Our pew, being on the South side of the altar, commanded a view of the greater part of the congregation. Every thing proceeded *secundum regulum et etiam consuetudines*, until the Elevation, when the startling clamor of an approaching mob was heard. Many a rosy countenance assumed the hue of the lily. . . .

I noticed that most of the men who occupied places within the pews at once arose quietly, and respectfully, and placed themselves next the door. Nearer and nearer came the cries,—a member of the city Council, who, on the evening before, when the commander of military had given the order to fire upon the mob, had stepped before the cannon's mouth and countermanded that order, and who had then been taken prisoner and incarcerated in the House of the God of peace, had been released from confinement, and was being carried in triumph by the mob to his dwelling near St. Mary's Church. Nearer and nearer came the shouts, but the celebrant, if he felt any fear, showed none, as the God of battles lay before him. Nearer and nearer yet came the yells, and as they passed behind the church the solemn *miserere nobis* was over, and the soothing *dona nobis pacem* of Di Monti in D floated melodiously upon our anxious ears. Further and further receded the tumult and when the *Ite missa est* was chanted all was still. . . .

All this while the neighborhood of St. Philip's Church was in a ferment of excitement. Queen Street and all the streets leading to it were filled with a disorderly mass of people, so that it was deemed advisable to make some concessions to the mob. A parley was beat and it was agreed that the Company of Hibernia Greens, occupying the Church, should march out with arms unloaded and reversed. All of them did not comply with the agreement. Unfortunately when they reached Second and Catharine Streets, provoked at the cruel taunts of the rabble, they turned and fired into the crowd, and believing that "he who fights and runs away may live to fight another day," they plied their heels and scattered ingloriously in every direction. Some did not stop running until they reached Germantown and Manayunk, and Norristown, and other suburban localities more agreeable for their security than for odors; it has been said that two of them continued their weary pedestrianism until they reached New York City.

Some of the yelping mob pursued the swift warriors. One poor fellow named Gallagher was chased to Sixth and Small Streets, about half a mile from the scene of bold and daring deeds, when running panting into a house, the good house mother hid him between two feather beds. At first the hounds were baffled in the search, and having lost the scent they were about retiring as well bred curs, when the glitter of his regimentals caught the sight of one whose snarl soon recalled the others. A rope was soon around his neck and down the stairs was he dragged and along the streets for fully three quarters of a mile to Christian and Fourth Streets where a culvert was building, when the inhuman wretches amused themselves in heaving large cobblestones upon him, varied at intervals by six or eight heavy men jumping upon him; twice they hanged him to a lamp-post, till after two hours of torture indescribable he was rescued and carried to the Pennsylvania Hospital. On the next Sunday I saw him apparently unscarred and unscathed. It has been remarked that in both these riots it was impossible to kill an Irishman. . . .

The firing of the brave "lads in Green" was the signal for the attack upon the Church. In ten minutes the interior was gutted. Lewis C. Levin, whose wife, daughter, and step-daughter have since been received into the Church by one of our fathers, mounting the sacred table in front of the tabernacle, delivered a harangue, which for blasphemy and ribaldry would have befitted the days of the French Revolution.

General Cadwalader, who commanded the military, had established his headquarters at the old Girard Bank in Third Street opposite Dock. Finding it necessary to be there, he with two of his officers, in citizen dress and unarmed, entered a close carriage at the Church, and had succeeded in passing through the mob, when they were recognized by an old woman, the wife of a Catholic who had not sense enough to hold his silence. At once the cry and hue was raised of "Old Cadwalader! Bloody Cadwalader! Irish Cadwalader!" and four or five hundred started in pursuit. The driver drove for life. When turning Second Street into Pine, a stalwart American citizen of Scotch birth caught the near horse by the bit, and the carriage was brought to a halt. My eldest brother, whose dormant Catholicity had been roused by the persecution, and whom my good mother imagined she had safely locked up in the second story back room, but who had climbed the pipe and was in the midst of the excitement, taking in the situation with a glance of the eye, although a slender, weak young man, seized the gentleman from Glasgow by the throat and dashed him to the ground, while the *noble* brutes dashed wildly on. Henry, Henry, why were you so reckless? As it was generally believed that my brother was anti-Catholic, acquaintances surrounded him and his bad reputation saved him from the fury of the mob, who would willingly have made him a victim to their baffled rage.

The majority of the mob pursued the fleeing commander-in-chief until they reached Third and Spruce Streets. Third Street between Spruce and Walnut was at that time paved with wooden blocks. The horses on reaching this smooth pavement made such speed that the mob, having a salutary fear of the loaded cannons that guarded the entrance to the bank, gave over the pursuit.

They halted and consulted as to their further proceedings. A part proposed to attack the Jesuit Church in Willing's Alley, but it was too near headquarters; some suggested St. Mary's, but the majority wished to return to the field of their preceding efforts; and the majority, as in all well regulated mobs, carried the day. . . .

In the meanwhile the rioters were not idle. They had gone to all the stores for squares, and made requisitions, collecting all the powder, shot, nails, chains, in fact everything that could be used in loading the cannon they had obtained. Then they waited for the night.

It was a night of more than ordinary darkness. The moon was ashamed to look upon such doings and the stars kept her company. At the usual hour the gas was lighted, but was soon extinguished by the rioters in their neighborhood. At this time the military were in the Church and guards were posted on all sides to meet the mob if it should attempt to regain possession. Poor soldiers! they were in a most trying position. On the roofs of all the surrounding buildings were men, and women, and boys, with muskets, and rifles, and pistols, and stones, and hot water to fire and pour down upon them. They stood out boldly in the light. Whilst the rabble at Queen and Front Streets could take easy aim, themselves being in the dark, the only thing the soldiers had to direct their aim was the flash of the cannon, which the rioters would load in Front Street, then suddenly wheel round into Queen Street, take deliberate aim, fire, and the man who applied the match was back in Front Street almost before the soldiers had seen the flash. . . .

In the small wee hours of July 7th, the weary mob, seeing that victory was not theirs, gradually dispersed, and by 4 o'clock, the soldiers were sleeping upon the pavements of Queen, Second and Third Streets, or talking together and partaking of refreshments furnished by the neighbors. . . .

For weeks a heavy gloom hung over Philadelphia. The city was still under martial law, and the streets leading to the Catholic churches being guarded by soldiers, not a little inconvenience was caused to pedestrians, and as then we had few omnibuses and no street cars, most people had to pedestrianize.

Pentecost Riot in Hoboken
1851

The nineteenth-century Turnverein was a German society which combined gymnastics and politics. Founded in Berlin in 1811 by Friedrich Ludwig Jahn, these clubs taught liberal and sometimes socialist ideals along with physical training. *Mens sana in corpore sano* was their motto. The first American branch was founded in 1824, and after the 1848 migration from Germany the organization flourished. By 1856, there were Turner organizations in twenty-eight states.

In the 1850's the Turners increasingly took on another function: to protect Germans against assaults by nativists and, ironically, by conservative Catholic Irish immigrants who hated Turners for their liberalism. In some cities Turners organized into paramilitary companies. In Hoboken, New Jersey, in 1851, a group of German workers and their families, including many Turners, celebrating Pentecost Sunday at a picnic were attacked by a mob of rowdies, nativists, and immigrants. The disciplined Turners' counterattack led to a wild melee in which one person was killed and dozens were wounded.

The following account is taken from the New York *Herald Tribune*, May 27, 1851. See Carl Wittke: *Refugees of Revolution: The German Forty-Eighters in America* (1952).

RIOT IN HOBOKEN

*Assault on the Germans, Several Persons Killed—Great Excitement—
The Military Called Out*

Yesterday was celebrated by the German residents of this City as the holiday of Pentecost—a day which in Germany is commemorated by festivals in the woods. A large number of Germans, ten to twelve thousand in all, perhaps, crossed to Hoboken in the morning, after assembling in the Park where they formed into line, displaying the national colors. They had leased for the day the "Cricket Ground," some distance from the village, and on the western side of the road. Here, under the trees, stands for the sale of beer and refreshments were erected, beside a platform for the orators of the day and a band of music which accompanied them. All parties present seemed to enjoy themselves, and the beer, especially, flowed in torrents from the barrels on tap down hundreds of thirsty throats.

Everything passed off peaceably till towards the close of the afternoon, when some difficulties occurred through the presence of a gang of rowdies belonging to the city, and known by the title of "the Short Boys." These scamps, whose existence as an organized body has disgraced this city for some time past, went on the ground in company with a number of lawless characters, some belonging to Hoboken and some to our side of the river, and very soon created a disturbance at the scene of the festival. According to different representations, there were about forty in all, some of them Germans, some Irish, and some Americans. They were armed, and evidently came for the purpose of assault, as they commenced, without provocation, to insult the females, overthrow the refreshment tables, and destroy the property of the vendors. This was about half past three in the afternoon at the Race Course. The Germans, who saw the object of the rowdies, had determined, at first, to avoid a collision, on account of the number of ladies and children who were present, but these outrages were not to be tolerated, and the offenders were driven off. The rowdies retreated toward the Elysian Fields, and were followed by the Germans. The Short Boys obtained access to the house at the Fields, kept by McCarthy, and a regular fight commenced. The Germans had now become infuriated, and after driving off the Short Boys from the house they commenced breaking the furniture. The keeper of the house and his wife were assaulted and driven off. McCarthy, we are told, made his retreat to a part of the house where he had a double-barreled gun, already loaded. With this he shot two of the Germans, killing them instantly, and he seriously injured another by knocking him over with his gun. The house was completely riddled, and everything that it contained thoroughly demolished.

After being driven from the Elysian Fields, the rowdies retreated towards the village, followed by the Germans, and a sort of running fight was kept up for the whole distance. The Zurn-verein [sic] (Society of Gymnasts) took an active part in the conflict, and were marked out as special subjects of resentment. On reaching the village, the rowdies were reinforced by others from this side of the river and by a gang of boys from 14 to 16 years of age. Towards evening, they assembled before the gates of the ferry, and prevented the Germans coming in from the festival from reaching the boat. For more than an hour they shut off all communication. About half-past six the procession, consisting of the Zurn-verein, the Liederkranz, (Musical Society) the Social Batallion and other associations, accompanied by large numbers of Germans with their families, came in from the woods for the purpose of returning to this city. The front of the procession had scarcely reached the Otto Cottage, before it was assailed by a shower of stones, the boys who were with the rowdies occupying themselves with assaulting the females, many of whom were struck and severely bruised. The procession halted and the Zurners, taking the lead, advanced against the mob, for the purpose of clearing a way to the ferry boat. A violent fight then commenced, which lasted with little intermission for two hours. The rowdies were armed with guns, pistols, swords, clubs and sling shots, and after the first attack the Germans entered the German beer-houses in the neighborhood and armed themselves. Two are known to be killed, one a Zurner and the other an Irish boy, one of the gang, about eighteen years of age. Another Zurner named Gabi, a Hungarian, received a charge of buckshot in his leg.

Previous to the arrival of the procession, all the returning Germans were assaulted indiscriminately, some of them being knocked down while walking with ladies. Sometimes they were asked if they were Germans, before being struck, and one who replied in the affirmative to the question whether he was a Turner immediately received a musket ball in his side. It is said that the house of a German named Beiner was attacked and the furniture demolished. A great number of persons were severely, and some mortally, injured. Many were stabbed in different parts of the body, or beaten with stones. One man had his head shockingly cut by a large pole, the end of which was covered with spikes. The fight was one of the most brutal and sanguinary which ever occurred in this vicinity. The Sheriff of the County was early on the ground, endeavoring to quell the riot. He made two applications to the police authorities on this side for assistance, but for some reason it was refused. He then ordered the citizens to assist him, and also ordered out the military from Jersey City. In their efforts to stop the fight, Justice Browning and a man named Hickey were wounded so badly that it is thought they will not recover. The Sheriff was also badly cut on the head. The riot was mostly over before the arrival of the military from Jersey City. . . .

The number of arrests made was near forty, a large portion of whom were Germans. They were bound hand and foot, and sent to the County Jail at Bergen. The militia remained on guard till half-past 11 o'clock, when everything appeared to be quiet, and they left. At 1 o'clock this morning, when our reporter left, there were no signs of disturbance in any part of the village, and the rioters of both parties had all returned to this city. It is impossible precisely to ascertain the number of killed and wounded. There are certainly four of the former and probably fifty of the latter, some of whom will not recover. Twelve or fifteen of the rowdies were badly injured.

Louisville
1855

In the 1850's large numbers of Germans emigrated to the United States. Many went to the mid-west, particularly to the cities of the Mississippi Valley, including Louisville, Kentucky.

Some were radicals, forced to leave when the revolution of
1848 failed. They advocated women's suffrage, direct election
of all officials, ending of prayer in Congress, ending of capital
punishment, public lands for colonists, and, most troublesome
of all, abolition of slavery and equality for blacks. Others were
Catholics, against whom there was considerable prejudice. In
1854, Louisville anti-German nativists organized a Know-
Nothing Party; in response the Germans organized a group
called the Sag-Nichts. At election times the two groups often
fought for control of the polls. An August 6, 1855, the Know-
Nothings captured the polls before dawn, and with the aid of
police and sympathetic local officials, pulled immigrant Americans out of voting lines and beat them. Gun fights began at noon
and spread over the city. By evening twenty people had been
killed and large numbers had been injured.

The following account is taken from the Louisville *Courier*,
an anti-Know-Nothing journal, as reprinted in *The New York
Times*, August 10, 1855. See also Charles E. Deusner: "The
Know Nothing Riots in Louisville," *Register of the Kentucky
Historical Society*, LXI (1963), 122–47.

We passed, yesterday, through the forms of an election. As provided by
the statute, the polls were opened, and privilege granted to such as were
"right upon the goose," with a few exceptions, to exercise their elective
franchise. Never, perhaps, was a greater farce, or as we should term it
tragedy, enacted. Hundreds and thousands were deterred from voting by
direct acts of intimidation, others through fear of consequences, and a
multitude from the lack of proper facilities. The city, indeed, was, during
the day, in possession of an armed mob, the base passions of which were
infuriated to the highest pitch by the incendiary appeals of the newspaper
organ and the popular leaders of the Know-Nothing party.

On Sunday night, large detachments of men were sent to the First
and Second Wards to see that the polls were properly opened. These men,
the "American Executive Committee," supplied with requisite *refreshments*,
and as may be imagined they were in very fit condition on yesterday
morning to see that the rights of freemen were respected. Indeed they
discharged the important trusts committed to them in such manner as
to commend them forever to the admiration of outlaws! They opened
the polls; they provided ways and means for their own party to vote;
they buffed and bullied all who could not show the sign; they in fact con-

verted the election into a perfect farce, without one redeeming or quali-
fying phase.

We do not know when or how their plan of operations was devised.
Indeed we do not care to know when such systems of outrage—such
perfidy—such dastardy—was conceived. We only blush for Kentucky
that her soil was the scene of such outrages, and that some of her sons
were participants in the nefarious swindle.

It would be impossible to know when or how this riot commenced. By
daybreak the polls were taken possession of by the American party, and
in pursuance of their preconcerted game, they used every stratagem or
device to hinder the vote of every man who could not manifest to the
"guardians of the polls" his soundness on the K. N. question. We were
personally witnesses to the procedure of the party in certain wards, and
of these we feel authorized to speak. At the Seventh Ward we discovered
that for three hours in the outset in the morning it was impossible for
those not "posted" to vote, without the greatest difficulty. In the Sixth
Ward a party of bullies were masters of the polls. We saw two foreigners
driven from the polls, forced to run a gauntlet, beat unmercifully, stoned
and stabbed. In the case of one fellow, Hon. Wm. Thomasson, formerly a
member of Congress from this District, interfered, and while appealing
to the maddened crowd to cease their acts of disorder and violence, Mr.
Thomasson was struck from behind and beat. His gray hairs, his long
public service, his manly presence, and his thorough Americanism, availed
nothing with the crazed mob. Other and serious fights occurred in the
Sixth Ward, of which we have no time to make mention now.

The more serious and disgraceful disturbances occurred in the upper
wards. The vote cast was but a partial one, and nearly altogether on one
side. No show was given to the friends of Preston, who were largely in
the majority, but who, in the face of cannon, musket and revolvers, could
not, being an unarmed and quiet populace, confront the mad mob. So the
vote was cast one way, and the result stands before the public.

In the morning as we stated elsewhere, George Berg, a carpenter,
living on the corner of Ninth and Market Streets, was killed near Hancock
Street. A German named Fitz, formerly a partner at the Galt House, was
severely, if not fatally, beaten.

In the afternoon a general row occurred on Shelby Street, extending
from Main to Broadway. We are unable to ascertain the facts concerning
the disturbance. Some fourteen or fifteen men were shot, including officer
Williams, Joe Selvage, and others. Two or three were killed, and a number of houses, chiefly German coffee-houses, broken into and pillaged.
About 4 o'clock, when the vast crowd, augmented by accessions from

every part of the city, and armed with shotguns, muskets and rifles, were proceeding to attack the Catholic Church on Shelby Street, Mayor Barbee arrested them with a speech, and the mob returned to the First Ward Polls. Presently a large party arrived with a piece of brass ordinance, followed by a number of men and boys with muskets. In an hour afterwards the large brewery on Jefferson Street near the junction of Greene, was set fire to.

In the lower part of the city the disturbances were characterized by a greater degree of bloody work. Late in the afternoon, three Irishmen going down Main Street near Eleventh, were attacked, and one knocked down. Then ensued a terrible scene; the Irish firing from the windows of their houses on Main Street, repeated volleys. Mr. Rhodes, a river man, was shot and killed by one in the upper story, and Mr. Graham met with a similar fate. An Irishman who discharged a pistol at the back of a man's head, was shot and then hung. He, however, survived both punishments. John Hudson, a carpenter, was shot dead during the fracas.

After dusk a row of frame houses on Main Street between Tenth and Eleventh, the property of Mr. Quinn, a well known Irishman, was set on fire. The flames extended across the street and twelve buildings were destroyed. These houses were chiefly tenanted by Irish, and upon any of the tenants venturing out to escape the flames they were immediately shot down. No idea could be formed of the number killed. We are advised that *five men* were roasted to death, having been so badly wounded by gun-shot wounds that they could not escape from the burning buildings.

Of all the enormities and outrages committed by the American party yesterday and last night we have not time now to write. The mob having satisfied its appetite for blood, repaired to Third Street, and until midnight made demonstrations against the *Times* and *Democrat* offices. The furious crowd satisfied itself, however, with breaking a few window panes and burning the sign of the *Times* office.

At one o'clock this morning a large fire is raging in the upper part of the city.

Upon the proceedings of yesterday and last night we have no time nor heart now to comment. We are sickened with the very thought of the men murdered and houses burned and pillaged, that signalized the American victory yesterday. Not less than twenty corpses form the trophies of this wonderful achievement.

Mountain Meadows Massacre
1857

After their migration from Illinois in 1846, the Mormons settled in Utah and prospered in the communal theocracy presided over by Brigham Young. They formed the state of Deseret in 1849, and were accepted into the United States as part of the Territory of Utah in 1850. But in the 1850's the feeling grew that the Mormons were not only immoral fanatics, but were too independent of the federal government. They often harassed or ignored federal officials, and they were intolerant of non-Mormon minorities in Utah. In 1857, President Buchanan, provoked by defiant remarks in the Mormon press, decided to assert federal authority in a forceful way; on May 26, he ordered 2,500 troops to Utah.

The Mormons were terrified; they feared they would be killed, their communities destroyed, their wives ravaged. Brigham Young issued a proclamation forbidding armed troops to enter his territory. He declared that Mormons would fight to the end, "in the mountains, in the canyons, upon the plains, on the hills, along the mighty streams, and by the rivulets." When the troops entered Utah, the Saints fought them and burned their crops wherever they were forced to retreat. They were so successful that the army was forced into winter quarters before reaching Salt Lake City. There it prepared for a spring campaign.

It was against this backdrop that the Mountain Meadows massacre took place. A wagon train of 140 emigrants bound for California was passing through the territory. Some of them abused the Indians, turned cattle into Mormon fields, and insulted Mormon women. On September 7, Indians attacked the wagon train. Seven of the emigrants were killed before they were able to beat off the Indians and form a barricade of wagons. Then a siege began. Three emigrants slipped out to get aid, but the Indians killed two and the third was killed by a Mormon.

The Indians asked John Lee, a part-time Mormon missionary, to help them. Lee called together about fifty Mormons who decided to help the Indians kill all the emigrants in order to prevent the first three murders from becoming known. They feared that if the murders were discovered, more federal troops would be sent. This grim plan, and its bloody execution—the slaughter of 120 men, women, and children—are described below by Lee himself. Although Lee's deed was disavowed by Young and the Mormon elders, it further inflamed anti-Mormon feeling throughout the country.

After the massacre, President Buchanan requested that five more regiments be sent against the Mormons, and thousands of Mormons fled from Utah. Hostilities were happily averted when Thomas L. Kane, a Philadelphia lawyer friendly to the Mormons, offered to act as a mediator, and Buchanan accepted. Kane went to Salt Lake City to confer with Brigham Young. They agreed that Washington would be accepted as supreme in temporal matters, and that in church affairs the Mormons would be unmolested. Lee was eventually tried and found guilty of murder. In 1877, twenty years after the event, he was executed at the place where the massacre had occurred.

For the document, see *Mormonism Unveiled, Including the Remarkable Life and Confessions of the Late Mormon Bishop John D. Lee* (1877), 236–45. See also Juanita Brooks: *The Mountain Meadows Massacre* (1962).

I was then told the plan of action. . . . The emigrants were to be decoyed from their strong–hold under a promise of protection. . . . I was to agree that the Mormons would protect the emigrants from the Indians and conduct them to Cedar City in safety. . . .

It was agreed that when I had made the full agreement and treaty, as the brethren called it, the wagons should start for Hamblin's Ranch with the arms, the wounded and the children. The women were to march on foot and follow the wagons in single file; the men were to follow behind the women, they also to march in single file. Major John M. Higbee was to stand with his militia company about two hundred yards from the camp, and stand in double file, open order, with about twenty feet space between the files, so that the wagons could pass between them. The drivers were to keep right along, and not stop at the troops. The women were not to stop there, but to follow the wagons. The troops were to halt the men for a few minutes, until the women were some distance ahead, out into the cedars, where the indians were hid in ambush. Then the march was to be resumed, the troops to form in single file, each soldier to walk by an emigrant, and on the right-hand side of his man, and the soldier was to carry his gun on his left arm, ready for instant use. The march was to continue until the wagons had passed beyond the ambush of the Indians, and until the women were right in the midst of the Indians. Higbee was then to give the orders and words, "Do Your Duty." At this the troops were to shoot down the men; the Indians were to kill all of the women and larger children, and the drivers of the wagons and I were to kill the wounded and sick men that were in the wagons. Two men were to be placed on horses near by, to overtake and kill any of the emigrants that might escape from the first assault. The Indians were to kill the women and large children, so that it would be certain that no Mormon would be guilty of shedding *innocent blood*—if it should happen that there was any innocent blood in the company that were to die. Our leading men all said that there was no innocent blood in the whole company. . . .

Bateman took a white flag and started for the emigrant camp. When he got about half way to the corral, he was met by one of the emigrants, that I afterwards learned was named Hamilton. They talked some time, but I never knew what was said between them.

Brother Bateman returned to the command and said that the emigrants would accept our terms, and surrender as we required them to do.

I was then ordered by Major Higbee to go to the corral and negotiate the treaty, and superintend the whole matter. I was again ordered to be certain and get all the arms and ammunition into the wagons. Also to put the children and the sick and wounded in the wagons, as had been agreed upon in council. . . .

As I entered the fortifications, men, women and children gathered around me in wild consternation. Some felt that the time of their happy deliverance had come, while others, though in deep distress, and all in tears, looked upon me with doubt, distrust and terror. My feelings at this time may be imagined (but I doubt the power of man being equal to even imagine how wretched I felt.) No language can describe my feelings. My position was painful, trying and awful; my brain seemed to be on fire; my nerves were for a moment unstrung; humanity was overpowered, as I thought of the cruel, unmanly part that I was acting. . . . Yet, my faith in the godliness of my leaders was such that it forced me to think that I was not sufficiently spiritual to act the important part I was commanded to perform. My hesitation was only momentary. Then feeling that duty compelled *obedience to orders*, I laid aside my weakness and my humanity, and became an instrument in the hands of my superiors and my leaders. . . . I hurried up the people and started the wagons off towards Cedar City. As we went out of the corral I ordered the wagons to turn to the left, so as to leave the troops to the right of us. Dan. McFarland rode before the women and led them right up to the troops, where they still stood in open order as I had left them. The women and larger children were walking ahead, as directed, and the men following them. The foremost man was about fifty yards behind the hindmost woman.

The women and children were hurried right on by the troops. When the men came up they cheered the soldiers as if they believed that they were acting honestly. Higbee then gave the orders for his men to form in single file and take their places as ordered before, that is, at the right of the emigrants. . . . Just as we were coming into the main road, I heard a volley of guns at the place where I knew the troops and emigrants were. Our teams were then going at a fast walk. I first heard one gun, then a volley at once followed.

McMurdy and Knight stopped their teams at once, for they were ordered by Higbee, the same as I was, to help kill all the sick and wounded who were in the wagons, and to do it as soon as they heard the guns of the troops. McMurdy was in front; his wagon was mostly loaded with the arms and small children. McMurdy and Knight got out of their wagons; each one had a rifle. McMurdy went up to Knight's wagon, where the sick and wounded were, and raising his rifle to his shoulder, said: *"O Lord, my God, receive their spirits, it is for thy Kingdom that I do this."* He then shot a man who was lying with his head on another man's breast; the ball killed both men.

I also went up to the wagon, intending to do my part of the killing. I drew my pistol and cocked it, but somehow it went off prematurely, and I shot McMurdy across the thigh, my pistol ball cutting his buck-skin pants. McMurdy turned to me and said:

"Brother Lee, keep cool, you are excited; you came very near killing me. Keep cool, there is no reason for being excited."

Knight then shot a man with his rifle; he shot the man in the head. Knight also brained a boy that was about fourteen years old. The boy came running up to our wagons, and Knight struck him on the head with the butt end of his gun, and crushed his skull. By this time many Indians reached our wagons, and all of the sick and wounded were killed almost instantly. I saw an Indian from Cedar City, called Joe, run up to the wagon and catch a man by the hair, and raise his head up and look into his face; the man shut his eyes, and Joe shot him in the head. The Indians then examined all of the wounded in the wagons, and all of the bodies, to see if any were alive, and all that showed signs of life were at once shot through the head. I did not kill any one there, but it was an accident that kept me from it, for I fully intended to do my part of the killing, but by the time I got over the excitement of coming so near killing McMurdy, the whole of the killing of the wounded was done. There is no truth in the statement of Nephi Johnson, where he says I cut a man's throat.

Just after the wounded were all killed I saw a girl, some ten or eleven years old, running towards us, from the direction where the troops had attacked the main body of emigrants; she was covered with blood. An Indian shot her before she got within sixty yards of us. That was the last person that I saw killed on that occasion.

While going back to the brethren, I passed the bodies of several women. In one place I saw six or seven bodies near each other; they were stripped perfectly naked, and all of their clothing was torn from their bodies by the Indians.

I walked along the line where the emigrants had been killed, and saw many bodies lying dead and naked on the field, near by where the women lay. I saw ten children; they had been killed close to each other; they were from ten to sixteen years of age. The bodies of the women and children were scattered along the ground for quite a distance before I came to where the men were killed.

When I reached the place where the dead man lay, I was told how the orders had been obeyed. Major Higbee said, "The boys have acted admirably, they took good aim, and all of the d—d Gentiles but two or three fell at the *first fire*."

He said that three or four got away some distance, but the men on horses soon overtook them and cut their throats. Higbee said the Indians did their part of the work well, that it did not take over a minute to finish up when they got fairly started. I found that the first orders had been carried out to the letter.

Orange Riot
1871

On July 11, 1690, William of Nassau, Prince of Orange, defeated James II at the Battle of the Boyne, and for centuries afterward the commemoration of that day provoked bloody clashes between Protestants and Catholics in Ireland. The animosities came to the United States with the Irish immigrants, and in both 1870 and 1871 there were Orange riots in New York City. In 1870 five people were killed and many severely injured. The following year there was an even more violent riot. The men of the Irish Hibernian Society publicly declared their intention to disrupt a parade of Orangemen. The Protestants asked Superintendent of Police James J. Kelso to protect them: he refused, and issued instead an order "to prevent the formation or progression" of a parade because of the possibility of violence. The issue now involved control of the city government. *The New York Times* protested that "The city authorities find their masters too much for them. . . . They now officially proclaim that the city is absolutely in the hands of the Irish Catholics." And, indeed, one leading Hibernian jubilantly proclaimed Kelso's order "the greatest concession ever given the Irish." Both sides prepared to fight once more. The day before the march the Governor of New York and the Mayor reversed the police order and said the Orangemen's parade would be protected. Seven hundred police (many of them Irish Catholics) and 5,000 militia escorted 100 Protestant marchers down Eighth Avenue. Although the Catholic clergy urged their parishioners to stay away, the Hibernians came out in strength to harass the paraders. When the procession reached 24th Street, a shot was fired, and the militia returned the fire, although they were not authorized to do so. In the ensuing fight, two militiamen were killed, and 24 wounded; 37 rioters were killed, and 67 wounded.

The following account is taken from a pro-Orange pamphlet, written shortly after the riot: *Civil Rights: The Hibernian Riot in New York City* (1871), 20–4. See Joel Tyler Headley: *The Great Riots of New York* (1873).

The fatal morning of the 12th of July arrived. New York City, in time of profound peace, wore the appearance of a place about to be stormed by a victorious enemy, when gathering his strength to make the final attack. And the cause of all this most disgraceful excitement, eventually to end in bloodshed and death, was a mob of brutalized foreigners who, transplanting their bigotry and their incapacity for self-government from the Old World, determined to renew their fight in the home of their adoption—proving for the thousandth time that they know nothing, and under their leaders learn nothing, and practice nothing, common to a liberty-loving citizen of the United States.

The cowardice of the leaders of Tammany, the hesitation and incompetency of its officials brought the terrible but natural fruits of sorrow and disgrace. The more than weak, the pusillanimous surrender of Mayor Hall to the mob, of course only encouraged it to more desperate resolution, for it was a thing to have been conquered by defiance; concession only flattered the hyra-headed monster and gave it strength. But after the fatal error of concession had been partially remedied, at the indignant demand of an outraged public sentiment, mismanagement almost as stupid led to results as painful, though not so momentous as those threatened by surrender.

Threatening demonstrations of the rioters early in the morning, revealed that the outraged cry of the people had not curbed them as completely as it frightened Tammany. Sullen groups gathered on the street corners in threatened districts or in the localities where the Irish reside in greater numbers. Among these groups women were most conspicuous by the vehemence with which they denounced Orangemen, police and soldiers alike; and children of both sexes gathered about them, ignorant alike of their own danger and the desperate resolution of those about them. The men generally were gruff and silent, evidently angry that their opportunities for pillage had been wrested from them by the enforced action of the men whom they had made Mayor and Governor. Separate gangs of ruffians, six or eight in number, moved from street to street, eager alike for fight or pillage. At the several rendezvous of the Hibernians many bore rifles without being interfered with or even reproved by the police. In the upper part of the city the rioters began to move southward at an early hour, compelling all workmen on their route to desist and join with

them. In one or two instances movements were made against the houses
of men who had protected the Orangemen during the riots of last year,
but as the rioters were without leadership they gradually dispersed before
carrying their threats into execution. Attacks were made by the rioters
on one or two armories where arms were known to be stored, but the
resistance of a few determined policemen cowed the mob. The rioters
were vicious and fierce enough for any purpose, but it was plain that they
were without the organization they had boasted. Still their demonstrations were so threatening before 10 o'clock that the police were compelled
to seize Hibernia Hall, and Gen. Shaler called for a regiment of troops from
Brooklyn, where, as in Jersey City, all had been comparatively quiet.

About noon the fact became known that the Orangemen had resolved
to parade, starting from their lodge in Eighth Avenue and Twenty-ninth
Street, and thither the rioters from all points of the city began to concen-
trate. Many marched in large bodies through the principal streets un-
dispersed. A large police force had previously been sent to protect the
Orange Lodge, and these kept the rioters at a distance. Later in the day
five regiments of troops marched to the same point, and by two o'clock
the entire brigade and a large body of police had formed in Eighth
Avenue, hemmed in at all the cross streets by an angry mob.

Shortly after 2 o'clock the Master of the Orange Lodge called it to
order, preliminary to forming in procession in the street. A resolution was
passed, that it was dangerous for the ladies present to take part in the
public demonstration as originally intended, and they were requested to
remove any lodge or other insignia calculated to provoke an assault, and
proceed unostentatiously to their homes. An impressive appeal to the
Supreme Being was then made by one of the members, asking aid and protection to those who were to risk martyrdom for the assertion of a principle.

Soon after the Orangemen made their appearance in the street, pre-
paratory to taking their places in the line of march, the mob in Twenty-
ninth Street began hooting, and the police at once put them to flight.
Subsequently Twenty-eighth Street was cleared in the same way, the
police acting with great spirit. But the rioters soon returned to the places
from which they had been driven, and prepared to renew their hooting,
or to indulge in more violent demonstrations. A few shots were fired from
houses in the avenue, before the procession moved, the police in one instance returning the fire by a single shot, but nothing really serious occurred until the head of the line had reached Twenty-third Street, and
the Orangemen were opposite Twenty-fourth Street. Here they were
fired upon from a tenement house on the corner of Twenty-fourth Street.

But not more than half a dozen shots were discharged in all, and none of them apparently took effect on troops or policemen. The 84th Regiment, however, immediately discharged their weapons at the house and at the crowd in the avenue and along the street. The members had previously loaded with ball cartridge in the open street, as if to intimidate the rioters, and the effect of their fire was murderous. At the same time the 9th and 6th Regiments in the rear of the Orangemen also began firing indiscriminately, sweeping Twenty-fifth, Twenty-sixth, Twenty-seventh, and Twenty-eighth Streets, the extreme rear of the 9th firing a few shots up Eighth Avenue, at Twenty-ninth Street. The troops of the 6th, 9th and 84th Regiments were for a moment thrown into confusion, as usual after firing, but at command of the officers, instantly fell into line and marched on, leaving the dead and wounded behind where they fell. The side streets, as might be expected, from Twenty-fifth to Twenty-eighth Streets had been instantly cleared by all who were able to fly, the rioters abandoning their friends without the slightest compunction.

This ended the conflict. The wretches who had defied the law and created all this ruin, discovered that the authorities were in earnest, and their cowardly spirit quailed within them, making the hesitation and subserviency of the Mayor and Superintendent Kelso doubly odious, as illustrating how easily a little firmness at the proper time, on their part, would have relieved the city of any riot whatever.

Anti-Chinese Riot in Los Angeles
1871

The discovery of gold in 1848 brought many Chinese to California to supply an urgent need for mine laborers and for cooks and laundrymen in the overwhelmingly male camps and towns. By the 1860's large-scale farms and railroads were employing hundreds of Chinese. By 1870 there were 50,000 Chinese, nearly all unattached males, in California.

As the Chinese community grew, whites began to object to the crowding and smells of the Chinese districts, their prostitution and gambling, their alien customs, and their alleged monarchism. The Chinese system of contract labor, in which gangs of workers were hired together, smacked of slavery to the Californians, who feared that a caste system would emerge which would strengthen the monopolies of the landlords and railroads. At one anti-Chinese meeting there were placards declaring: "We want no Slaves or Aristocrats." Prejudice was economic as well as cultural. The Chinese, forced to endure low standards of living, depressed wages and made unionization difficult. One labor paper warned that if capitalists were allowed to import Chinese labor "the equilibrium is destroyed, capital is triumphant, and the laboring poor of America must submit to the unholy sacrifice." Whites began to agitate for immigration restriction, and politicians began to respond. Governor Stanford said in 1862 that "The settlement among us of an inferior race is to be discouraged by every legitimate means." The movement grew and in 1882 succeeded in persuading Congress to pass an Exclusion Act, which barred Chinese immigration for ten years.

Along with the political campaign went a campaign of violence, which began in the late 1860's. All along the California coast there were frequent assaults on Chinese in the streets, and new immigrants were often stoned at the docks when they arrived. Rival Chinese groups, or Tongs, sometimes fought each other, and in Los Angeles in 1871 such a fight precipitated a bloody anti-Chinese riot. When the Tong fight broke out the police tried to stop it, but both Chinese groups shot at them; several policemen were wounded and one civilian killed. The Chinese then barricaded themselves in their district, known as "Nigger Alley," which was then surrounded by infuriated white mobs. A day-long slaughter began which left eighteen Chinese shot or lynched. Aggravated by the depression of 1873, violence continued throughout much of California in the early 1870's. In 1876 and 1877 a wave of raids and riots swept the state, as white laborers in town after town drove out Chinese, burning their quarters and killing many of them.

The following account is taken from the Los Angeles *Daily News*, October 25, 1871. See Paul M. De Falla: "Lantern in the Western Sky," *Historical Society of Southern California Quarterly*, XLII (March and June 1960), 57-88, 161-85; C. P. Dorland: "Chinese Massacre at Los Angeles in 1871," *Annual Publication of the Historical Society of Southern California*, III (1894), 22-6; and E. C. Sandmeyer: *The Anti-Chinese Movement in California* (1939).

The difficulty which occurred yesterday at Negro Alley, between two opposition Chinese companies, in which pistols were then freely used, again broke out afresh about five o'clock last evening. The difficulty of yesterday had been taken into court where it was supposed that it would be properly disposed of. It appears, however, that after coming from Justice Gray's Court where the preliminary examination was commenced yesterday afternoon, they renewed their quarrel and again resorted to the pistol for settlement. Immediately after the first shots were fired, officers and citizens rushed to the scene, and an attempt was made to arrest the parties engaged in the melee. Instead of surrendering, these miscreants at once turned to bay, and discharged the contents of their revolvers at those attempting to arrest them. This dispersed the crowd quicker than it had collected; but two of the Chinese still stood at the door of one of their dens, and discharged their weapons at the retreating crowds. One of the officers—Bilderrain—in a gallant attempt, with one or two others of the officers and some volunteers, to enter this den, was shot in the right shoulder and badly wounded. His brother, a boy about 15 years of age, received a ball in his right leg below the knee. Another man, a well known and respected citizen—named Robert Thompson, who was called upon to assist—while endeavoring to enter was confronted by a Chinaman with a loaded pistol in each hand. These he placed against Thompson's breast, and fired, one of the balls entering the right breast, the wound resulting fatally in about an hour and a half. This repeated firing was the signal for the closing of the iron shutters of neighboring stores.

Knots of men congregated at the street corners; and, in less time than it takes to be told, the entire block was surrounded, so as to permit none to escape. A string of men extended across Los Angeles Street along the east side of Negro Alley and on the western side of the block along Sanchez Street; and an unbroken line formed around the Plaza connecting with both the ends of the lines on Sanchez Street and Negro Alley. The wildest excitement prevailed. The mob was demoralized and uncontrollable. No definite organization existed. There seemed to be an under-standing on the part of some few to drive the inmates of the blockaded houses up to the upper end of the block and allow them to escape into the Plaza where parties were stationed to receive them.

A Capture—The Captive Lynched

Shortly after the line had been formed, one of the inmates of the den in which these Chinamen had taken refuge, was observed endeavoring to escape across Los Angeles Street. The cry was raised; and he was quickly captured by one Romo Sortorel. He had evidently made up his mind to cut his way through the circle, being armed at the time with a hatchet. When arrested, someone made an attempt to stab him with a knife, cutting the hand of Sortorel. Others took him in charge, with the view of placing him in jail. The infuriated mob followed. Cries of "Hang him!" "Take him from Harris!" "Shoot him!" rose in every direction. The officers proceeded safely with their prisoner until they arrived at the junction of Temple and Spring Streets. Here they were surrounded, and the China-man forcibly taken from them, and dragged up Temple Street to New High Street. The frame of the sliding doors of a corral at the corner of this street afford a convenient gallows. A rope was soon at hand, and amid his own wailings and the hootings and imprecations of the crowd, he was elevated. The cord broke, however, but another was at hand, and he was again hoisted to the beam, and there left to swing.

The Multitude Maddened

Returning to the scene, efforts were made by the Sheriff to organize a body of men to watch the place until morning, when more efficient means would be used for capturing those remaining in the houses. But all his efforts failed. Parties then proceeded on the roofs of the Chinese dens, breaking them in with axes, and discharging their pistols into the interior, hoping thereby to succeed in driving them out. In the center of the block, behind the Chinese residences, is a corral. Last evening this contained some seven or eight horses, behind which some of the Chinamen were discovered secreting themselves, and four of them were summarily des-patched. The demoniacal desire to set the block on fire and burn them out was broached, but a better spirit prevailed, and the repeated cries of "Burn the S—— of B——s out," were answered by more numerous ones, in the negative. The dread of a conflagration was, providentially, predominant in the minds of the majority. Two attempts, nevertheless, were made by throwing fireballs into the open doorways, and through the holes in the roofs, but they were expeditiously extinguished.

For three hours, that portion of the city was a pandemonium. Yells, shouts, curses, and pistol shots rent the air in every direction. A novel idea at last suggested itself to some-one's mind, viz.: that water through the firemen's hose be brought to play upon their retreat, to try and drive them out in that manner. The effort was made, but was unsuccessful, as it was impossible to get any concert of action.

Ferreted Out

About half past nine, some person ventured to enter one of the houses, and presently emerged with a prisoner. The crowd instantly seized him, and hurried him off down to Los Angeles Street to the point south of Commercial Street. At this point were several empty wagons; and in lieu of any more convenient place, a rope was attached to his neck, and he was raised from the ground. Further search resulted in the capture, as far as we could ascertain, of fourteen others, who were similarly dealt with, four of them being taken to the place of execution on New High Street and the other ten to Los Angeles and Commercial Streets. The dwellings on Los Angeles Street, where these scenes were enacted, have an awning projecting over the sidewalk. Six of these Chinamen— one a mere child—swung from it in a row, three hanging together in a bunch. An empty wagon close by had four others hanging to its sides. So furious had the mob become, that they placed the ropes around the necks of their captives as soon as they got them into their hands, and then dragged them along the street to the places of execution, where, more dead than alive, their existence was ended. An effort to stay the proceedings, as possible innocence was being sacrificed for guilt, was squelched, and the humanitarian, threatened with having a place given him among the ghastly row of victims hanging there before him. Such was the terrible vengeance that overtook these men. The bodies of those who were shot were lying on the street and sidewalk last night. . . .

As might be expected, thieves were not idle. Upon breaking open the Chinese establishment, and obtaining complete mastery over the inmates, they commenced to ply their trade, helping themselves to everything they could lay their hands upon. "Help yourself, boys," was the advice boldly given by one, who was actively putting same into practice. When he proceeded to retire, however, the crowd marched him back and forced him to disgorge.

It was currently reported that during the melee about forty of the opposition party of Chinamen, or the Yo Hing Company had decamped, crossing the Los Angeles River, and going in an eastward direction.

Latest

At the time of going to press, seventeen bodies are reported at the jail, and three wounded, besides a large number of women and children in custody.

Everything is now quiet in Negro Alley and the neighborhood, and a strong special force will keep guard throughout the rest of the night.

Rock Springs Massacre
1885

Rock Springs, Wyoming, was a coal town run by the Union Pacific Railroad. Before 1875 the mines there had been worked by white laborers. That year they struck for a wage increase. The company imported 150 Chinese, fired the strikers, and reopened the mines. For ten years whites and Chinese worked peacefully together. But the mid-1880's were a time of rising labor militancy and rapid growth in the membership of the Knights of Labor. When the Knights formed a local in Rock Springs in 1883, their attempt to organize the mines was blocked by the refusal of the Chinese to join the union or to strike. Pent-up hatred exploded on September 2, 1885, in a massacre in which twenty-eight Chinese were killed, fifteen wounded, and hundreds driven out of town. Most of the aggressors were themselves immigrants, mainly Welsh, Cornishmen, and Swedes. The local grand jury brought in no indictment.

Many of the Chinese who fled were saved from further assault by the arrival of federal troops, sent by President Cleveland at the request of the Governor of Wyoming. The soldiers escorted them back to Rock Springs, and they were soon at work in the mines again; the Union Pacific discharged forty-five whites who were believed to have taken part in the massacre. The Knights of Labor then asked the railroad to remove all Chinese laborers, but the General Manager replied: "When the company can be assured against strikes . . . at the hands of persons who deny its owners the right to manage their property, it may consider the expediency of abandoning Chinese labor."

The Chinese government asked for punishment of the rioters, and for indemnification; indemnity was granted in 1887 by Congress. The following document is a statement by Ralph Zwicky, an eye-witness, submitted to a Congressional Committee inquiring into the justice of the indemnity: House Report No. 2044 "Providing Indemnity to Certain Chinese Subjects," 49th Congress, 1st Session, May 1, 1886. See Paul Crane and Alfred Larson: "The Chinese Massacre," *Annals of Wyoming*, XII (January and April 1940), 47-55, 153-60.

In the forenoon of September 2 our clerk reported from No. 6 mine that a fight had taken place in the mine between white and Chinese miners; that several Chinamen had been seriously hurt, and that the men were all leaving the mines.

About one-half hour afterwards an armed body of men from No. 6 came marching down the track towards the town. At the bridge crossing Bitter Creek the men halted and held a conference. Upon persuasion by a few citizens, they left their arms in the store nearby and continued their march up town and down Front Street towards the hall of the Knights of Labor, shouting, while marching, "White men fall in." Their number was augmented by several tradesmen and miners from other mines. The word was then passed around, "A miners' meeting will be held at 6 o'clock in the evening to settle the Chinese question." The men then dispersed in the different saloons. It becoming evident that the men were imbibing freely, all stores and saloons agreed not to sell any more intoxicating drinks that day. A good deal of talk was indulged in about making the Chinese leave camp, but no outsider took it seriously. In the afternoon, about 2 o'clock, the same body of men came marching past the store again, armed with their rifles. They crossed the railroad towards the Chinese section-house, driving the men out towards Chinatown.

Soon the rioters came abreast the outlying houses of Chinatown, about

150 strong, half of them carrying Winchester rifles. There they halted, as it seemed, for consultation. In a little while several revolver shots were fired, whether by whites or Chinamen I could not say, but I began to realize the seriousness of the situation. What appeared first to be the mad frolic of ignorant men was turning into an inhuman butchery of innocent beings. The rioters now cautiously advanced. Now a rifle-shot, followed by another and still another, was heard, and then a volley was fired. The Chinamen were fleeing like a herd of hunted antelopes, making no resistance. Volley upon volley was fired after the fugitives. In a few minutes the hill east of the town was literally blue with the hunted Chinamen. In the mean time fire broke out in a China [sic] house, and one after another followed in being laid into ashes. Some houses may have caught fire from others, but it was also evident that many separate fires were laid. Shooting and burning continued uninterrupted until no more Chinamen were in sight and half the houses were gone up in flames.

Towards 5 o'clock the rioters headed for the town again, crossing Bitter Creek, stopping on the bank, where stood a Chinaman's wash-house. The rioters surrounded it, and fired several shots through the roof. It was evident that a poor Chinaman was hid away, for a revolver shot made the crowd more cautious. A good many more shots were fired into the house, and then the bloody work was finished; the poor fellow was shot in the back of the head. The rioters took up their march towards Sonquie's house, in the midst of the town. All the Chinamen being gone, they order Sonquie's wife to leave town. From here the rioters went to No. 1 mine. A few wretches had sought safety there, but they were driven out, while the rioters fired their rifles into the air. It was too public a place for any rioter to aim low, and this fact probably saved the lives of the Chinamen. The rioters then went to foreman Evans and told him to leave town first train east; also gave the same order to William H. O'Donnell, foreman of the Chinese, and employed by Beckwith, Quinn & Co.

The first act was now over, and the rioters dispersed for supper. But it was plain to be seen that their bad blood was up, and could only be cooled down by further destruction. A little after nightfall the firing of the remaining China houses commenced, and continued until after midnight. All this time men, women, and children were engaged in looting and plundering. The next morning a horrible sight presented itself to the visitor in Chinatown. In one place lay three burnt bodies, and one or two in several others. One body was almost eaten by hogs. It had been roasted by the fire. Another body, shot through the back, lay in the sagebrush, and others were found in different directions. Altogether the number of those known to have lost their lives reached twenty-one. Thirty-nine houses were burned at No. 3 mine, with a large number of dugouts belonging to Chinamen. Five houses were burnt at No. 6 mine, and one section-house in town.

Anti-Italian Riot in New Orleans
1891

On October 15, 1890, the Chief of Police of New Orleans was murdered. The Italian Mafia in the city, which he had been investigating, was suspected, and nineteen Italians were charged with the murder. Despite strong evidence of guilt, their skillful lawyers won an acquittal. A group of prominent citizens called for a mass protest meeting on March 14, 1891. Over 6,000 citizens came and listened to indignant speeches. One civil leader, attorney William Parkerson, told the crowd: "When the law is powerless the rights delegated by the people are relegated back to the people, and they are justified in doing that which the courts have failed to do." Parkerson then led fifty men to the jail and, as authorities stood by, they killed eleven of the Italians. Most were shot inside the jail, but some were dragged outside where the crowd lynched them.

Three of the victims were Italian citizens, and the Italian government officially protested their deaths, and recalled the Italian Ambassador. A settlement was reached when the United States paid Italy an indemnity of 125,000 lire. Many New Orleans civic leaders denied having any animosity toward Italians, but there were violent anti-Italian incidents in Louisiana before and after 1891. Three Italians were lynched in 1896, and five more were murdered in 1899.

The following account was given by William Parkerson, the mob leader, in an interview in a New York magazine, the New York *Illustrated American*, VI (April 4, 1891), 320-2. See J. S. Kendall: "Who Killa de Chief?" *Louisiana Historical Quarterly*, XXII (April 1939), 492-530; and J. A. Karlin: "The New Orleans Lynchings of 1891, and the American Press," *Louisiana Historical Quarterly*, XXIV (January 1941), 187-204.

"Your name is very much before the public just now," the correspondent remarked, as he was offered a seat.

"Yes; we had a thirty-minute experience that Saturday," he said with a smile. "The most wonderful thing about it is that it was over so soon. I take more credit for that than anything else."

He gave his version of the outbreak, bit by bit, and not without reluctance, although he seems to consider his work a public service.

"I did not take the initiative," he said, in answer to questions. "I could not tell who did. It was all done by others. I was in court Friday morning in a distant building, attending to some business, and came back to this office after the verdict acquitting the Italians. When I got here I found a large number of citizens awaiting me, some of them old enough to be my grandfather. With those who came in afterward, there were perhaps sixty or seventy. They were talking about the outragious verdict, and told me they had come to ask me to take some measure to right it. After fifteen minutes' conversation we adjourned to meet again that evening. I had no connection with the case beyond taking a good citizen's interest in it, and dropping into court once or twice to see how it was getting along. That evening we met in the rooms of a young man, whose name I don't care to give. There were about one hundred and fifty of us, among them the same men who were here in the morning. We stood up and were packed like sardines. They made me chairman. There was some more talking about the verdict and I was again appealed to. None of us drank anything and there were no refreshments in the room. We all signed a call that was published in the next morning's papers, asking the citizens to assemble at 10 o'clock A.M., Saturday, at Clay statue, and saying that we would be prepared to carry out their instructions."

"Meaning that you would be ready to kill the prisoners."

"That was the feeling, we understood, of the public pulse. On Saturday I came to my office at 8:45, and at 9:45 started for the rendezvous at our friend's room. I was a little ahead of time. Four or five of us went from there to the statue, where we found a muttering mob of many thousands.

We walked around outside the railings two or three times to give our own people a chance to fall in. Then I went through the gate of the railings and up the steps. As soon as I took off my hat the people began to cheer. I don't remember exactly what I said, but I made a little speech, telling them we had a duty to perform; that it was the most terrible duty I had ever undertaken; that the law had miscarried, and that we were prepared to do whatever they desired. They shouted, 'Come on!' "

"What did you understand from that?"

"That we were to go to the prison."

"Did anybody say so in so many words?"

"Oh, it was known well enough. At the meeting on Friday night they tried to get me to the prison, but I refused to do anything that night. From the statue we started for the prison, I leading, and the crowd following us. We had to walk about a mile, and as we walked along, people came from side streets and fell into the procession. The women were crying, and the men were cheering. It was the most terrible thing I ever saw, the quiet determination of the crowd. There was no disorder. We stopped on the way at our friend's room, where we found guns awaiting us. I had my own gun there. There were about one hundred and fifty Winchesters and shot-guns, I think, given out. I never carry a revolver, but that morning I put one in my pocket. I took a Winchester besides. At this moment I am unarmed. At the prison gate, Lem Davis, I think that is his name, came to the door. I asked him for the keys to let us in. He said he could not give them up, and we said if he did not we would break in the prison. He still refused, and I ordered the crowd to make ready to break, sent for some gunpowder, and also sent a detachment to break in at the side door, which was about a block away, the building being an immense one and covering more than a square of ground. Meantime, we got some wood and used it to batter the main door. That resisted, but the side door was forced. Then I went around to the side door, placed three men on guard, one a legal officer of this municipality, telling them whom to allow to enter, and asking the crowd to be orderly. The guards all had Winchesters.

The crowd was composed of lawyers, doctors, bankers, and prominent citizens generally. It was the most obedient crowd you ever saw. They obeyed me implicitly, just as if I was a military commander. If there was any riff-raff it was all on the outside. The intention had been not to shoot any of them, but when my men were inside—about fifty of them—they got very furious, and after the first taste of blood it was impossible to keep them back."

"If you did not mean to shoot, why did you take the guns?"

"Because we did not know what resistance we might encounter from the officers in charge—from anybody. We meant to get into the prison, and we would have burned it down if necessary."

"Did you kill anybody with your own hands?"

"No, I did not fire a shot. In fact, at the meeting the night before I had said that Matranga and another should be spared, the two declared innocent by Judge Baker, in whose integrity we had perfect confidence. I said I would defend these men with my own life if necessary, and they were not harmed."

"Did it not strike you as not courageous to shoot the lot of unarmed men in a hole?"

"Well," said the young lawyer, quietly, "there was no doubt of the courage of any man in our party. Of course, it is not a courageous thing to attack a man who is not armed, but we looked upon these as so many reptiles. Why, I was told that on Friday, after the verdict, the Italian fruit and oyster schooners along the wharfs hoisted the sicilian flag over the stars and stripes, and the prisoners themselves had an oyster supper."

"Do you regret what you have done?" asked the correspondent after a pause.

"Not a bit," said Parkerson, promptly. "This was a great emergency; greater than has ever happened in New York, Cincinnati, or Chicago. I did not act through a sentimental or personal interest for Hennessy. I knew him well, and asked Mayor Shakespeare to appoint him. He was a fine man and an efficient officer, and we felt that when he was killed there was no telling who would go next. While the Mafia confined itself to killing its own members we did not resort to violence. But Hennessy's killing struck at the very root of American institutions. The intimidation of the Mafia and the corruption of our juries are to be met only with strong measures. Moreover, I recognize no power above the people. Under our constitution the people are the sovereign authority, and when the courts, the agents, fail to carry out the law the authority is relegated back to the people, who gave it. In this case I look upon it that we represented the people—not the people of the whole United States, perhaps, but the people of the state of Louisiana. . . ."

Zoot-Suit Riot
1943

On the evenings of June 3–June 7, 1943, crowds attacked Mexicans and Negroes in Los Angeles, particularly youths wearing "zoot-suits." On June 7, a mob of over a thousand soldiers, sailors, and civilians broke into movie theaters, street-cars, and homes, dragged Mexicans into the street and stripped and beat them. During all this time, the police stood by or on occasion arrested the victims.

These riots were touched off by the assault of a group of sailors by a group of Mexican youths; but Southern California had a long history of tension between Mexicans and whites, tensions which had been increased by the press and the police. The Hearst papers, in particular, headlined every incident which reflected badly on Mexicans. When in 1942 the Office of War Information remonstrated with the Hearst publishers, pointing out that Mexico was our ally, the Hearst papers substituted the word "zoot-suiter" for "Mexican." The word, which referred to elaborate clothes worn by some Mexicans, became a synonym for all young Mexicans.

Much of the city condoned the riot. The Los Angeles County Supervisor told newsmen: "All that is needed to end lawless-ness is more of the same action as is being exercised by the servicemen." The District Attorney proclaimed that "zoot-suits are an open indication of subversive character," and the Los Angeles City Council made the wearing of zoot-suits a mis-demeanor.

The following account of the riot is taken from Carey Mc-Williams: *North from Mexico* (1949).

The stage was now set for the really serious rioting of June seventh and eighth. Having featured the preliminary rioting as an offensive launched by sailors, soldiers and marines, the press now whipped public opinion into a frenzy by dire warnings that Mexican zoot-suiters planned mass retaliations. To insure a riot, the precise street corners were named at which retaliatory action was expected and the time of the anticipated action was carefully specified. In effect these stories announced a riot and invited public participation. "Zooters Planning to Attack More Servicemen," headlined the *Daily News*; "Would jab broken bottlenecks in the faces of their victims. . . . Beating sailors' brains out with hammers also on the program." Concerned for the safety of the Army, the Navy, and the Marine Corps, the *Herald Express* warned that "Zooters . . . would mass 500 strong."

On Monday evening, June seventh, thousands of *Angelenos*, in response to twelve hours' advance notice in the press, turned out for a mass lynching. Marching through the streets of downtown Los Angeles, a mob of several thousand soldiers, sailors, and civilians, proceeded to beat up every zoot-suiter they could find. Pushing its way into the important motion picture theaters, the mob ordered the management to turn on the house lights and then ranged up and down the aisles dragging Mexicans out of their seats. Street cars were halted while Mexicans, and some Filipinos and Negroes, were jerked out of their seats, pushed into the streets, and beaten with sadistic frenzy. If the victims wore zoot-suits, they were stripped of their clothing and left naked or half-naked on the streets, bleeding and bruised. Proceeding down Main Street from First to Twelfth, the mob stopped on the edge of the Negro district. Learning that the Negroes planned a warm reception for them, the mobsters turned back and marched through the Mexican east side spreading panic and terror.

Here is one of numerous eye-witness accounts written by Al Waxman, editor of *The Eastside Journal*:

At Twelfth and Central I came upon a scene that will long live in my memory. Police were swinging clubs and servicemen were fighting with civilians. Wholesale arrests were being made by the officers.

Four boys came out of a pool hall. They were wearing zoot-suits that have become the symbol of a fighting flag. Police ordered them into arrest cars. One refused. He asked: "Why am I being arrested?" The police officer answered with three swift blows of the night-stick across the boy's head and he went down. As he sprawled, he was kicked in the face. Police had difficulty loading his body into the vehicle because he was one-legged and wore a wooden limb. Maybe the officer didn't know he was attacking a cripple.

At the next corner a Mexican mother cried out, "Don't take my boy, he did nothing. He's only fifteen years old. Don't take him." She was struck across the jaw with a night-stick and almost dropped the two and a half year old baby that was clinging in her arms. . . .

Rushing back to the east side to make sure that things were quiet here, I came upon a band of servicemen making a systematic tour of East First Street. They had just come out of a cocktail bar where four men were nursing bruises. Three autos loaded with Los Angeles policemen were on the scene but the soldiers were not molested. Farther down the street the men stopped a streetcar, forcing the motorman to open the door and proceeded to inspect the clothing of the male passengers. "We're looking for zoot-suits to burn," they shouted. Again the police did not interfere. . . . Half a block away . . . I pleaded with the men of the local police sub-station to put a stop to these activities. "It is a matter for the military police," they said.

Throughout the night the Mexican communities were in the wildest possible turmoil. Scores of Mexican mothers were trying to locate their youngsters and several hundred Mexicans milled around each of the police substations and the Central Jail trying to get word of missing members of their families. Boys came into the police stations saying: "Charge me with vagrancy or anything, but don't send me out there!" pointing to the streets where other boys, as young as twelve and thirteen years of age, were being beaten and stripped of their clothes. From affidavits which I helped prepare at the time, I should say that not more than half of the victims were actually wearing zoot-suits. A Negro defense worker, wearing a defense-plant identification badge on his workclothes, was taken from a street car and one of his eyes was gouged out with a knife. Huge half-page photographs, showing Mexican boys stripped of their clothes, cowering on the pavements, often bleeding profusely, surrounded by jeering mobs of men and women, appeared in all the Los Angeles newspapers. As Al Waxman most truthfully reported, blood had been "spilled on the streets of the city."

At midnight on June seventh, the military authorities decided that the local police were completely unable or unwilling to handle the situation, despite the fact that a thousand reserve officers had been called up. The entire downtown area of Los Angeles was then declared "out of bounds" for military personnel. This order immediately slowed down the pace of the rioting. The moment the Military Police and Shore Patrol went into action, the rioting quieted down.

PART V

Anti-Radical
and Police Violence

Anti-Abolition Riot in New York
1834

Abolitionist leaders were frequently mobbed, their presses smashed, their homes burned. Theodore Weld was repeatedly attacked with stones, clubs, and eggs. Henry B. Stanton was mobbed countless times before 1840, Garrison was dragged through the streets of Boston, Samuel May was stoned, the English abolitionist George Thompson narrowly escaped a mob at Concord, and Elijah Lovejoy was murdered at Alton, Illinois. Sometimes the protests became full-scale riots, and often hatreds were vented on blacks. Repressive laws were passed by Congress, among them the banning of abolitionist literature from the mails and the gag rule, which forbade all discussion of slavery in the House of Representatives.

The New York anti-abolition riot began in July, 1834, with an assault on abolitionist Lewis Tappan's store and moved to several churches sympathetic to abolition. Crowds stoned and tore down black homes, a school, and churches, and destroyed about $20,000 worth of property. In addition they attacked whorehouses and wrecked homes whose inhabitants did not place lit candles in their windows to signify their approval of the crowd's work.

The following account is taken from the New York *Journal of Commerce*, July 12, 1834, as reprinted in the Albany *Argus*, July 15, 1834. See Aileen Kraditor: *Means and Ends in American Abolitionism* (1969); Louis Filler: *The Crusade Against Slavery, 1830-1860* (1960); Linda Kerber: "Abolitionists and Amalgamation: The New York City Race Riots of 1834," *New*

York History, XLVIII (1967), 28-39; and Leonard L. Richards:
Gentlemen of Property and Standing (1970).

The worst anticipations of the day have been realized. For five hours our city has been the prey of an infuriated mob, or rather mobs, who have been carrying destruction before them in every direction. All the efforts of the watch, and of the military, as they were conducted, have not availed to stay the work of desolation, nor scarcely to retard its progress. Probably not less than one thousand troops have been on duty, includihg two squadrons of cavalry,—but so general was the impression among the mob, of the illegality of firing upon them without the presence of the Governor, that they were rather disposed to laugh than to tremble at their approach. If this impression is erroneous, it ought to be immediately removed. Affairs have come to such a pitch, that severe measures must be adopted, or our government is at an end.

Mr. Tappan's store was attacked at half past nine last evening, by a number of boys and men, who fired volleyes of stones and broke the upper windows, but did not attempt to force the doors. The mob were suspicious that there were things behind the doors, to which they did not wish to be introduced. As it was, they put themselves out of the pale of the law, and may thank a better spirit than their own, that they were not treated as they deserved.

On the first appearance of the watch they scattered, and after standing about in squads for some time, dispersed, and before 11 o'clock had all withdrawn to other scenes of action. The missiles, only in one instance, were sufficiently powerful to break the window shutters.

Between 10 and 11 a large mob assembled at Dr. Cox's church in Laight Street, and smashed in the doors and windows. From the church they proceeded to Charlton Street where he resides, but a strong detachment of watchmen were placed in line across the east end of the street and prevented all ingress to it. After remaining some time about Charlton Street the mob proceeded to Spring Street and attacked Rev. Mr. Ludlow's church, the doors and windows of which they began to batter in, when a small party of watchmen arrived and put a momentary stop to their proceedings and took one or two of the ringleaders into custody. Their companions however soon liberated them, beat the watchmen off and maltreated some of them. They then recommenced the work of destruction, broke in the doors, shattered the windows to atoms, and entered the church. In a short time they broke up the interior of it, destroying whatever they could. The session house adjoining, shared the same fate. A small party of horse now arrived, who appeared deterred from acting, on account of the immense disparity of numbers, as the mob then amounted to several thousands—and galloped off without attempting to interfere. In order to prevent their return, the mob erected a strong barrier, composed of carts and pieces of timber, across the street at each side of the church. About half past eleven, a strong detachment of cavalry and infantry arrived on the ground, and the cavalry charged at full gallop against the first barrier, which gave way, and they passed on to the second, against which several of their horses fell before they got through it. They then cleared the middle of the street, and the infantry took possession of the church, the interior of which was already nearly demolished. . . .

A sort of compact was then agreed on between them and the mob, by which the military were to leave the ground, and the mob immediately to disperse. The military then marched off; but the mob, instead of fulfilling their part of the agreement, returned into the church, rang the bell in token of triumph, and again began to destroy whatever remained undemolished. In about twenty minutes the military again returned, and took possession of the church. About midnight the mob began to disperse, but neither willingly nor in large numbers, nor in such a manner as to do away the impression that they might not renew the attack. . . .

About 11 o'clock, another mob attacked St. Phillip's African Episcopal church in Centre St.—Rev. Peter Williams, a colored man, pastor,—and demolished it almost entirely, including a fine organ. The furniture they took out and burned it in the street.

The windows of the African Baptist church in Anthony St. were broken to atoms.

The African school-house in Orange St., which is also used as a Methodist meeting house, was totally demolished.

Several houses where colored people resided, in Orange and Mulberry Sts., between Anthony and Walker, and about the Five Points, were greatly injured or totally destroyed. The mob compelled occupants of houses to set lights at the windows, and wherever colored people were seen, or no lights were shown, the work of destruction commenced. In one case a colored woman advanced to the window with her light, when in an instant some missile was sent which knocked her down and extinguished the light. . . .

About 9 o'clock, a detachment of the mob at the Five Points commenced an assault upon a small wooden building in Orange, near Bayard St., occupied as a barber's shop, by a colored man named Marsh, the front and interior of which they soon demolished. The black intrepidly kept possession of his premises, discharging a pistol three times at his assailants, the

last of which unfortunately took effect, and severely wounded Elisha
Spence in the leg, as he was passing on the opposite side of the street on
his way home. The rioters then joined the main body in Leonard Street.
A strong body of the watch shortly afterwards arrived at the spot, and
succeeded, with little difficulty, in putting the rioters to flight, and dispersing a much more numerous body of spectators. . . .

A watchman by the name of Philip Marks was badly wounded in the
stomach by a paving stone, in a conflict with the mob near Spring Street
Church. He was carried to the watch-house, and to our inquiry if he was
a good deal hurt, replied "yes:" but we hope not dangerously. Capt.
Archer, of the 3rd district watch, was considerably injured. It was reported
that a person was killed by a watchman in the same engagement; but we
trust it will prove to be an error. Mr. Lawson, inspector of the 1st Ward,
was badly wounded by a blow from a watchman inflicted through mistake.
A good many other persons, on both sides, were more or less hurt. The
conflict near Spring Street Church, before the arrival of the military, was
very obstinate.

A colored man, connected with one of the steamboats, was carrying
a trunk for a passenger to some part of the city, ignorant of what was
going on, when he was attacked by a fraction of the mob, his trunk taken
from him, and he shamefully abused. The trunk was afterwards restored.
Many other blacks were injured, some of them severely.

A great number of blacks repaired to the watch-house in the Park for
protection.

The mob was composed in part of sailors.

At this late hour we have not time for a word of comment,—further
than to say, that years cannot wash away the deep injury and disgrace
which our city is suffering,—and to call upon every good citizen to exert
his influence, by every means in his power, to prevent a continuance of
these scenes of violence and outrage. At the rate things are going on, it
will soon be as much as a man's life is worth, to reside in the city of New
York.

Tompkins Square
1874

During the depression of 1873, groups of unemployed workers organized to ask for government assistance, particularly for programs of public works which would create jobs for them. In New York City such a group, calling itself a Committee of Safety, was established in December 1873; among its members were socialists, reformers, and trade unionists. When this group petitioned the city government for aid, local officials refused to meet with them. The Committee then planned a march from Tompkins Square to City Hall, but the police refused to issue a permit for the march. "You have the same rights as any body of men," they were told, "but we want to avoid . . . annoyance to the business community and the public." The Committee then asked for a permit to hold a demonstration in Tompkins Square. The night before the meeting the police officials decided to refuse this permit also, but they did not so inform the Committee until the next morning. On a sub-freezing January day small Tompkins Square Park was jammed with over 7,000 workers, most of them immigrants, many women and children. At 10:30 a detachment of police appeared and began clubbing the demonstrators; mounted police charged the crowd repeatedly.

The response to the event reflected the fears that had been aroused by the Paris Commune. Commissioner of Police Abram Duryee was elated: "It was the most glorious sight I ever saw the way the police broke and drove the crowd. Their order was perfect as they charged with their clubs uplifted." The press was equally pleased, in New York and across the country. Editors advocated complete suppression of radicals and the unemployed. Should a communistic spirit emerge again, said one editor, the city should "club it to death at the hands of the police or shoot it to death at the hands of the militia." The attempt of the unemployed to organize and propose a program of public works ceased shortly afterwards.

The following description was written by Samuel Gompers, who was present at Tompkins Square, and who concluded from what happened there that radical methods of protest would not succeed: Gompers: *Seventy Years of Life and Labor* (1925). See Herbert Gutman: "The Tompkins Square 'Riot' in New York City on January 13, 1874: A Re-examination of Its Causes and Its Aftermath," *Labor History*, VI (Winter 1965), 44-70.

Next morning people began assembling early in the Square. I reached the Square a little after ten. It had been a drill field and playground and, though a bit out of repair, was commonly used by the working people for general gatherings and speeches. A high iron fence surrounded the park with wide gate entrances. Soon the park was packed and all the avenues leading to it crowded. The people were quiet. There was nothing out of harmony with the spirit of friendly conferences between the chief public official and workless and breadless citizens. The gathering was planned as visible proof of suffering and destitution among New York unemployed. A paper was edited for this special meeting by Lucien Sanial and P. J. McGuire. The paper, widely circulated among the unemployed, the working people, and the city authorities, contained the program proposed by the workers. The *Volcano* was also conspicuously for sale. Tom-ri-John, everybody in New York in the early 'seventies will remember as a Communist or Socialist or a reformer of some kind. Tom was also a journalistic reformer. He ran a newspaper called the *Volcano*. It was printed on bright yellow paper and its articles set up in red ink. In accord with their distribution of family responsibility, it was Mrs. Tom-ri-John's business to sell these papers, and her working dress (masculine garb) served to attract attention, while the big stick she always carried was her rod and staff of defense and support. The couple had three children Eruptor, Vesuvia, and Emancipator.

It was about 10:30 when a detachment of police surrounded the park. Hardly had they taken position before a group of workers marched into the park from Avenue A. They carried a banner bearing the words "TENTH WARD UNION LABOR." Just after they entered the park the police sergeant led an attack on them. He was followed by police mounted and on foot with drawn night-sticks. Without a word of warning they swept down the defenseless workers, striking down the standard-bearer and using their clubs right and left indiscriminately on the heads of all they could reach.

Shortly afterwards the mounted police charged the crowd on Eighth Street, riding them down and attacking men, women, and children without discrimination. It was an orgy of brutality. I was caught in the crowd on the street and barely saved my head from being cracked by jumping down a cellarway. The attacks of the police kept up all day long—wherever the police saw a group of poorly dressed persons standing or moving together. Laurrell went to Tompkins Square and received a blow from the police across his back, the effect of which remained with him for several months.

The next few days disclosed revolting stories of police brutality inflicted on the sick, the lame, the innocent bystander. Mounted police and guards had repeatedly charged down crowded avenues and streets. To this day I cannot think of that wild scene without my blood surging in indignation at the brutality of the police on that day. They justified their policy by the charge that Communism was rearing its head.

The Internationals replied with the ugly charge that they had been sold out by George Blair and others of the Workingmen's Union who they said had told the authorities that they were dynamiters trying to organize a Commune, a charge that never died until it was thrashed out in the Central Labor Union years later and Blair exonerated. Blair was a boxmaker by trade and was then operating a co-operative establishment. He was an ardent Knight of Labor which then, of course, was a wholly secret body. I always thought him honest and loyal to the best interests of labor. He did not look with friendliness upon any attempt to turn the labor movement into opera bouffe. He may have asked for police protection to have the workers properly protected—but I am perfectly confident he betrayed no trust.

The Tompkins Square outrage was followed by a period of extreme repression. The New York police borrowed continental methods of espionage. Private indoor meetings were invaded and summarily ended by the ejection of those present. The police frustrated several meetings held to protest police brutality and in defense of the right of free assemblage for a lawful purpose.

Everett Massacre
1916

Few American radical organizations have been so feared as the "Wobblies," the Industrial Workers of the World. The Wobblies' ideology was an amalgam of revolution and industrial unionism; they seldom discussed bread-and-butter issues—higher wages or shorter hours. They never had a large following, except in certain areas, particularly the Northwest, and for certain types of laborers, particularly migrant lumbermen. The local business-men of the West and Northwest often organized against the Wobblies, most often by denying them permission to hold street meetings. In return, the Wobblies organized "Free Speech" fights. Large numbers of Wobblies would go to a town, hold meetings, and get arrested until they literally filled the jails to overflowing. Often this tactic brought about some sort of accommodation with local officials. There were many such battles in California in the early 1900's, and the "Free Speech" campaign spread to the Northwest, to Spokane in 1999, and Aberdeen, Washington, in 1911.

The resistance the Wobblies encountered when they tried to help out a shingle weavers' strike in Everett, Washington, in August 1916, was particularly fierce. Street speakers were arrested and put on boats to Seattle. The Wobblies rented a launch and tried to land in the town but were caught by armed deputies organized by the town officials and the business lead-ers of the Commercial Club, and deported. On October 30 they tried again. Armed deputies met their boat and beat the Wob-blies with clubs and gun butts, then drove them to the outskirts of town and forced them to run a gauntlet of blackjacks. When local citizens organized a meeting to protest the violence, the Wobblies announced that they would attend. They organized another expedition, 280 strong, hired the steamer *Verona*, and headed for Everett. This time seven men were killed and many injured.

The following description was written by Walker C. Smith:
"The Voyage of the Verona," *International Socialist Review*,
XVII (1916-17), 340-6. See also Robert L. Tyler: *Rebels of
the Woods: The I.W.W. in the Pacific Northwest* (1967), 62-
84; Melvyn Dubofsky: *We Shall Be All* (1969); and Norman H.
Clark: "Everett, 1911, and After," *Pacific Northwest Quarterly*,
LVII (April 1966), 57-64.

Five workers and two vigilantes dead, thirty-one workers and nineteen
vigilantes wounded, from four to seven workers missing and probably
drowned, two hundred ninety-four men and three women of the working
class in jail—this is the tribute to the class struggle in Everett, Wash., on
Sunday, November 5. Other contributions made almost daily during the
past six months have indicated the character of the Everett authorities,
but the protagonists of the open shop and the antagonists of free speech
did not stand forth in all their hideous nakedness until the tragic trip of
the steamer Verona. Not until then was Darkest Russia robbed of its
claim to "Bloody Sunday."

Early Sunday morning on November 5 the steamer Verona started for
Everett from Seattle with 260 members of the Industrial Workers of the
World as a part of its passenger list. On the steamer Calista, which followed, were 38 more I.W.W. men, for whom no room could be found
on the crowded Verona. Songs of the One Big Union rang out over the
waters of Puget Sound, giving evidence that no thought of violence was
present.

It was in answer to a call for volunteers to enter Everett to establish
free speech and the right to organize that the band of crusaders were
making the trip. They thought their large numbers would prevent any
attempt to stop the street meeting that had been advertised for that afternoon at Hewitt and Wetmore Avenues in handbills previously distributed
in Everett. Their mission was an open and peaceable one. . . .

When the singers, together with the other passengers, crowded to the
rail so they might land the more quickly, Sheriff McRae called out to
them:

"Who is your leader?"

Immediate and unmistakable was the answer from every I.W.W.:

"We are all leaders!"

Angrily drawing his gun from its holster and flourishing it in a threatening manner, McRae cried:

"You can't land here."

"Like hell we can't!" came the reply from the men as they stepped toward the partly thrown off gang plank.

A volley of shots sent them staggering backward and many fell to the deck. The waving of McRae's revolver evidently was the prearranged signal for the carnage to commence.

The few armed men on board, according to many of the eye-witnesses, then drew revolvers and returned the fire, causing consternation in the ranks of the cowardly murderers barricaded on the dock. Until the contents of their revolvers were exhausted, the workers stood firm. They had no ammunition in reserve. The unarmed men sought cover but were subjected to a veritable hail of steel jacketed soft-nosed bullets from the high power rifles of the vigilantes. The sudden rush to the off-shore side of the boat caused it to list to about thirty degrees. Bullets from the dock to the south and from the scab tugboats moored there apparently got in their destructive work, for a number of men were seen to fall overboard and the water was reddened with their blood. No bodies were recovered when the harbor was dragged the next day. On the tugboat Edison, the scab cook, a mulatto, fired shot after shot with careful and deadly aim at the men on the off-shore side of the boat, according to the Pacific Coast Longshoreman, the official I.L.A. paper. This man had not even a deputy badge to give a semblance of legality to his murders. That the gunmen on the two docks and on the scab boats were partly the victims of their own cross fire is quite likely.

After ten minutes of steady firing, during which hundreds of rounds of ammunition were expended, the further murder of unarmed men was prevented by the action of Engineer Ernest Skelgren, who backed the boat away from the dock with no pilot at the wheel. The vigilantes kept up their gunfire as long as the boat was within reach.

On a hilltop overlooking the scene thousands of Everett citizens witnessed the whole affair. The consensus of their opinion is that the vigilante mob started the affair and are wholly responsible.

May Day Riot in Cleveland
1919

In the decade before World War I, the Socialist party was a vital political force, large enough to enter candidates in local, state and national elections. In 1912, almost 900,000 people voted for Eugene V. Debs for President. When the United States entered the war in 1917 the Socialists, like the Wobblies, opposed the war effort; moreover their resistance won support and Socialist candidates made a strong showing in the municipal elections of 1917. But to many of those who were caught up in a fervor of patriotism in support of the war, all opponents were betraying America. Congress passed an Espionage Act in June 1917 and a harsh Sedition Act in May 1918. Throughout the country Socialist meetings were raided; Socialists were beaten, tarred and feathered, and on occasion tortured. Under the new laws immigrants were rounded up and deported, and over 1,500 people were arrested, including Eugene Debs, Victor Berger, and Wobbly Leader "Big Bill" Haywood. Employers took advantage of wartime hysteria to suppress radical labor organizers, as in the Tulsa, Oklahoma, oil country where seventeen I.W.W. members were tarred and feathered and shipped out.

Anti-radical feeling continued high after the Armistice in November, 1918. The first major post-war show of strength by Socialists was a nationwide effort to hold May Day celebrations in 1919. Wherever there were celebrations, there were also violent attacks on the Socialists. In Boston, crowds attacked the May Day parade, killing one person and wounding several, and also destroyed the local Socialist headquarters. The police arrested 116 paraders, but not one of their assailants. In New York City, mobs wrecked the office of the Socialist *Call* and the Russian Peoples' House. The Cleveland, Ohio, parade was attacked by victory loan workers and army veterans, and for two hours the central part of the city was in chaos. Socialist offices were wrecked, one person was killed, and forty injured. Again, 106 paraders were arrested, but none of their assailants.

The following account of the Cleveland riots is taken from the Ohio *Socialist*, May 8, 1919. See William Preston, Jr.: *Aliens and Dissenters* (1963); James Weinstein: *The Decline of Socialism in America, 1912-1925* (1967); and National Civil Liberties Bureau: *War-Time Prosecutions and Mob Violence . . . from April 1, 1917 to May 1, 1918* (1918).

The greatest parade ever staged by the Socialists of Cleveland ended in red riot and bloodshed on Thursday afternoon, May 1st. Hundreds of arrests were made, scores were taken to the hospitals, including seventeen policemen. Many more only slightly injured were taken home by friends. Riots and mobs ruled in the downtown section of the city for two hours. Shots were fired, police clubs cracked scores of heads and fist fights innumerable were principal parts of the debauch to which this section of the city was given over when the first division of the parade, numbering 35,000 marchers, entered the Public Square in the heart of the business section.

Paraders Peaceful and Happy

In five great divisions the 35,000 Socialists and sympathizers, including the Bakers' union, on strike for day work only, the Machinists, one local of the Carpenters, members of the Workmen's Sick and Death Benefit Fund, converged near Acme Hall and began their march toward the Public Square. Thousands carried small red pennants. Dozens of banners demanding release of political prisoners, withdrawal of troops from Russia and similar emblems were carried. Great red silk banners together with the national emblem were carried at the head of the parade and by the different divisions.

Smiles and happiness were on every face, cheers were given for the workers' cause and the spirit of the New Day was seen to shine in every comrade's face and bearing. The parade was one of happy men, women and children, bent upon a peaceful and happy celebration of our International holiday.

First Riot Starts

The parade was passing East 9th Street on Superior Street when soldiers on the sidewalk rushed into the parade, tearing the red banners from the hands of the marchers. In a few minutes Superior Street was the scene of riot and disorder from this point to the Public Square.

When the head of the parade reached the Square an immense cheering rose up from the thousands who packed the grounds. At the same moment the soldiers who carried the Socialist banners were attacked by others from the crowds. Their banners were wrested from them. When C. E. Ruthenberg, who was to be the principal speaker, interceded for the Socialists, he was arrested. Scarcely had the applause of the vast throng died down when a shriek of terror rose from thousands of throats as a platoon of mounted police dashed into the melee, wielding clubs without discrimination upon men and women alike. Instantly, bedlam broke loose. Army trucks and tanks, police autos, ambulances and police patrol wagons were dashing helter-skelter through the crowds, overrunning and injuring many in an attempt to disperse the crowds. Autos carrying police and mounted police dashed up and down the sidewalks to clear them. Men, women and children fled through by-streets and alleys for safety.

Workers Fight Back

While police were freely using their clubs upon the heads of the Socialists, some fought back with naked hands and what weapons they could find. Mounted police were pulled from their mounts and other officers were beaten into unconsciousness. In a short while, however, the crowd had been dispersed from the Square, but small riots and fights occurred in many adjacent streets all afternoon as mobs searched out individuals and groups of known Socialists.

Local Headquarters Demolished

During the riots downtown the local headquarters at Prospect and Bolivar Rd. was a scene of destruction. Mobs stormed the local headquarters, demolishing it almost completely. Windows were smashed out, furniture made into kindling wood. Thousands of books and pamphlets, records and files were carried away or ruined. The scene at the finish was one of utter desolation.

Centralia

1919

Wartime anti-radical feeling ran highest against the "Wobblies" (see p. 348). Their opposition to the war made it possible to call them traitors and German spies and to stir up popular sentiment against them. What happened in Centralia, Washington, is typical of many anti-Wobbly outbursts, although it was more dramatic in its outcome than most. When Wobblies first appeared in Centralia in 1918 they were denounced as an insult to patriotic sensibilities. Some men marching in a Red Cross parade attacked the newly opened I.W.W. Hall, beat up the Wobblies, and drove them out of town. The next year the Wobblies made plans to return, and in preparation the businessmen of Centralia, at the urging of the employers' association of the state, formed a Citizens Protective League. In September, 1919, the IWW reopened its hall; in November, a secret committee of the Protective League, together with an American Legion unit, arranged for the Armistice Day parade to pass the Wobbly headquarters. When the Legionnaires reached the hall, they broke ranks and charged; the waiting Wobblies opened fire, killing three on the spot. Now the hall was destroyed, and Wobblies in Centralia and throughout the state were rounded up and jailed. One Wobbly, Wesley Everest, was taken from the Centralia jail and lynched.

The following account is taken from an IWW pamphlet by Walker C. Smith: *Centralia* (1925). See Robert Tyler: *Rebels of the Woods: the IWW in the Pacific Northwest* (1967).

The Chehalis division again passed the hall and kept on marching. The Centralia contingent on command stopped directly in front of the hall. Marshall Cormier—member of the secret committee—from his vantage point on a bay here cried in vexation to the Chahalis marchers, "What is the matter with you fellows? Aren't you in on this?" Immediately he signaled with shrill whistle, there were shouts from the crowd, "Come on boys! Let's get them!" and the mob rushed the I.W.W. hall, smashing the windows and breaking down the door. Then at last came the belated defense by I.W.W. members.

Grimm, shot in the abdomen, staggered unassisted to a nearby store and from there was taken to a hospital, where he died. Some claim he made a dying statement accepting blame for his actions.

McElfresh died almost instantly from a bullet wound in the head. Here again the testimony conflicts, some claiming that McElfresh was taken from inside the doorway of the I.W.W. hall where a bullet fired by Wesley Everest had laid him low.

Casagranda was shot while in the vicinity of the hall outside the line of march. Several others among the attacking party received slight wounds.

Dr. Bickford's testimony at the inquest, as already given in these pages, is substantiated by the statements of Dr. Harold Y. Bell, another of the paraders. Bell said he heard shouts, saw the ranks break, and there followed a concerted move toward the I.W.W. hall.

"It seemed to me that it was at the same moment that I heard shots. The shooting and the movement of the men was as nearly simultaneous as any human acts could be."

From a man favorable to the prosecution comes this evidence that the shouts and the breaking of ranks preceded any gunfire. From Bickford, also favorable to the prosecution, comes the vital fact that a raid upon the hall was the thought uppermost in the minds of the Centralia paraders. He had offered to head the paraders.

As before, the hall was gutted and its contents destroyed, with the exception of records from the desk of the I.W.W. secretary, which were put into the hands of Prosecutor Allen as he stood on the street at Second and Tower Avenue watching the property destruction.

Bert Faulkner attempted to leave the hall after the first onslaught had been checked by the firing. With one other exception the occupants of the hall sought refuge in a large disused ice-box in the rear of the hall, surrendering later to the authorities. The exception was Wesley Everest —quiet, grim, game; an ex-service man who seemed not to know such a thing as fear.

Everest left the hall by the rear door, firing as he went. He was through the mob at the rear before they recovered from their surprise. Threatening his pursuers with a still smoking revolver, he sped down the alley, rifle bullets zipping around him. The mob mistook Everest for Britt Smith, the I.W.W. secretary, against whom the conspirators had a deep grudge. The pursued man stopped to reload his weapon, then continued the running fight until the river was reached. He tried to ford the stream, but found the water too deep. Turning on his assailants, he waded to the bank and stood waiting with the last of his ammunition in the overheated gun. Raising his voice, he declared his willingness to submit to arrest to any constituted authority. But it was merely a mob that confronted the man at bay. On came the pursuing group, one man in a soldier's uniform some distance in the lead. Everest took careful aim and fired. The crowd halted, but the single man sped on. Twice more Everest pierced the on-coming man. Twice again he fired and Dale Hubbard, nephew of the chief conspirator in the raid, fell dead at his very feet. Game as grit, the defenseless ex-soldier awaited the coming of his mob-maddened "buddies."

Everest's trip to the jail was marked by blows, kicks, and curses. With the butt of a rifle his front teeth were rammed into his throat. A rope was thrown around his neck, but with the defiance that had been his throughout the whole time of the raid, Everest said: "You haven't got the guts to lynch a man in the daytime."

The Lynching of Wesley Everest

Night told a different story, however. Maimed and bleeding in the cell next to his fellow workers, the hours passed slowly for Everest. Late that night the lights of the city were suddenly extinguished from the power plant. The outer door of the city jail was smashed in. No attempt was made to stop the lynchers. Staggering erect, Wesley Everest said to the other prisoners, "Tell the boys I died for my class."

A brief struggle. Many blows. A sound of dragging. The purring of high powered automobiles. Then a sudden return of light to the darkened city.

The autos reached the Chehalis River bridge. To the steel framework one end of a rope was tied, the other end being noosed around Everest's neck. With a brutal kick the semi-conscious man was hurled from the bridge. A pause. The body was hauled up, revealing the fact that Everest still had a spark of life. A longer rope was attached to the first and the brutal process repeated. With Everest dead, the corpse was raised and a third rope attached before the ghouls again flung the body from the bridge. An automobile headlight was trained upon the dead man, plainly revealing that some sadist more demoniacal than his fellow degenerates had ripped Everest's sexual organs almost loose from the body with some sharp instrument during the auto trip to the bridge. There under the glare of that headlight the corpse was riddled with bullets.

Later the rope was cut, allowing the mutilated body to fall into the river.

Dearborn Massacre
1932

In March, 1932, Detroit was seething with labor unrest, much of it directed against the Ford Motor Company. On March 7, a crowd of three to five thousand unemployed workmen organized by the Communist party, marched from downtown Detroit to the Ford plant in Dearborn. They intended to ask for jobs for all laid-off Ford workers, immediate payment of fifty percent of their wages, a seven-hour day, the end of the production-line speed-up, two fifteen-minute rest periods, equal hiring rights for Negroes, and free medical care at the Ford hospital. The Mayor of Dearborn, a cousin of Henry Ford's, ordered the Chief of Police, a former detective on Ford's payroll, to halt the marchers at the Dearborn line. The marchers ignored the order to halt, and managed to reach the Ford plant; there firehoses, pistols, and a machine gun were used to drive them off. Four were killed and a score or more injured. On March 12 the murdered men were laid in coffins under a huge picture of Lenin, and a banner proclaiming that "Ford gave Bullets for Bread." Over thirty thousand people attended the funeral. Said the Detroit *Times*: "The killing of innocent workmen . . . is a blow directed at the very heart of American institutions."

The following account is taken from *The New York Times*, March 8, 1932. See Irving Bernstein: *The Lean Years* (1966); and Keith Sward: *The Legend of Henry Ford* (1948).

Nearly 3,000 of Detroit's unemployed, with Communists in their midst, took part in a riot today at the gates of the Ford Motor Company's plant in Dearborn. Their demonstration culminated in a furious fight in which four men were killed and at least fifty others were injured.

The demonstration by the unemployed, who had planned to ask Ford company officials, through a committee, to give them work, started quietly, but before it was over Dearborn pavements were stained with blood, streets were littered with broken glass and the wreckage of bullet-ridden automobiles and nearly every window in the Ford plant's employment building had been broken. . . .

The march, plans for which were completed on Sunday evening, according to one of the wounded demonstrators, was orderly at the start. In accordance with the program, the work-seekers gathered at Fort Street and Oakland Boulevard at about 2 o'clock this afternoon and set out for the Ford plant in Dearborn, more than two miles away, where they intended to send a committee of officials to the factory with the demand that the company immediately employ a large number of those out of work.

Carrying banners and signs demanding jobs, the demonstrators marched in orderly fashion along Fort Street to Miller Road, where they halted for a few minutes to hold a conference. The conference was soon over and once more they resumed the march, swinging along Miller Road to the Dearborn city limits.

There they encountered a squad of Dearborn police, who warned them to turn back to Detriot.

Ignoring the warning, the marchers surged over the city lines, and instantly the fighting broke out. The police hurled a barrage of tear bombs into the crowd, causing the vanguard of the parade to fall back along the Rouge River and the railroad tracks.

Wind Carries Off Gas Fumes

But in a few minutes the police had exhausted their supply of bombs and, to add to their troubles, the prevailing high winds quickly cleared the air of tear-gas fumes.

Quick to take advantage of the situation, the marchers began a second charge, hurling rocks and jagged chunks of frozen mud at the police.

Dodging the missiles, the police drew their guns, pointing them threateningly at the angry mob. Once more the marchers scattered, this time along Miller Road to Dearborn Road, where they encountered more gas bombs which had been rushed to the scene during the lull of their first retreat.

Meanwhile, Dearborn firemen had stationed themselves on an overhead walk that crosses Miller Road at Gate 3, in front of the main plant, around which the worst of the fighting took place.

On the viaduct, out of reach of the missiles flung by the rioters, the firemen turned a hose on them, holding them back temporarily with the icy stream of water.

But the rioters were held at bay only for a few minutes. Soon they swarmed up the embankment and were surging to the gate of the Ford Motor Company's employment office.

Shot Starts General Melee

There they were met by squads of police with drawn guns and by the Ford Company's fire department.

The demonstrators had just made their request for a hearing in the employment office, when someone started to shoot. The report of the pistol shot started a general melee. Hand-to-hand fighting began, the police defensive being aided by streams of water from the firemen's hoses.

Men fell with gunshot wounds in their legs and were carried out of further harm's way by their comrades, who tried to commandeer automobiles to take the wounded away. When automobile drivers refused to help, their cars were stoned.

The fighting continued meanwhile, but it was finally checked with the arrival, in answer to calls for aid, of reinforcements of State and Detroit police. . . .

One man declared that the marchers were fired upon by the Ford police before they could present their appeal.

Bonus Army
1932

In 1924 Congress authorized a bonus for World War I veterans, to be paid twenty years later. In the depths of the Depression, when local and state measures to combat unemployment and hunger were proving futile, veterans' groups began to demand immediate payment of their bonus as a relief measure. In the spring of 1932 thousands of jobless men, most of them veterans, went to Washington to demonstrate for immediate payment. The Bonus Expeditionary Force, as it came to be called, eventually numbered over 20,000, and included many veterans' families. The Washington Police Department, under the sympathetic leadership of Chief Pelham D. Glassford, helped them to build a community of shacks on Anacostia Flats. On June 15, the House passed a Bonus Bill, but on June 17, as 12,000 men waited outside the Capitol, the Senate overwhelmingly rejected it. Disappointed, the men went peacefully back to their shacks, but refused to leave Washington. President Hoover persuaded Congress to authorize loans to pay for transportation back home, but only a few men left. Weeks passed, and Hoover became increasingly uneasy; he seems to have feared a communist-led insurrection. His anxiety was increased by the War Department. Army Intelligence insisted that a veterans' riot would be the "signal for a communist uprising in all large cities, thus initiating a revolution." On July 28 Hoover ordered the reluctant Glassford to clear the men out of some abandoned buildings. The veterans fought back and two were killed. Declaring that law and order had broken down, Hoover ordered troops under the command of General Douglas MacArthur to clear the riot area and return the veterans to their camps. There, under Army guard, they would be investigated to identify the communists Hoover assumed were responsible for the disorder. MacArthur, however, ignored the President's order, and told Glassford "We are going to break the back of the B.E.F." Assisted by Dwight D. Eisenhower and George S. Patton, MacArthur led a force of four troops of cavalry, four companies of steel-helmeted infantry with fixed bayonets, and six tanks to the Bonus Camps. They used tear gas to force the men out, and burned the camps to the ground. A baby of eleven weeks died, an eight-year-old was partially blinded by the gas, and several people were wounded by bayonets or sabers.

Hoover was angered and dismayed but decided to accept full responsibility for MacArthur's actions, and insisted publicly that many of the marchers were Communists and criminals. MacArthur issued his own statement, declaring that the mob "was animated by the essence of revolution." If the Administration had waited another week, "the institutions of our Government would have been severely threatened." The press thought otherwise. Many who had visited the camp said rather that the men had been crushed by the Depression and joined the march to flee from the realities of hunger. Mauritz Hallgren found no spirit of revolt, "no fire, not even smouldering resentment." Communist party leaders had organized a front group, the Workers Ex-Service Mens' League, which had tried to convert the march into a revolutionary striking force; but the leaders of the Bonus Army, particularly Walter W. Waters, who were vehemently anti-communist, organized squads of veterans to beat up the radicals. The radicals did have an impact on some of the veterans: some members moved beyond demands for a lump sum handout to demands for unemployment insurance, and toward a deeper questioning of the roots of the Depression.

The story of the rout of the Bonus Army is told by the Washington *Post*, July 29, 1932. On the B.E.F., see Irving Bernstein: *The Lean Years* (1960); Arthur C. Hennessy: "The Bonus Army: Its Roots, Growth, and Demise," doctoral dissertation, Georgetown, 1957; W. W. Waters (as told to William C. White): *B.E.F.: The Whole Story of the Bonus Army* (1933); Felix Morrow: *The Bonus March* (1932); James F. and Jean H. Vivian: "The Bonus March of 1932: The Role of General George Van Horn Moseley," *Wisconsin Magazine of History*, LI (Autumn 1967), 26-36; and Donald J. Lisio: "A Blunder Becomes Catastrophe: Hoover, the Legion, and the Bonus Army," ibid., 37-50.

Tear gas bombs and torches, unleashed by Federal troops in a sweeping offensive, routed the ragged bonus army yesterday from every major encampment in the Capital in a day of wild disorder that took the life of one veteran.

In a relentless drive, infantrymen, cavalrymen and tanks opened the drive against the veterans on Pennsylvania Avenue, herded them from the Southwest section and stopped their offensive at Camp Marks, the largest of the bonus army encampments. . . .

Dropping tear gas bombs to the right of them and to the left of them, the infantrymen had routed the veterans from every camp in the western section of the city, and the desolation was completed by soldiers who laid waste the encampment with torches.

Toward midnight the cavalrymen and foot soldiers were in possession of all encampments in the city, with the exception of Camp Bartlett in Anacostia, which is privately owned, and to which the veterans were flocking for shelter.

As in their tactics against the other camps, the soldiers at Anacostia laid down a heavy barrage of tear gas as the veterans fled for cover. Women and children had been removed from the camp an hour before.

The troops reached the Anacostia camp shortly after 10 o'clock. As they reached the Anacostia end of the bridge a crowd impeded their way: the troops hurled tear gas bombs.

Cheers and boos from the thousands of onlookers greeted their arrival. Women and children ran back screaming. They turned into the parkway, with the cavalry in their wake. In a few minutes the torches were touched to several shacks near the entrance to the camp.

In the Pennsylvania Avenue onset tear gas bombs were thrown into the stubborn ranks of the veterans as they refused to budge, while infantrymen, with fixed bayonets, moved into the disputed area. As the acrid fumes of the bombs settled through the hovels the men began to retreat.

Gas masks were donned by the 300 infantrymen from Fort Washington as they moved through the billets. The bombs were hurled into the ranks of the veterans, whose resistance was mostly in the form of taunts and maledictions.

The foot soldiers were in the first line of attack, with the cavalry backing them up and holding the regained territory. Eyes of police, veterans and spectators were seared as the fumes spread over the area.

Shacks Are Fired

Fire broke out in a number of shacks on the southwest corner of the area, adding to the confusion. The fire is thought to have been started by veterans who spread gasoline over the shacks and put a torch to them before they evacuated.

A blue haze of gas hovered over the area as the veterans retreated. Another detachment of infantrymen began a flanking movement and they pushed the veterans south to Maryland and Maine Avenues.

Bomb after bomb was thrown as the soldiers moved quickly through the main building of the camp at 344 Pennsylvania Avenue. The fumes routed the veterans from the upper floors of the building.

Thousands of spectators fled from the tear gas. Women and children in the crowd were affected. Storekeepers were ordered to lock their doors.

There was one casualty from the tear gas and the heat. An ambulance quickly took the victim away. As the troops moved toward the southeast corner of the area, the tanks moved behind the infantrymen.

Scenes reminiscent of the days of the World War were enacted as the troops rushed through the billets. As the fires broke out, the fire department was called to prevent spread of the flames.

In a futile gesture to halt the advance of the soldiers, some of the retreating bonus veterans, above whose heads waved an American flag, picked up a number of the gas shells before they could explode and threw them back into the ranks; but the soldiers pressed on.

Ordered to Get Out

Cavalrymen moved through the area mopping up the work of the infantry. A cavalryman with a saber drawn espied a veteran in one of the shanties. "Get out of here," he said, pointing his sword.

The man held aloft his shoes and said he was putting them on. "It makes no difference," said the officer. Women and children in the huts were also evacuated. Some of them left with pots and pans and a few household belongings clutched in their arms.

The firemen, called into action by the blaze, drove into the midst of the flames. Screeching sirens added to the din. Boos and jeers of the veterans echoed throughout the sector, sprinkled with faint cheers and jeers of spectators.

Cavalry Horses Unruly

Cavalry horses, frightened at the shouting and confusion, the gas and the flames, became unruly. One of them broke through a door to a drug store, carrying its rider over the sidewalk and into the store.

The cavalry came into view down historic Pennsylvania Avenue shortly before 5 o'clock with pennants and flags flying above the horses' heads. The horses were halted at Sixth and Pennsylvania Avenue. Then they [entered] Third Street and in their rear came five whippet tanks, clattering and sputtering down the Avenue. Another moved into the affected area as Gen. Glassford ordered all spectators moved back from the scene of action.

The horses were spread clear across the avenue, placing a halt on all vehicular movements. As they marched past the billets between Third and Fourth Streets northwest, they were cheered and slightly booed by the veterans.

The head of the column stopped, a cavalry unit followed them, and then came a machine gun company. All of these were from Fort Myer.

Then came several companies of infantry from Fort Washington, equipped with trench helmets, rifles and fixed bayonets. Over their shoulders were strung sacks of tear gas bombs.

The mounted men carried carbines, sabers, pistols and tear gas bombs.

The khaki-clad men were grim-faced and quiet. Bonus marchers shot "wise cracks" at them. Maj. George Patton, astride a horse, was jeered and cheered as he trotted down the avenue. He surveyed the situation and then returned to Gen. MacArthur.

Mounted orderlies trotted up and down, carrying messages between the various unit commanders. One veteran shouted. "The first move they make, boys, get down on your bellies!"

Some veterans broke out with "Hail, Hail, the Gang's All Here." There was a short conference betweeen Gen. Glassford and Army officials. Then the detachments of soldiers took their positions around the block. . . .

Army trucks rolled up with new supplies of gas bombs. They were issued to the troops, the soldiers filling their pouches with them.

Throughout the entire movement in the southwest sections, the veterans were kept on the move, prodded by the rifles of soldiers.

A few minutes after the exodus from the Pennsylvania Avenue billets began, a group of the veterans moved toward the Peace Monument. One man, carrying a blanket over his shoulder, started to sing "Pack Up Your Troubles." He was silenced by angry shouts of his companions.

Near the Peace Monument a woman sat on a packing box filled with clothing. She started to harangue the troopers, police, and then the veterans.

Some of the veterans were challenging the soldiers to get down from their horses and fight. Behind a towering Negro, carrying an American flag, a group of the bonus veterans surged across the street between two of the cavalrymen who were holding the line.

The Negro, dressed in riding boots and trousers, held the flag aloft and shouted he would not move. He was the point of a triangle about which the 100 or more veterans gathered.

Break Through Lines

After the cavalrymen had tried unsuccessfully to push the Negro back, they put their horses squarely into the crowd, five of them breaking through the lines and scattering the men.

At another point several veterans tried to drag a cavalry captain from his mount, but other soldiers dashed up and pushed back the rioters.

Peekskill Riot

1949

On August 28, 1949, the Communist party planned to hold an open-air concert in Peekskill, New York, about 50 miles north of New York City. Paul Robeson was to be one of the singers. First, the concert had to be postponed when a local mob attacked a group of sponsors who were viewing the proposed site. The concert was held a week later on September 4, and the sponsors, knowing that there was likely to be trouble, provided guards for protection. The concert went on as planned, but as the audience left it was attacked. For miles along the road to New York City, cars were assaulted by American Legionnaires, Westchester police, and local anti-Communists. They hurled rocks at windshields, beat members of the departing audience, and shouted anti-radical, anti-Negro, anti-Semitic epithets. The first account which follows was written by Howard Fast, a novelist and one-time Communist party member, who was one of the organizers of the concert. The other accounts are taken from a Westchester Citizens' Committee Report, as reprinted in Fast: *Peekskill, U.S.A., A Personal Experience* (1951), 82-9, 105-7.

. . . our concert went smoothly enough, and with all the difficulties there was good music there that day. The great voice of Paul Robeson echoed back from the hills; the music of Handel and Bach was played there; and Pete Seeger and his friends sang those fine old songs of a time when treason and hatred and tyranny were not the most admired virtues of Americans. And the police did what they could. When they saw that they were not able to prevent the concert, they brought in a helicopter and it hovered over our sound truck constantly, swooping down to buzz us again and again, trying to drown out the sound of our music with the noise of its motor. To some extent they succeeded, but we were fortunate that the motor of a helicopter is less noisy than that of a regular airplane. It did not spoil the concert. . . .

Cars were moving now and the afternoon was wearing on. R——, who has spent the best years of his life being a soldier in two wars and an industrial organizer, has a better nose for danger than I have, and now he was shaking his head.

"I don't like it, I don't like it," he kept saying. . . .

Two of the security guards passed down the line of cars, telling each driver, "Close all windows as you approach the exit. They seem to be throwing things."

The situation was new to us, and Fords and Plymouths and Pontiacs were not built as military weapons. If people were throwing things, it seemed eminently correct that the windows should be closed protectively, and motorists as a whole have a rather child-like faith in the much-touted and widely advertised shatter-proof glass. No one questioned the advice, but even if they had, the damage would have simply taken other forms.

The line would move a few feet, then stop; a wait of about five minutes and then a few feet more. Driving an old car and depending on it, I was afraid of overheating, so I cut my motor constantly. But then suddenly we were in motion and the entrance was in sight and we rolled up and through it and out. A small cluster of hell was at work at the entrance; cops, in a craze of hate, were beating cars, not people, with their long clubs, smashing fenders, lashing out against windshields, doing a dance of frenzy as the autos rolled out of the place. Even through our closed windows we could hear the flood of insanely vile language from the police, the unprintable oaths, the race words, the slime and filth of America's underworld of race hatred compressed into these "guardians" of the law, and released now. There were about thirty of them grouped there at the entrance, and they flogged the cars as if the automobiles were living objects of their resentment.

(That was the experience, incidently, of the car which carried Paul Robeson. The police beat in the windshield and smashed at the car itself in their desire to get at the occupants.)

But that was only the beginning. . . .

It happened more quickly than it takes to tell it, but it must be told slowly. About thirty yards after I turned right on the state road, it began. On the left side of the road there were two policemen. The two policemen were about twenty feet apart, and between them were six or seven legionnaires with a great pile of heavy rocks. As my car came within range, they began to throw. The cops did not throw. They watched, smiling approval, and it became evident that these two policemen had been detached as guards for the group of rock-throwers—just in case a car should stop and turn on the rock-throwers. . . .

One reacts slowly, and I only comprehended what was happening when the first rocks crashed against the car. The first hit the door frame, between the front and rear windows; the second hit the frame of the windshield; two more heavy rocks crashed into the body of the car. The cops held their bellies and howled with mirth. . . .

And so it went, from group to group, through that nightmare gauntlet.

Then, suddenly, we had to slow down. The car ahead of us had fared worse than we; every window was smashed, even the rear window. I remember saying to R——,

"The road is wet. They must have gotten the gas tank or the radiator."

There was a dark wetness that flowed out of the car ahead of us; and then we realized that it was blood, but an enormous flow of blood that ran from the car that way and onto the road.

The rocks began again, and I jockeyed on. We had gone over a mile now. The car ahead pulled over to the side and the driver sat with his head hanging over the wheel. His head was bloody all over. . . .

Two miles or so from the concert grounds, a car had pulled into a gas station. This car, like so many others, left a trail of blood behind it. Five adults and one child emerged, and they were all covered with blood from head to foot. The child was weeping softly and they stood like people dazed, and a few feet away a group of young hoodlums hurled rocks at the passing cars. I pulled over to the gas station to stop and see if we could help the wounded people, but a cop stationed there ran at us, screaming oaths and beating the car with his club. When he started to draw his revolver, we drove on. Another car stopped and R——, turning around, saw the policeman beat the windshield of the car in with his club while he drew his revolver with his other hand. It was behavior which bordered on the paranoid, and though I have many times in the past seen police go into their frenzied dance of hatred against workers or progressives, I never saw anything to equal this display. And I must make the point that these were not single instances, for a while later when we stopped at a crossroad, we saw another policeman smashing in the windshield of a car which had halted for directions.

In Peekskill, in Buchanan and in Croton-on-Hudson, we continued to run the gauntlet of rocks, and the road we traveled was running with blood and littered with broken glass. Never in all my life have I seen so much blood; never have I seen so many people so cruelly cut and bleeding so badly. At another service station we saw three cars parked in a great spreading pool of blood and the people trying to staunch the flow of it.

Eyewitnesses: Quoted by Westchester Committee

Rose C., Brooklyn: "Another rock smashed through the front and hit the wife of the driver, seated on the front seat. Glass cut her right arm, blood was streaming, and she became quite hysterical. The driver, upset by his wife's condition and the condition of the car as well, stopped the car and told the state trooper he would go no further unless he was given protection. The state trooper said, 'You god damn bastard, run ahead or I'll club you.'"

. . . . .

Henry F., of Brooklyn, arrived with some other World War II veterans to help prepare for the concert. "The paraders were shouting all kinds of profane language. One shouted, 'We'll give you solidarity, we'll make you eat it!' Then, with a grin on his face, 'Dewey is going to protect you, oh yeah!'"

After the concert, he and other concert guards started to ride toward the entrance. "Suddenly, as if from out of nowhere a bunch of troopers swooped down on our cars and yelled, 'Get out of the cars!' Before we could comply, however, they were pulling us out to the side of the road. I saw the driver in the car in front of our car get hit in the kidneys by a cop for protesting the rough treatment. The troopers threw out everything in the car that wasn't fastened down, from the glove compartment and from the trunk. They ordered us back into the cars.

"A moment later another bunch of about fifteen deputies and police ordered us out of the cars again, this time roughing us up worse than the troopers. Some of them evidently had had something to drink. Their faces were red and they were wild, and swinging indiscriminately at everyone with their clubs.

"They ordered us into the cars once more. A moment later another group of deputies and police ordered us out of the car. This time I remarked to my companions, 'Here we go, out again and in again.' One cop overheard me and yelled, 'Hey, this son of a bitch is talking back!' Whereupon a group of cops and deputies set upon me and the car occupants in the most violent and vicious manner that I have ever experienced. One grabbed me by the collar and throat at the same time, and threw me to the ground, face down in the dirt, a distance of about eight feet from the car, and started beating us all. My shirt and suit were badly torn. Another cop dragged me to my feet and said, 'Get in and get going, you red bastard!' Another, who was obviously a captain of police, said, 'Go back to Jew town, and if we ever catch you up here again we'll kill you!' "

John N., New Jersey: "One of the troopers said, 'Let's get these bastards.' One of them stopped at the front right window where I sat. He took careful aim and shoved his nightstick, point first, at my left eye. I ducked my head when I saw it coming. The club missed the eyeball and caught the corner of the lid. It began to bleed, and when I brought my head up, he aimed at the eye again. I fended the club off with my arm.

"The police ordered us out of the car. Then, as we got out, they began to club us over the head.

"I was forced to run through a gauntlet of 15 to 20 policemen. Each of them clubbed me across the head or back. I tried to escape. They threw me to the ground and continued the beating. One of the policemen noticed a bandage on my left hand, which had been burned a week before. He jumped on the hand and ground his heel into the bandage, fracturing one of the burned fingers."

Sarah M., Bronx: "I saw several injured people ask the troopers and policemen for help. They were not only refused help, but were laughed at, called such names as 'Dirty Jew,' 'Dirty n——,' and some of those injured were hit with the billies of the policemen. I also saw some troopers and policemen throw rocks at the cars and buses."

William G., Queens: "As we were riding by, several of the state troopers cursed at us with epithets like 'Get out of here, you dirty so-and-so's.' 'You got what was coming to you, you dirty n—— lovers.' I saw the state troopers joking and talking to the very hoodlums who were endangering our lives."

Marvin L., Flushing, L.I.: "During all of this, the cops used all kinds of vile epithets, *i.e.*, 'Spread their legs and hit them in the groin.' This last was to the cops who were beating the men in the car ahead."

Irving W., Corona, N.Y.: "Repeatedly, men in their late twenties and also middle aged, wearing American Legion hats, and light blue overseas caps of another organization, came up to the low stone wall near me, screamed fifthy unprintable remarks, shook their fists and threatened. 'You'll never get out of here alive!' and 'Wait till you yellow bastards try to leave tonight!' These were definitely mature participants of the parade and not teen-age boys."

Freedom Riders
1961

When, in the late fifties, a new campaign for civil rights began in the South, one of its first goals was the desegregation of transportation facilities and restaurants. In 1961 civil rights workers tried to win enforcement of a 1958 Supreme Court ruling ordering stations and waiting rooms of bus lines to be desegregated. Led by James Farmer and the Congress of Racial Equality (CORE) two buses carrying thirteen freedom riders— six white and seven black—left Washington on May 4th for New Orleans. When they reached Alabama, one bus was fire-bombed and the demonstrators were beaten several times. This account of attacks in Anniston and Birmingham, Alabama, was written by James Peck, one of the Freedom Riders; it was published first in the New York *Post*, May 16, 1961. See Louis Lomax: *The Negro Revolt* (1962); Howard Zinn: *SNCC: The New Abolitionists* (1964); and Lester A. Sobel, ed.: *Civil Rights, 1960-66* (1967).

The thing you must remember to do when you get involved in one of these things is always to remain non-violent.

Another thing you should remember is to protect your head and face with your hands. I remembered the first—and I think I remembered the second too—but I guess I just didn't do too good a job of covering up. I'm pretty stiff today. They put 50 stitches in my head and face to put me back together again.

To be honest, it hurts just a little to smile today. . . .

We were riding in two buses from Atlanta, and our first stop was Anniston. My group—there were seven of us—was in the second bus, a Trailways bus. The other group (of ten) was in a Greyhound bus and got to Anniston first. That was the bus that was burned.

We didn't know there had been any trouble until we were about to leave Anniston, where we had stopped for over 15 minutes. When we first rolled into the town, it looked quiet, dead, like any other Sunday in a small town in the afternoon. There were no crowds or anything like that.

Then, just as we were about to leave, these eight white hoodlums came onto the bus. The bus driver then told us about the trouble the first bus had, and said he wasn't going to drive us unless the Negroes with us moved to the back. Well, of course, they didn't, and that's when these eight hoodlums started in.

The Negroes were sitting up front and the eight white men started hitting them and pushing. I ran up to help—to help ward off the blows—and all you could hear was the sound of flesh being smashed and bone being hit by clubs.

But there were no screams from us. And the others, the white hoodlums, they were shouting the usual stuff like, "Goddam niggers" and "why don't you white Communists stay up North?"

Finally we were pushed to the back four seats in the bus and these eight whites—they were pretty young—sat up front, and in between us there was this gap of empty seats, like a no-man's-land. The whites kept glaring back at us and muttering, and looking like they wanted to kill us.

In fact, I was thinking, after we were on the road toward Birmingham for a while, that maybe these boys have a little party in store for us before we get to Birmingham. Maybe we'll never get to Birmingham, I thought once. Maybe we'll be ordered out of the bus and worked over again.

But we weren't. They just sat there, the eight of them, glaring back at us and muttering.

I don't know about the others, but I wasn't scared. I guess I'm getting used to these things, so I don't get scared. You just make up your mind not to. . . .

As we started approaching Birmingham, passing from the suburbs into the town itself, we started getting ourselves together. I was pretty bloody from the business in Anniston, and I tried to clean myself up a little. And the others straightened themselves out, too—as if they were going to a party or something—. . . .

Well, when we got in, there they were. We spotted them right away. They were drawn up in a sort of semi-circle, maybe 25 or so, all young and grinning at each other. And, I swear, almost licking their lips. They weren't—I don't want to exaggerate—but they had that appearance.

I remember I looked at Charlie Person and he looked at me. And we both sort of shrugged, sort of like "here we go again," and then the bus stopped.

And then we had to get out. Person—he's a Negro—and I were the first two out. We had planned it that way. We started to walk toward the lunch counter. One of the mob came up and told me, "You're a shame to the white race" and another went up to Person and said, "You're a shame to the nigger race." We both kept walking.

We were in the waiting room by then, and then they cut us off, just as we were about to get to the lunch counter. They pushed us back, toward an alley, and about six of them started slugging me.

It was really rough. I put my hands over my face and head, but there were so many of them, and they just kept pounding away. One of them kept shouting, "get him, get him. Jesus, get him good."

And they didn't just use their fists. The doctor later at the hospital told me they must have used chains and brass knucks to do what they did to the back of my head. But I was lucky that on my face it was pretty much just fists.

I was dripping blood by this time, and I fell into a daze. Then I was taken to a private home, but finally they thought I ought to be taken to a hospital. They were nice at the hospital and did their job well, I guess.

I don't know what I was thinking in the hospital when they worked on me. Nothing special, I don't think, except that it hurt like hell and I wasn't going to be the handsomest guy in the world.

Oxford, Mississippi
1962

In May 1954, a unanimous Supreme Court decision ordered the elimination of segregation in public schools "with all deliberate speed." In the South, a vigorous campaign of resistance began, touched off by Senator James O. Eastland of Mississippi, who counseled defiance of the Court. Business and professional men organized White Citizens Councils, whose members often encouraged violent resistance on the part of lower-class Southern whites. In some areas, the Ku Klux Klan was reborn.

In 1962 James Meredith, a black student, attempted to enroll in the University of Mississippi at Oxford. On June 26, 1962, the University was ordered to admit him. In defiance of the courts and the federal government, Governor Ross Barnett announced that he would use the power of the state to bar Meredith. Business and professional men in the state, however, were alarmed at the prospect of defying the national government and attempted to stop Barnett, who then secretly negotiated with President Kennedy for a staged surrender. He would allow himself to be forced to back down by federal marshals. Nevertheless, shortly before the marshals were to arrive, he announced at a football game: "I love Mississippi! I love her people! I love her customs!" General Edwin Walker called for 10,000 volunteers to come to Oxford to aid Barnett, and thousands responded. On the night of September 30, a throng of students and others from Mississippi and the South, who compared themselves to the Hungarian Freedom Fighters, attacked the small force of federal marshals who had escorted Meredith onto the campus. The attack continued for fifteen hours, although President Kennedy spoke to the students on television to urge them to comply with the law. The riot was finally halted by 3,000 federal troops and federalized National Guards. Two persons were killed and over 70 wounded. Federal troops remained in Oxford for more than a year to maintain order and to protect Meredith.

The following account, by George B. Leonard, T. George Harris, and Christopher Wren: "How a Secret Deal Prevented a Massacre at Ole Miss," is taken from *Look*, December 31, 1962, 19-33. See James W. Silver: Mississippi: *The Closed Society* (1964); Hodding Carter III: *The South Strikes Back* (1959); American Friends Service Committee, National Council of the Churches of Christ, Southern Regional Council: *Intimidation, Reprisal, and Violence in the South's Racial Crisis* (1959); and James Howard Meredith: *Three Years in Mississippi* (1966).

Meredith ate lunch calmly at the Naval Air Station cafeteria. His companion, John Doar, was on the phone to receive orders from the Justice Department: Be ready to take off with Meredith by 3:30. Later came the order to be over Oxford at 5:50. Circle until ordered to land.

Doar could hear the engines of four transports that would take the first 170 marshals to Oxford. A convoy of 30 U.S. border-patrol cars with two-way radios was ready to take 60 more men to Ole Miss.

. . . a Jetstar from Washington touched down at the Oxford airport. The Justice Department task force, Nick Katzenbach in charge, stepped out. Katzenbach telephoned the Attorney General. The operation was still on.

Between the airport and the campus, the convoy of marshals led by Katzenbach met the state-patrol head, Col. T. B. Birdsong. Katzenbach and Chief Marshal McShane got out to exchange pleasantries. Much of the Government's hope for that night lay with the elderly colonel's steadfastness and ability.

The convoy—seven olive-drab trucks—rolled on. A marshal with a smile as broad as his shoulders rode the running board of the third truck. Clarence Albert (Al) Butler, 33, was one of four group leaders. With practiced eyes, he judged the mood and intent of the crowd that lined both sides of the road.

"You'll be sorry," a young man shouted. Butler smiled. "Nigger lover," another yelled. Butler smiled. Compared with other mobs he had seen, this one did not seem so bad. Some people even applauded. Maybe it was sarcastic, but they applauded.

Ahead, Butler spied a boy of about five wearing a cowboy hat. Butler, not liking the look of fear on the child's face, waved and called, "Hi, Cowboy." Cowboy laughed and waved back.

Highway patrolmen stood guard at the Sorority Row entrance to the university. Obeying Birdsong's orders, they let the marshals through. The trucks rolled past stately white sorority houses, then swung around a grove that sloped gently up to the classic white-columned Lyceum. This was the university's administration building, the marshals' first objective. The only sign of life was an occasional squirrel gathering acorns in streaks of sun and shadow on the grass of the grove. Butler was dazzled by the beauty and stillness of the place.

At 4:15 P.M., the marshals dismounted and formed a cordon around the Lyceum. Butler's group of 48 held the area directly in the front, facing the grove. Butler paced up and down the street before his men. A crowd gathered. Within a half hour, Butler estimated the number at around 500, almost all students. The first shots fired were verbal, and Butler was a main target.

"Marshal, where is you wife tonight? Home with a nigger?"

Butler's broad grin quickly earned him the name "Smiley."

"You have a nigger mistress, Smiley. You have nigger children."

Nick Katzenbach quickly set up a phone line from the Lyceum to Robert Kennedy's office in Washington and another to the White House. He told the Attorney General that Meredith could now come onto the campus, preferably via plane to the airport, then by car from there.

The airport. It was like a bad dream. The waiting Katzenbach looked up at the twilight sky to see three almost identical light planes circling. Which was Meredith's? The first, a blue and white Cessna 310, landed. Katzenbach and Guthman [of the Department of Justice] ran toward it. Not their man. They turned and ran to the next plane. It was Meredith. With the help of Birdsong, they drove him onto the campus without incident and took him to his room in Baxter Hall. . . .

When they got word that Meredith was safely on campus, Robert Kennedy and Burke Marshall [of the Department of Justice] drove to the White House. The President's office was crowded with TV equipment and technicians. The speech had been delayed to 10 P.M., Washington time, to be sure Meredith was first safely on the campus. Robert Kennedy and Marshall met the President and several of his assistants in the Cabinet Room.

All agreed on the content and tone of the proposed address to the nation. Robert Kennedy suggested adding an appeal to the students of Ole Miss. The reports coming over the phone from the Lyceum were still fairly reassuring.

Standing in front of the Lyceum, however, Marshal Al Butler was beginning to worry. Just as darkness fell, he was hit on the left leg with a poorly made Molotov cocktail, a soda bottle filled with lighter fluid. The fuse went out when the bottle smashed on the pavement. A few minutes later, an empty bottle hit his left arm.

The crowd swelled to 1,000, then to over 2,000. Students flipped lighted cigarettes onto the canvas tops of the Army trucks parked in front of the Lyceum. One truck was set aflame by a burning piece of paper. The driver put out the fire.

The Mississippi state troopers stood, widely spaced, between the marshals and the mob. When Butler asked the troopers to move the crowd back, they did. But members of the mob began slipping through the line of Mississippi lawmen.

The verbiage thrown at the marshals now reached the limits of obscenity. Butler was particularly shocked to hear foul epithets from the lips of pretty young girls in the crowd. Butler kept smiling. He would be thankful, he thought, if words were all he had to contend with. Nor did he particularly mind the spittle aimed at him, or the coins thrown by jeering mob members.

Chief Marshal McShane looked at the mob and sensed danger. He thought the state troopers were unable or unwilling to move the crowd back. Some troopers seemed mixed with the crowd as far back as the fourth or fifth rank. About the time Yarbrough reentered the Lyceum, McShane saw a two-foot length of pipe arch over the crowd and strike a marshal's helmet. He shouted "Gas!"—the order for gas masks. As the marshals put on their masks, the crowd fell back for a moment.

Just then, a bottle hit Al Butler on the arm. A milkly liquid sprayed on his hand, then ran under his sleeve. Hours later, Butler realized that acid was searing his flesh.

"*Fire!*"

McShane's command was almost lost in the roar of the mob. The marshals near the center of the line fired first. Ragged salvos followed from right, then left. The cartridges in the marshals' guns emitted a blast of raw tear gas over a range of 35 feet. Wax wadding in the cartridges struck several people, who thought they had been hit by projectiles. Several gas canisters thrown by hand also hit people, including state troopers who were directly in the line of fire.

It was 7:58 P.M. in Oxford. The Battle of Ole Miss was on. . . .

Reporter Fred Powledge of the Atlanta *Journal* was trapped in an automobile between the marshals and the mob. Powledge had been slugged earlier. The crowd was on the prowl for reporters.

Now, crouched down in the car, he tried to figure what to do next. If he ran toward the marshals, they would think he was attacking them, and he would be plugged with tear gas. But if he went toward the mob, he would be a dead rat in a gang of cats.

He slumped lower in the seat and switched on the car radio. The President was speaking, addressing himself to the students of Ole Miss.:

"The eyes of the nation and all the world are upon you and upon all of us. And the honor of your university—and state—are in the balance. . . ."

Pomp! Pomp! Pomp! Three tear-gas guns went off.

". . . I am certain the great majority of the students will uphold that honor. . . ."

A volley of stones whistled over the car.

". . . There is, in short, no reason why the books on this case cannot now be quickly and quietly closed in the manner directed by the Court. . . ."

A cloud of tear gas floated over the car. Powledge, in spite of his own predicament, felt sorry for the President.

The feeling was short-lived. He heard a voice behind him: "Let's get that son of a bitch in the car." There seemed to be no escape. Just then, three marshals rushed toward him. The first jumped up in the air and fired over the top of the car. Powledge saw "a beautiful burst of smoke" billowing over his attackers. Someone yelled, "Kennedy is a son of a bitch." The crowd fell back. . . .

Bullets began to splatter against the Lyceum. Anyone appearing at a window drew fire. The marshals crouched behind the trucks in front of the Lyceum. Some asked permission to return fire with their pistols. The request was phoned to the White House. Permission denied.

Strangely, only a few rioters attacked Baxter Hall, which was far more vulnerable than the Lyceum. Only 24 marshals guarded it, and its only sure communication with the Lyceum was the radio in a border-patrol car parked outside. But the marshals at Baxter had secret permission to use pistols as a last resort. Meredith was there. . . .

Katzenbach held off asking for troops as long as he could. Before 10 P.M., as the gunfire became intense, he told Robert Kennedy they had better get the Army. Then, Katzenbach phoned the National Guard armory in Oxford and asked Capt. Murray Falkner, nephew of the late novelist William Faulkner, to bring his men to the Lyceum.

Al Butler gasped for breath. "Mr. Katzenbach," he said, "that's not a riot out there anymore, it's an armed insurrection."

At 10:45, Butler saw the lights of four jeeps and three trucks coming up toward the grove. It was Falkner, running a gauntlet of brickbats, Molotov cocktails and roadblocks. His 55 Mississippi guardsmen tried unsuccessfully to fend off the volleys of bricks and bottles. A Molotov cocktail hit Falkners jeep, but did not go off. Falkner raised his left arm to shield his face; a brick struck the arm, breaking two bones. By the time they reached the Lyceum, 13 guardsmen were wounded. Six vehicles had broken windshields. One jeep collectd six bullet holes. . . .

The rioters burned their first car, a professor's station wagon, as a fiery roadblock. The entire north side of the grove was bathed in an eerie light. The crowd fell silent. The lull was a godsend to the marshals, who again were almost out of tear gas.

As the rioters stood there holding bricks and stones, the horn of the burning automobile started blowing. For ten minutes, it wailed, as if the car were crying out in agony. Shivering, many dropped their bricks and began drifting away. By midnight, most students had returned to dormitories or fraternity houses, shaken by what they had done.

The outsiders took over the fight. Hidden snipers increased their fire. One lay in a flower bed on the northeast border of the grove and emptied his .22 rifle at the Lyceum. Miraculously, no marshals were killed. At least five cars were burning at one time. Some 200 more Mississippi guardsmen made a heroic entry through roadblocks, brick barrages, gunfire, plus—this time—a wall of flaming gasoline. But they, like Captain Falkner's group, were not equipped or trained for riot control and had little effect.

Several hundred yards to the southeast, Ray Gunter, 23, an Oxford juke-box repairman, watched the fight. Quietly, he slumped forward, a .38 bullet in his forehead. He died on the way to the hospital. . . .

In the White House, the President, the Attorney General and Burke Marshall moved from telephone to telephone, from the President's office to the Cabinet Room. They felt frustration, along with concern and horror. Angrily, the President told the Army to get moving. . . .

At 2:04, four gray Navy buses stopped just inside the Sorority Row entrance of the campus. Donnie Bowman led his men, grim and tight-lipped, out of the first and second buses. The marshals there told the MP's the buses could never make it through the mob. The men would have to march in. A small knot of onlookers ominously heckled the soldiers: "You'll get hurt up there." A state patrolman turned his powerful flashlight into the eyes of one of Bowman's five Negro soldiers and said, "What you doing down here, nigger?"

The soldiers fixed bayonets on their loaded rifles. About every fifth man carried a loaded riot shotgun. The MP's slipped on gas masks and moved into wedge formation. In silence, they began the half-mile march to the Lyceum, past the dimly lit sorority houses and ghostly trees. The only sound was the shuffle of boots and the grunt and breath through gas masks.

From nowhere a volley of bricks and rocks hit them. *Ambush.* Molotov cocktails exploded just in front of them. The soldiers marched through the flames. A Molotov cocktail shattered against an MP's helmet, but failed to ignite. Gasoline trickled down his face and shirt. Several men were knocked down. Others picked them up and dragged them on. "Take it, men, just take it," said Lt. Col. John Flanagan, the commander of the 503rd Battalion. . . . As the soldiers—still in formation, bayonets at ready—hove into sight, the marshals cheered.

General Billingslea had followed the MP's to the Lyceum in a border-patrol sedan. He reported to Nick Katzenbach, who told him the President wanted him on the open line. The General's voice, on the phone that had brought so much bad news, led the President and his brother to sense that the battle was ending, though, actually, it had many hours to go.

Chicago
1968

Anger at the Vietnamese war led numerous anti-war groups to plan a huge protest rally at the Democratic Convention in Chicago, August, 1968. Thousands came, among them various groups of radicals, Yippies, supporters of Senator Eugene McCarthy, and non-radicals opposed to the war. Speakers denounced the war, the Democratic Party and Vice President Hubert Humphrey. Mayor Daley's decision not to allow peace marches or to let protestors sleep in the parks, and to use the police to prevent violations of these orders, set the stage for these violent clashes.

An investigating committee chaired by a Chicago lawyer, Daniel Walker, called the violence a "police riot." But in the judgment of many people, the primary responsibility for the outbreak was the city administration's. The Chicago police had behaved with restraint in the riots following the assassination of Martin Luther King in April, 1968, and had afterwards been rebuked by Mayor Daley for their leniency; he had ordered them "to shoot to kill arsonists and shoot to maim looters." Most of the anti-war groups seem not to have planned any violence, although many of them apparently expected violence to occur, and a few hoped for the sort of police violence that would lend credence to their views. Before the Convention opened, early arrivals from the peace groups practiced defense tactics in the park, while Mayor Daley mustered 6,000 police, 6,000 Illinois National Guardsmen, and 6,000 regular army troops armed with rifles, flame throwers, and bazookas. On Saturday night, August 25, the police cleared Lincoln Park at 11 p.m., the curfew hour, with little difficulty. Protest leaders advised compliance. The next night, however, people began to refuse to leave, chanting "The parks belong to the people," and screaming obscenities. The first episode of violence started. The culmination came on Wednesday, August 28, when a march was being organized to go to the Ampitheater where the Convention was being held. Violence started in the park when the police clubbed youths who were lowering an American flag. The crowd threw sticks, shoes, clods of earth, and bottles at the police, who retaliated with tear gas attacks, and blocked the march to the Amphitheater. The crowds then converged on the Loop and the Conrad Hilton Hotel, and there the police lost control, venting their fury at the protestors. The police also attacked journalists and news photographers, smashing their equipment and beating them. Angry condemnations of the behavior of the police were made by many persons, even on the floor of the Convention itself, where Senator Abraham Ribicoff denounced "Gestapo tactics in the streets of Chicago." By Friday the violence was over.

The following account is taken from the Walker Report: *Rights in Conflict: The Violent Confrontation of Demonstrators and Police in the Parks and Streets of Chicago During the Week of the Democratic National Convention of 1968. A Report submitted by Daniel Walker, Director of the Chicago Study Team, to the National Commission on the Causes and Prevention of Violence* (1968), 255-65.

. . . at 7:57 P.M., with two groups of club-wielding police converging simultaneously and independently, the battle was joined. The portions of the throng out of the immediate area of conflict largely stayed put and took up the chant, "The whole world is watching," but the intersection fragmented into a collage of violence.

Re-creating the precise chronology of the next few moments is impossible. But there is no question that a violent street battle ensued.

People ran for cover and were struck by police as they passed. Clubs were swung indiscriminately.

Two Assistant U.S. Attorneys who were on the scene characterized the police as "hostile and aggressive." Some witnesses cited particularly dramatic personal stories.

"I saw squadrols [sic] of policemen coming from everywhere," a secretary quoted earlier said. "The crowd around me suddenly began to run. Some of us, including myself, were pushed back onto the sidewalk and then all the way up against . . . the Blackstone Hotel along Michigan Avenue. I thought the crowd had panicked."

"Fearing that I would be crushed against the wall of the building . . .

I somehow managed to work my way . . . to the edge of the street . . . and saw policemen everywhere.

"As I looked up I was hit for the first time on the head from behind by what must have been a billy club. I was then knocked down and while on my hands and knees, I was hit around the shoulders. I got up again, stumbling and was hit again. As I was falling, I heard words to the effect of 'move, move' and the horrible sound of cracking billy clubs."

"After my second fall, I remember being kicked in the back, and I looked up and noticed that many policemen around me had no badges on. The police kept hitting me on the head."

Eventually she made her way to an alley behind the Blackstone and finally, "bleeding badly from my head wound," was driven by a friend to a hospital emergency room. Her treatment included the placing of 12 stitches.

Another young woman, who had been among those who sat down in the intersection, ran south on Michigan, a "Yippie flag" in her hand, when she saw the police. "I fell in the center of the intersection," she says. "Two policemen ran up on me, stopped and hit me on the shoulder, arm and leg about five or six times, severely. They were swearing and one of them broke my flag over his knee." By fleeing into Grant Park, she managed eventually to escape.

Another witness said: "To my left, the police caught a man, beat him to the ground and smashed their clubs on the back of his unprotected head. I stopped to help him. He was elderly, somewhere in his mid-50's. He was kneeling and holding his bleeding head. As I stopped to help him, the police turned on me. "Get that cock sucker out of here!" This command was accompanied by four blows from clubs—one on the middle of my back, one on the bottom of my back, one on my left buttock, and one on the back of my leg. No attempt was made to arrest me or anybody else in the vicinity. All the blows that I saw inflicted by the police were on the backs of heads, arms, legs, etc. It was the most slow and confused, and the least experienced people who got caught and beaten.

"The police were angry. Their anger was neither disinterestd nor instrumental. It was deep, expressive and personal. 'Get out of here you cock suckers' seemed to be their most common cry.

"To my right, four policemen beat a young man as he lay on the ground. They beat him and at the same time told him to 'get up and get the hell out of here.' Meanwhile, I struggled with the injured man whom I had stopped to help. . . ."

One demonstrator said that several policemen were coming toward a group in which he was standing when one of the officers yelled, "Hey, there's a nigger over there we can get." They then are said to have veered off and grabbed a middle-aged Negro man, whom they beat.

A lawyer says that he was in group of demonstrators in the park just south of Balbo when he head a police officer shout, "Let's get 'em!" Three policemen ran up, "singled out one girl and as she was running away from them, beat her on the back of the head. As she fell to the ground, she was struck by the nightsticks of these officers." A male friend of hers then came up yelling at the police. The witness said, "He was arrested. The girl was left in the area lying on the ground."

The beating of two other girls was witnessed from a hotel window. The witness says, he saw one girl "trying to shield a demonstrator who had been beaten to the ground," whereupon a policeman came up "hitting her with a billy club." The officer also kicked the girl in the shoulder, the witness said.

A *Milwaukee Journal* reporter says in his statement, "when the police managed to break up groups of protesters they pursued individuals and beat them with clubs. Some police pursued individual demonstrators as far as a block . . . and beat them. . . . In many cases it appeared to me that when police had finished beating the protesters they were pursuing, they then attacked, indiscriminately, any civilian who happened to be standing nearby. Many of these were not involved in the demonstrations." . . .

"It seemed to me," an observer says, "that only a saint could have swallowed the vile remarks to the officers. However, they went to extremes in clubbing the Yippies. I saw them move into the park, swatting away with clubs at boys and girls lying in the grass. More than once I witnessed two officers pulling at the arms of a Yippie until the arms almost left their sockets, then, as the officers put the Yippie in a police van, a third jabbed a riot stick into the groin of the youth being arrested. It was evident that the Yippie was not resisting arrest." . . .

While violence was exploding in the street, the crowd wedged behind the police sawhorses along the northeast edge of the Hilton, was experiencing a terror all its own. . . .

"I was crowded in with the group of screaming, frightened people," an onlooker states. "We jammed against each other, trying to press into the brick wall of the hotel. As we stood there breathing hard . . . a policeman calmly walked the length of the barricade with a can of chemical spray [evidently mace] in his hand. Unbelievably, he was spraying at us." Photos reveal several policemen using mace against the crowd.

Another witness, a graduate student, said she was on the periphery of the crowd and could see that "police sprayed mace randomly along the first line of people along the curb." A reporter who was present said a woman cried, "Oh no, not mace!" He said a youth moaned, "Stop it! We're not doing anything!" "Others," recalls another witness, "pleaded with the police to tell them where they should move and allow them to move there."

. . . a part of the crowd was trapped in front of the Conrad Hilton and pressed hard against a big plate glass window of the Haymarket Lounge. A reporter who was sitting inside said, "Frightened men and women banged . . . against the window. A captain of the fire department inside told us to get back from the window, that it might get knocked in. As I backed away a few feet I could see a smudge of blood on the glass outside."

With a sickening crack, the window shattered, and screaming men and women tumbled through, some cut badly by the jagged glass. The police came after them.

"I was pushed through by the force of large numbers of people," one victim said. "I got a deep cut on my right leg, diagnosed later by Eugene McCarthy's doctor as a severed artery. . . . I fell to the floor of the bar. There were ten to 20 people who had come through . . . I could not stand on the leg. It was bleeding profusely.

"A squad of policemen burst into the bar, clubbing all those who looked to them like demonstrators, at the same time screaming over and over, 'We've got to clear this area.' The police acted literally like mad dogs looking for objects to attack. . . ."

There is little doubt that during this whole period, beginning at 7:57 P.M., and lasting nearly 20 minutes, the preponderance of violence came from the police. It was not entirely a one-way battle, however. . . .

"Some hippies," said a patrolman in his statement, "were hit by other hippies who were throwing rocks at the police." Films reveal that when police were chasing demonstrators into Grant Park, one young man upended a sawhorse and heaved it at advancing officers. At one point the deputy superintendent of police was knocked down by a thrown sawhorse. At least one police three-wheeler was tipped over. One of the demonstrators says that "people in the park were prying up cobblestones and breaking them. One person piled up cobblestones in his arms and headed toward the police." Witnesses reported that people were throwing "anything they could lay their hands on. From the windows of the Hilton and Blackstone hotels, toilet paper, wet towels, even ash trays came raining down." A police lieutenant stated that he saw policemen bombarded with "rocks, cherry bombs, jars of vaseline, jars of mayonnaise and pieces of wood torn from the yellow barricades falling in the street." He, too, noticed debris falling from the hotel windows.

A patrolman on duty during the melee states that among the objects he saw thrown at police officers were "rocks, bottles, shoes, a telephone and a garbage can cover. Rolls of toilet paper were thrown from hotel windows. I saw a number of plastic practice golf balls, studded with nails, on the street as well as plastic bags filled with what appeared to be human excrement." He said he saw two policemen, one of them wearing a soft hat, get hit with bricks.

A sergeant states that during the fracas, two men under his command had their plastic faceguards (which they pay for themselves) shattered by bricks or rocks.

A number of police officers were injured, either by flying missiles or in personal attacks. One, for example, was helping a fellow officer "pick up a hippie when another hippie gave [me] a heavy kick, aiming for my groin." The blow struck the officer partly on the leg and partly in the testicles. He went down, and the "hippie" who kicked him escaped.

PART VI

Personal Violence

Hamilton-Burr Duel
1804

The duel at Weehawken which cost Alexander Hamilton his life ended many years of political antagonism between Hamilton and Aaron Burr. Hamilton on two occasions used his influence to block Burr's advancement. In 1800, when Burr and Jefferson were tied in the Electoral College and the choice of a President was thrown into the House of Representatives, Hamilton swung such weight as he still had with the Federalists against Burr. In 1804, Hamilton was instrumental in defeating Burr when he ran for the Governorship of New York. A letter found its way into the newspapers which referred to the "despicable opinion which General Hamilton has expressed of Mr. Burr." When Burr requested an acknowledgement or denial, Hamilton temporized but finally the correspondence ended in a challenge and acceptance. Hamilton drafted his will, and also wrote a letter of explanation, in which he declared his abhorrence of dueling, but said he would fight because he believed that a public show of cowardice would end his ability to be politically useful in the future. On July 11 he met Burr in New Jersey and was mortally wounded. The following description of the duel was prepared immediately afterwards for the press by the seconds, Nathaniel Pendleton and William P. Van Ness. See Harold C. Syrett and Jacob Cooke: *Interview in Weehawken* (1960).

Col. Burr arrived on the ground as had been previously agreed. When Gen. Hamilton arrived the parties exchanged salutations and the seconds proceeded to make their arrangements. They measured the distance, ten full paces, and cast lots for the choice of position as also to determine by whom the word should be given, both of which fell to the second of Gen. Hamilton. They then proceeded to load the pistols in each others presence, after which the parties took their stations. The gentleman who was to give the word, then explained to the parties the rules which were to govern them in firing, which were as follows:

The parties being placed at their stations—The second who gives the word shall ask them whether they are ready—being answered in the affirmative, he shall say "*present*" after which the parties shall present & fire when they please. If one fires before, the opposite second shall say one, two, three, fire, and he shall fire or loose his fire.

And asked if they were prepared, being answered in the affirmative he gave the word *present* as had been agreed on, and both of the parties took aim & fired in succession. The intervening time is not expressed, as the seconds do not precisely agree on that point. The pistols were discharged within a few seconds of each other and the fire of Col. Burr took effect; Gen. Hamilton almost instantly fell, Col. Burr then advanced toward Genl H——n with a manner and gesture that appeared to Gen. Hamilton's friend to be expressive of regret, but without speaking turned & withdrew—Being urged from the field by his friend as has been subsequently stated, with a view to prevent his being recognized by the surgeon and bargemen who were then approaching. No further communication took place between the principals, and the barge that carried Col. Burr immediately returned to the city. We conceive it proper to add that the conduct of the parties in that interview was perfectly proper as suited the occasion.

Jackson-Dickinson Duel
1806

John Dickinson was a successful lawyer and fashionable gentleman of Nashville, Tennessee. His quarrel with Andrew Jackson arose out of political differences, but was exacerbated when he made insulting comments about Jackson's wife. After a series of disputes, Jackson denounced Dickinson as "a worthless drunken, blackguard scoundrel," and Dickinson, although he was already a good shot, began practicing marksmanship. He publicly called Jackson "a worthless scoundrel, a poltroon and a coward," and challenge and acceptance immediately followed. The duel took place a day's ride from Nashville. The following description of the duel is by James Parton, a contemporary biographer of Jackson who talked to people with first-hand knowledge of this quarrel. See James Parton: *Life of Andrew Jackson* (1860), I, 298-301.

The horsemen rode about a mile along the river; then turned down toward the river to a point on the bank where they had expected to find a ferryman. No ferryman appearing, Jackson spurred his horse into the stream and dashed across, followed by all his party. They rode into the poplar forest, two hundred yards or less, to a spot near the center of a level platform or river bottom, then covered with forest, now smiling with cultivated fields. The horsemen halted and dismounted just before reaching the appointed place. Jackson, Overton, and a surgeon who had come with them from home, walked on together, and the rest led their horses a short distance in an opposite direction.

"How do you feel about it now, General?" asked one of the party, as Jackson turned to go.

"Oh, all right," replied Jackson, gayly; "I shall wing him, never fear."

Dickinson's second won the choice of position, and Jackson's the office of giving the word. The astute Overton considered this giving of the word a matter of great importance, and he had already determined *how* he would give it, if the lot fell to him. The eight paces were measured off, and the men placed. Both were perfectly collected. All the politenesses of such occasions were very strictly and elegantly performed. Jackson was dressed in a loose frock-coat, buttoned carelessly over his chest, and concealing in some degree the extreme slenderness of his figure. Dickinson was the younger and handsomer man of the two. But Jackson's tall, erect figure, and the still intensity of his demeanor, it is said, gave him a most superior and commanding air, as he stood under the tall poplars on this bright May morning, silently awaiting the moment of doom.

"Are you ready?" said Overton.

"I am ready," replied Dickinson.

"I am ready," said Jackson.

The words were no sooner pronounced than Overton, with a sudden shout, cried, using his old-country pronunciation,

"Fere!"

Dickinson raised his pistol quickly and fired. Overton, who was looking with anxiety and dread at Jackson, saw a puff of dust fly from the breast of his coat, and saw him raise his left arm and place it tightly across his chest. He is surely hit, thought Overton, and in a bad place, too; but no; he does not fall. Erect and grim as Fate he stood, his teeth clenched, raising his pistol. Overton glanced at Dickinson. Amazed at the unwonted failure of his aim, and apparently appalled at the awful figure and face before him, Dickinson had unconsciously recoiled a pace or two.

"Great God!" he faltered, "have I missed him?"

"Back to the MARK, sir!" shrieked Overton, with his hand upon his pistol.

Dickinson recovered his composure, stepped forward to the peg, and stood with his eyes averted from his antagonist. All this was the work of a moment, though it requires many words to tell it.

General Jackson took deliberate aim, and pulled the trigger. The pistol neither snapped nor went off. He looked at the trigger, and discovered that it had stopped at half cock. He drew it back to its place, and took aim a second time. He fired. Dickinson's face blanched; he reeled; his friends rushed toward him, caught him in their arms, and gently seated him on the ground, leaning against a bush. His trowsers reddened. They stripped off his clothes. The blood was gushing from his side in a torrent. And, alas! here is the ball, not near the wound, but above the *opposite* hip, just under the skin. The ball had passed through the body, below the ribs. Such a wound could not but be fatal.

Overton went forward and learned the condition of the wounded man. Rejoining his principal, he said, "He won't want anything more of you, General," and conducted him from the ground. They had gone a hundred yards, Overton walking on one side of Jackson, the surgeon on the other, and neither speaking a word, when the surgeon observed that one of Jackson's shoes was full of blood.

"My God! General Jackson, are you hit?" he exclaimed, pointing to the blood.

"Oh! I believe," replied Jackson, "that he has pinked me a little. Let's look at it. But say nothing about it *there*," pointing to the house.

He opened his coat. Dickinson's aim had been perfect. He had sent the ball precisely where he supposed Jackson's heart was beating. But the thinness of his body and the looseness of his coat combining to deceive Dickinson, the ball had only broken a rib or two, and raked the breastbone. It was a somewhat painful, bad-looking wound, but neither severe nor dangerous, and he was able to ride to the tavern without much inconvenience. Upon approaching the house, he went up to one of the negro women who was churning, and asked her if the butter had come. She said it was just coming. He asked for some buttermilk. While she was getting it for him, she observed him furtively open his coat and look within it. She saw that his shirt was soaked with blood, and she stood gazing in blank horror at the sight, dipper in hand. He caught her eye, and hastily buttoned his coat again. She dipped out a quart measure full of buttermilk, and gave it to him. He drank it off at a draught; then went in, took off his coat, and had his wound carefully examined and dressed. That done, he dispatched one of his retinue to Dr. Catlett, to inquire respecting the condition of Dickinson, and to say that the surgeon attending himself would be glad to contribute his aid toward Mr. Dickinson's relief. Polite reply was returned that Mr. Dickinson's case was past surgery. In the course of the day, General Jackson sent a bottle of wine to Dr. Catlett for the use of his patient.

But there was one gratification which Jackson could not, even in such circumstances, grant him. A very old friend of General Jackson writes to me thus: "Although the General had been wounded, he did not desire it should be known until he had left the neighborhood, and had therefore concealed it at first from his own friends. His reason for this, as he once stated to me, was that as Dickinson considered himself the best shot in the world, and was certain of killing him at the first fire, *he did not want him to have the gratification even of knowing that he had touched him.*"

Poor Dickinson bled to death. The flowing of blood was stanched, but could not be stopped. He was conveyed to the house in which he had passed the night, and placed upon a mattress, which was soon drenched with blood. He suffered extreme agony, and uttered horrible cries all that long day. At nine o'clock in the evening he suddenly asked why they had put out the lights. The doctor knew then that the end was at hand; that the wife, who had been sent for in the morning, would not arrive in time to close her husband's eyes. He died five minutes after, cursing, it is said, with his last breath, the ball that had entered his body. The poor wife hurried away on hearing that her husband was "dangerously wounded," and met, as she rode toward the scene of the duel, a procession of silent horsemen escorting a rough emigrant wagon that contained her husband's remains.

Sand Bar Gun Battle
1827

Duels and other personal encounters were often unrestrained on the frontier. Fights were sometimes brutal: eyes were gouged out, noses and ears bitten off. Even contests between men of good social standing could become bloody. This brawl among twelve "gentlemen," one of whom was James Bowie, seems to have begun as a duel between Dr. Thomas H. Maddox and Samuel L. Wells, a brother of the Governor of Louisiana. It degenerated into a wild knife and gun battle in which two were killed and two wounded. This celebrated affair gave Colonel Bowie's knife its deadly reputation.

Robert A. Crain, Maddox's second and fellow combatant, told the following story of the fight to General Joseph Walker in a letter dated October 3, 1827, reprinted in Robert Dabney Calhoun: "A History of Concordia Parish," *Louisiana Historical Quarterly*, XV (1932), 638-42.

Dear Walker—

Yours of the 23rd of September, in reply to mine of the 19th previous, received last night, and will now proceed to give you a detailed account of the unfortunate occurrence of the 18th, to convince you that it was not my wish to meet those men. I said to Mr. Wells and his friend, McWhorter, in the presence of Dr. Denny, that there must not be permitted but three of a side on the ground. "You know that I cannot meet certain men that are on the other side of the river," (this was at the steam saw mill where we met to make arrangements for the interview between Maddox and Wells). Wells said to me, "Sir, I know to whom you allude. They shall not be on the ground." This I took as a pledge of his honor, but, to our astonishment, when we got on the ground, within eighty yards of the spot where the fight took place, there stood Jim Bowie, Sam Cuney and Jeff Wells. Dr. Maddox asked Dr. Cuney what they were doing there. He replied: "They will not approach any nearer." The affair proceeded, and after two shots apiece, the matter was honorably settled to both, Sam Wells withdrawing his carte blanche and all offensive language previously applied to the Doctor. I will now remark for Sam Wells that his conduct seemed highly honorable and that of a gentleman. He proposed that we should go up to the willows and take a glass of wine. I observed immediately: "No, Mr. Wells, you know that I cannot meet certain gentlemen that are there, but let us go down the river to our friends" (who were during the fight at least a quarter of a mile off, but who were then approaching, as a servant had informed them of the result), "and drink and bury the hatchet." "Agreed, sir," said he; and after collecting the pistols that were used, a brace of which I gave to the boy, the others I held, one in each hand, well loaded, of course. We proceeded down the river, angling across the Sand Bar, and having Bowie, Cuney and Jeff Wells immediately at right angles from where we started under the willows. They started and ran down the hill and in a quick running walk intercepted us, or rather me. Drs. Denny and Maddox were some ten or fifteen steps ahead, Maddox entirely unarmed. Cuney remarked: "Now is the time to settle our affair," I think, swearing at me at the same time, and commenced drawing his pistol. I drew away from him. Sam Wells got hold of him, and Dr. Cuney got immediately between me and his brother, so that I could not shoot at him then. Bowie, at the same time, was drawing his pistol. I drew away at him. I shot him through the body as he shot. I could not miss him, shooting not further than ten feet. . . . I wheeled and jumped six or eight steps across some little washes in the sand bar and faced Cuney. We fired at the same moment. His bullet cut the shirt and grazed the skin on my left arm. He fell. Jim Bowie was at that time within a few feet of me, with his big knife raised to lunge. I again wheeled and sprang a few steps, changed the butt of the pistol, and as he rushed upon me, I wheeled and threw the pistol at him, which struck him on the left side of the forehead, which circumstance alone saved me from his savage fury and big knife. At that moment, Major Wright and the two Blanchards rushed up. Bowie sheered off to a leaning stump, by which he took a stand. Wright and Bowie exchanged shots at about ten paces, without any chance of Wright hitting him, he behind the log, and the other exhausted by running at least a hundred yards. He shot poor Wright through the body, who exclaimed, "The damned rascal has killed me," and then rushing upon Bowie with his sword cane, who caught him by the collar and plunged his knife into his bosom. At that moment Wright shot Bowie in the hip, who fell instantly. Wright wheeled, made a lunge at him, and fell over him dead. Hostilities then ceased. They say that I fired three pistols—I had but two. When I fired the first at Bowie, I dropped it to cock and use the other on Cuney, and when I threw the pistol at Bowie I was completely unarmed, without even a knife. They say we ran. Yesterday morning, upon receipt of your letter, I went in company with three other gentlemen to the ground, and I pledge my honor that the fight took place in an area of less than thirty yards square, as the blood where Cuney fell, and where Bowie and Wright fell, which is still there, proves. There could be little running in the small place. I set immediately about getting certificates, which shall be headed by a statement of my own and Maddox . . ."

Assault on Charles Sumner
1856

One incident of personal violence that was to have wide political repercussions was the assault on Senator Charles Sumner of Massachusetts by Congressman Preston Brooks of South Carolina. Sumner had given a two-day address to the Senate on the current troubles in Kansas, "The Crime Against Kansas," a painstaking document, 112 printed pages long, in which the anti-slavery Senator denounced "the rape of a virgin territory." In calling for the immediate admittance of Kansas as a free state, Sumner denounced some of his colleagues, particularly Senator Butler of South Carolina, who was absent.

Butler's cousin, Preston Brooks, decided to avenge his aged relative, and on May 22 he made his way into the Senate Chamber and beat Sumner into insensibility with a gutta-percha cane. Sumner was incapacitated and absent from the Senate for three years. Brooks at once became a hero in the South. Groups of Southerners, among them students at the University of Virginia, sent him emblematic canes; the Richmond *Whig* regretted only that "Mr. Brooks did not employ a horsewhip or cowhide upon [Sumner's] slanderous back instead of a cane." A House Committee proposed Brooks's expulsion, but failed to win the necessary two-thirds vote when all Southern Congressmen but one voted against it. In the North, "Bleeding Sumner and Bleeding Kansas" became a new battle cry. There were mass meetings of tribute to Sumner in Boston and New York, and perhaps as many as a million copies of "The Crime Against Kansas" were distributed.

The following description is Sumner's, given in testimony before a Congressional Committee investigating the incident: "Alleged Assault upon Senator Sumner," 34th Congress, 1st Session, H. R. No. 182. See David Donald: *Charles Sumner and the Coming of the Civil War* (1960).

Hon. Charles Sumner sworn.

Question (by Mr. Campbell). What do you know of the facts connected with the assault alleged to have been made upon you in the Senate chamber by Hon. Mr. Brooks, of South Carolina, on Thursday, May 22, 1856?

Answer. I attended the Senate as usual on Thursday, the 22d of May. After some formal business, a message was received from the House of Representatives, announcing the death of a member of that body from Missouri. This was followed by a brief tribute to the deceased from Mr. Geyer, of Missouri, when, according to usage, and out of respect to the deceased, the Senate adjourned.

Instead of leaving the chamber with the rest on the adjournment, I continued in my seat, occupied with my pen. While thus intent, in order to be in season for the mail, which was soon to close, I was approached by several persons who desired to speak with me; but I answered them promptly and briefly, excusing myself for the reason that I was much engaged. When the last of these left me, I drew my arm-chair close to my desk and with my legs under the desk continued writing. My attention at this time was so entirely withdrawn from all other objects, that, though there must have been many persons on the floor of the Senate, I saw nobody.

While thus intent, with my head bent over my writing, I was addressed by a person who had approached the front of my desk, so entirely unobserved that I was not aware of his presence until I heard my name pronounced. As I looked up, with pen in hand, I saw a tall man, whose countenance was not familiar, standing directly over me, and at the same moment, caught these words: "I have read your speech twice over carefully. It is a libel on South Carolina, and Mr. Butler, who is a relative of mine—." While these words were still passing from his lips, he commenced a succession of blows with a heavy cane on my bare head, by the first of which I was stunned so as to lose sight. I no longer saw my assailant nor any person or object in the room. What I did afterwards was done almost unconsciously, acting under the instinct of self defence. With head already bent down, I rose from my seat, wrenching up my desk, which was screwed to the floor, and then pressed forward, while my assailant continued his blows. I have no other consciousness until I found myself ten feet forward, in front of my desk, lying on the floor of the Senate, with my bleeding head supported on the knee of a gentleman, whom I soon recognized, by voice and countenance, as Mr. Morgan, of New York. Other persons there were about me offering me friendly assistance; but I did not recognize any of them. Others there were at a distance, looking on and offering no assistance, of whom I recognized only Mr. Douglas, of Illinois, Mr. Toombs, of Georgia, and I thought also my assailant, standing between them.

I was helped from the floor and conducted into the lobby of the Senate, where I was placed upon a sofa. Of those who helped me to this place I have no recollection. As I entered the lobby, I recognized Mr. Slidell of Louisana who retreated; but recognized no one else until some time later, as I supposed, when I felt a friendly grasp of the hand, which seemed to come from Mr. Campbell, of Ohio. I have a vague impression that Mr. Bright, President of the Senate, spoke to me while I was lying on the floor of the Senate or in the lobby.

I make this statement in answer to the interrogatory of the committee, and offer it as presenting completely all my recollections of the assault and of the attending circumstances, whether immediately before or immediately after. I desire to add that, besides the words which I have given as uttered by my assailant, I have an indistinct recollection of the words "old man;" but these are so enveloped in the mist which ensued from the first blow, that I am not sure whether they were uttered or not.

The Hatfields and the McCoys
1873–1888

The great family feuds—such as the Hatfield-McCoy, Martin-Tolliver, Hargis-Cockrell, Sutton-Taylor, and Horrell-Higgins feuds, which lasted from ten to thirty years and killed many people—were intensely personal, but many had been started by Civil War animosities, particularly in the Southern Appalachians. In Kentucky and West Virginia guerilla bands of Confederate and Union sympathizers had fought in the mountain wilderness. In addition to these inherited hatreds, the poverty and isolation, the backward education and law enforcement of the area, led to sustained feuds, of which the most notorious took place between the Hatfields and the McCoys.

The Hatfields and McCoys lived on opposite sides of a stream dividing West Virginia from Kentucky. The Hatfield chief was William Anderson (Devil Anse) Hatfield, who had been a Confederate captain. Randolph (Ran'l) McCoy, the opposing clan leader, had been a Union guerrilla. They lived in peace for a time after Appomattox, industriously producing moonshine. Trouble started in 1873, as Devil Anse recalled later, "when a difficulty arose between Floyd Hatfield . . . and Randolph McCoy, over a sow and some pigs." McCoy accused Hatfield of stealing his pigs; the accusation led to scuffles, brawls, and eventually guns, and the feud was on.

The following document tells of an incident in 1888, when nine of the Hatfields went to Randolph McCoy's cabin to murder two McCoys who could give material evidence against a Hatfield who had murdered three McCoys in 1882. It is a confession by Charles Gillespie of his part in the incident. The account is taken from a book by a New York *World* reporter who visited the feud site in 1888 and talked to Devil Anse: Theron C. Crawford: *An American Vendetta: A Story of Barbarism in the United States* (1889), 179-85. See Virgil Carrington Jones: *The Hatfields and the McCoys* (1948).

"On the first day of last January I was at home, when 'Cap' Hatfield came along and said: 'Charley, we are going over into Kentucky to-night to have some fun. Get a horse and meet us, and go along.' Well, I did not know what was up, but I told 'Cap' I would be on hand, and after a little trouble I got a horse and was at the rendezvous, where I found 'Cap,' 'Johns,' Ellis, 'Bob,' and Ellett Hatfield, 'Old Jim' Vance, Ellison Mounts, and a man who goes by the name of both Mitchell and Chambers, whom I know by the name of the 'Guerilla.' 'Jim' Vance was in command of the party, and it was agreed at the start, before the real object of the trip was disclosed, that all should yield to everything he said and do all he might order us to do. It has been claimed that the whole Hatfield neighborhood was with us that night. This is not true. There were just nine of us, and the nine I have mentioned.

"Arriving at a convenient distance from the McCoy house, I was first made acquainted with the real object of our trip. Vance told us that, if old Randall McCoy and his son 'Cal' were out of the road, every material witness against the men who had taken part in the murder of the three McCoy boys would be removed, and there could be no conviction of any of them, even if they might at some time be arrested for it. All had become tired of dodging the officers of the law, and wished to be able to sleep at home beside better bedfellows than Winchester rifles, and to occasionally take off their boots when they went to bed. This was the reason which 'Old Jim' Vance gave us, and 'Cap' and 'Johns' Hatfield agreed with him.

"Well, we determined, if the family would not come out when we should warn them to, to shoot through the windows and doors of the house from the ends and sides, with our Winchesters, volley after volley, until all inside would be either dead or disabled. The only reply the McCoys made to our demand to come out was to bar and barricade the doors and to prepare to fight us till the last. We shot through the windows and doors and our shooting was responded to by 'Old Ran'l' and 'Cal,' the former with a double-barreled shot-gun and the other with a Winchester. We had to be very careful, as both were good shots.

"I must tell you right here that I was not one of those who were doing the shooting. Me and one of the other Hatfields was put out along the road to act as guards to see that no one came up or that no one got past us. We never went near the house until the house was burning and all was on their way back to Hatfield's house. When they came up, Ellison Mounts said to me: 'Well, we killed the boy and the girl, and I am sorry of it. We have made a bad job of it. We didn't get the man we wanted at all (meaning "Old Ran'l"). If we had got him, it would have been all right and our work would not have been lost. There will be trouble over this.'

I asked him about the fight as we went along home, and he told me how Chambers had crawled up on the roof to get at those inside and to fire the house, when Ran'l McCoy heard him, and, firing at him through the shingles, shot his hand off behind the knuckles. He said Chambers got down, tied his hurt hand, and, taking his Winchester, began shooting again. It took some time to get the McCoys out, but finally the door opened and 'Cal' ran out at the top of his speed toward a corn-crib. Several banged away at him, but none of the shots took effect, and one or two more shots were fired, when he was seen to jump up and fall forward. We went to him and found him dead, with a big hole in the back of his head. The girl came out of one of the two dwelling-houses, and wanted to get into the one where the family was, and some of the men told her to go back; but she knew them and named them, and she was killed. 'Cap' was blamed for this, but I think Mounts did it. I could not find out who struck old Mrs. McCoy with the butt of the revolver, but I think Mounts did this too. The hammer of the revolver penetrated her skull, and when she fell several of the men jumped upon her, breaking her ribs, and when they left her thought she was dead.

"I had let my horse go on the way to the house of the McCoys, and had to get up behind Mounts, better known as 'Cotton-Top' and 'Cotton-Eye,' because he has white hair and white eyes. On the way home he talked a great deal. Once he said: 'If John Hatfield had not shot before we were ready, there would not have been one of the McCoys in that house alive now. That shot gave them inside a correct idea of the location of some of the men, and they kept us well in sight right along thereafter. They kept us so far away that it was a long time before we got up to the house and were able to do anything.'

"Mounts told me that he himself made the first move toward getting into the house, breaking into the annex to the cabin, where he found Alfaro McCoy and the little children. He demanded that the men in there should come out. She told him there were no men about the annex, but Mounts insisted that she make a light. She told him to give her a match and she would satisfy him of the truth of her words. Then 'Cap' Hatfield yelled, 'Shoot her,—her, and let's go on.' Then Mounts shot her, and she fell dead without a word. They then began shooting through the doors and windows of the cabin, thinking that some of those in it would be looking to see what was going on in the annex, and by the promiscuous shooting to kill all within the house. After this volley nothing was done for several minutes.

" 'Cal' McCoy, from the loft of the cabin, in the meantime got sight of the men and began firing at them so rapidly that they all got behind a log pig-pen for safety. There they concluded to burn the house, and Mitchell, by dodging around for a little while, managed to get to the roof with a torch and fire the roof, but not till 'Old Ran'l' had shot off one of his hands, as I have described. This was done with a revolver, and the old man was not two feet from Mitchell when he fired. He could see only his hand, and he did the best he could at the distance.

"Well, we all went back to 'Cap' Hatfield's, and most of us stayed in his house all night, leaving early in the morning. I did not see the gang again. There was one of the nine missing, but I could not tell who it was, and none of us spoke of the fact but once.

"I left home within a day or two and have not been back since, and have had no means of knowing what is going on."

Gunfight at the O.K. Corral
1881

Among legendary Western heroes it is often hard to tell the good guys from the bad guys. Wyatt Earp, for example, whose good-guy reputation is a recent invention, apparently acted on both sides of the law. Various persons have said he was a professional gambler, a stage robber, and a murderer; in any case, he was never the heroic peace officer he is now said to have been. The story of his celebrated gun fight in Tombstone, Arizona, on October 26, 1881, is also more ambiguous than the legend would have it. It is clear that Virgil Earp, town marshal, his brothers Wyatt, a saloon-keeper, and Morgan, a gambler, together with John H. (Doc) Holliday, gambler, dentist, and reputed pimp, clashed with Ike and Bill Clanton and Frank and Tom McLaury. Bill Clanton and both McLaurys were killed, Virgil and Morgan Earp badly wounded. Everything else is uncertain. According to one account, Virgil, acting as peace officer, with his brothers and Holliday as deputies, went to disarm the others; when they were shot at they opened fire. Another version claims the Earps were out to kill Ike Clanton, who had seen them try to rob a stagecoach; still another explanation is that the Earps and Clantons were feuding over women; another, that gangs of cowboys were in Tombstone threatening to kill the Earps, the four at the O.K. Corral acting as their vanguard. Some called it a fair fight, others a cold-blooded massacre. Afterwards, the Earps were arrested for murder, Virgil was fired as marshal, but after a month-long hearing all were acquitted. The Earps soon left Tombstone. Wyatt died in 1929 at the age of 81.

Wyatt Earp's account of the gun fight at his trial was recorded by the Tombstone *Epitaph,* and reprinted in Douglas D. Martin: *The Earps of Tombstone* (1959), 38-40. See Frank Waters: *The Earp Brothers of Tombstone* (1960); and Kent L. Steckmesser: *The Western Hero in History and Legend* (1965).

"I was tired of being threatened by Ike Clanton and his gang. I believed from what they had said to others and to me, and from their movements, that they intended to assassinate me the first chance they had, and I thought if I had to fight for my life against them I had better make them face me in an open fight. So I said to Ike Clanton, who was then sitting about eight feet away from me, "you d—d dirty cur thief, you have been threatening our lives and I know it. I think I should be justified in shooting you down any place I should meet you, but if you are anxious to make a fight, I will go anywhere on earth to make a fight with you, even over to the San Simon among your own crowd." He replied, "All right, I'll see you after I get through here. I only want four feet of ground to fight on." I walked out just then and outside the court room, near the Justice's office, I met Tom McLowry. He came up to me and said to me, "If you want to make a fight I will make a fight with you anywhere." . . . I felt just as I did about Ike Clanton, that if the fight had to come I had better have it come when I had an even show to defend myself, so I said to him, "all right, make a fight right here," and at the same time I slapped him in the face with my left hand, and drew my pistol with my right. He had a pistol in plain sight on his hip, but made no move to draw it. I said to him, "jerk your gun and use it." He made no reply, and I hit him on the head with my six-shooter, and walked away, down to Hafford's corner. I went into Hafford's and got a cigar, and came out and stood by the door. Pretty soon I saw Tom McLowry, Frank McLowry and Wm. Clanton. They passed me and went down Fourth Street to the gunsmith shop. I followed them to see what they were going to do . . . Ike Clanton came up about that time and they all walked into the gunsmith's shop. I saw them in the shop changing cartridges into their belts. . . .

Virgil Earp was then city marshal; Morgan Earp was a special policeman for six weeks, wore a badge and drew pay. I had been sworn in in Virgil's place to act for him while Virgil had gone to Tucson on Stilwell's trial. Virgil had been back several days but I was still acting. I knew it was Virgil's duty to disarm these men. I expected he would have trouble in doing so and I followed up to give assistance if necessary especially as they had been threatening us, as I have already stated. About ten minutes afterwards, and while Virgil, Morgan, Doc Holliday and myself were standing on the corner of Fourth and Allen Streets, several people said, "There is going to be trouble with those fellows," and one man named Coleman, said to Virgil Earp, "They mean trouble. They have just gone from Dunbar's corral into the O.K. Corral, all armed. I think you had better go and disarm them." Virgil turned around to Doc Holliday, Morgan Earp and myself and told us to come and assist him in disarming them. Morgan Earp said to me, "They have horses, had we not better get some horses ourselves, so that if they make a running fight we can catch them?" I said, "No, if they try to make a running fight we can kill their horses and then capture them." We four then started through Fourth to Fremont Street. When we turned the corner of Fourth and Fremont we could see them. . . . We came up on them close—Frank McLowry, Tom McLowry and Bill Clanton standing all in a row against the east side of the building on the opposite side of the vacant space west of Fly's photograph gallery. Ike Clanton and Billy Claiborne and a man I did not know were standing in the vacant space about half way between the photograph gallery and the next building west. I saw that Billy Clanton and Fred McLowry and Tom McLowry had their hands by their sides, and Frank McLowry's and Billy Clanton's six-shooters were in plain sight. Virgil said, "Throw up your hands I have come to disarm you." Billy Clanton and Frank McLowry laid their hands on their six-shooters. Virgil said, "Hold, I don't mean that; I have come to disarm you."

They—Billy Clanton and Frank McLowry—commenced to draw their pistols, at the same time Tom McLowry threw his hand to his right hip and jumped behind a horse. . . . When I saw Billy and Frank draw their pistols I drew my pistol. Billy Clanton leveled his pistol at me but I did not aim at him. I knew that Frank McLowry had the reputation of being a good shot and a dangerous man and I aimed at Frank McLowry. The first two shots which were fired were fired by Billy Clanton and myself; he shot at me and I shot at Frank McLowry. I do not know which shot was first; we fired almost together.

The fight then became general. After about four shots were fired Ike Clanton ran up and grabbed my right arm. I could see no weapon in his hand and thought at the time he had none and I said to him. "The fight has now commenced; go to shooting or get away;" at the same time I pushed him off with my left hand. He started and ran down the side of the building and disappeared between the lodging house and the photograph gallery. My first shot struck Frank McLowry in the belly. He staggered off on the sidewalk but first fired one shot at me. When we told them to throw up their hands Claiborne held up his left hand and then broke and ran. I never drew my pistol or made a motion to shoot until after Billy Clanton and Frank McLowry drew their pistols.

"If Tom McLowry was unarmed I did not know it. I believe he was armed and that he fired two shots at our party before Holliday, who had the shotgun, fired at and killed him. . . . I never fired at Ike Clanton, even after the shooting commenced because I thought he was unarmed. I believed then and believe now from the acts I have stated and the threats I have related and other threats communicated to me by different persons, as having been made by Tom McLowry, Frank McLowry and Isaac Clanton, that these men last named had formed a conspiracy to murder my brothers Morgan and Virgil and Doc Holliday and myself. I believe I would have been legally and morally justifiable in shooting any of them on sight, but I did not do so or attempt to do so; I sought no advantage. When I went as deputy marshal to help disarm them and arrest them, I went as part of my duty and under the direction of my brother the marshal. I did not intend to fight unless it became necessary in self defense and in the performance of official duty. When Billy Clanton and Frank McLowry drew their pistols I knew it was a fight for life and I drew and fired in defense of my own life, and lives of my brothers and Doc Holliday."

PART VII

Assassinations, Terrorism, Political Murders

Murder of Lovejoy

1837

Most assaults on abolitionists were not meant to kill but to silence them. Elijah P. Lovejoy was never silenced until he was killed. Lovejoy was not an abolitionist when he went to St. Louis in 1833 to edit a religious weekly, the St. Louis *Observer;* indeed he was known as a spokesman of anti-Catholic bigotry. But on October 1, 1835, he published and endorsed the credo of the American Anti-Slavery Society. A group of eminent local citizens then asked him "to pass over in silence every thing connected with the subject of slavery," a matter too close to their "vital interests" to suffer criticism. Lovejoy refused, and was then asked by the owners of the *Observer* to resign. Again he refused and stayed on. In May, 1836, he denounced the burning-alive of a Negro in St. Louis. This time his office was sacked, and he moved to Alton in Southern Illinois. His printing press happened to arrive in Alton on a Sunday, and had to be left on a wharf. When it was unguarded, a mob dumped it in the river. However, some citizens of Alton paid for a new printing press, and soon, in the Alton *Observer,* Lovejoy was speaking out once more for abolition. On July 4, 1837, he called for the formation of a local branch of the American Anti-Slavery Society. Much of the town was outraged. Lovejoy's press was destroyed, replaced, and destroyed again. When the Ohio Anti-Slavery Society sent another replacement, Lovejoy, aided by sixty young armed abolitionists, prepared to defend it. It arrived on November 7, and Lovejoy died defending it, giving abolitionism its first martyr.

The following description of Lovejoy's murder is taken

from Edward Beecher: *Narrative of the Riots at Alton* (1838; edn. 1965), 63-5. See Russel B. Nye: *Fettered Freedom* (1949).

About ten o'clock a mob, *already armed*, came and formed a line at the end of the store in Water Street, and hailed those within. Mr. Gilman opened the end door of the third story, and asked what they wanted. They demanded the press. He, of course, refused to give it up; and earnestly entreated them to use no violence. He told them that the property was committed to his care, and that they should defend it at the risk and sacrifice of their lives. At the same time they had no ill will against them, and should deprecate doing them an injury. One of them, a leading individual among the friends of free inquiry at the late convention, replied, that they would have it at the sacrifice of their lives, and presented a pistol at him: upon which he retired.

They then went to the other end of the store and commenced an attack. They demolished two or three windows with stones and fired two or three guns. As those within threw back the stones, one without was distinctly recognized and seen taking aim at one within: for it was a moonlight evening, and persons could be distinctly seen and recognized.

A few guns were then fired by individuals from within, by which Lyman Bishop, one of the mob, was killed. The story that he was a mere stranger waiting for a boat, and that Mr. Lovejoy shot him, are alike incapable of proof. He was heard during the day, by a person in whose employ he was, to express his intention to join the mob.

After this the mob retired for a few moments, and then returned with ladders which they lashed together to make them the proper length, and prepared to set fire to the roof. . . .

It now became evident to the defenders that their means of defense, so long as they remained within, was cut off; and nothing remained but to attack the assailants without. It was a hazardous step; but they determined to take it. A select number, of whom Mr. Lovejoy was one, undertook the work. They went out at the end, turned the corner, and saw one of the incendiaries on the ladder, and a number standing at the foot. They fired and it is supposed wounded, but did not kill him, and then, after continuing their fire some minutes and dispersing the mob, returned to load their guns. When they went out again no one was near the ladder, the assailants having so secreted themselves as to be able to fire, unseen, on the defenders of the press as they came out. No assailants being in sight Mr. Lovejoy stood, and was looking round. Yet, though he saw no assailant, the eye of his murderer was on him. The object of hatred, deep, malignant, and long continued, was fully before him—and the bloody tragedy was consummated. Five balls were lodged in his body, and he soon breathed his last. Yet after his mortal wound he had strength remaining to return to the building and ascend one flight of stairs before he fell and expired. They then attempted to capitulate, but were refused with curses by the mob, who threatened to burn the store and shoot them as they came out. Mr. Roff now determined at all hazards to go out and make some terms, but he was wounded as soon as he set his foot over the threshold.

The defenders then held a consultation. They were shut up within the building, unable to resist the ferocious mode of attack now adopted, and seemed to be devoted to destruction. At length Mr. West came to the door, informed them that the building was actually on fire, and urged them to escape by passing down the riverbank; saying that he would stand between them and the assailants so that if they fired they must fire on him. This was done. All but two or three marched out and ran down Water Street, being fired on by the mob as they went. Two, who were wounded, were left in the building, and one, who was not, remained to take care of the body of their murdered brother. The mob then entered, destroyed the press, and retired. Among them were seen some of those leading "friends of free inquiry" who had taken an active part in the convention.

Assassination of Lincoln
1865

During the Civil War, John Wilkes Booth, a fanatic Southerner and an actor of note, hoped to save the Confederacy by kidnapping President Lincoln; his ransom would be the recognition of Southern independence. When the Confederacy surrendered, Booth wanted vengeance. In Ford's Theater in Washington on Good Friday, April 14, 1865, he mortally wounded the President. A fellow conspirator shot Secretary of State William E. Seward, but he survived. Booth, his leg broken when he leapt from the President's box to the theater stage, got away from Washington, but was trapped in a Virginia tobacco barn where he was killed, or possibly shot himself. Three men and one woman, accused of being co–conspirators, were convicted at a military trial and hanged. Four others received long prison terms, though three survived to benefit by a pardon from Andrew Johnson.

The following account is taken from the testimony of Major Henry R. Rathbone before the Military Tribunal; Rathbone was with the President and his wife in the box at Ford's, and was himself wounded by Booth. Benjamin Pitman, comp.: *The Assassination of President Lincoln and the Trial of the Conspirators* (1865), 78-9. For a discussion of some of the ambiguities surrounding the assassination and trial, see Richard Current: *The Lincoln Nobody Knows* (1958), Chapter 11.

On the evening of the 14th of April last, at about twenty minutes past 8 o'clock, I, in company with Miss Harris, left my residence at the corner of Fifteenth and H Streets, and joined the President and Mrs. Lincoln, and went with them, in their carriage, to Ford's Theater, on Tenth Street. On reaching the theater, when the presence of the President became known, the actors stopped playing, the band struck up "Hall to the Chief," and the audience rose and received him with vociferous cheering. The party proceeded along in the rear of the dress-circle and entered the box that had been set apart for their reception. On entering the box, there was a large arm-chair that was placed nearest the audience, farthest from the stage, which the President took and occupied during the whole of the evening, with one exception, when he got up to put on his coat, and returned and sat down again. When the second scene of the third act was being performed, and while I was intently observing the proceedings upon the stage, with my back toward the door, I heard the discharge of a pistol behind me, and, looking round, saw through the smoke a man between the door and the President. The distance from the door to where the President sat was about four feet. At the same time I heard the man shout some word, which I thought was "Freedom!" I instantly sprang toward him and seized him. He wrested himself from my grasp, and made a violent thrust at my breast with a large knife. I parried the blow by striking it up, and received a wound several inches deep in my left arm. . . . The man rushed to the front of the box, and I endeavored to seize him again, but only caught his clothes as he was leaping over the railing of the box. The clothes, as I believe, were torn in the attempt to hold him. As he went over upon the stage, I cried out, "Stop that man." I then turned to the President; his position was not changed; his head was slightly bent forward and his eyes were closed. I saw that he was unconscious, and, supposing him mortally wounded, rushed to the door for the purpose of calling medical aid.

On reaching the outer door of the passage way, I found it barred by a heavy piece of plank, one end of which was secured in the wall, and the other resting against the door. It had been so securely fastened that it required considerable force to remove it. This wedge or bar was about four feet from the floor. Persons upon the outside were beating against the door for the purpose of entering. I removed the bar, and the door was opened. Several persons, who represented themselves as surgeons, were allowed to enter. I saw there Colonel Crawford, and requested him to prevent other persons from entering the box.

I then returned to the box, and found the surgeons examining the President's person. They had not yet discovered the wound. As soon as it was discovered, it was determined to remove him from the theater. He was carried out, and I then proceeded to assist Mrs. Lincoln, who was intensely excited, to leave the theater. On reaching the head of the stairs, I requested Major Potter to aid me in assisting Mrs. Lincoln across the street to the house where the President was being conveyed. . . .

In a review of the transactions, it is my confident belief that the time which elapsed between the discharge of the pistol and the time when the assassin leaped from the box did not exceed thirty seconds. Neither Mrs. Lincoln nor Miss Harris had left their seats.

Assassination of Garfield
1881

Charles Jules Guiteau, who assassinated President Garfield, is usually described as a disappointed office-seeker who wanted revenge. In reality, however, Guiteau was a victim of mental illness, probably paranoid schizophrenia. He lived for a long time in the utopian Oneida Community, but was unable to cope with life there, and subsequently became, in succession, a lawyer, a bill collector, a writer of abstruse theological tracts, a lecturer, and a petty swindler. Turning to politics in 1880, he joined the Stalwart faction of the Republican party in their campaign to run Grant for a third term, spending most of his time lounging around campaign headquarters, but also giving occasional partisan talks. When Garfield won the Republican nomination, Guiteau supported him. On November 11, 1880, he wrote politely to Secretary of State William Evarts, asking for the ministry in Vienna in return for his work in the campaign, which, he said, had been of critical importance. He moved to Washington, slept on park benches, haunted the State Department, now demanding to be made Consul at Paris. He wrote insistent letters to the President, and more and more included in them criticisms of Garfield's policies. In mid-May, 1881, he seems to have decided that Garfield, who had aligned himself with the Half-Breed faction of the Republican Party, enemies of the Stalwarts, should be assassinated. He planned twice to kill Garfield, but was unable to bring himself to act. Then on July 2, when Garfield was in the Washington railroad station waiting for a train, Guiteau shot him. The President lived in pain through the summer, but died on September 19.

On November 14 the trial of Guiteau began. It proved to be an important one in the development of criminal justice because Guiteau pleaded insanity, and the legal status of such a plea was still uncertain. Guiteau, who assisted at his own defense, was found guilty on January 5, 1882, and executed on July 30.

The following account of the assassination is Guiteau's own, taken from the autobiography he wrote while in prison: H. H. Alexander: *The Life of Guiteau and the Official History of the Most Exciting Case on Record* . . . (1882). See Charles E. Rosenberg: *The Trial of the Assassin Guiteau: Psychiatry and Law in the Gilded Age* (1968).

"I have not," he says, "used the words 'assassination' or 'assassin' in this work. These words grate on the mind and produce a bad feeling. I think of General Garfield's condition as a removal and not as an assassination. My idea simply stated was to remove as easily as possible Mr. James A. Garfield, a quiet and good-natured citizen of Ohio, who temporarily occupied the position of President of the United States, and substitute in his place Mr. Chester A. Arthur, of New York, a distinguished and highly estimable gentleman. . . .

"Two weeks after I conceived the idea my mind was thoroughly settled on the intention to remove the President. I then prepared myself. I sent to Boston for a copy of my book, 'The Truth,' and I spent a week in preparing that. I cut out a paragraph and a line and a word here and there and added one or two new chapters, put some new ideas in it and I greatly improved it. I knew that it would probably have a large sale on account of the notoriety that the act of removing the President would give me, and I wished the book to go out to the public in proper shape. That was one preparation for it.

"Another preparation was to think the matter all out in detail and to buy a revolver and to prepare myself for executing the idea. This required some two or three weeks, and I gave my entire time and mind in preparing myself to execute the conception of removing the President. . . . My mind was perfectly clear in regard to removing the President; I had not the slightest doubt about my duty to the Lord and to the American people in trying to remove the President, and I want to say here, as emphatically as words can make it, that, from the moment when I fully decided to remove the President, I have never had the slightest shadow on my mind; my purpose had been just as clear and just as determined as anything could be. I believed that I was acting under a special Divine authority to remove him, and this Divine pressure was upon me from the time when I fully resolved to remove him until I actually shot him. It was only by nerving myself to the utmost that I did it at all, and I never had the slightest doubt as the Divine inspiration of the act, and that it was for the best interest of the American people."

Nearing the End

"Having heard on Friday from the papers, and also by my inquiries of the doorkeeper at the White House, Friday evening, that the President was going to Long Branch Saturday morning, I resolved to remove him at the depot. I took my breakfast at the Riggs House about eight o'clock. I ate well and felt well in body and mind. I went into Lafayette Square and sat there some little time after breakfast, waiting for nine o'clock to come, and then I went to the depot and I got there about ten minutes after nine. . . .

"I examined my revolver to see that it was all right, and took off the paper that I had wrapped around it to keep the moisture off. I waited five or six minutes longer, sat down on a seat in the ladies' room, and very soon the President drove up. He was in company with a gentleman who, I understand, was Mr. Blaine. . . .

"The President got out on the pavement side and Mr. Blaine on the other side. They entered the ladies' room; I stood there watching the President and they passed by me. Before they reached the depot I had been promenading up and down the ladies' room between the ticket office door and the news stand door, a space of some ten or twelve feet. I walked up and down there I should say two or three times working myself up, as I knew the hour was at hand. The President and Mr. Blaine came into the ladies' room and walked right by me; they did not notice me as there were quite a number of ladies and children in the room.

"There was quite a large crowd of ticket-purchasers at the gentlemen's ticket office in the adjoining room; the depot seemed to be quite full of people. There was quite a crowd and commotion around, and the President was in the act of passing from the ladies' room to the main entrance through the door. I should say he was about four or five feet from the door nearest the ticket office, in the act of passing through the door to get through the depot to the cars. He was about three or four feet from the door. It stood five or six feet behind him, right in the middle of the room, and as he was in the act of walking away from me I pulled out the revolver and fired. He straightened up and threw his head back and seemed to be perfectly bewildered. He did not seem to know what struck him. I looked at him; he did not drop; I thereupon pulled again. He dropped his head, seemed to reel, and fell over. I do not know where the first shot hit; I aimed at the hollow of his back; I did not aim for any particular place, but I knew if I got those two bullets in his back he would certainly go. I was in a diagonal direction from the President, to the northwest, and supposed both shots struck.

"I was in the act of putting my revolver back into my pocket when the depot policeman seized me and said, 'You shot the President of the United States.' He was terribly excited; he hardly knew his head from his feet, and I said, 'Keep quiet, my friend; keep quiet, my friend. I want to go to jail.' A moment after the policeman seized me by the left arm; clutched me with terrible force. Another gentleman—an older man, I should say, and less robust—seized me by the right ram. At this moment the ticket agent and a great crowd of people rushed around me, and the ticket agent said, 'That's him; that's him'; and he pushed out his arm to seize me around the neck, and I says, 'Keep quiet, my friends; I want to go to jail; and the officers, one on each side of me, rushed me right off to the Police Headquarters, and the officer who first seized me by the hand says, 'This man has just shot the President of the United States,' and he was terribly excited. And I said, 'Keep quiet, my friend; keep quiet; I have got some papers which will explain the whole matter.'

"They held my hands up—one policeman on one side and one on the other—and they went through me, took away my revolver and what little change I had, my comb and my toothpick, all my papers, and I gave them my letter to the White House; told them that I wished they would send that letter to the White House at once, and the officer began to read my letter to the White House, and in this envelope containing my letter to the White House was my speech 'Garfield against Hancock.' He glanced his eye over the letter and I was telling him about sending it at once to the White House to explain the matter and he said, 'We will put you into the White House!' So I said nothing after that.

Haymarket
1886

The 1880's were a time of rising labor unionization, spurred by growing unemployment. Organized labor had some spectacular successes, among them the strike against Jay Gould's Southwest-

ern Railroad System in 1885. The Knights of Labor membership
soared from 100,000 in that year to 700,000 the next. One of the
chief goals of the labor movement in this period was the eight-
hour day, and a nation-wide strike in its support was planned
for May 1, 1886.

Chicago was the center of the eight-hour movement, and
also of the anarchist and other radical movements in the United
States. Leftists were divided over the place of violence in the
class struggle. The anarchist Johann Most insisted that the class
struggle "must have a violent revolutionary character, and the
wage struggle alone will not lead us to our goal." Among
revolutionaries his was an influential voice, and in the mid-
1880's the powers of dynamite were eulogized in the anarchist
press. The anarchist *Alarm* told its readers: "It will be your
most powerful weapon; a weapon of the weak against the
strong. . . . Use it unstintingly, unsparingly." Another writer
said: "Dynamite! . . . stuff several pounds of the sublime stuff
into an inch cap . . . place this in the immediate neighborhood of
a lot of rich loafers who live by the sweat of other people's
brows, and light the fuse. A most cheerful result will follow."
At mass meetings in Chicago the red and black flags were waved,
private property was denounced, and violence advocated. Yet
there were other voices on the left, including those of the
revolutionary socialists, August Spies and Albert Parsons arguing for less spectacular methods, such as propaganda, political
action, and "infiltration" of the labor movement. This group
was instrumental in organizing the eight-hour movement in
Chicago.

On May 1, 1886, between 200,000 and 300,000 workers
across the country struck or demonstrated for the eight-hour
movement. In Chicago a peaceful pro–eight–hour meeting was
addressed by anarchist speakers. However, violence did begin
in Chicago on May 3—but accidentally. During a strike of
packing house workers at the McCormick Harvester Plant, a
strike unrelated to the eight–hour movement, police broke up
a fight between scabs and strikers by shooting into the strikers,
killing one and seriously wounding others. Delegates of labor unions immediately sent out 2,000 circulars in German and English
calling for a mass meeting at Haymarket Square the next day
"to denounce the latest atrocious acts of the police." This meeting, which was small and peaceful, was on the point of breaking

up when 180 police arrived and ordered persons who were still there to disperse. At that moment someone threw a bomb at the police; seventy were seriously wounded, and seven ultimately died. The police then charged the crowd, shooting and clubbing; several were killed, uncounted numbers wounded. There was an immediate round-up of anarchists. Eight of them were promptly tried for murder. A biased judge and a packed jury found the defendants guilty, although no evidence was presented that connected them with the bomb thrower. Four were hanged, one committed suicide in prison, and three were jailed for life, but were pardoned in 1893 by Governor John P. Altgeld.

The Haymarket explosion was disastrous for the labor movement, since it led the public to equate anarchism, violence, and unionism. This identification was fostered by employers who used the anarchist theory of violence to blacken the Knights of Labor. Although the Knights tried to dissociate themselves from the anarchists, the labor movement suffered a serious setback.

The following trial testimony of an eye-witness, Barton Simonson, was reprinted in Dyer D. Lum: *Concise History of the Great Trial of the Chicago Anarchists in 1886* (1886), 112– 14. See Henry David: *The History of the Haymarket Affair* (1936).

I reached the Haymarket about 7:30. I found no meeting there. I walked around among the crowd, which was scattered over the Haymarket, then I went to the DesPlaines Street station and shook hands with Captain Ward, whom I knew. He introduced me to Inspector Bonfield and I had a conversation with him. Later on I went back and remained throughout the whole meeting until the bomb had exploded. The speakers were northeast of me in front of Crane Brothers' building, a few feet north of the alley. I remember the alley particularly. As far as I remember Spies' speech, he said: "Please come to order. This meeting is not called to incite any riot." [Witness then gave a synopsis of the speech, which in no wise differs from that previously given as written out by Spies.]

He thought Mr. Parsons did say: "To arms, To arms," but in what connection could not remember. "Somebody in the crowd said 'shoot' or 'hang Gould,' and he says, 'No, a great many will jump up and take his place. What socialism aims at is not the death of individuals but of the system.'

Fielden spoke very loud, and as I had never attended a Socialist meeting before in my life, I thought they were a little wild. Fielden spoke about a Congressman from Ohio who had been elected by the workingmen and confessed that no legislation could be enacted in favor of the workingmen, consequently he said there was no use trying to do anything by legislation. After he had talked a while a dark cloud with cold wind came up from the north. Many people had left before, but when that cloud came a great many people left. Somebody said, "Let's adjourn"—to someplace— I can't remember the name of the place. Fielden said he was about through, there was no need of adjourning. He said two or three times, "Now in conclusion," or something like that and became impatient. Then I heard a commotion and a good deal of noise in the audience, and somebody said "police." I looked south and saw a line of police. The police moved along until the front of the column got about up to the speaker's wagon. I heard somebody near the wagon say something about dispersing. I saw some persons upon the wagon. I could not tell who they were. About the time somebody was giving that command to disperse, I distinctly heard two words coming from the vicinity of the wagon or from the wagon. I don't know who uttered them. The words were, "peaceable meeting." That was a few seconds before the explosion of the bomb. I did not hear any such exclamation as, "Here come the bloodhounds of the police; you do your duty and I'll do mine," from the locality of the wagon or from Mr. Fielden. I heard nothing of the sort that night. At the time the bomb exploded I was still in my position upon the stairs. There was no pistol firing by any person upon the wagon before the bomb exploded. No pistol shots anywhere before the explosion of the bomb.

Just after the command to disperse had been given, I saw a lighted fuse, or something—I didn't know what it was at the time—come up from a point *twenty feet south* of the south line of Crane's alley, from about the center of the sidewalk on the east side of the street, from behind some boxes. I am positive it was *not* thrown from the alley. I first noticed it about six or seven feet in the air, a little above a man's head. It went in a northwest course and up about fifteen feet from the ground, and fell about the middle of the street. The explosion followed almost immediately. Something of a cloud of smoke followed the explosion. After the bomb exploded there was pistol shooting. From my position I could distinctly see the flashes of the pistols. My head was about fifteen feet above the ground. There might have been fifty to one hundred and fifty pistol shots. They proceeded from about the center of where the police were. I did not observe either the flashes of the pistol shot or hear the report of any shots from the crowd upon the police prior to the firing by the police.

The police were not only shooting at the crowd but I noticed several of them shoot just as they happened to throw their arms. I concluded that my position was possibly more dangerous than down in the crowd, and then I ran down to the foot of the stairs, ran west on the sidewalk on Randolph Street a short distance, and then in the road. A crowd was running in the same direction. I had to jump over a man lying down, and I saw another man fall in front of me about 150 to 200 feet west of DesPlaines Street. I took hold of his arm and wanted to help him, but the firing was so lively behind me that I just let go and ran. I was in the rear of the crowd running west, the police still behind us. There were no shots from the direction to which I was running.

I am not and never have been a member of any Socialistic party or association. Walking through the crowd before the meeting, I noticed that the meeting was composed principally of ordinary workingmen, mechanics, etc. The audience listened and once in a while there would be yells of "Shoot him, hang him." The violent ones seemed to be in the vicinity of the wagon. My impression is that some were making fun of the meeting. I noticed no demonstration of violence, no fighting or anything of that kind on the part of the crowd.

I heard about half a dozen or perhaps a few more of such expressions as "Hang him" or "Shoot him" from the audience. I did not find any difference in the bearing of the crowd during Fielden's speech from what it was during Parsons' or Spies'. In the course of the conversation with Capt. Bonfield at the station before the meeting that night, I asked him about the trouble in the southwestern part of the city. He says: "The trouble there is that these"—whether he used the word Socialist or strikers, I don't know—"get their women and children mixed up with them and around them and in front of them, and we can't get at them. I would like to get three thousand of them in a crowd without their women and children"—and to the best of my recollection he added—"and I will make short work of them." I noticed a few women and children at the bottom of the steps where I was.

Upon cross-examination this graphic and evidently truthful narration was not weakened in the least.

Attempted Murder of Henry Clay Frick
1892

Industrial violence in America usually took the form of fights between laborers and the agents of employers, private or public. Rarely was violence directed against leaders of American industry themselves. One important exception was the attack on Henry C. Frick by Alexander Berkman, a young, Russian-born anarchist active in New York. Outraged by Frick's role in the Homestead strike, Berkman decided that Frick was the ideal object for the kind of terroristic act called for by the anarchist theory of propaganda-by-deed. On July 23, 1892, he entered Frick's office in Pittsburgh and shot and stabbed him, wounding him seriously but not mortally. Berkman refused counsel at his trial, and was sentenced to twenty-two years in prison. A campaign for his pardon began in the late 1890's, leading to his release in May, 1906.

The attempt on Frick had little effect on the Homestead strike. Strike leaders quickly disavowed the act, denounced "the unlawful act of the wounding of Henry Clay Frick," and extended their sympathy to the industrialist.

The following account is taken from Berkman's: *Prison Memoirs of an Anarchist* (1912), 31–5.

East End, the fashionable residence quarter of Pittsburgh, lies basking in the afternoon sun. The broad avenue looks cool and inviting: the stately trees touch their shadows across the carriage road, gently nodding their heads in mutual approval. A steady procession of equipages fills the avenue, the richly caparisoned horses and uniformed flunkies lending color and life to the scene. A cavalcade is passing me. The laughter of the ladies sounds joyous and care-free. Their happiness irritates me. I am thinking of Homestead. In mind I see the sombre fence, the fortifications and cannon; the piteous figure of the widow rises before me, the little children weep-

ing, and again I hear the anguished cry of a broken heart, a shattered
brain. . . .

Ah, life could be made livable, beautiful! Why should it not be? Why
so much misery and strife? Sunshine, flowers, beautiful things are all
around me. That is life! Joy and peace. . . . No! There can be no peace
with such as Frick and these parasites in carriages riding on our backs,
and sucking the blood of the workers. Fricks, vampires, all of them—I
almost shout aloud—they are all one class. All in a cabal against *my* class,
the toilers, the producers. An impersonal conspiracy, perhaps; but a conspiracy nevertheless. And the fine ladies on horseback smile and laugh.
What is the misery of the People to *them*? Probably they are laughing at
me. Laugh! Laugh! You despise me. I am of the People, but you belong
to the Fricks. Well, it may soon be our turn to laugh. . . .

The door of Frick's private office, to the left of the reception-room,
swings open as the colored attendant emerges, and I catch a flitting glimpse
of a black-bearded, well-knit figure at a table in the back of the room.

"Mistah Frick is engaged. He can't see you now, sah," the negro says,
handing back my card.

I take the pasteboard, return it to my case, and walk slowly out of the
reception-room. But quickly retracing my steps, I pass through the gate
separating the clerks from the visitors, and, brushing the astounded attendant aside, I step into the office on the left, and find myself facing Frick.

For an instant the sunlight, streaming through the windows, dazzles
me. I discern two men at the further end of the long table.

"Fr—," I begin. The look of terror on his face strikes me speechless. It
is the dread of the conscious presence of death. "He understands," it flashes
through my mind. With a quick motion I draw the revolver. As I raise the
weapon, I see Frick clutch with both hands the arm of the chair, and
attempt to rise. I aim at his head. "Perhaps he wears armor," I reflect. With
a look of horror he quickly averts his face, as I pull the trigger. There
is a flash, and the high-ceilinged room reverberates as with the booming of
cannon. I hear a sharp, piercing cry, and see Frick on his knees, his head
against the arm of the chair. I feel calm and possessed, intent upon every
movement of the man. He is lying head and shoulders under the large
armchair, without sound or motion. "Dead?" I wonder. I must make sure.
About twenty-five feet separate us. I take a few steps toward him, when
suddenly the other man, whose presence I had quite forgotten, leaps upon
me. I struggle to loosen his hold. He looks slender and small. I would
not hurt him: I have no business with him. Suddenly I hear the cry,
"Murder! Help!" My heart stands still as I realize that it is Frick shouting.

"Alive?" I wonder. I hurl the stranger aside and fire at the crawling figure of Frick. The man struck my hand,—I have missed! He grapples with me, and we wrestle across the room. I try to throw him, but spying an opening between his arm and body, I thrust the revolver against his side and aim at Frick cowering behind the chair. I pull the trigger. There is a click— but no explosion! By the throat I catch the stranger, still clinging to me, when suddenly something heavy strikes me on the back of the head. Sharp pains shoot through my eyes. I sink to the floor, vaguely conscious of the weapon slipping from my hands.

"Where is the hammer? Hit him, carpenter!" Confused voices ring in my ears. Painfully I strive to rise. The weight of many bodies is pressing on me. Now—it's Frick's voice! Not dead? . . . I crawl in the direction of the sound, dragging the struggling men with me. I must get the dagger from my pocket—I have it! Repeatedly I strike with it at the legs of the man near the window. I hear Frick cry out in pain—there is much shouting and stamping—my arms are pulled and twisted, and I am lifted bodily from the floor.

Police, clerks, workmen in overalls, surround me. An officer pulls my head back by the hair, and my eyes meet Frick's. He stands in front of me, supported by several men. His face is ashen gray; the black beard is streaked with red, and blood is oozing from his neck. For an instant a strange feeling, as of shame comes over me; but the next moment I am filled with anger at the sentiment, so unworthy of a revolutionist. With defiant hatred I look him full in the face.

"Mr. Frick, do you identify this man as your assailant?"

Frick nods weakly.

The street is lined with a dense, excited crowd. A young man in civilian dress, who is accompanying the police, inquires, not unkindly:

"Are you hurt? You're bleeding."

I pass my hand over my face. I feel no pain, but there is a peculiar sensation about my eyes.

"I've lost my glasses," I remark, involuntarily.

"You'll be damn lucky if you don't lose your head," an officer retorts.

Assassination of Frank Steunenberg
1905

Frank Steunenberg was elected Governor of Idaho in 1896 and 1898 with heavy labor support, but he was instrumental in crushing the Coeur d'Alene strike in 1899, and crippling the Western Federation of Miners. When the Governor was killed by a bomb explosion six years later (December 30, 1905) many accused the W.F.M. of settling an old grudge. This they denied, but the Idaho police caught the assassin, Albert E. Horsley, alias Harry Orchard, who proved to be a miner and a member of the W.F.M. Orchard at first denied everything, but the state sent James McParland, the Pinkerton detective who had infiltrated, exposed, and destroyed the Molly McGuires, to visit Orchard in his cell. McParland hinted to Orchard that he could save his neck if he implicated the leaders of the union in the assassination. Orchard did so, charging that Charles H. Moyer, President, William D. Haywood, Secretary-Treasurer, and George Pettibone, adviser to the Western Federation of Miners were instigators of the crime. In addition, he confessed to murdering twenty-six other men on union orders. The three men named by Orchard were in Colorado, but they were arrested and brought to Idaho without legal extradition to stand trial. Orchard's charges and the kidnapping by the Idaho officials touched off an uproar in the labor and radical press. Eugene Debs threatened that "If they do attempt to murder Moyer, Haywood, and their brothers, a million revolutionists, at least, will meet them with guns." Marches were held in Boston, New York, and San Francisco to protest the first trial in which Haywood was the defendant—which began on May 7, 1907, in Boise. Clarence Darrow was the attorney for the defense, and Senator William E. Borah for the prosecution. Borah produced much oratory but little evidence aside from Orchard's testimony against the union leader. The jury found Haywood not guilty. Another jury acquitted Pettibone in 1908, and Moyer was never tried. Orchard was sentenced to hang, but his penalty was commuted to life imprisonment. He died in jail in 1954 at the age of eighty-eight.

The following account of the assassination is taken from the *Confessions and Autobiography of Harry Orchard* (1907), 216–18. See David H. Grover: *Debaters and Dynamiters: A Story of the Haywood Trial* (1964); Philip S. Foner: *History of the Labor Movement in the United States*, IV, 40–60; and Abe C. Ravitz and James N. Primm, eds.: *The Haywood Case* (1960).

I did not see Mr. Steunenberg again until the next Thursday. I did not know where he went when he was away, and I saw his son on the street one day, and I spoke to him and asked him if they had any sheep to sell. I thought I would find out this way where his father went. He told me that he knew nothing about it, as his father attended to that, but he said I could find out by telephoning to his father at the company ranch at Bliss. But he said he would be home the next day, and I could see him if I was there. I told him I just wanted to find out where some sheep could be bought, as a friend of mine wanted them to feed.

The next day, Friday, I went to Nampa and thought I might get a chance to put the bomb under Governor Steunenberg's seat, if I found him on the train, as the train usually stops fifteen to twenty minutes at Nampa. I had taken the powder out of the wooden box, and packed it in a little, light, sheet-iron box with a lock on, and I had a hole cut in the top of this and a little clock on one side. Both this and the bottle of acid were set in plaster [of] Paris on the other side of the hole from the clock, with a wire from the key which winds the alarm to the cork in the bottle. The giant-caps were put in the powder underneath this hole, and all I had to do was to wind up the alarm and set it and, when it went off, it would wind up the fine wire on the key, and pull out the cork, and spill the acid on the caps. I had this fitted in a little grip and was going to set it, grip and all, under his seat in the coach, if I got a chance. I went through the train when it arrived at Nampa, but did not see Mr. Steunenberg, and the train was crowded, so I would not have had any chance, anyway. I saw Mr. Steunenberg get off the train at Caldwell, but missed him on the train.

I saw him again around Caldwell Saturday afternoon. I was playing cards in the saloon at the Saratoga, and came out in the hotel lobby at just dusk, and Mr. Steunenberg was sitting there talking. I went over to the post-office and came right back, and he was still there. I went up to my room and took this bomb out of my grip and wrapped it up in a newspaper and put it under my arm and went downstairs, and Mr. Steunenberg was still there. I hurried as fast as I could up to his residence, and laid this bomb close to the gate-post, and tied a cord into a screw-eye in the cork and around a picket of the gate, so when the gate was opened, it would jerk the cork out of the bottle and let the acid run out and set off the bomb. This was set in such a way, that if he did not open the gate wide enough to pull it out, he would strike the cord with his feet, as he went to pass in. I pulled some snow over the bomb after laying the paper over it, and hurried back as fast as I could.

I met Mr. Steunenberg about two and a half blocks from his residence. I then ran as fast as I could, to get back to the hotel if possible before he got to the gate. I was about a block and a half from the hotel on the foot-bridge when the explosion of the bomb occurred, and I hurried to the hotel as fast as I could. I went into the bar-room, and the bartender was alone, and asked me to help him tie up a little package, and I did, and then went up to my room, intending to come right down to dinner, as nearly everyone was in at dinner.

Dynamiting of Los Angeles *Times*
1910

Harrison Gray Otis, publisher of the Los Angeles *Times*, was a vehement foe of labor unions. In his editorial page and through the Los Angeles Merchants and Manufacturers Association, Otis fought unionism effectively for twenty years; during this period, Los Angeles industry maintained open shops. The AFL Convention of 1907 denounced Otis as "the most unfair, un-scrupulous, and malignant enemy of organized labor in America." In 1910, AFL leaders decided to try once more to bring unionism to Los Angeles. Aided by skilled labor organizers from San Francisco, funds from the national office, and by the guidance of a General Strike Committee, strikes were started in a large number of industries employing skilled workers.

In response, Otis and the Merchants and Manufacturers Association persuaded the City Council to outlaw picketing, and the police began to arrest strikers. After the strikes failed, the unions turned to politics, allied themselves with the Socialist party, and supported the Socialist leader, Job Harriman, for Mayor. Harriman scored a dramatic upset in the Democratic primary, and labor confidently looked forward to victory in the mayoral election.

Then, shortly after midnight on October 1, 1910, the Los Angeles *Times* building was dynamited. Twenty persons were killed. Otis immediately blamed the dynamiting on the unions, and said bombs had also been found at his home and that of the Secretary of the Merchants and Manufacturers Association. The union denied his charges, and in the absence of proof their political chances still seemed promising. Private detective William J. Burns was hired by the incumbent Mayor to find the bomber. Noticing a similarity in pattern between the Los Angeles attack and a series of bombings initiated elsewhere by the Bridge and Structural Iron Workers Union against United States Steel, Burns investigated the activities of John J. McNamara, Secretary-Treasurer of the Bridge and Structural Iron Workers Union. Burns found incriminating evidence, and, using means of dubious legality, sent McNamara and his younger brother James to Los Angeles for trial. Labor organizations mobilized to defend the McNamara brothers; Samuel Gompers called the trial a "capitalist conspiracy," and Clarence Darrow was retained for the defense. Millions believed the McNamaras were innocent.

On December 1, to the shock of the labor movement, Darrow announced that his clients were reversing their pleas and admitting their guilt. This disclosure halted the labor drive in Los Angeles and Harriman lost by a wide margin. James B. McNamara, who had set the bomb, ("I did not intend to take the life of anyone," he said) was sentenced for life to San Quentin; J. J. McNamara was sentenced to fifteen years, served ten, and was released in May, 1921.

The following account of the bombing is from the issue of

the Los Angeles *Times* printed on the day of the bombing, October 1, 1910. (The paper had an auxiliary printing plant, and the other journals of the city lent assistance.) See Graham Adams: *Age of Industrial Violence* (1966); Louis Adamic: *Dynamite* (rev. edn. 1934); Clarence Darrow: *The Story of My Life* (1932); and Grace H. Stimson: *Rise of the Labor Movement in Los Angeles* (1955).

Many lives were jeopardized and half a million dollars' worth of property was sacrificed on the altar of hatred of the labor unions at 1 o'clock this morning, when the plant of the Los Angeles *Times* was blown up and burned, following numerous threats by the laborites.

Not quite as many of the employees were on duty as would have been the case earlier in the night, when all departments were working in full blast, but even so the murderous cowards knew that fully one hundred people were in the building at the time. With the suddenness of an earthquake, an explosion, of which the dry, snappy sound left no room to doubt of its origin in dynamite, tore down the whole first floor of the building on Broadway, just back of the entrance to the business offices. In as many seconds, four or five other explosions of lesser volume were heard.

In the time it took to run at full speed from the police station to the corner of First and Broadway, a distance of less than half a block, the entire building was in flames on three floors. Almost in the same instant flames and smoke filled the east stairway on First Street, driving down in a frenzied panic those employes of the composing room who had been so fortunate as to reach the landing in time.

Elbowing past the last of these fugitives, men fought their way up to the first floor with flash lights and handkerchiefs over their faces. There efforts were unavailing, the blistering hot smoke and the lurid light of the flames almost upon them and licking down at them fiercely, drove the would-be rescuers back, hurriedly.

Although they could hear clearly the cries of distress, the groans and screams of the men and women, who, mangled and crippled by flying debris from the explosion, lay imprisoned by the flames, about to be cremated alive.

Along the shadows of the editorial and city rooms, on the south side of the building, through a choking volume of black smoke, could be seen men and women crowding each other about the windows of the third floor. The cries for ladders went up, frantic.

A fire wagon drove up at full speed. Groans greeted it when it was seen that it was but a hose wagon instead of the hook and ladder truck. "Nets; get nets, nets!" was the yell.

A policeman came running up from headquarters, carrying a short ladder, pathetically inadequate. Someone called him a fool. But the ladder saved the live of Lovelace, the country editor, who jumped upon it and escaped with a broken leg and some minor burns.

Other fire apparatus thundered up. The nets were jerked out in less time than it takes to tell, but by that time the fire had surged through the building with such rapidity that it was impossible to approach the reddening walls with them, and those unfortunates who had not jumped with Lovelace were doomed.

In less than four minutes from the time the explosion was heard the entire building was ablaze.

The Work of Demons

It recked little to the man who placed the bombs which wrecked a splendid newspaper that one hundred men were at work on the various floors, busily engaged in getting out the great newspaper. That the instant that the bombs were exploded their lives were in peril; that as a result of the hellish work lives were probably lost and other lives precious to wives, children and relatives were in deadly peril.

The bombs were planted by experienced hands. They did the work for which they were intended, at least temporarily, to cripple a great newspaper.

At 1 o'clock the *Times* plant was humming in every department. Forms were being closed up, stereotyped and sent down to the press room. An hour later the great presses would run at lightning speed to print the many thousands of papers which carriers were waiting to serve to their customers.

A second later hell broke loose. A deafening detonation, a sickening uplift of men's hearts and lungs, then vivid tongues of flames, dense, stifling smoke which obscured the electric lights on every floor.

One instant busy occupation, lights, the whirr of machinery, the next, black midnight, smoke that overpowers, flames that shot their wicked tongues from basement to roof.

Trapped on all floors, the men of the *Times*, picked men they were, preserved their coolness in the midst of this appalling scene.

But it would seem that there was no escape. The murderers had planned with hellish cunning. The broad stairways were filled with deadly smoke almost as soon as the echo of the dynamite bomb had died away. The building was on fire on every side. But there was a way out for brave men, and they took the desperate chance.

The explosion caught the working force unawares and many were buried in the ruins, while others jumped from windows, fell through the elevator chutes or climbed down fire escapes after receiving terrible injuries from flying timbers and debris.

A few in the building escaped uninjured. . . .

The explosions were heard throughout the business district, and scores of persons going home in the 1 o'clock cars jumped out and joined the thousands of citizens who were pouring from downtown houses and hurrying to the fire.

Within five minutes the scene of the explosion presented a terrible spectacle, as the big building had burst immediately into flame and was doomed. Great excitement seized the multitude and word quickly passed that scores of doomed persons were within the seething furnace. Desperate attempts were made by policemen, firemen and citizens to rescue those within, but the flames drove them back. The terrible spectacle of persons attempting to escape from windows in the upper stories was turned to a horror when they were seen to jump to the ground. One man was seen framed in a window casing; he threw up his hands and fell backward into the seething cauldron behind and beneath him.

Men poured from doors dragging broken limbs and holding battered heads and bodies. Those who tottered forth were seized by eager hands and borne to places of safety.

Men begged to be permitted to dash into the burning building, but officers with drawn revolvers and riot guns forced them back and cleared the streets. A few moments later the flames licked up the woodwork of the structure, the walls began to fall and electric wires fell, sputtering to the pavements, and endangered those in the vicinity. . . .

For those in the wreck there was no aid; God only could care for their souls. Human agencies were of no avail.

Wall Street Bombing
1920

1919 was a year of fear for many Americans and of hysteria for some. The Bolshevik Revolution abroad, the increased activity of American labor at home—the steel strike, the Boston police strike, the Seattle general strike—suggested that revolutionary ideas were spreading in the United States. A number of terrorist incidents added to the climate of fear. In April, a servant in the employ of a Georgia senator opened a package and had her hands blown off; thirty-six other bombs were discovered in post offices through the country addressed to important persons. These were the events that led to the great Red Scare of 1919, a product of both hysteria and calculation. During this year, hundreds of radicals and immigrants were rounded up, arrested, and deported on the sole orders of Attorney-General A. Mitchell Palmer. These and other denials of civil liberties were protested by many prominent and respected men, and by 1920 much of the hysteria had passed. But on September 16, 1920, a bomb went off outside the House of Morgan on Wall Street, killing thirty-four people and injuring over two hundred. The interior of the building was wrecked, and repairs cost about $2,000,000. Palmer pronounced it part of a plot to overthrow capitalism and to establish a Soviet order in the United States, but after a national flurry of indignation the matter was laid to rest, along with the innocent victims. The bombers were never discovered. The following account is from *The New York Times*, September 17, 1920. See William Preston, Jr.: *Aliens and Dissenters* (1963); and Robert Murray: *Red Scare* (1955).

An explosion, believed to have been caused by a time bomb, killed thirty persons and injured probably 300 others at Broad and Wall Streets yesterday at noon.

The blast shattered windows for blocks around, threw the financial district into a panic and strewed the streets in the immediate vicinity with the bodies of the dead and injuried victims.

Twelve hours later investigating authorities were almost certain the disaster was due to an infernal machine left on an uncovered one-horse vehicle on Wall Street directly in front of the United States Assay Office nextdoor to the Sub-Treasury, and directly across the street from the J. P. Morgan Building.

While no arrest had been made up to last midnight, Federal, State and City authorities were agreed that the devastating blast signaled the long threatened Red outrages.

Throughout the nation the same interpretation was placed upon the explosion, and public buildings and great storehouses of wealth, as well as conspicuous men in several cities, were placed under vigilant guard.

A guard of thirty detectives was placed around the Morgan home on Madison Avenue last night. Pedestrians were not allowed to pass in front of the house. It was said the guard would be kept on duty all night.

Accident Theories Doubted

Rumors that a red wagon loaded with explosives had collided with an automobile or that its cargo had ignited spontaneously had been very nearly dissipated by the criminal investigators, working at unprecedented high pressure. It had been established that no vehicle freighted with such materials was lawfully in the vicinity at that hour, and no other accident theory, supported by the least plausibility, had been advanced.

Against this negative foundation for any hypothesis of accident stood the positive fact that the explosion rained death through the neighborhood in the form of short heavy slugs of cast iron window weights. These were of a cheap make, easily obtainable, rust on their fractured ends showing that they had not been broken by the explosion itself, and a minute, exhaustive examination of the many damaged buildings in the neighborhood proved that no such weights had fallen from their torn and twisted steel window casings.

Slow identification of the dead, many of them mangled beyond ready recognition retarded the investigation. That there was a one-horse truck, probably with lattice sides, standing directly in front of the Assay Office, where the explosion occurred, is known. Parts of the dead horse were found, as well as the axles and hubs of the wheels, with a few stubs of spokes still sticking in them. But whether the driver was a victim of the blast or whether he is an escaped conspirator is a point of vital importance that remains in doubt.

Police Convinced of Plot

So the investigators became more and more convinced that they faced a piece of organized deviltry, executed with a terrible effectiveness that dwarfed such anarchist and other radical crimes of the past as the attempts on the lives of Russell Sage and Henry C. Frick, and the bombs in Union Square, St. Patrick's Cathedral and St. Alphonsus's Church.

If their interpretation was correct, the conspirators in large measure failed of whatever direct object they had beyond sheer terrorization. They evidently timed their infernal machine for an hour when the streets of the financial district were crowded, but they chose as well the hour when not the captains of industry but their clerks and messengers were on the street. J. P. Morgan himself, who already had escaped one attempt at assassination when he was shot by Mrs. Muenter, was in Europe. . . .

Thus it was throughout the district. Men of wealth and prominence escaped, some by miles and some by narrow coincidence and the great force of the blow fell on middle-class workers. . . .

Stock Exchange Is Closed

Almost within seconds of the tragedy the financial work of the nation was halted and the work of rescue or guarding the billions of money and securities endangered was underway.

Around in Broad Street the Stock Exchange was running full blast. Trading centered about the Redding post at the center of the pit and William H. Remick, President of the institution, stood nearby chatting with one of the Governors. He heard the terrible detonation, saw the glass raining everywhere, listened a second to cries and groans and excited shouting and running feet, then said quickly:

"I think we had better stop trading for the day."

A second later he had stepped over and rung the gong that brought the financial operations of the city to an end. The wires flashed the news and a few moments later other big cities were following suit. They will reopen today.

Meantime hundreds had been overtaken by swift disaster and the first few moments of wild panic had gripped many thousands. From the excited, oft-times incoherent stories of eye witnesses and the first rescuers to arrive there developed a composite picture of frightfulness that recalled the days of German raids and long distance bombardments of unprotected allied cities.

First a blinding flash of bluish-white light that illuminated the whole of Wall Street, then the deafening, bewildering roar of the explosion, carrying with it dozens of those iron plugs with all the velocity of a high explosive shell.

Smoke Blots Out the Scene

It seemed, the eye witnesses said, as if there was just the slightest lull after that, through which was heard the tinkle and smash of glass as hundreds of windows showered down over the stone fronts of buildings, or were blown back through rooms where busy men and women bent over desks.

Those who went through those dread moments heard the glass before they saw it. A great cloud of smoke surrounded the immediate seat of the explosion, a great cloud of dust blotted out the whole of the street.

That cleared and there, many eye witnesses say, lay hundreds of men and women, most of them prone on their faces. Some were dead. Some writhed in agony. Some already were scrambling to their feet. Some were badly hurt and silent. Others screamed in pain or fright, some moaned, some cried for help for themselves. One little messenger, badly hurt, begged that someone would look after the little fortune of securities he clutched in an injured hand.

According to the clock in the Assay Office, which stopped from the force of the explosion, it was 12:01. Gray Trinity, over at Broadway was not yet done tolling the hour. From every office the lunch clouds of clerks and messengers who report for work early were jamming their way into the street.

There seemed to be just that little instant after the dust cleared away when everyone stood still, dazed, puzzled, frightened. Then, as window after window, with now and then a chunk of stone, came tumbling down they ran—ran in blind fear. That was the second phase, as many described it.

Thousands Crowd into Street

Again it was but seconds until the third phase, with its returning sanity. Nothing dreadful was happening, the worst was over, and those who raced to corners and turning to see from what they had fled, saw the stricken lying on the streets and in the sidewalk. Back they tore, thousands of them, jamming into the narrow alley, getting into one another's way, trying almost aimlessly to help.

Murder of Medgar Evers
1963

While Southern opponents of racial equality have on occasion turned out in mass protests, a few have also resorted to political murder. The list of martyrs, black and white, to the civil rights movement includes, as well as Evers, Rev. George E. Leeb (1955), Lamar Smith (1955), Thomas H. Brewer (1956), Herbert Lee (1961), William L. Moore (1963), Louis Allen, James Chaney, Andrew Goodman, Michael Schwerner (1964), Jonathan M. Daniels, Jimmie Lee Jackson, Viola Liuzzo, James Reed (1965), Vernon Dahmer (1966), Samuel Younge, Jr., (1966), Wharlest Jackson (1967), and Martin Luther King (1968). Medgar Evers, NAACP field secretary for nine years, announced an anti-segregation drive in Jackson, Mississippi, on May 12, 1963. He requested the appointment of a bi-racial committee to discuss grievances; the Mayor, after consulting with seventy-five business leaders, rejected the request, asserting that it would lead to "compliance with the demands of racial agitators from outside," and he banned demonstrations as well. Evers launched his campaign on May 28 with a sit-in at a Woolworth's lunch counter. His group was beaten up, others were arrested, and a bomb was exploded at one of the integrationist leaders' homes. Next, black school children marched in support of civil rights; 600 of them were arrested. On June 1 some concessions were made, but the demand for a bi-racial committee was again rejected. On June 12, returning home from an integration rally, Evers was shot in the back. Governor Ross Barnett called Evers's murder a "dastardly act." Congressman William Colmer, however, felt it was the "inevitable result of agitation by politicians, do-gooders and those who sail under the false flag of liberalism."

The F.B.I. arrested Byron de la Beckwith, a resident of Mississippi for thirty-eight years, on the charge of murder. At Beckwith's trial, Governor Barnett strode into the courtroom, greeted Beckwith warmly, and shook hands with him. On February 7, 1964, the jury reported itself deadlocked; a second trial also resulted in a hung jury. Beckwith, now free, continued harassing civil rights workers; in February 1967 he announced his candidacy for the Democratic nomination for Lieutenant Governor of Mississippi, and running while under indictment for murder finished (with 30,000 loyal supporters) last in a field of five.

The following account was written by Mrs. Medgar Evers (with William Peters) in *For Us, the Living* (1967), 301-4. See Pat Watters and Reese Cleghorn: *Climbing Jacob's Ladder: The Arrival of Negroes in Southern Politics* (1967).

It was a moving speech, the most direct and urgent appeal for racial justice any President of the United States had ever made. It moved me and gave me hope and made what Medgar was doing seem more important than ever before. I remember wondering what the white people of Mississippi were thinking as I lay back on the bed and the children switched the set to another channel. I must have drifted off into a light sleep, because I woke, later, to settle an argument over which program was to be watched next. Then, still buoyed up by the President's words, I relaxed, to watch with the children. Darrell heard the car first.

"Here comes Daddy."

We listened to the familiar sound of the car. I roused myself as the tires reached the gravel driveway, stretched, and then heard the car door close. I wondered what Medgar would have to say about the speech, and I sat up on the bed.

A shot rang out, loud and menacing. The children, true to their training, sprawled on the floor. I knew in my heart what it must mean.

I flew to the door, praying to be wrong. I switched on the light. Medgar lay face down at the doorway drenched with blood.

I screamed, went to him, calling his name.

There was another shot, much closer, and I dropped to my knees. Medgar didn't move.

The children were around me now, pleading with him. "Please, Daddy, please get up!"

Behind Medgar on the floor of the carport were the papers he had dropped and some sweatshirts. Crazily, across the front of one, I read the words, "Jim Crow Must Go." In his hand, stretched out toward the door, was the door key. There was blood everywhere.

I left the children and ran to the telephone. I dialed "O" and tried to breathe and screamed at the operator for the police and gave her the address and ran back outside.

The Youngs were there and the Wellses and more people were coming and someone had turned Medgar over and he was breathing heavily, in short spurts, and his eyes were open, but they were set and unmoving.

I called and called to him, but if he heard me he showed no sign.

I heard the children being led away, screaming and crying for their father, and I remember some men carrying the mattress from Rena's bed from the house, putting Medgar on it and carrying him to Houston Wells' station wagon. I followed and tried to get in beside him, still calling to him, but they held me back, and as the car pulled off, I fell trying to reach him and someone picked me up and I ran back into the house. There had been a police car in front of the Wells' car as it tore away through the night, but I had not yet seen a policeman.

I ran to the living room and fell to my knees and prayed. I prayed for Medgar and I fought for breath and I prayed that God's will be done and I sobbed and I prayed that whatever happened I would be able to accept it.

Someone found me there, and I got up and ran to the telephone and called Attorney Young's house where Gloster Current was staying. "They've killed my husband!" I screamed. "They've killed my husband!"

A woman took the telephone from me, and I wandered off to the bedroom, dazed with grief. One of the women followed and found me packing Medgar's toothbrush and some pajamas for the hospital and asking out loud how many pairs he would need.

Jean Wells took my arm and said that Dr. Britton had called from Ole Miss Hospital. Medgar had regained consciousness, I searched the room for my clothes and began to dress.

Then Hattie Tate came in the door and looked at me and I knew.

"Is he gone?"

She couldn't speak. She tried but she couldn't speak. She turned and ran from the room, and I slumped like a marionette whose strings had been cut.

Murder of Malcolm X
1965

Malcolm Little, who was converted to the Nation of Islam in 1948, became, as Malcolm X, one of its most effective national leaders, and in that role a rival to its leader, Elijah Muhammed. In March 1964, Malcolm broke with the Muslims because he wanted a broader crusade for human rights, and founded his own black nationalist organization. Later he also made a pilgrimage to Mecca, and upon his return he became convinced that the Black Muslims were trying to kill him, sometimes publicly predicting that he would be murdered. On February 13, 1965, his house was wrecked by fire bombs (he accused some Muslims of the assault), but he and his family were unhurt. On February 21 he was shot and killed while speaking in the Audubon Ballroom in New York.

Three men were arrested for the murder. Two, Norman 3X Butler and Thomas 15X Johnson, were Black Muslims: the third, Talmage Hayer, denied that he was. At trial all pleaded not guilty, but on February 28, 1966, Hayer changed his plea, saying that he had killed Malcolm with two confederates, but that they were not the two men on trial with him. The Muslims had nothing to do with the killing, he said; he had been paid to do the job, but he would not say by whom. All three were convicted and sentenced to life imprisonment.

The account is that of an eye-witness, Thomas Skinner, in the New York *Post*, February 22, 1965. See Malcolm X: *The Autobiography of Malcolm X* (1964); and *The New York Times*, March 11, 1966.

They came early to the Audubon Ballroom, perhaps drawn by the expectation that Malcolm X would name the men who firebombed his home last Sunday; streaming from the bright afternoon sunlight into the darkness of the hall.

The crowd was larger than was usual for Malcolm's recent meetings, the 400 filling three-quarters of the wooden folding seats, feet scuffling the worn floor as they waited impatiently, docilely obeying the orders of Malcolm's guards as they were directed to the seats.

I sat at the left in the 12th row and, as we waited, the man next to me spoke of Malcolm and his followers:

"Malcolm is our only hope," he said. "You can depend on him to tell it like it is and to give Whitey hell."

Then a man was on the stage, saying:

". . . I now give you Brother Malcolm. I hope you will listen, hear, and understand."

There was a prolonged ovation as Malcolm walked to the rostrum past a piano and a set of drums waiting for an evening dance and stood in front of a mural of a landscape as dingy as the rest of the ballroom.

When, after more than a minute the crowd quieted, Malcolm looked up and said "A salaam aleikum" (Peace be unto you), and the audience replied "Wo aleikum salaam (And unto you, peace).

Bespectacled and dapper in a dark suit, his sandy hair glinting in the light, Malcolm said:

"Brothers and sisters . . ." He was interrupted by two men in the center of the ballroom, about four rows in front and to the right of me who rose and, arguing with each other, moved forward. Then there was a scuffle in the back of the room and, as I turned my head to see what was happening, I heard Malcolm X say his last words:

"Now, now brothers, break it up," he said softly. "Be cool, be calm."

Then all hell broke loose. There was a muffled sound of shots and Malcolm, blood on his face and chest, fell limply back over the chairs behind him. The two men who had approached him ran to the exit on my side of the room, shooting wildly behind them as they ran.

I fell to the floor, got up, tried to find a way out of the bedlam.

Malcolm's wife, Betty, was near the stage, screaming in a frenzy. "They're killing my husband," she cried, "They're killing my husband."

Groping my way through the first frightened, then enraged crowd, I heard people screaming. "Don't let them kill him." "Kill those bastards." "Don't let him get away." "Get him."

At an exit I saw some of Malcolm's men beating with all their strength on two men. Police were trying to fight their way toward the two. The press of the crowd forced me back inside.

I saw a half-dozen of Malcolm's followers bending over his inert body on the stage, their clothes stained with their leader's blood. Then they put him on a litter while guards kept everyone off the platform. A woman bending over him said: "He's still alive. His heart's beating."

Four policemen took the stretcher and carried Malcolm through the crowd and some of the women came out of their shock long enough to moan and one said: "I don't think he's going to make it. I hope he doesn't die, but I don't think he's going to make it."

I spotted a phone booth in the rear of the hall, fumbled for a dime, and called a photographer. Then I sat there, the surprise wearing off a bit, and tried desperately to remember what had happened. One of my first thoughts was that this was the first day of National Brotherhood Week.

Assassination of Robert F. Kennedy
1968

At 12:13 A.M. on Wednesday, June 5, 1968, Senator Robert F. Kennedy was shot in the Ambassador Hotel in Los Angeles a few minutes after giving a victory address to supporters and television newsmen. He had just narrowly defeated Senator Eugene McCarthy in the California primary race for the Democratic nomination for the Presidency. Kennedy aides wrested away the assassin's gun and captured him. Doctors undertook a three-hour operation to save Kennedy's life, but in the early morning of June 6, a little more than twenty-five hours after he had been wounded, he died at the age of forty-two.

The assassin, a Jordanese immigrant, Sirhan Bishara Sirhan, was immediately indicted for first degree murder. At his trial his lawyers tried to plead temporary insanity, but he repeatedly demurred, asserting that he had committed a political murder to retaliate for Kennedy's sympathy with Israel, and in particular for Kennedy's promise that he would send jets to Israel if elected. After a long trial, Sirhan was convicted of first degree murder, and the jury recommended the death penalty.

This transcript of a recording made by Andrew West, a Mutual Broadcasting System correspondent who had just interviewed Kennedy, is reprinted in Francine Klagsbrun and David C. Whitney: *Assassination: Robert F. Kennedy, 1925–68* (1968). See Jules Witcover: *85 Days: The Last Campaign of Robert Kennedy* (1969).

Seconds before Senator Kennedy was shot, Mutual Broadcasting System correspondent Andrew West interviewed him amidst his jubilant supporters. As the interview ended, West followed Kennedy through a hallway into the hotel kitchen. There he turned his tape recorder back on just as crowds began to scream that Kennedy had been shot. In a highly emotional voice, West continued to report and describe the scene. At the same time he shouted directions to bystanders, ordering them to disarm the assailant and to shut the doors to the kitchen. Here is the text of the tape that was later broadcast, copyrighted by station KRKD and the Mutual Broadcasting System:

"Senator Kennedy has been shot . . . Senator Kennedy has been shot . . . is that possible, is that possible? It is possible, ladies and gentlemen. It is possible. He has. Not only Senator Kennedy . . . Oh, my God . . . Senator Kennedy has been shot and another man . . . a Kennedy campaign manager . . . and possibly shot in the head. I am right here and Rafer Johnson has hold of the man who apparently has fired the shot. He has fired the shot . . . He still has the gun, the gun is pointed at me right this moment. I hope they can get the gun out of his hand. Be very careful. Get the gun . . . Get the gun . . . Get the gun . . . Stay away from the gun . . . Stay away from the gun

"His hand is frozen . . . Get his thumb . . . Get his thumb . . . Get his thumb . . . Get his thumb . . . Get his thumb. Take a hold of his thumb . . . and break if it you have to . . . Get his thumb. Get away from the barrel. Get away from the barrel, man. Look out for the gun. OK . . . all right. That's it Rafer, get it. Get the gun Rafer. OK now hold on to the gun. Hold on to him. Hold on to him.

"Ladies and gentlemen they have the gun away from the man. In this . . . they've got the gun. I can't see the man. I can't see who it is. Senator Kennedy right now is on the ground. He has been shot. This is a . . . this is . . . what is it? Wait a minute. Hold him . . . hold him . . . Hold him. We don't want another Oswald. Hold him, Rafer. Keep people away from him. Keep people away from him. All right, ladies and gentlemen. This is a . . . make room, make room, make room, make room. make room. The Senator is on the ground. He's bleeding profusely . . . from apparently . . . clear back . . . apparently the Senator has been shot from the frontal area. We can't see exactly where the Senator has been shot. But come on, push back, grab a hold of me, grab hold of me and let's pull back. That's it. Come on. Get hold of my arms. Let's pull back. Let's pull back. All right. They . . . the Senator is now . . . the ambulance has been called for and the ambulance is bringing the ambulance in this entrance. And this is a terrible thing. It's reminiscent of the valley the other day when the Senator was out there and somebody hit him in the head with a rock. And people couldn't believe it at that time. But it is a fact.

"Keep room. Ethel Kennedy is standing by. She is calm. She's raising her hand high to motion people back. She is attempting to get calm. A woman with a tremendous amount of presence. A tremendous amount of presence. It's impossible to believe. It's impossible to believe. There's a certain amount of fanaticism here now . . . as this has occurred no one . . . we're trying to run everybody back. Clear the area. Clear the area. Right at this moment . . . the Senator apparently . . . we can't see if he is still conscious or not. Can you see if he is conscious?"

Observer—"What?"

West—"I don't know . . . no, no . . . he is half conscious."

West—"He is half conscious, and ladies, we can't see . . . ladies and gentlemen . . . one of the men, apparently a Kennedy supporter, is going berserk. Come on . . . come on . . . out, out, out. Is there some way to close these doors, Jess? Is there any doors here? Out through the . . . out through the exit . . . let's go. Out we go . . . unbelievable situation. They're clearing the halls.

"One man has blood on himself. We're walking down the corridors here. Repetition in my speech . . . I have no alternative. The shock is so great. My mouth is dry. I can only say that here in the kitchen of the Ambassador Hotel . . . the back entrance . . . from the podium . . . in the Press Room. The Senator walked out the back. I was directly behind him. You heard a balloon go off and a shot. You didn't really realize that the shot was a shot. Screams went up . . . Two men were on the ground . . . both bleeding profusely. One of them was Senator Robert Kennedy. At this moment, we are stunned. We are shaking as is everyone else. In this kitchen corridor at the Ambassador Hotel in Los Angeles . . . they're blocking off the entrance now. Supposedly to make room for the ambulance. That's all we can report at this moment. I do not know if the Senator is dead or if he is alive. We do not know the name of the gentleman concerned. This is Andrew West, Mutual News, Los Angeles."

PART VIII

Violence in the Name of Law, Order, and Morality

Doctors' Riot
1788

Before dissection was legalized, medical schools had to find subjects for anatomy courses by robbing graves, a practice popularly known as "body snatching" or "resurrection." In the nineteenth century, medical schools would at times resort to professional grave robbers, but at first the students themselves pillaged cemetaries. The first riot protesting such activities came in 1765 when the carriage and house of Dr. William Shippen of Philadelphia were attacked by an angry mob. Riots continued into the next century. In 1807, a newly founded Baltimore medical college was demolished, and had to be abandoned for seven years. In 1839 a mob forced the closing of a college in Worthington, Ohio. In 1849 another attacked the anatomy professor of Franklin Medical College in St. Charles, Illinois, and killed him and one of his students. Probably the bloodiest "resurrection riot" took place in New York City, in April, 1788. Some boys observed a limb imprudently hung up to dry in a hospital window. A crowd formed, entered the hospital, and destroyed part of it; some additional corpses discovered by the crowd were buried that evening. So much feeling was aroused against the doctors that they had to be protected by being lodged in the jail. The next day mobs searched the physicians' houses, trying to find the doctors. The militia was called out to defend the jail. In the several determined assaults made by the mob on the jail, four persons were killed and several wounded.

The following account is a reminiscence by an eye witness, William A. Duer: *New York as it was during the Latter Part*

of the Last Century (1849). See also James J. Walsh: *History
of Medicine in New York* (1919), II, 378–92; and L. F. Edwards:
"Resurrection Riots during the Heroic Age of Anatomy in
America," *Bulletin of the History of Medicine*, XXV (March-
April 1951), 174–84.

The public occurrence that made the earliest, if not the deepest impression
upon my memory was the famous "*Doctors' Mob;*" so called, not because
the members of that grave faculty were *actors*, but because they were
sufferers in that outbreak. It was, indeed, provoked by the reckless and
wanton imprudence of some young surgeons at the Hospital, who from one
of its upper windows exhibited the dissected arm of a *subject* to some boys
who were at play on the green below. One of them, whose curiosity was
thus excited, mounted upon a ladder used for some repairs, and as he
reached the window, was told by one of the doctors to look *at his mother's
arm*. It happened unfortunately that the boy's mother had recently died,
and the horror which had now taken the place of his curiosity, induced him
to run to his father, who was at work as a mason, at a building in Broadway, with the information of what he had seen and heard. Upon receiving
the intelligence, the father repaired to his wife's grave, and upon opening
it, found that the body had been removed. He returned forthwith to the
place where he had been at work, and informed his fellow-laborers of
the circumstances; their indignation and horror at the relation were nearly
equal to his own. Armed with the tools of their trade, they marched in a
body to the Hospital, gathering recruits by the way in number amounting
to a formidable mob. The doctors in the meantime had taken the alarm,
and decamped. The theatre of their operations, however, was ransacked,
and several *subjects*, in various states of mutilation, were discovered.
Driven to frenzy by the spectacle, the mob issued forth in pursuit of the
doctors, who, had they fallen into the hands of the enraged multitude,
would speedily have been made *subjects* of themselves. They had the good
fortune, however, to elude the search, though some of them escaped by the
breadth of a hair. They took refuge in the gaol, and the militia were
ordered out to protect them, and quell the riot. This was not effected
without a specimen of civil war in the streets, which had the mob been
acquainted with the modern art of constructing barricades, might have
proved more serious and of longer continuance. As it was, it lasted for
three or four days, during which the city may be said to have been in a
state of siege. Never shall I forget the charge I saw made upon a body of

the rioters by Stakes's light-horse. From our residence opposite St. Paul's, I first perceived the troop as it debouched from Fair, now Fulton Street, and attacked the masses collected at the entrance of the "fields," whence they were soon scattered, some of them retreating into the church-yard, —driven sword in hand through the portico, by the troopers striking right and left with the backs of their sabres. The rioters had received a temporary check, but were by no means subdued. Apprised of the retreat of the doctors, they rallied and advanced to attack the gaol; but the militia arrived there before them, and were drawn up to defend it, with loaded muskets and fixed bayonets. The Governor, the Mayor, the Recorder, and other city magistrates, were also on the ground, with many of the principal citizens, who repaired to the assistance of the civil authority. Some of them were severely wounded by missiles from the mob. Mr. Jay received a serious wound in the head. The Baron de Steuben was struck by a stone which knocked him down, inflicted a flesh wound upon his forehead, and wrought a sudden change in the compassionate feelings he had previously entertained towards the mob. At the moment of receiving it, he was earnestly remonstrating with the Governor against ordering the militia to fire on the people; but, as soon as he was struck, the Baron's benevolence deserted him, and as he fell he lustily cries out, *"fire! Governor, fire!"*

Portland Whorehouse Riot

1825

Americans have sometimes denounced and always patronized prostitutes; on some occasions they have rioted against them. Throughout the eighteenth and nineteenth centuries the whorehouse riot was a common occurrence. One of the first took place in Boston in 1737, when crowds demolished several houses.

New York City was the scene of one bloody battle between would-be smiters of evil and the defenders of a whorehouse, in which several were wounded in 1793, and another battle in 1799. In Boston over 2,000 rioters tore down houses of prostitution in 1825 and beat up officers who tried to intervene. There were assaults in Lenox, Pennsylvania, in 1829, in St. Louis, Missouri, in 1831, and in Troy, New York, in 1850. In Chicago in 1857, elite volunteer companies led by Mayor John Wentworth burnt down a whole district, and in the same year half a dozen houses were destroyed in Detroit. In 1825 there were three successive riots in Portland, Maine; after each, the ladies relocated and recommenced business—perhaps, since the town was so small, with some of the very people who had lately demolished their houses. On the third occasion the ladies were defended. A gunfight took place in which one man was killed and several wounded.

The following account is taken from the Portland *Eastern Argus*, November 11, 1825.

We are again called upon to record the proceedings of a disgraceful riot, making the third which has occurred in this town, in the space of little more than a year, and the last of a more atrocious and aggravated character than either of the former, inasmuch as deadly weapons were used and life taken. If these affairs are suffered to go on at this rate, Portland will soon receive and *deserve* the name of mob-town. It is high time something effectual was done to put a stop to occurrences of this kind. If we have laws sufficient to preserve order in the community, let them be enforced; if we have not, let application be made to the Legislature for the enactment of laws of a more severe and efficacious nature. We have generally been in the habit of considering the standard of public morals in this town as high and tense as in any of our seaport towns, and are at a loss to account for the repetition of scenes which indicate a want of moral energy in the community, and which are universally condemned, though not prevented. . . . *Every* good citizen should make it his business, and be willing to raise his voice and his hand against these enormous outrages upon the peace and security of society. It is said most of the offenders in this last riot were foreigners, principally Irishmen. Be it so, it does not remove the stain from the reputation of the town; public peace has been outraged, no matter by whom. . . .

These outrageous riots and highanded breaches of the peace have grown out of a well-meant, but ill advised step of some individuals about a year ago to do what they no doubt thought a good deed. There was . . . a nest of little, mean, filthy boxes, of that description commonly called houses of ill-fame, tenanted by the most loathsome and vicious of the human species, and made a common resort for drunken sailors and the lowest off-scouring of society. These buildings in the heart of the town were an *eye-sore* to the neighborhood, and even the owners of some of the buildings wished them torn away. . . . Instead of taking the proper steps of the law to abate these nuisances, a company of laboring people, truckmen, boys &c. understanding the feelings of the owners and the wishes of the neighbors, assembled in the evening, turned out the tenants and tore the buildings to the ground, while some hundreds of citizens stood looking on and sanctioning the whole proceeding by their presence and their silence. The operators in this transaction becoming a little warm and excited, grew over zealous in the good work and repaired to other parts of the town and demolished other buildings of a like character. The affair passed off and but little was said or done about it. But the example was left to work its effect upon the minds of lower classes of people, the idle, the mischievous, and the vicious, and having learnt their lesson they began last spring to put it in practice. It was a kind of sport that had peculiar attractions for idle roaring boys and raw Irishmen; and the watchword being past, a throng assembled one night and tore several more houses of ill-fame, *all for public good*, mind ye; till coming to a long 2 story house in Crabtree's wharf, which contained several families, and which proved so firmly built that they were unable to pull it down, and in their zeal for serving the public they set it on fire, and the whole town was alarmed in the dead of night by the ringing of bells and the cry of fire. It was now thought to be rather a serious matter and the feelings of the citizens were very much excited. The selectmen called a town meeting, and a committee was appointed to investigate the subject and to commence legal prosecutions. Accordingly several were arrested, examined, and bound over for trial. One black man, not being able to procure bonds, was committed to jail for a few months until the Common Pleas was in session. All of them were finally discharged without any penalty, and it was thought, the law had shown its *teeth* at the rioters, they would be deterred from a repetition of their offenses.

But time has proved the opinion fallacious. . . . On Saturday night last, the *reformers* attacked a two story house on Fore Street occupied by a colored barber by the name of Gray. Gray had been convicted at the Common Pleas Court of keeping a house of ill-fame, and had appealed to the Supreme Court which is now in session, and in which he has also been convicted the present week. But the mob chose to render more speedy justice than the laws would do and accordingly on Saturday night they threw a few rocks into Gray's house, broke the windows, &c., but either from the want of sufficient forces or from meeting more resistance than they expected, they desisted till Monday evening, when they renewed their attack with increased force. In the meantime Gray had armed himself with guns and other weapons. He and his family, with some others remained in the house. In the course of the assault, the mob fired guns into the house, and guns were fired from the house upon the mob. Which fired first we are not informed. One man in the street, an Englishman by the name of Joseph Fuller, was killed almost instantly and six or eight others were wounded, some severely. After this the crowd soon dispersed. We examined the house on Tuesday morning, and found the windows mostly stove in, rocks scattered about the floors and lead shot in the plastering opposite the windows.

Vicksburg Gamblers
1835

During the 1830's the Mississippi River towns were plagued by gamblers, who sometimes branched out into robbery and murder, often in an organized and systematic fashion. The gambling dens and saloons were a constant irritation to the increasing numbers of respectable people who were moving to the towns. In 1835, five gamblers were murdered by a vigilante mob in Vicksburg, and an anti-gambling crusade swept the Mississippi Valley. By legal or illegal means the faro dealers and their kind were banished from New Orleans, Clinton, Natchez, Louisville, Cincinnati, and Chicago.

This account of the Vicksburg murders, "prepared by a wit-

ness of the acts detailed," was printed in the Vicksburg *Register*,
July 9, and reprinted in the Mobile *Commercial Register*, July
10, 1835.

For years past, professional gamblers, destitute of all sense of moral obli-
gations . . . have made Vicksburg their place of rendezvous—and, in the
very bosom of our society, boldly plotted their vile and lawless machin-
ations. . . .

Our streets everywhere resounded with the echoes of their drunken
and obscene mirth, and no citizen was secure from their villainy. Frequently in armed bodies, they have disturbed the good order of public
assemblages, insulted our citizens, and defied our civil authorities. Thus
had they continued to grow bolder in their wickedness, and more formidable in their numbers, until Saturday, the fourth of July, instant,
when our citizens had assembled together with a corps of Vicksburg
volunteers, at the barbecue to celebrate the day by the usual festivities.
After dinner, and during the delivery of the toasts, one of the officers
attempted to enforce order and silence at the table, when one of these
gamblers, whose name is Cakler, who had impudently thrust himself into
the company, insulted the officer, and struck one of the citizens. Indignation immediately rose high, and it was only by the interference of the
commandant that he was saved from instantaneous punishment. He was,
however, permitted to retire, and the company dispersed.

The military corps proceeded to the public square of the city, and
information was received that Cakler was coming up armed, and resolved
to kill one of the volunteers who had been most active in expelling him
from the table. Knowing his desperate character—two of the corps instantly stepped forward and arrested him. A loaded pistol, a large knife
and a dagger were found on his person, all of which he had procured since
he had separated from the company. To liberate him would have been to
devote several of the most respectable members of the company to his
vengeance, and to proceed against him at law would have been mere
mockery, inasmuch as, not having had the opportunity of consumating
his design, no adequate punishment could have been inflicted on him. Consequently it was determined to take him into the woods and *Lynch* him
—which is a mode of punishment provided for such as become obnoxious
in a manner which the law cannot reach. He was immediately carried
out under a guard, attended by a crowd of respectable citizens—tied to
a tree, punished with stripes—tarred and feathered; and ordered to leave
the city in forty-eight hours. . . .

Having thus aggravated the whole band of these desperados, and feeling no security against their vengeance, the citizens met at night in the court house, in a large number, and there passed the following resolutions:

Resolved, That a notice be given to all professional gamblers, that the citizens of Vicksburg are *resolved* to exclude them from this place and its vicinity; and that twenty-four hours notice be given them to leave the place. . . .

On Sunday morning, one of these notices was posted at the corners of each square of the city. During that day (the 5th instant) a majority of the gang, terrified by the threats of the citizens, dispersed in different directions, without making any opposition. It was sincerely hoped that the remainder would follow their example, and thus prevent a bloody termination of the strife which had commenced. On the morning of the 6th, the military corps, followed by a file of several hundred citizens, marched to each suspected house, and, sending in an examining committee, dragged out every faro table and other gambling apparatus that could be found. At length they approached a house which was occupied by one of the most profligate of the gang, whose name was North, and in which it was understood that a garrison of armed men had been stationed. All hoped that these wretches would be intimidated by the superior numbers of their assailants, and surrender themselves at discretion, rather than attempt a desperate defense. The house being surrounded, the back door was first opened, when four or five shots were fired from the interior, one of which instantly killed Dr. Hugh S. Bodley, a citizen universally loved and respected. The interior was so dark that the villains could not be seen; but several of the citizens, guided by the flash of their guns, returned their fire. A yell from one of the party announced that one of these shots had been effectual; and by this time a crowd of citizens, their indignation overcoming all other feelings, burst open every door of the building, and dragged into the light those who had not been wounded.

North, the ringleader, who had contrived this desperate plot, could not be found in the building, but was apprehended by a citizen, while attempting, in company with another, to make his escape at a place not far distant. Himself, with the rest of the prisoners, were then conducted in silence to the scaffold. One of them, not having been in the building before it was attacked, nor appearing to be concerned with the rest, except that he was the brother of one of them, was liberated. The remaining number of five, among whom was the individual who had been shot, but who still lived, were immediately executed in presence of the assembled multitude. All sympathy for the wretches was completely merged in the detestation and horror of their crime. The whole procession then returned to the city, collected all the faro tables into a pile and burnt them. . . .

[The] bodies were cut down on the morning after execution, and buried in a ditch.

Astor Place Riot
1849

Theater riots, common in the first half of the nineteenth century, expressed a mixture of xenophobia, ethnic rivalries, and class antagonism. Political animosities left over from the Revolution and the War of 1812 fed attacks on British actors, as in that made against Edmund Keane in 1821. In addition, British actors symbolized aristocracy to the mass of American playgoers. Irish audiences had their own political and ethnic reasons for hating the British. All these animosities came to a dramatic focus in the Astor Place Riot in New York City, May 10, 1849. William C. Macready, a British actor, publicly expressed his contempt for most American audiences. His leading rival in the theater was Edwin Forrest, a passionate American patriot and an equally passionate democrat. When Macready played at New York's Astor Place Theater to the applause of polite society, Forrest played to a working class audience at the "democratic" Bowery Theater. In London, Forrest was hissed by "groaners" hired by Macready, while in Edinburgh Macready was hissed by Forrest himself. Their fulminations against each other were the delight of theatergoers. When Macready went on an American tour in 1848 Forrest too went on tour, and the two crisscrossed the country trading insults, until their paths met in New York City. On Monday night, May 7, 1849, Macready opened in *Macbeth* at Astor Place. The working class of the city, who were organized in various clubs or gangs—particularly the Irish or the Bowery B'hoys—turned up *en masse*. Screaming "huzzah for native talent," and "three groans for the English bulldog," and heaving rotten eggs, potatoes, and chairs, they closed down the performance. The enraged Macready was about to leave for England when a group of prominent citizens asked him to stay and give a repeat performance, guaranteeing that order would be maintained. Macready agreed. To many in the city, this animated various grievances against the local elite as well as the English. The city gangs distributed notices and placards calling their supporters to the "English Aristocratic Opera House," and urging them to "burn the damned den of the Aristocracy." The theater refused to sell tickets to un-kempt applicants. When the curtain rose, some anti-Macready men who had slipped in started yelling, but were quickly ar-rested. After a short time, an immense crowd of perhaps 10,000–15,000 which had gathered outside, began hurling rocks and smashing windows, but Macready continued amidst the din. The militia was then summoned, but was stoned by the crowd. Militiamen first fired in the air, but as stones continued to be thrown, fired directly into the crowd four times until it broke ranks and scattered. Thirty-one people were killed and more than one hundred wounded.

At a rally the following day speakers denounced the "aris-tocracy of the city" for the shooting and asserted that "law and order become a curse when they bring death and desolation into families." But the crowd had had enough, and dispersed in relative peace. Class antagonisms, however, could no longer be ignored. The Philadelphia *Public Ledger* noted that "There is now in our country, in New York City, what every good patriot hitherto has considered it his duty to deny—a *high* and a *low* class."

The following account is taken from the New York *Herald*, May 11, 1849, as reprinted in a pamphlet entitled *A Rejoinder to 'Replies from England' . . . Together with an Impartial His-tory and Review of the Lamentable Occurrences at the Astor Place Opera House . . .* (1849). See Richard Moody: *The Astor Place Riot* (1958); Herbert Asbury: *The Gangs of New York* (1927); Joel Tyler Headley: *The Great Riots of New York* (1873); and Douglas T. Miller: *Jacksonian Aristocracy* (1967).

The house itself was filled to the dome. A great portion of the assemblage in the theatre consisted of policemen, who had been distributed all over the house in detached parties. There was not any appearance of an organized party of rioters in the house. When the curtain rose, there was an outburst of hisses, groans, cheers, and miscellaneous sounds, similar to those which interrupted the performance on Monday night. The opening scenes, however, were got through with after a fashion, several persons who hissed and hooted having been siezed by the police, and immediately conveyed to an apartment underneath the boxes, where they were placed in confinement, under the charge of a posse of the police officers. Macready's appearance was the signal for a great explosion of feeling. Hisses, groans, shouts of derision assailed him, intermingled with loud cries of "Out with him!" "Out with him!" Large numbers of the auditory started to their feet, and called on the police to eject the individuals who had expressed their disapprobation, and several arrests were made in the manner we have described, each arrest being followed by loud cheers and applause all over the house. It was speedily apparent that those unfriendly to Mr. Macready were in the minority.

Thus the play proceeded through the first two acts. There had been a great deal of trepidation behind the scenes, but the heroism with which the actors and actresses sustained themselves on the stage is worthy of all praise. The manner of Mrs. Pope, the Lady Macbeth of this melancholy night, deserves the most honorable mention. It was, indeed, a trying scene. Mr. Macready repeatedly expressed to Mr. Hackett his wish to desist, and his desire to avoid any further collision with those who were opposed to his appearance; but, amid the shouts, groans, hisses and arrests by the police, the play, as we have said, went on much of it in dumb show, but portions of it without much interruption. It was supposed, at this moment, that the tumult would be effectually quelled, for the disturbance in the house became less and less, and even some passages of Mr. Macready's part were heard, with a tolerable degree of order. . . .

At this moment a shower of stones assailed the windows of the theatre. News then came in from the street through Captain Tilley, of the 13th ward, that a man known to be Edward Z. C. Judson, was heading the mob outside, and calling upon them to stone the building. The Chief of Police immediately ordered his arrest, which was promptly effected. In the meantime the assault upon the doors and windows was continued. Volley after volley of large paving stones were discharged against the windows. The glass was, of course, in a few moments, all smashed to atoms; but having been barricaded, the windows resisted the attack for some minutes; at last yielding however, the fragments of glass, and blinds, and barricades being driven with violence into the body of the house, great alarm began to pervade the audience. Rumors of all kinds—that the house would be fired—that it was to be blown up, and so on, were circulated. The ladies, seven in number, who were present, and who, with a heroism that did infinite credit to their sex, had till this moment preserved their equanimity, now became alarmed, as well they might, and shifted their seats to the part of the house not in the range of any of the windows through which the stones and fragments of glass and wood were now flying.

At this time, the scene within the house was indeed most exciting. In front and rear the fierce assaults of the mob, as they thundered at the doors, resounded all over the theatre, whilst the shouts and yells of the assailants were terrific. . . .

As the mob increased in magnitude and in the ferocity with which they assailed the building the cry arose inside, and also outside, among the peaceable citizens attracted by a curiosity, which in such a case was most culpable—"Where are the military?" "Can nothing be done to disperse the rioters?" "Where's the Mayor?" Several dispatches were sent to the City Hall, where the military were stationed. At length, about nine o'clock, the sound of a troop of cavalry coming up Broadway was heard; and in a few minutes afterwards, two troops of cavalry of the First Division of the State Militia, and a battalion of the National Guard were approaching the scene of the riot.

Appearance of the Military

A troop of horses then turned from Broadway in Astor Place, and rode through the crowd to the Bowery, receiving showers of stones and other missiles, on their way. The horses became unmanageable, and the troops did not again make its appearance on the ground. In a few minutes afterwards, the National Guard, one of our independent volunteer companies, made their appearance on the ground, and attempted to force a passage through the crowd to the theatre. The mob hissed and hooted at them, and finally attacked them with stones, which were at hand in consequence of the building of a sewer in the neighborhood. The company were at this period thrown into disorder by the attack made upon them, and retired to Broadway, where they rallied and made another attempt to reach the theatre. They were hissed and pelted as before, with stones, but they succeeded in reaching the desired point. They then endeavored to form in line on the side-walk, and while doing so, five or six of them were felled to the ground by paving stones and taken into the theatre in a state of insensibility. Captain Pond, the Captain of the company, was one of those thus injured.

The next officer in command then said to the Sheriff, who was on the ground, that if he did not get orders to fire, he and his men would abandon the streets. Accordingly that officer directed the company to fire a round over the heads of the people, which was accordingly done, but without effect. The people continued to pelt them with paving stones as before. An order was then given to the company to fire at the crowd, and it was done, two falling, one shot in the arm, and the other through the right cheek. The first was sent to the hospital, but the other was found to be dead. After the volley, the mob retreated a short distance, but rallied and renewed the attack with greater vigor than before. Paving stones and other missiles were discharged at them in great quantities; and while the mob was going on, another volley was fired by the military, killing and wounding several more, some of whom were taken by their friends to the drugstore on the corner of Ninth Street and Broadway. One young man named John McKinley, of no. 147 Third Avenue, was shot through the body, and taken to a public house in the neighborhood.

After this volley the crowd retreated again, and the military and the police took advantage of it to form a line across the street at both ends of Astor Place, so as to prevent any connection between Broadway and the Bowery. Major General Sandford then issued an order for more troops and two brass pieces loaded with grape to be brought to the scene immediately, as it was rumored that the crowd intended to arm themselves and renew the attack. It was at this time half past eleven o'clock and the additional troops consisting of several companies and the artillery, reached the scene of disorder. The cannon loaded with grape were replaced in front of the theatre, ready in case of a renewal of the attack.

San Francisco Vigilance Committee
1856

The mining camps that sprang up during the gold rush of 1849 in California were plagued by thieves. To deal with thievery in the absence of courts, the miners formed extra-legal bodies which carried out their own sentences by summary whipping, banishment, or hanging. The booming city of San Francisco was particularly plagued with criminals. One group known as the Hounds harassed the city in 1849, and in 1850 the Sydney Coves robbed and killed almost at will: over 100 persons were killed in a few months. Witnesses were intimidated and convictions were rare. In 1851, prominent men organized a Committee of Vigilance, established a constitution, and issued warnings to criminals. They banished some and hung others. They checked incoming boats to examine passengers and deport convicts. Having done their appointed task effectively they dissolved in 1853.

The Committee was reborn in 1856, in part because of a high crime rate and several particularly flagrant murders. In November 1855 a gambler, Charles Cora, shot William Richardson, a United States Marshal. Many called for a lynching, but the majority of the city preferred to let the law handle Cora. When he was tried in January, 1856, a fixed jury heard several perjured witnesses, and the jury would come to no decision. The trial was heatedly denounced in the *Bulletin*, edited by James King. On May 14, King was shot by James P. Casey, a city supervisor. A group of citizens called for the formation of a Committee of Vigilance and within two days 5,500 had been enrolled. The vigilantes marched to the jail with a cannon in tow, removed Cora and Casey, tried them, and then hung them. The committee deported many whom they considered criminals, and hung two more murderers. In August, after 6,000 members marched in a triumphal parade, the Committee virtually ceased to exist.

Besides its desire to fight crime, the Committee of Vigilance of 1856 was moved by the hope of wresting control of the city from the dominant Irish Catholic Democratic machine. The bulk of the members were middle- and upper-class Protestants, old-line Whigs and Know-Nothings, and were predominantly Northerners. Their hero, James King, was an anti-Catholic editor, and most victims of vigilantism were Catholics. They were opposed by the Democrats under David C. Broderick and by the Law and Order party which drew its strength from the Southern-oriented wing of the Democrats.

The following account of the Committee's activities by a resident of San Francisco, Minor King, is a letter written August 2, 1856: "The San Francisco Committee of Vigilance of 1856: An Estimate of A Private Citizen," Historical Society of Southern California *Quarterly*, XXXI (1949), 292–5. See Richard Maxwell Brown: "Pivot of American Vigilantism: The San Francisco Vigilance Committee of 1856," in John A. Carroll, ed.: *Reflections of Western Historians* (1969); Wayne Gard: *Frontier Justice* (1949); Hubert Howe Bancroft: *Popular Tribunals* (1887); and Mary Floyd Williams: *History of the San Francisco Committee of Vigilance of 1851: A Study of Social Control on the California Frontier in the Days of the Gold Rush* (1921).

. . . you have no doubt ere this heard of the very exciting times we have had in this city for the last two months, the fact is San Francisco is undergoing a purification, and is now in a measure regulated; the work is still going on but when the end will be no one can tell—For a long time the city has ben under the control of the vilest of creation, desperados of every caste, the gambler, the thief, the murderer and assassin have been our rulers, from the judge on the bench to the smallest police officer. All have pandered to their influence and obtained their positions through it—A good citizen has stood no chance whatever he has not dared to speak his sentiments, lest some shoulder striker at his elbow should check him with pistol or knife—but a change has taken place, retribution has come upon them at last, and thus far it has ben fearful—

The last feather that broke the camel's back was added when James King of Wm. was shot down in broad daylight in the open street. King was the Editor of the Evening Bulletin and in his paper had ben most fearless and energetic in denouncing these scoundrels; his assassin was J. P. Casey a man who from '49 to '51 was a convict in Sing Sing Prison, N.Y.; immediately after his release, he came to this country, where it did not take him long to obtain a controling influence among his class. It is said he had amassed quite a fortune and has never ben known to do an honest days work since he came here.

As soon as he had committed the awful deed he was hurried off to jail by several policemen who seemed to (be) convinetly by and who it is believed were prievously aware of his intentions—Soon the citizens began to assemble in the vicinity of the jail, such an intensly exciting crowd was never seen before, some urging an immediate attack on the jail, and some demanding the prisoner (be) brought forth and delivered to the people, some counselling one thing and some another. In the meantime the Sheriff (himself a noted Irish gambler) had organized a strong force of gamblers and shoulder strikers within the jail, and had called on the military companies to assist him in securing the prisnor against harm. After a while the people or at least the great mass of them left the ground, leaving a strong gard to watch the jail lest the Sherriff should take him out and secrete him in some other place; this was on Wednesday Evening, on the next morning the honest citizens began to organize a Vigilence Committee. After Enrolling about 3,000 Men and fully equipping them (which took them three days) they marched up to the jail surrounded the same planted a nine pounder cannon in front of the main door, loaded the same with double shot, then demanded the prisner Casey the murderer of King and the Prisner Cora the murderer of Gen Richardson the United States Marshall of this District; the murder was committed last November; the prisner was tried, but the jury failed to agree & he was in jail awaiting another trial, which we all knew would be but a mere farce, for Cora was one of the first gamblers in the place. I will here state there has (been) 76 cold blooded murders committed in this city within the last two years and only one man executed, and he the poor dog had no money or he too would have gone clear. After a short consultation the Sheriff thought it wise to bring out the prisoners, they were taken to the committee rooms had a fair trial, they were both convicted and executed, these procedings so enraged the gamblers they called on the Gov. for help, who by the by is a miserable apology for a Governor; he orders out the military of the whole state to put down the good citizens of San Francisco; the call was disregarded by all good respectable people, and was only obey'd by *Gamblers, Murderers*, some *Lawyers, Judges* and *Thieves* of every grade; they assembled in this city and hired rooms in different parts of the town where they met for drill, the Gov. sending them arms and ammunition to shoot down the best citizens of the place; the Law and Murder Party now amounted to about 500 all told and now quite sure they were able to put down the Mob as they were pleased to call it—but the Peoples Committee have not ben idle, they having forti- fied their rooms and increased their numbers to 6,000 good able bodied men well armed, they pay'd no attention to the Govs. troops, but were pushing on the good work of purification, by arresting some of the worst characters in town, such as ballot box stuffers and robbers, thieves, and shoulder strikers, and confining them in their rooms and giving them a trial, and if found guilty banish them out of Country. One of our Supreme Court judges by the name of David S. Terry came down from the Capital (Sacramento) and joined himself to the Law and Murder Party armed with double barrel gun revolver and Bowie Knife; thus equipt he paraded our street to protect his brother gambler; while one of the Vigilence Police by the name of Hopkins was about to arrest one of the worst scoundrels in Town by the name of Malony, Judge Terry presented his gun to Hopkins breast, "Hopkins" says Judge "I have nothing to do with you" at the same time caught the gun by the muzzle and jerkd it out of his hands; the rowdy Judge now draws his knife and plunges it into Hopkins' neck and left him for dead, and fled to one of the armories of the Murder Party for protection; the alarm was given at the Vigilants' rooms, the bell rung, and in less than 15 minutes 5,000 infantry, 200 calvalry all well armed with guns & bayonetts, cutlasses and four pieces brass cannon were surrounding the different armories of the murderers. I assure you it was not long before his judgeship and compatriots in arms were on their way to the committees rooms, after the vigilants had sur- rounded the buildings in which the govs. troops were or at least a por- tion of them they were ordered to surrender and were given 5 minutes to do it in. I tell you there was no use parlying; the different garrisons surrendered and lay down their arms without firing a shot—the people triumphed, victory perched upon their banner, and the result was that the vigilants took 150 prisners, 500 rifles and muskets, about 100 cutlasses, one Gen., two Majors, and a Supreme Court judge.

. . . Since the surrender of Governor Johnsons' troops the Committee have had things their own way, and for the first time in this city for three years past have I felt that there was any safety for person or property. Ladies can now walk the streets with their husbands without the fear of being insulted by a gang of loaffers at every corner of the streets; the Committee have hung four, the notorious Yankey Sulivan committed sui- cide in his cell, they have banished 20 or more and have frightened more than one hundred from the city. Consequently the gambling houses are shut up and forsaken and a degree of quietness reigns throughout the entire city.

Montana Vigilantes
1863–1865

In the 1860's the towns of Bannack and Virginia City, Montana, on the eastern slope of the Rocky Mountains were rugged frontier communities. Hundreds of miners worked the nearby gold fields, and many outlaws preyed upon them with little hindrance from the law. On May 24, 1863, the citizens of Bannack met together and elected town officials. Most of those elected were respectable men; but the newly chosen sheriff, Henry Plummer, a recent arrival, was secretly the leader of a network of highwaymen, horsethieves, and murderers. A hundred or more of his "road agents" terrorized travelers and miners, and his spies were everywhere.

Plummer's first act was to deputize three of his toughest bandits. This aroused some suspicion; and slowly, as a reign of robberies and murders proceeded unchecked, the people of the community began to realize what sort of man Plummer was. In late November 1863, George Ives, Plummer's chief lieutenant, went on a rampage, killed several men, and was hanged by a group of citizens from Nevada City. This spurred the organization of vigilante groups in surrounding towns, who began to round up criminals. Some of their captives confessed, implicating Plummer among others. Hangings went on throughout the winter, and on January 10, 1864, the vigilantes caught up with Plummer. In all, over thirty criminals were caught and hung.

The vigilante organizations acted openly, electing officers, keeping records, holding trials, making their forays in daylight and without masks. Many people defended their behavior vigorously. The Montana *Post* declared: "Upon general principle the majority of a community can be justified in taking the law into their own hands. . . . Our vigilance committee is not a mob. Until justice can be reached through the ordinary channels, our citizens will be fully protected against these evil desperadoes, even if the sun of every morning should rise upon the morbid picture of a malefactor dangling in the air."

The following account of the capture and execution of Plummer is from Thomas J. Dimsdale: *The Vigilantes of Montana or Popular Justice in the Rocky Mountains* . . . (1866), 147–50. Dimsdale was an Englishman who opened a private school in Virginia City and in 1864 was appointed Superintendent of Public Instruction. He ran a series of articles on vigilantes in the Montana *Post* which he later collected and published in this volume. On vigilante movements, see Richard M. Brown: "The American Vigilante Tradition," in *Violence in America, Historical and Comparative Perspectives*, A Report to the National Committee on the Causes and Prevention of Violence (1969), 144–218.

At dusk, three horses were brought into town, belonging severally and respectively to the three marauders so often mentioned, Plummer, Stinson, and Ray. It was truly conjectured that they had determined to leave the country, and it was at once settled that they should be arrested that night. Parties were detailed for the work. Those entrusted with the duty performed it admirably. Plummer was undressing when taken at his house. His pistol (a self-cocking weapon) was broken and useless. Had he been armed, resistance would have been futile; for he was seized the moment the door was opened in answer to the knocking from without. Stinson was arrested at Toland's, where he was spending the evening. He would willingly have done a little firing, but his captors were too quick for him. Ray was lying on a gambling table when seized. The three details marched their men to a given point, en route to the gallows. Here a halt was made. The leader of the Vigilantes and some others, who wished to save all unnecessary hard feeling, were sitting in a cabin, designing not to speak to Plummer, with whom they were so well acquainted. A halt was made, however, and at the door appeared Plummer. The light was extinguished;

when the party moved on, but soon halted. The crisis had come. Seeing that the circumstances were such as admitted of neither vacillation nor delay, the citizen leader, summoning his friends, went up to the party and gave the military command, "Company! forward—march!" This was at once obeyed. A rope taken from a noted functionary's bed had been mislaid and could not be found. A nigger boy was sent off for some of that highly necessary but unpleasant remedy for crime and the bearer made such good time that some hundreds of feet of hempen necktie were on the ground before the arrival of the party at the gallows. On the road Plummer heard the voice and recognized the person of the leader. He came to him and begged for his life; but was told, "It is useless for you to beg for your life; that affair is settled and cannot be altered. You are to be hanged. You cannot feel harder about it than I do; but I cannot help it if I would." Ned Ray, clothed with curses as with a garment, actually tried fighting, but found that he was in the wrong company for such demonstrations; and Buck Stinson made the air ring with the blasphemous and filthy expletives which he used in addressing his captors. Plummer exhausted every argument and plea that his imagination could suggest, in order to induce his captors to spare his life. He begged to be chained down in the meanest cabin; offered to leave the country forever; wanted a jury trial; implored time to settle his affairs; asked to see his sister-in-law; and, falling on his knees, with tears and sighs declared to God that he was too wicked to die. He confessed his numerous murders and crimes, and seemed almost frantic at the prospect of death.

The first rope being thrown over the cross-beam, and the noose being rove, the order was given to "Bring up Ned Ray." This desperado was run up with curses on his lips. Being loosely pinioned, he got his fingers between the rope and his neck, and thus prolonged his misery.

Buck Stinson saw his comrade robber swinging in the death agony, and blubbered out, "There goes poor Ned Ray." Scant mercy had he shown to his numerous victims. By a sudden twist of his head at the moment of his elevation, the knot slipped under his chin, and he was some minutes dying.

The order to "Bring up Plummer" was then passed and repeated; but no one stirred. The leader went over to this "perfect gentleman," as his friends called him, and was met by a request to "Give a man time to pray." Well knowing that Plummer relied for a rescue upon other than Divine aid, he said briefly and decidedly, "Certainly; but let him say his prayers up here." Finding all efforts to avoid death were useless, Plummer rose and said no more prayers. Standing under the gallows which he had erected for the execution of Horan, this second Haman slipped off his necktie and threw it over his shoulder to a young friend who had boarded at his house, and who believed him innocent of crime, saying as he tossed it to him, "Here is something to remember me by." In the extremity of his grief, the young man threw himself weeping and wailing upon the ground. Plummer requested that the men would give him a good drop, which was done, as high as circumstances permitted, by hoisting him up as far as possible in their arms, and letting him fall suddenly. He died quickly and without much struggle.

It was necessary to seize Ned Ray's hand, and by a violent effort to draw his fingers from between the noose and his neck before he died. Probably he was the last to expire of the guilty trio.

The news of a man's being hanged flies faster than any other intelligence in a Western country, and several had gathered round the gallows on that fatal Sabbath evening—many of them friends of the road agents. The spectators were allowed to come up to a certain point, and were then halted by the guard, who refused permission either to depart or to approach nearer that the "dead line," on pain of their being instantly shot.

The weather was intensely cold, but the party stood for a long time round the bodies of the suspended malefactors, determined that rescue should be impossible.

Loud groans and cries uttered in the vicinity attracted their attention, and a small squad started in the direction from which the sound proceeded. The detachment soon met Madam Hall, a noted courtezan—the mistress of Ned Ray—who was "making the night hideous" with her doleful wailings. Being at once stopped, she began inquiring for her paramour, and was thus informed of his fate, "Well, if you must know, he is hung." A volcanic eruption of oaths and abuse was her reply to this information; but the men were on "short time," and escorted her towards her dwelling without superfluous display of courtesy. Having arrived at the brow of a short descent, at the foot of which stood her cabin, stern necessity compelled a rapid and final progress in that direction.

Soon after, the party formed and returned to town, leaving the corpses stiffening in the icy blast. The bodies were eventually cut down by the friends of the road agents and buried. The "Reign of Terror" in Bannack was over.

Cincinnati Riot
1884

On March 28, 1884, William Berner, a confessed murderer in Cincinnati, received a twenty-year sentence rather than the customary death penalty. "At the call of reputable citizens," 10,000 indignant persons held a mass meeting to denounce the "disgraceful verdict." Afterwards a crowd of several thousand streamed toward the jail, unaware that Berner had been spirited away to safety in the state penitentiary. At midnight they broke into the jail, but were fired on by the militia stationed within. The enraged crowd set the jail ablaze, but were dispersed by further fire from the militia and the police.

The next night a crowd assembled at the Courthouse and burned it down. Gunfire was exchanged with the militia and finally Gatling guns were turned on the crowd. A third night of rioting followed. At least fifty people were killed in the course of the three-day riot.

What gives this incident significance is the attitude taken toward the rioters by local leaders. When the purpose of the mob was to take justice into their own hands, prominent citizens seemed to approve, describing the rioters as "respectable laboring men" who "spared private property." But when the mob burned the courthouse and fought the militia, they were denounced as members of "the dangerous classes" among whom "there was much socialist talk." It was not until then that Cincinnati's Mayor called on a group of the "leading two hundred businessmen" and officers of the Grand Army of the Republic to put the riot down.

The following account of the second night's violence is from J. S. Tunison: *The Cincinnati Riot: Its Causes and Results* (Cincinnati, 1886).

The crowd had been dense all day, and it gathered numbers and confidence as dark fell. The barricades looked ugly, and the crowd gathered chiefly in front of the Court-house. The riot began with the throwing of bowlders and brick-bats at the Court-house, while some fired pistols and shot-guns at the windows. Gaining confidence, a storming party was formed, and the iron doors in the Court-house front were battered down in a few minutes. About the same time a crowd of boys began breaking in the County Treasurer's office, which was in the north-west corner of the basement. The idea of firing the Court-house began with this crowd of boys and half-grown men, who are said to have been led by men and boys from Kentucky. The furniture and broken counters were piled up in the middle of the room, and coal-oil was poured upon them. The match was applied, and a small flame shot forth. It leaped from one article to another, gathered head, and roared with increasing strength. The crowd cheered and yelled. One office after another was fired, and soon the flames were dancing in every apartment of the front basement. When the crowd reached South Court Street it rushed along the side of the Court-house, intending to fire the offices on that side. It was met by a volley of musketry which made it stagger and rush around the corner again. Soon after a white handkerchief tied to a stick was waved, and then a number of the rioters cautiously appeared and carried off the dead and wounded. In a few minutes afterward the sheriff's red auction flag, through which the crowd had been firing bullets, was waved and again the mob surged around the corner, emptying its fire-arms at the barricade. "Fire!" Another crash made every wall in the narrow street tremble, and the multitude rushed back, some reeling and falling, others tripping over them, then picking themselves up and continuing the flight. Again the white flag was waved. "Make way, gentlemen, make way for the wounded," called out several surgeons, whom a sense of professional duty had called to the scene. "Make way," and the crowd opened lanes through which was carried many a poor fellow who had rushed around the corner but a minute before. Soon the tables of the Debolt Exchange were covered with mangled bodies, some from which life had fled, others which were gasping with feeble and perishing breath. The surgeons busied themselves with these while the battle went on without. After this the militia kept up a dropping fire on the crowd whenever it showed itself, and continually the number of the wounded grew. The Debolt could not hold them all. Burdsal's drug-store, below Canal, and a saloon on Ninth Street were turned into temporary hospitals. This sort of skirmishing continued for hours, and amid it all the Court-house burned slowly. Slowly the flames crept from room to room through a building alleged to be fire-proof. Anon the flames pierced the roof, dense volumes of smoke roared through the ventilator over the rotunda, iron shutters bent in the heat, iron girders sprang from their seats on iron pillars with loud explosions, records which were eloquent with human joys and sorrows turned into bright flame and vanished, while passions as hot as the fire raged around the devoted pile. Nothing could be done to stay the flames—the mob would not allow it.

But another turning point had been reached, and the insulted majesty of law and order began to assert itself with greater force. Soldiers began to arrive from other parts of the State who a few hours before had been plying the peaceful arts of the citizen. First came the Fourth Regiment, but only to teach Dayton how little reliance she might place in her citizen-soldiery. Appalled by the hostility of the crowd, which would have made respectful room before a gleaming line of bayonets, this regiment halted within sight almost of the building, which was only beginning to burn then, and ingloriously returned to the depot from which it came. Captain Frank Brown, of Company A, after trying vainly to rally the command, returned with several members of his Dayton company to the lines the next day and did good service. The remainder of that company left for their homes in Dayton. Companies of the regiment from Springfield and other points retrieved their fame by assisting in quelling the following day, and some of the Daytonians were forced to return by the scorn of their wives and fellow-townsmen. But most of them would not risk their precious lives.

Not so the gallant Fourteenth, of Columbus. This regiment arrived at half-past ten, an hour after the Fourth, and marched from the Little Miami Depot to the scene of conflict. They were ordered to clear the street before the Court-house. Marching down South Court Street, they drove the crowd before them. Company A pushed the mob up Main Street. Companies B and F wheeled to the left upon the crowd in Court Street and found themselves engaged with the real rioters. At first the mob gave way; then sixteen or twenty rioters separated themselves from the mass, precipitated themselves through the first company, several falling dead in their tracks at the first volley, and were caught by the colored company, the Duffy Guard, and pushed aside.

Ten of their regiment were soon wounded under the fire of the mob, and the command devolved from one officer to another until the third who took command gave the order to fire. With the precision of veterans platoon after platoon delivered its fire. It was about midnight when the rapid succession of crashing volleys told that the tables had turned, and many an anxious citizen ejaculated his thanks, as he divined that the mob had met its master. The crowd rushed up Court Street. Every volley found its victims, and Kinzbach's drug-store, at the corner of Court and Walnut Streets, was soon filled with the dead and dying. The rush of fugitives into the store and the crashing of bullets through the windows imperiled the lives of the wounded and the surgeons, who were mostly devoting themselves to suffering humanity. It was too much for the mob. The Fourteenth held the ground it had captured, and the Gatling gun was brought up from its post near the jail to support the militia. Then the skirmishing continued. Occasionally some section of the mob, with reckless daring, sprang from behind a sheltering corner to fire on the troops. The troops returned the fire, not in volley, now, for the discharge of two or three guns was enough to disperse the crowd, and almost every such episode added to the list of the dead and wounded. Thus the night wore away, and with the gray dawn the firing gradually ceased.

Lynching at Memphis
1893

After Reconstruction, lynching became a primary means of upholding white supremacy in the South. Between 1882, when records were first kept, and 1927, 4,951 people were lynched by mobs. While most of the lynchings, particularly in the North and West were by summary hanging or shooting, many were of a more hideous nature. There were spectacles of sadism: in 1893 a crowd of 10,000 came to Paris, Texas, on special trains to watch the execution of a mentally–retarded black man who had killed a little girl—red-hot irons were thrust into his body, his eyes were burned out, hot pokers were shoved down his throat, and after nearly an hour of such torture he was set on fire. In 1899 at Palmetto, Georgia, excursion trains brought thousands on a Sunday afternoon to see a black man burned alive. His ears, toes, and fingers were first cut off and passed to the crowd; afterward his heart was cut out and slices were sold for souvenirs. In May 1911, a black charged with murder was taken to the local opera house in Livermore, Kentucky, and tied to a stake on stage. Tickets were sold for orchestra seats, which entitled men to empty their revolvers into the victim, and for gallery seats, good for one shot. In 1918 there was a five-day orgy of killing in Georgia, in which eight blacks died, one pregnant woman was slowly roasted alive, and her baby cut out and trampled. The alleged crimes so atrociously punished ranged from murder and rape to such offenses as striking or talking back to whites (two victims were "saucy" to white people), testifying against whites, making boastful remarks, and using offensive language.

Lynchings declined steadily after the 1890's. This decline has never been fully explained. Some have suggested the growing distaste of Southern elites for brutality, particularly Southern women and businessmen; others invoke the increasing urbanization of the South and increasingly effective protest and publicity by the National Association for the Advancement of Colored People. Further, statewide police systems were developed which were willing to oppose local mobs, the National Guard was increasingly called to stop lynchings, and Southern editors began frequently to denounce them.

The following account of a lynching in Memphis on July 22, 1893, is taken from a pamphlet, *A Red Record* (1895) written by Ida Wells-Barnett. She was editor of a black Memphis newspaper until she was driven out by a mob in 1892; she then devoted her energies to a one-woman anti-lynching lecture crusade. This pamphlet and two others have been reprinted in one volume: *On Lynching* (1969). See Walter A. White: *Rope and Faggot; A Biography of Judge Lynch* (1929); Arthur Raper: *The Tragedy of Lynching* (1933); James E. Cutler: *Lynch-Law: An Investigation into the History of Lynching in the United States* (1905); and John G. Van Deusen: *The Black Man in White America* (1944).

Memphis is one of the queen cities of the south, with a population of about seventy thousand souls—easily one of the twenty largest, most progressive and wealthiest cities of the United States. And yet in its streets there occurred a scene of shocking savagery which would have disgraced the Congo. No woman was harmed, no serious indignity suffered. Two women driving to town in a wagon, were suddenly accosted by Lee Walker. He claimed that he demanded something to eat. The women claimed that he attempted to assault them. They gave such an alarm that he ran away. At once the dispatches spread over the entire country that a big, burly Negro had brutally assaulted two women. Crowds began to search for the alleged fiend. While hunting him they shot another Negro dead in his tracks for refusing to stop when ordered to do so. After a few days Lee Walker was found, and put in jail in Memphis until the mob there was ready for him.

The Memphis Commercial of Sunday, July 23, contains a full account of the tragedy from which the following extracts are made:

At 12 o'clock last night, Lee Walker, who attempted to outrage Miss Mollie McCadden, last Tuesday morning, was taken from the county jail and hanged to a telegraph pole just north of the prison. All day rumors were afloat that with nightfall an attack would be made upon the jail, and as everyone anticipated that a vigorous resistance would be made, a conflict between the mob and the authorities was feared.

At 10 o'clock Capt. O'Haver, Sergt. Horan and several patrolmen were on hand, but they could do nothing with the crowd. An attack by the mob was made on the door in the south wall, and it yielded. Sheriff McLendon and several of his men threw themselves into the breach, but two or three of the storming party shoved by. They were seized by the police, but were not subdued, the officers refraining from using their clubs. The entire mob might at first have been dispersed by ten policemen who would use their clubs, but the sheriff insisted that no violence be done.

The mob got an iron rail and used it as a battering ram against the lobby doors. Sheriff McLendon tried to stop them, and some one of the mob knocked him down with a chair. Still he counseled moderation and would not order his deputies and the police to disperse the crowd by force. The pacific policy of the sheriff impressed the mob with the idea that the officers were afraid, or at least would do them no harm, and they redoubled their efforts, urged on by a big switchman. At 12 o'clock the door of the prison was broken in with a rail.

Walker made a desperate resistance. Two men entered his cell first and ordered him to come forth. He refused, and they failing to drag him out, others entered. He scratched and bit his assailants, wounding several of them severely with his teeth. The mob retaliated by striking and cutting him with fists and knives. When he reached the steps leading down to the door he made another stand and was stabbed again and again. By the time he reached the lobby his power to resist was gone, and he was shoved along through the mob of yelling, cursing men and boys, who beat, spat upon and slashed the wretch-like demon. . . .

The mob proceeded north on Front Street with the victim, stopping at Sycamore Street to get a rope from a grocery. "Take him to the iron bridge on Main Street," yelled several men. The men who had hold of the Negro were in a hurry to finish the job, however, and when they reached the telephone pole at the corner of Front Street and the first alley north of Sycamore they stopped. A hastily improvised noose was slipped over the Negro's head, and several young men mounted a pile of lumber near the pole and threw the rope over one of the iron stepping pins. The Negro was lifted up until his feet was three feet above the ground, the rope was made taut, and a corpse dangled in midair. A big fellow who helped lead the mob pulled the Negro's legs until his neck cracked. The wretch's clothes had been torn off, and, as he swung, the man who pulled his legs mutilated the corpse.

One or two knife cuts, more or less, made little difference in the appearance of the dead rapist, however, for before the rope was around his neck his skin was cut almost to ribbons. One pistol shot was fired while the corpse was hanging. A dozen voices protested against the use of fire-arms, and there was no more shooting. The body was permitted to hang for half an hour, then it was cut down . . . The body fell in a ghastly heap, and the crowd laughed at the sound and crowded around the prostrate body, a few kicking the inanimate carcass. . . . Then some one raised the cry of "Burn him!" It was quickly taken up and soon resounded from a hundred throats. Detective Richardson, for a long time, single-handed, stood the crowd off. He talked and begged the men not to bring disgrace on the city by burning the body, arguing that all the vengeance possible had been wrought.

While this was going on a small crowd was busy starting a fire in the middle of the street. The material was handy. Some bundles of staves were taken from the adjoining lumber yard for kindling. Heavier wood was obtained from the same source, and coal oil from a neighboring grocery. Then the cries of "Burn him! Burn him!" were redoubled.

Half a dozen men seized the naked body. The crowd cheered. They marched to the fire, and giving the body a swing, it was landed in the middle of the fire. There was a cry for more wood, as the fire had begun to die owing to the long delay. Willing hands procured the wood, and it was piled up on the Negro, almost, for a time, obscuring him from view. The head was in plain view, as also were the limbs, and one arm which stood out high above the body, the elbow crooked, held in that position by a stick of wood. In a few moments the hands began to swell, then came great blisters over all the exposed parts of the body; then in places the flesh was burned away and the bones began to show through. It was a horrible sight, one which, perhaps, no one there had ever witnessed before. It proved too much for a large part of the crowd and the majority of the mob left very shortly after the burning began.

But a large number stayed, and were not a bit set back by the sight of a human body being burned to ashes. Two or three white women, accompanied by their escorts, pushed to the front to obtain an unobstructed view, and looked on with astonishing coolness and nonchalance. One man and woman brought a little girl, not over 12 years old, apparently their daughter, to view a scene which was calculated to drive sleep from the child's eyes for many nights, if not to produce a permanent injury to her nervous system. The comments of the crowd were varied. Some remarked on the efficacy of this style of cure for rapists, others rejoiced that men's wives and daughters were now safe from this wretch. Some laughed as the flesh cracked and blistered and while a large number pronounced the burning of a dead body as a useless episode, not in all that throng was a word of sympathy heard for the wretch himself.

The rope that was used to hang the Negro, and also that which was used to lead him from the jail, were eagerly sought by relic hunters. They almost fought for a chance to cut off a piece of rope, and in an incredibly short time both ropes had disappeared and were scattered in the pockets of the crowd in sections of from an inch to six inches long. Others of the relic hunters remained until the ashes cooled to obtain such ghastly relics as the teeth, nails, and bits of charred skin of the immolated victim of his own lust. After burning the body the mob tied a rope around the charred trunk and dragged it down Main Street to the court house, where it was hanged to a center pole. The rope broke and the corpse dropped with a thud, but it was again hoisted, the charred legs barely touching the ground. The teeth were knocked out and the finger nails cut off as souvenirs. The crowd made so much noise that the police interfered. Undertaker Walsh was telephoned for, who took charge of the body and carried it to his establishment, where it will be prepared for burial in the potter's field today.

Epilogue

It is a grim and sometimes distasteful course over which the reader has been led, one that inspires compassion for the victims of violence and, to say the least, a certain wry curiosity about the perpetrators. The primary point of such an expedition into the past will be lost if these episodes are looked at for their sensational quality or as material for the muckraker. Violence has been used repeatedly in our past, often quite purposefully, and a full reckoning with the fact is a necessary ingredient in any realistic national self-image. In pursuit of their goals substantial groups of Americans—more often than not well situated in the social order—have from time to time preferred direct action to law, and violence to peaceful accommodation. Our recent concern with the problem may have reached unprecedented levels of intensity, but such concern is hardly new. A general anxiety about American lawlessness and a particular dismay over the level of industrial violence was a common theme of the age of Theodore Roosevelt and Woodrow Wilson. The violence of the Reconstruction era was the despair of many men who thought of slavery as a relic of barbarism and who had hoped that reunion and the abolition of slavery would set the United States on the path to a more admirable civilization. The startling outburst of anti-Irish, anti-Negro, and anti-abolitionist rioting in the 1830's, which alarmed many men, brought Abraham Lincoln to his first important political speech and his first significant utterance on the character and fate of the United States. In a speech delivered to the young men of Springfield in January 1838, Lincoln, then twenty-eight, took as his theme the prevalence of violence and lawlessness in the country and its threat to the survival of free institutions. His address was a heartfelt cry for law and order.

The United States, Lincoln pointed out, faced no serious dangers from abroad. Any danger that one could anticipate to its institutions "must spring up amongst us. . . . If destruction be our lot, we must ourselves be its author and finisher. As a nation of freemen, we must live through all time, or die by suicide." Even at that time, Lincoln went on, he could see an ill omen: "The increasing disregard for law which pervades the country; the growing disposition to substitute the wild and furious passions, in lieu of the sober judgment of Courts; and the worse than savage mobs, for the executive ministers of justice. . . . Accounts of outrages committed by mobs form the every-day news of the times."

Whatever the cause of such outrages, Lincoln pointed out that they were common to the entire country. The rising mob spirit, the tendency toward vigilantism, the contempt for law, the readiness to hang members of both races, were, he thought, the primary danger to America. "By the operation of this mobocratic spirit, which all must admit, is now abroad in the land, the strongest bulwark of any Government, and particularly of those constituted like ours, may effectually be broken down and destroyed—I mean the *attachment* of the People. Whenever this effect shall be produced among us; whenever the vicious portion of [the] population shall be permitted to gather in bands of hundreds and thousands, and burn churches, ravage and rob provision stores, throw printing presses into rivers, shoot editors, and hang and burn obnoxious persons at pleasure, and with impunity; depend on it, this Government cannot last. By such things, the feelings of the best citizens will become more or less alienated from it; and thus it will be left without friends, or with too few, and those few too weak, to make their friendship effectual. At such a time and under such circumstances, men of sufficient talent and ambition will not be wanting to seize the opportunity, strike the blow, and overturn that fair fabric, which for the last half century, has been the fondest hope of the lovers of freedom throughout the world."

Lincoln's only prescription for checking violence was to urge all Americans to "swear by the blood of the Revolution, never to violate in the least particular the laws of the country; and never to tolerate their violation by others." He hoped that by constant indoctrination in homes, schools, colleges, churches, and legislative halls and courts of justice, reverence for the laws might be made "the political religion of the nation." In an interesting passage he pointed out that the country had been established on the strength of a unifying passion, hatred of the British nation, but that the scenes of the Revolution, though unforgotten, were losing their emotional force and their unifying effect. These had been "the pillars of the temple of liberty." What would replace them? Passion, he argued, was now useless as a sustaining force, and had in fact become an enemy rather than a friend. Only reason, "cold, calculating, unimpassioned reason" would furnish the materials for the future support and defense of the country, and reason must mould a national morality in which reverence for the Constitution and the laws would be a central tenet. But establishing reverence through reason had its own difficulties; and to preach cold reason to the Americans of the 1830's was to preach asceticism to the Sybarites. Lawlessness and violence continued at a high pitch in the 1840's and 1850's, and they were followed by the disaster of the 1860's.

Lincoln was wrong in expecting that a group of ambitious usurpers would take advantage of men's alienation from free government to overthrow it and establish a tyranny. The American people—perhaps it is a hopeful sign—had even less capacity for establishing tyranny than they had for keeping order. But Lincoln seems to have been right in seeing the exceptional disorder around him as the symptom of a dangerously rising inability to work consistently through pacific means, and to abide dissent, discussion, and compromise.

It would be far too much to say that the violence Lincoln saw rising in the 1830's was a primary "cause" of the disaster of the Civil War. It was rather a symptom of the same basic pathology in American life that hastened the war itself—the pathology of a nation growing at a speed that defied control, governed by an ineffective leadership, impatient with authority, bedeviled by its internal heterogeneity, and above all cursed by an ancient and gloomy wrong that many of its people had even come to cherish as a right. Lincoln at an early age read the surface agitations correctly as signs of a profoundly dangerous condition; but he then had a faith, which he would one day outgrow, in the power of exhortation and indoctrination in and of itself. His cure—urging that men should be taught everywhere from the nursery to the churches and legislative halls to be lawful and orderly—was not much different from urging that they be taught everywhere to be moral and good. Such exhortations can, of course, have some effect, but only in a social setting that gives them coherence and plausibility, and by the late 1830's governmental authority in the United States was losing rather than gaining in its ability to provide such a setting. Leaders in business and government were increasing in their willfulness and their vast carelessness, the nation was splitting into two separate political cultures, and the few institutions that might have held it together and enabled it to resolve its problems in peaceful ways were beginning to snap. Twenty years after Lincoln's speech, the last of these institutions, the two national parties, were in one case dead and in the other hopelessly split. It became Lincoln's fate in the 1860's to preside over the climactic failure of the American political system. In the end he could only arrive at the melancholy and prophetic fatalism expressed in his second inaugural address, in which he concluded that "the Almighty has His own purposes," and that the war had been ordained for Americans as a terrible but just way of ridding them of the "offence" of slavery. A fatalism of this kind was perhaps natural to one who had experienced such a catastrophe at the storm center and had suffered from it to his very marrow. But it is hardly suitable to those who sense a potential catastrophe that they can still hope to avert. The metapolitics of divine judgment are the last resort of those who have failed; the appeal to human judgment must be the first resort of those who expect to succeed. In the search for grounds of judgment there is reason to think that the historical study of violence and its consequences has something important and chastening to tell us. For historians the records are voluminous enough.

RICHARD HOFSTADTER

INDEX

A NOTE ABOUT THE EDITORS

Richard Hofstadter, DeWitt Clinton Professor of American History at Columbia University, was the author of THE AMERICAN POLITICAL TRADITION, THE AGE OF REFORM, ANTI-INTELLECTUALISM IN AMERICAN LIFE, THE PROGRESSIVE HISTORIANS, THE IDEA OF A PARTY SYSTEM, THE PARANOID STYLE IN AMERICAN POLITICS, *and other works. He served as Pitt Professor of American History and Institutions at Cambridge University in 1958–9, and lectured widely in American and English Universities. He died in October 1970.*

Michael Wallace, a graduate student in history at Columbia University, is completing a dissertation on the development of ideas on the two-party system in the nineteenth century, of which one chapter appeared in the American Historical Review, December 1968. *He is the author of "The Uses of Violence in American History," published in the* American Scholar, Summer 1970, *and co-editor (with Dennis van Essendelft) of the forthcoming* DICTIONARY OF AMERICAN VIOLENCE.

VINTAGE POLITICAL SCIENCE
AND SOCIAL CRITICISM